Women and Political Violence

This book directly challenges the stereotype that women are inherently peaceable by examining female combatants' involvement in ethno-national conflicts.

Drawing upon empirical case studies of Sri Lanka and Northern Ireland, this study explores the ways in which women have traditionally been depicted. Whereas women have predominantly been seen as victims of conflict, this book acknowledges the reality of women as active combatants. Indeed, female soldiers/irregulars are features of most modern conflicts, and particularly in ethno-nationalist violence – until now largely ignored by mainstream scholarship.

Original interview material from the author's extensive fieldwork addresses why, and how, some women choose to become violently engaged in nationalist conflicts. It also highlights the personal/political costs and benefits incurred by such women. This book provides a valuable insight into female combatants, and is a significant contribution to the literature.

This book will be of great interest to students and scholars of political violence, ethnic conflict, gender studies and international relations in general.

Miranda H. Alison is Associate Professor in Politics and International Studies at the University of Warwick. She completed her PhD at Queen's University Belfast.

Contemporary security studies
Series Editors: James Gow and Rachel Kerr
King's College London

This series focuses on new research across the spectrum of international peace and security, in an era where each year throws up multiple examples of conflicts that present new security challenges in the world around them.

NATO's Secret Armies
Operation Gladio and terrorism in Western Europe
Daniele Ganser

The US, NATO and Military Burden-Sharing
Peter Kent Forster and Stephen J. Cimbala

Russian Governance in the Twenty-First Century
Geo-strategy, geopolitics and new governance
Irina Isakova

The Foreign Office and Finland 1938–1940
Diplomatic sideshow
Craig Gerrard

Rethinking the Nature of War
Edited by Isabelle Duyvesteyn and Jan Angstrom

Perception and Reality in the Modern Yugoslav Conflict
Myth, falsehood and deceit 1991–1995
Brendan O'Shea

The Political Economy of Peacebuilding in Post-Dayton Bosnia
Tim Donais

The Distracted Eagle
The rift between America and old Europe
Peter H. Merkl

The Iraq War
European perspectives on politics, strategy, and operations
Edited by Jan Hallenberg and Håkan Karlsson

Strategic Contest
Weapons proliferation and war in the greater Middle East
Richard L. Russell

Propaganda, the Press and Conflict
The Gulf War and Kosovo
David R. Willcox

Missile Defence
International, regional and national implications
Edited by Bertel Heurlin and Sten Rynning

Globalising Justice for Mass Atrocities
A revolution in accountability
Chandra Lekha Sriram

Ethnic Conflict and Terrorism
The origins and dynamics of civil wars
Joseph L. Soeters

Globalisation and the Future of Terrorism
Patterns and predictions
Brynjar Lia

Nuclear Weapons and Strategy
The evolution of American nuclear policy
Stephen J. Cimbala

Nasser and the Missile Age in the Middle East
Owen L. Sirrs

War as Risk Management
Strategy and conflict in an age of globalised risks
Yee-Kuang Heng

Military Nanotechnology
Potential applications and preventive arms control
Jurgen Altmann

NATO and Weapons of Mass Destruction
Regional alliance, global threats
Eric R. Terzuolo

Europeanisation of National Security Identity
The EU and the changing security identities of the Nordic states
Pernille Rieker

International Conflict Prevention and Peace-building
Sustaining the peace in post-conflict societies
Edited by T. David Mason and James D. Meernik

Controlling the Weapons of War
Politics, persuasion, and the prohibition of inhumanity
Brian Rappert

Changing Transatlantic Security Relations
Do the US, the EU and Russia form a new strategic triangle?
Edited by Jan Hallenberg and Håkan Karlsson

Theoretical Roots of US Foreign Policy
Machiavelli and American unilateralism
Thomas M. Kane

Corporate Soldiers and International Security
The rise of private military companies
Christopher Kinsey

Transforming European Militaries
Coalition operations and the technology gap
Gordon Adams and Guy Ben-Ari

Globalization and Conflict
National security in a 'new' strategic era
Edited by Robert G. Patman

Military Forces in 21st Century Peace Operations
No job for a soldier?
James V. Arbuckle

The Political Road to War with Iraq
Bush, 9/11 and the drive to overthrow Saddam
Nick Ritchie and Paul Rogers

Bosnian Security after Dayton
New perspectives
Edited by Michael A. Innes

Kennedy, Johnson and NATO
Britain, America and the dynamics of alliance, 1962–68
Andrew Priest

Small Arms and Security
New emerging international norms
Denise Garcia

The United States and Europe
Beyond the neo-conservative divide?
Edited by John Baylis and Jon Roper

Russia, NATO and Cooperative Security
Bridging the gap
Lionel Ponsard

International Law and International Relations
Bridging theory and practice
Edited by Tom Bierstecker, Peter Spiro, Chandra Lekha Sriram and Veronica Raffo

Deterring International Terrorism and Rogue States
US national security policy after 9/11
James H. Lebovic

Vietnam in Iraq
Tactics, lessons, legacies and ghosts
Edited by John Dumbrell and David Ryan

Understanding Victory and Defeat in Contemporary War
Edited by Jan Angstrom and Isabelle Duyvesteyn

Propaganda and Information Warfare in the Twenty-first Century
Altered images and deception operations
Scot Macdonald

Governance in Post-Conflict Societies
Rebuilding fragile states
Edited by Derick W. Brinkerhoff

European Security in the Twenty-first Century
The challenge of multipolarity
Adrian Hyde-Price

Ethics, Technology and the American Way of War
Cruise missiles and US security policy
Reuben E. Brigety II

International Law and the Use of Armed Force
The UN charter and the major powers
Joel H. Westra

Disease and Security
Natural plagues and biological weapons in East Asia
Christian Enermark

Explaining War and Peace
Case studies and necessary condition counterfactuals
Jack Levy and Gary Goertz

War, Image and Legitimacy
Viewing contemporary conflict
James Gow and Milena Michalski

Information Strategy and Warfare
A guide to theory and practice
John Arquilla and Douglas A. Borer

Countering the Proliferation of Weapons of Mass Destruction
NATO and EU options in the Mediterranean and the Middle East
Thanos P. Dokos

Security and the War on Terror
Edited by Alex J. Bellamy, Roland Bleiker, Sara E. Davies and Richard Devetak

The European Union and Strategy
An emerging actor
Edited by Jan Hallenberg and Kjell Engelbrekt

Causes and Consequences of International Conflict
Data, methods and theory
Edited by Glenn Palmer

Russian Energy Policy and Military Power
Putin's quest for greatness
Pavel Baev

The Baltic Question During the Cold War
Edited by John Hiden, Vahur Made, and David J. Smith

America, the EU and Strategic Culture
Renegotiating the transatlantic bargain
Asle Toje

Afghanistan, Arms and Conflict
Post-9/11 security and insurgency
Michael Bhatia and Mark Sedra

Punishment, Justice and International Relations
Ethics and order after the Cold War
Anthony F. Lang, Jr.

Intra-State Conflict, Governments and Security
Dilemmas of deterrence and assurance
Edited by Stephen M. Saideman and Marie-Joëlle J. Zahar

Democracy and Security
Preferences, norms and policy-making
Edited by Matthew Evangelista, Harald Müller and Niklas Schörnig

The Homeland Security Dilemma
Fear, failure and the future of American security
Frank P. Harvey

Military Transformation and Strategy
Revolutions in military affairs and small states
Edited by Bernard Loo

Peace Operations and International Criminal Justice
Building peace after mass atrocities
Majbritt Lyck

NATO, Security and Risk Management
From Kosovo to Khandahar
M.J. Williams

Cyber-Conflict and Global Politics
Edited by Athina Karatzogianni

Globalisation and Defence in the Asia-Pacific
Arms across Asia
Edited by Geoffrey Till, Emrys Chew and Joshua Ho

Security Strategies and American World Order
Lost power
Birthe Hansen, Peter Toft and Anders Wivel

War, Torture and Terrorism
Rethinking the rules of international security
Edited by Anthony F. Lang, Jr. and Amanda Russell Beattie

America and Iraq
Policy making, intervention and regional politics
Edited by David Ryan and Patrick Kiely

European Security in a Global Context
Internal and external dynamics
Edited by Thierry Tardy

Women and Political Violence
Female combatants in ethno-national conflict
Miranda H. Alison

Women and Political Violence

Female combatants in ethno-national conflict

Miranda H. Alison

Routledge
Taylor & Francis Group
LONDON AND NEW YORK

First published 2009
by Routledge
2 Park Square, Milton Park, Abingdon, Oxon, OX14 4RN

Simultaneously published in the USA and Canada
by Routledge
270 Madison Ave, New York NY 10016

Routledge is an imprint of the Taylor & Francis Group, an informa business

Transferred to Digital Printing 2010

Typeset in Times by Wearset Ltd, Boldon, Tyne and Wear

British Library Cataloguing in Publication Data
A catalogue record for this book is available from the British Library

Library of Congress Cataloging in Publication Data
A catalog record for this book has been requested

ISBN10: 0-415-36313-6 (hbk)
ISBN10: 0-415-59242-9 (pbk)
ISBN10: 0-203-01345-X (ebk)

ISBN13: 978-0-415-36313-6 (hbk)
ISBN13: 978-0-415-59242-0 (pbk)
ISBN13: 978-0-203-01345-8 (ebk)

For Kieran, who keeps me sane every day and never lets me take myself too seriously

Contents

Acknowledgements

Primary thanks go to all the women who participated in my research by allowing themselves to be interviewed and giving of their time, energy and patience. I can never say thank you enough for sharing a part of your lives with me.

Thanks also to the numerous individuals and community organizations which so kindly helped put me in touch with interviewees, gave me access to resources, extended to me their warm hospitality or assisted in other ways. In Sri Lanka, sincere thanks to the political wings of the Liberation Tigers of Tamil Eelam, the Manoharan family (Jaffna), Saroja Sivachandran (Jaffna), Suriya Women's Development Centre (Batticaloa), Reverend Jeyanesan and Sounthi Azariah at the American Ceylon Mission, St John's Church (Batticaloa), Women's Education and Resource Centre (Colombo), Social Scientists' Association (Colombo), International War-Related Trauma and Humanitarian Intervention Trust (Colombo), Sanjana Hattotuwa at the Centre for Policy Alternatives (Colombo), the Coomaraswamy family for taking me safely to Jaffna on their first journey home in almost 20 years, and the Panos Institute (London) for access to their oral testimony records of interviews with women in Sri Lanka. Also to my interpreters: S. Pathmanathan, Krishnadevy Manoharan, Mrs Somadeva, T. Subashini, Thilak Ranasingha, and Mr Deen. In Northern Ireland, sincere thanks to React (Armagh), Ex-Prisoners' Interpretive Centre (Belfast), Families of Displaced, Dispersed and Distressed (Belfast), Prisoners' Aid (Belfast), Gae Lairn (Belfast), Coiste na n-Iarchimí (Belfast), Tar Anall (Belfast), Springfield Inter-Community Development Project (Belfast), EX-PAC (Monaghan), Sinn Féin, the Irish Republican Socialist Party, Stephen Bloomer, Katy Radford, Ian Woods and those who cannot be named.

Finally, thanks to Queen's University Belfast for a wonderful doctoral experience, where this book began; and to my publishers, for their almost endless patience.

Abbreviations

Sri Lanka

ACTC	All Ceylon Tamil Congress
CWC	Ceylon Workers' Congress
ENDLF	Eelam National Democratic Liberation Front
ENLF	Eelam National Liberation Front
EPDP	Eelam People's Democratic Party
EPRLF	Eelam People's Revolutionary Liberation Front
EROS	Eelam Revolutionary Organization
FP	Federal Party
IPKF	Indian Peace Keeping Force
JVP	Janatha Vimukthi Peramuna (People's Liberation Front)
LTTE	Liberation Tigers of Tamil Eelam
PA	People's Alliance
PLOTE	People's Liberation Organization of Tamil Eelam
PTA	Prevention of Terrorism Act
RAW	Research and Analysis Wing
SLA	Sri Lankan Army
SLFP	Sri Lanka Freedom Party
SLMC	Sri Lanka Muslim Congress
SLMM	Sri Lanka Monitoring Mission
STF	Special Task Force (Police)
TEA	Tamil Eelam Army
TELA	Tamil Eelam Liberation Army
TELF	Tamil Eelam Liberation Front
TELO	Tamil Eelam Liberation Organization
TNA	Tamil National Alliance
TUF	Tamil United Front
TULF	Tamil United Liberation Front
UNP	United National Party

Northern Ireland

APNI	Alliance Party of Northern Ireland
ASU	IRA active service unit
CIRA	Continuity IRA
CLMC	Combined Loyalist Military Command
CSJ	Campaign for Social Justice
DUP	Democratic Unionist Party
GFA	Good Friday Agreement (also called the Belfast Agreement)
INLA	Irish National Liberation Army
IPP	Irish Parliamentary Party
IRA	Irish Republican Army
IRSP	Irish Republican Socialist Party
MLA	Member of Local Assembly (Northern Ireland Assembly at Stormont)
NICRA	Northern Ireland Civil Rights Association
OIRA	Official IRA
PD	People's Democracy
PIRA	Provisional IRA
PSNI	Police Service of Northern Ireland
PUP	Progressive Unionist Party
RIRA	Real IRA
RUC	Royal Ulster Constabulary
SDLP	Social Democratic and Labour Party
SF	Sinn Féin
UDA	Ulster Defence Force
UDP	Ulster Democratic Party
UDR	Ulster Defence Regiment
UFF	Ulster Freedom Fighters
UKUP	United Kingdom Unionist Party
UPNI	Unionist Party of Northern Ireland
UPRG	Ulster Political Research Group
USC	Ulster Special Constabulary
UUP	Ulster Unionist Party
UVF	Ulster Volunteer Force

1 Introduction

The assumption that women are generally more peaceful and less aggressive or warlike than men is a familiar one. The belief in women as nurturing, non-violent beings (whether it is argued that this arises through biology or socialization) has been expressed by a variety of people and groups in the West, even those in conflict with each other on almost every other social and political issue. It has been used by social conservatives to continue to restrict women's life choices and career options to the domestic; by traditional militarists to argue against the inclusion of women in combat roles in the military; and by some (certainly not all) feminists to maintain that peace is somehow a 'women's issue' and to argue that having more women in powerful decision-making positions nationally and internationally would lead to less war. This book is premised on the claim that this belief in women's peacefulness is mistaken. A more nuanced picture of the variable ways that women participate in specific conflicts and wars is important and also necessary for effective peace work. In this introductory chapter I first briefly outline the background context to the book and my motivations for undertaking the research. I then outline the structure of the book and the issues that will be addressed. In the remainder of the chapter I attend to methodological issues relating to the process of doing feminist research, including discussion of how the research for this book was undertaken.

The bulk of the research for this book was carried out for the purposes of my doctoral dissertation (Alison 2003c). I conducted fieldwork in Sri Lanka August–September 2002, and in Northern Ireland January–June 2003 (though the whole time I lived in Northern Ireland between 2000 and 2004 had an impact on my work and might constitute fieldwork in the broader observational sense). After the doctorate was completed I interviewed a further woman in Northern Ireland and conducted another period of fieldwork in Sri Lanka June–July 2004. With regard to Northern Ireland a small amount of the fieldwork material that is utilized here is drawn on in a previous publication (Alison 2004b) but most of it is presented here for the first time. With regard to Sri Lanka some of the material used has been drawn on in previous publications (Alison 2003a, 2003b, 2004b) but the material arising from the second period of fieldwork has not been presented before. Furthermore, some of the earlier interview material has been altered in light of interesting re-translations of the interview tapes which were done in 2007, revealing some misunderstandings or mistranslations on the part of interpreters.[1]

Context and motivations

The academic field studying women, gender and armed conflict is still relatively new and the research and literature has tended to emphasize and focus on women as victims of armed conflict – as victims of sexual violence, widows, refugees and internally displaced women. These are extremely important areas of research. However with this focus on victimization there has been a corresponding emphasis on representations of women as somehow inherently or 'naturally' more peaceful and peace-loving and less violent than men. This has meant that the issue of women as agents of political violence or war has been very much neglected. The focus of this book is on a particular form of women's violent political agency – participation as combatants in ethno-nationalist movements. This has been largely ignored in the mainstream literature on nationalism and political violence. Here, too, an image has been perpetuated of women as being almost inevitably victims, and *only* victims, during armed conflict.

I believe that research on female combatants is necessary for various reasons. If we see women as only victims of, not also as perpetrators of violence and perpetuators of conflict, we see only part of the story. Even though it is clear that being a victim of violence does not mean one has no agency (Coulter 2008: 66), nevertheless it has been rightly argued that 'the prevalent view of women as victims of conflict … tends to overlook, explicitly or implicitly, women's power and agency' (Sharoni 2001: 86), and that '[v]iewing women as homogeneously powerless and as implicit victims, does not allow us to theorize women as the benefactors of oppression, or the perpetrators of catastrophes' (Lentin 1997a: 12). This also prevents us from addressing and responding to the effects of women's violence, alongside men's violence, which makes attempts at peacemaking, peacebuilding, or post-conflict reconstruction less effective. A greater acknowledgement and understanding of women's involvement as combatants is needed as part of an overall struggle towards peace. This book challenges the idea that women are necessarily more peaceful than men through an exploration of female combatants, as a group of women who do not fit the mould expected of them by most societies. Women who choose to become combatants do not sit well with the image of Woman the Peacemaker, regardless of whether this peacemaking role is assumed to be something biologically innate or socially constructed. My interest is specifically in non-conscripted, non-state military members who have engaged in active combat or are/were trained and prepared to do so: those women who have stretched our notions of femininity to breaking point by engaging in political violence. Ethno-national conflict is examined because anti-state 'liberatory' nationalisms seem to attract greater activism by women than state nationalisms and these conflicts often produce comparatively high numbers of female combatants; thus, they are interesting in terms of how this fits with theories of gender and nationalism.

Enloe contends, challengingly, that

> [w]omen *in* the military has never been an easy topic ... But gradually I began to realize that paying attention only to women as soldiers was simply too confining. Militaries – and militarized civilian elites – have relied not just on sporadic infusions of a 'few good women.' Military policy makers have depended on – and thus maneuvered to control – varieties of women, and on the very notion of femininity in all its myriad guises.
>
> (2000b: x, emphasis in original)

Therefore, she says, '[t]o invest one's curiosity solely in women as soldiers is to treat the militarization of so many other women as normal. If I slipped into that naive presumption, I probably would be allowing my own curiosity to become militarized' (ibid.: xii). As always from Enloe, these are significant and thought-provoking comments. I am certainly not suggesting here that combatant is the only women's role that has any significance in militarized socio-political mobilizations. Nor do I suggest that stark binary categories of 'woman-warrior' versus 'woman-peacemaker' are the only forms of agency or political activism available to women in war. Nor do I wish to imply, by focusing primarily on women in combat roles, that women's more common auxiliary military roles are less important (or less problematic) in the service of war. As de Pauw notes in her history of women in war, '[a]lthough some women in war appear in conventional combat roles, most do not' (1998: 17). Nevertheless, I support her suggestion that '[t]he reality of women's experience is distorted by focusing exclusively on exceptional females, but it is also distorted by focusing only on the most typical' (ibid.). It remains the case that women who engage in organized political violence challenge, more than any other women, the enduring image of women as natural peacemakers. These women have also been consistently under-examined. If we fail to consider and try to understand the full range of women's responses to and roles in war in varied contexts, including as combatants, we are missing vital pieces of the puzzle of violent human conflict. Accordingly, it is both justified and important to examine women combatants as part of the broader study of war and peace.

Given the focus here on ethno-national conflict, which is frequently asymmetric and includes non-conventional guerrilla forms of warfare and 'terrorist' tactics, in this book 'combat' is conceptualized broadly to include things like bomb-making and planting, assassinations, and suicide bombs, as well as more conventional forms of battle. 'Combatant', therefore, is equally used in a fairly broad sense to include all people engaged in such activities or trained to do so. I deliberately use the relatively neutral term 'combatant' throughout this work and actively avoid the word 'terrorist'. I side with those who argue that the word 'terrorist' has no internationally acceptable or agreed definition, is highly contested and is often used (selectively) because an author disagrees with the aims of a particular group, while the words 'guerrilla' or 'freedom fighter' are used for groups the author has more sympathy with (see Guelke 1995, among many others). As Meehan notes, it is not possible to avoid labelling in social science but we need to recognize that this has political implications and think about which label is used and by whom (1986: 124). The two case studies examined in the book are Sri Lanka and Northern Ireland, both having experienced long-drawn-out violent ethno-national conflicts. In the case of Northern Ireland, some loyalist women are discussed who engaged in the conflict in more auxiliary military roles (such as moving and hiding arms and ammunition, first aid and so on), rather than active combat as outlined above, but the primary focus is on combatants.

It has been alleged that when a violent armed conflict between groups becomes designated a war 'is the prerogative of dominant nations and groups' (Kelly 2000: 48–9). The persistent labelling of a violent conflict as a war is often a political tactic used by subversive, less powerful groups; however, the control over when a conflict is generally recognized as a war is usually held by the dominant group. In the 'Troubles' in Northern Ireland, for example, the Irish Republican Army (IRA) has consistently referred to its activities as a war against the British state, while this period has not always been recognized as a war by successive British governments and indeed some have actively refused to acknowledge it as such. It is clear that the naming of wars is a highly contested and political matter. Furthermore, it has been claimed that among military specialists, agreeing a definition of war is difficult and frequently arbitrary (de Pauw 1998: 9, 14). In this book, to an extent the terms 'conflict' and 'war' are used interchangeably, although 'conflict' is used more frequently to try and encompass all armed struggles without making a political judgement about which should qualify as 'wars'. It should be noted, however, that I do consider the armed ethno-national conflicts in both Sri Lanka and Northern Ireland to be wars, but in fact 'conflict' is a more useful word because it can also encompass the non-physical political and social struggles between groups that are as central to the overall picture as military conflict. Following on from this, it is also clear that for many people the definition of 'peace' has been evolving to encompass much more than the absence of violence, much more than the ending of war in the sense of a cessation of military hostilities. Newer conceptualizations of peace include ideas to do with cooperation, tolerance, mutual respect, possibly social justice and so forth (Reardon 1993; Ognibene 1998), which hint at a concern to address conflicts holistically and to try and resolve the underlying causes rather than just end military clashes, and which stem in no small part from Galtung's notion of 'positive peace' versus 'negative peace' (Galtung 1969, 1985).

A related point here is to clarify what I mean by violence and political violence. There is a messy debate about how violence is best conceptualized, ranging from a narrow understanding to do with coercive physical force against humans to a broad understanding entailing social injustices, structural economic inequalities and so forth (sometimes called 'structural violence'), and a whole lot of disagreement in the middle about whether there has to be intention to constitute violence and whether harm to property counts as violence in the same way as harm to people. I do not engage in this debate here. In this book 'violence' is generally used in a fairly narrow way to mean deliberately using physical force with the intention of hurting or killing another human being or damaging or destroying property. Furthermore, the focus is on *political* violence and when I refer in this work to women who commit violence, I usually specifically mean as combatants in the context of a society in conflict. Moser defines political violence as 'the commission of violent acts motivated by a desire, conscious or unconscious, to obtain or maintain political power' (2001: 36); de Silva emphasizes the use or threat of force 'by organised groups or members of such entities, to their perceived political enemies' (1995: 178). A broad view is taken of agents of political violence, which includes state forces (regular and extra-judicial) as potential agents as well as non-state paramilitary[2] groups, political parties, and, potentially, private armies. An equally open view is taken of manifestations of political violence, which include guerrilla and paramilitary conflict as well as more targeted or limited acts such as the use of suicide bombs, pipe bombs and other incendiary devices, politically motivated rape and sexual assault, assassinations, kidnappings and so forth.

In many ways this book is a personal exploration for me, as I continue to struggle to reconcile my conflicting beliefs about war and violence. On the one hand, to an extent I agree with liberal feminists who argue that women everywhere should be permitted and enabled to participate in military struggles in the same way as men, should they so choose. Furthermore, I do believe that there are certain situations of oppression and abuse where it may be justified to take up arms (though deciding when we have reached that situation, and when we have exhausted all other options, is so difficult as to be almost impossible). On the other hand, I also have sympathy with a more critical feminist perspective that views militaries and militarization as strongly masculinized and repressive institutions and processes, and I favour non-violence over violence whenever and wherever it is reasonably possible. I most certainly do not in any way wish to denigrate women's individual actions or collective movements for peace; my problem lies with arguments that women are or *should be* more disposed in this direction than men. I do not believe that peace and non-violence are 'women's issues' – or even feminist issues – exclusively. This work is part of an ongoing process of unpacking and thinking through the way I perceive war, violence and peace, and the implications this has for my thinking about feminism(s).

Structure and key concerns

This book attempts to address some primary themes and questions, from both a theoretical perspective and a more empirical one: how do feminists, as the primary scholars of women's experiences of war, approach and analyse women's relationship to war, peace and nationalism, and what are the main areas of disagreement here? What sort of factors seem to impel and/or enable some women in ethno-national conflicts to become combatants? What kinds of experiences do they have as combatants and within these ethno-national movements more broadly? Are these experiences any sort of catalyst towards developing a feminist perspective and, if so, of what kind? This work helps to highlight the fact that despite the strong cultural expectation that recurs in many societies that women are or should be less violent or aggressive than men, and should not be combatants in war, in ethno-national conflicts many women *do* choose to involve themselves as combatants. More importantly, I hope the work will contribute to advancing our knowledge of why this is the case and of the complicated interactions between processes of nationalist mobilization and gender constructions.

In Chapter 2 of the book I provide an overview of the two case study conflicts, Sri Lanka and Northern Ireland. This is primarily a narrative of the respective conflicts to provide context for the later chapters examining female combatants, but there are some underlying premises and contested areas which recur in Chapter 2, and elsewhere in the book, that I will briefly outline here. A significant premise is that the conflicts in both Sri Lanka and Northern Ireland are ethno-national in nature, so I will briefly discuss here the concepts of ethnicity, nation and nationalism.

Ethnicity, by Horowitz's definition, 'embraces differences identified by color, language, religion, or some other attribute of common origin' (2000: 41). An ethnic group is a human collectivity which identifies itself or is identified by others in ethnic terms. The particular social characteristics that become significant to group ethnic identity, and to differentiation between groups, vary between contexts and can have complicated interactions; furthermore, ethnic groups are never as homogeneous as they are sometimes presented. Ethnicity is conceptualized here as a relational and situational construct: ethnic identities are formed in contrast or opposition to others (though this should not be taken to imply a primordial view of inevitable conflict between ethnic groups), in specific historical times and places. It should be clear that ethnicity, then, like gender, is being viewed in this book as socially constructed rather than essential or primordial. Social constructionism argues that the way that people are is constructed through interaction with our surroundings (encompassing social, economic, cultural, historical and political factors), rather than being given by nature. It views people and social worlds as changeable, and 'is based on an ontological scepticism to what is considered natural or given' (Skjelsbæk 2001: 50). In this way it differs from essentialism, which has been described as 'not so much a theory or a philosophy as a largely unrecognised mind-set' (Smith 2001: 34), based on the idea that some objects have certain immutable, timeless qualities (Skjelsbæk 2001: 49). This perspective entails a philosophy and strategy of politics based on the assumption that people hold particular views and preferences because of their 'essence', a core of identity that makes them who they are. Certain characteristics come to be 'seen not only as the definitive component of that group's make-up and identity, but also as unavoidable and given by nature' (Smith 2001: 34). Dan Smith points out that essentialism is a difficult concept to think through analytically: '[a]s an object of discussion, essentialism has many of the features of a wet bar of soap: it seems to get all over the place but is often hard to take hold of firmly' (ibid.: 33). Clearly, an essentialist viewpoint assumes immutable qualities of people in relation to various characteristics, but in this book the two most relevant concerns are essentialist presumptions about gender and ethnic characteristics and differences.

Although it is contended that ethnicity is socially constructed and variable, an ethnic group's conception of ethnicity is generally based on 'a myth of collective ancestry, which usually carries with it traits believed to be innate' (Horowitz 2000: 52). Because of this, ethnic groups can 'think in terms of family resemblances – traits held in common, on a supposedly genetic basis, or cultural features acquired in early childhood'. Thus, an ethnic grouping is often viewed in terms of kinship, as 'an extension of family, however imperfect' (ibid.: 57, 62). For Anthony D. Smith, an ethnic community or 'ethnie' is 'a named human population with a myth of common ancestry, shared memories, and cultural elements; a link with an historic territory or homeland; and a measure of solidarity' (1993: 28–9). For other scholars the political aspect to ethnicity is central. Yuval-Davis describes ethnicity as 'a political phenomenon which uses cultural resources to promote its specific purposes' (1994: 411). Cockburn views ethnicity as a historical, cultural, and linguistic process whereby a sense of collective identity is created and transmitted through generations, but is always changing and adapting. Like Yuval-Davis, Cockburn says '[w]hen ethnic differences are stressed, it is always possible to detect a political project' (1998: 35–6). The relational nature of ethnicity (and nationalism) means that boundaries are continually drawn, and 'processes of exclusion and inclusion are in operation wherever a delineation of boundaries takes place' (Yuval-Davis 1998: 25).

The concept of nation is related to ethnicity and ethnic groups, but is not the same. Yuval-Davis points out that some definitions of 'the nation' read 'like a shopping list' of features, whereas others argue that national identity comes down simply to the conception of membership in 'a people' (1998: 25), much like ethnicity. For Smith, along with shared myths and memories, attributes of a nation include 'a clearly delimited, compact, and recognized homeland; a mass, public culture; a centralized economy with mobility throughout; and common rights and duties for all conationals, usually to the exclusion of outsiders' (1993: 34). As Pettman notes, '[n]ationalism speaks of a people, of "us", of belonging.... It frequently posits a people–time–land connection – we have been here forever – which presents a particular problem for settler-state nationalisms' (1996: 46). However Yuval-Davis highlights a sense of 'common destiny' as being equally important as the myth of common origins in the construction of nations, an orientation towards the future as well as the past (1998: 25), which can explain 'a subjective sense of commitment of people to collectivities and nations, such as in settler societies or in post-colonial states, in which there is no myth of common origin' (1997: 19; 1998: 25).

For Anderson, famously, the nation is 'an imagined political community – and imagined as both inherently limited and sovereign' (1991: 6). He views it as 'imagined' (which does not mean illusory) because each member will never know or meet most of their fellow-members, 'yet in the minds of each lives the image of their communion'. The imagined nation is 'limited' because even the largest 'has finite, if elastic, boundaries, beyond which lie other nations', and it is imagined as 'sovereign', he argues, because of the historical development of the concept during the Enlightenment and its interrelationship to ideas of the modern sovereign state (ibid.: 6–7).[3] In contrast, 'primordialist' theorists of nations and nationalism have a naturalized image of the nation, maintaining that 'nations not only are eternal and universal but also constitute a natural extension of family and kinship relations' (Yuval-Davis 1997: 15). 'Modernist' theorists of nations and nationalism (of which Anderson is one) view nations not as a timeless and universal phenomenon but as specifically modern, the result of certain developments in European history (though people *feel* their membership in the nation is 'natural') (Breuilly 1993; Anderson 1991; Tilly 1975; Smith 1991a, 1993). Nevertheless, Smith has persistently argued for the significance of premodern ethnic ties for modern nationalism (1986, 1991a, 1993, 1996).

Smith distinguishes between 'civic' and 'ethnic' conceptions of the nation (and variants of nationalism), though his own analysis, as suggested above, generally treats ethnic communities as building blocks for nations in nationalist projects and he is sceptical that any civic nationalism is completely free from ethnic elements (1986, 1991a, 1993, 1996). Smith notes that

> civic and territorial conceptions of the nation regard it as a community of shared culture, common laws, and territorial citizenship, [while] ethnic concepts of the nation focus on the genealogy of its members, however fictive; on popular mobilization of 'the folk'; on native history and customs; and on the vernacular culture.
>
> (1993: 34)

The first conceptions of nationalism were primarily, Smith argues, civic and territorial (though there was always an ethnic element), thus 'residence and political participation in a public culture tended to determine citizenship and membership of the nation'. Smith maintains that during the nineteenth century, however, ethnic nationalism rose in importance in various parts of the world (1993: 37). Ethnonationalism (or ethnic nationalism) involves the politicization of ethnicity and very often entails specific territorial as well as political claims. The ethnic group is assumed to be coterminous with the nation, and frequently it is further assumed that each nation should have its own state. The nation is not the same as the state, however, though the problematic 'nation-state' concept assumes perfect correspondence between the boundaries of a nation and the boundaries of those living in a particular state – which as Yuval-Davis notes 'is virtually everywhere a fiction', though it is the basis of most nationalist ideologies (1997: 11). The continuing primacy of the state can be seen in the fact that most nationalist movements are centred round some kind of claim to political representation for the collective, and this 'often – but not always – takes the form of a claim for a separate state and/or territory' (ibid.: 16). As Cockburn notes, a nation may want out of a state, it may want more autonomy within a state, it may want unification across state borders, control of an existing state, or to create a new state (1998: 37); these are very different political demands but they all focus on statehood in some way.

In Chapter 3 of the book I engage in the first half of the chapter with some of the main feminist debates about women, gender and peace. I look particularly at ideas that suggest women are inherently more peaceful than men, particularly by virtue of their capacity for motherhood or social role as mothers. I also look at arguments relating to the connection between military participation and citizenship, and women's integration into conventional state militaries. As noted earlier, this book takes a socially constructed view of gender as well as ethnicity. The basic understanding, outlined succinctly by Peterson, is that:

> [g]ender refers not to anatomical or biological distinctions but to the social construction, which is always culturally specific, of masculine and feminine as hierarchical and oppositional categories. Symbols, theories, practices, institutions, and, of course, individuals are gendered, meaning that their characteristics can be associated with, or construed as manifestations of, masculinity or femininity. A gender-sensitive lens enables us to see how gender hierarchy shapes our ways of thinking, knowing, and doing and therefore has patterned consequences.
>
> (1998: 41)

Thus, the argument is that gender identity is not given by nature and is negotiable; indeed the whole concept of 'gender' is inherently anti-essentialist. As Skjelsbæk puts it, '[m]asculinity and femininity are *negotiated interpretations* of what it means to be a man or a woman. These interpretations determine male and female actions, behaviour, perceptions and rationality' (2001: 47). Gender, like ethnicity, is a relational and situational construct. Gender differences can be conceptualized as 'the *construction of masculinity and femininity in their distinction from each other*' (ibid.: 50–1, emphasis in original). Who is centrally involved in the negotiation of these hegemonic interpretations is affected by complex intersections of power, particularly as it relates to 'race', ethnicity, class, and sexuality.

In the second half of Chapter 3 I examine and analyse feminist debates about gender, nationalism(s) and armed conflict, looking largely at how feminists have responded to and theorized women's participation in nationalist movements and the relationship between feminism(s) and nationalism(s), as well as what has been suggested so far about female combatants in nationalist movements. I end by drawing out some significant points for approaching the study of female combatants in ethno-national conflicts. Chapters 4, 5 and 6 of the book focus on female combatants in Sri Lanka and Northern Ireland, drawing on my research and fieldwork. Chapter 4 looks largely at the reasons for women's enlistment in the various military groups while Chapters 5 and 6 looks at their experiences within these groups, particularly in regard to gender relations and the question of nationalist feminisms. Finally, the concluding Chapter 7 tries to draw together comparative elements of the phenomenon of female combatants in the case studies, in relation to the body of feminist theory discussed.

The remainder of this introductory chapter addresses methodological issues and the research for this book, but first a brief note on the choice of case studies.

It doesn't require much initial research to realize that Sri Lanka and Northern Ireland are very different. Nevertheless, despite their differences there are many similarities between them in terms of histories of colonialism, identity formation, nationalist mobilization, ethno-national politics and factors that led to armed conflict. These things will be drawn out more in the next chapter; here I merely wanted to highlight the fact that each conflict is interesting in respect to the issue of female combatants. Sri Lanka has been widely noted for the phenomenon of large numbers of female combatants in the Liberation Tigers of Tamil Eelam (LTTE), yet serious research on this remains scarce. In regard to Northern Ireland, the role of women in the peacemaking process has attracted a relative amount of media publicity and academic attention. The participation of women as combatants in that conflict has not yet received the same degree of attention; though there is a certain body of work on women in the republican movement, virtually nothing has been written on loyalist women in this respect.

Feminist research and the research for this book

This work, like me, is unashamedly feminist. Feminism is, however, 'a multifaceted social movement in the process of change and self-creation' (Ruddick 1989: 234). It is a social movement with its roots in activism rather than theory, although theory is central as well. Feminism is extremely diverse, and as a concept has always had problems with definition (Carroll and Hall 1993: 11). Nevertheless, Evans asserts that

> [w]hile there are deep and sometimes bitter ideological disagreements between feminists, any feminist is, at the very minimum, committed to some form of reappraisal of the position of women in society. Feminism, then, is avowedly not value-neutral, but politically engaged.
>
> (1986a: 2)

Ruddick explains that when speaking of feminism, she refers 'minimally, to a politics that is dedicated to transforming those social and domestic arrangements that deliberately or unwittingly penalize women because of their sex' and, furthermore, 'whatever their other politics and interests, feminists focus seriously on the ways that gender – the social construction of masculinity and femininity – organizes political, personal, and intellectual life' (1989: 234). However it is also clear that women are divided in numerous ways, including 'differences ... [of] race, class, ethnicity, ability, sexual orientation, and sociohistorical context' (Carroll and Hall 1993: 11–12), which shape their experiences, and gender constructions vary between cultures and across time periods.

As well as the many differences between *women*, frequently *feminists* also fundamentally disagree amongst themselves on important political issues. Ruddick points out that usually 'people who are feminists under any general definition of the term also have other, sometimes more primary, political allegiances and identities that "modify" or "hyphenate" their feminism' (1998: 214–15). One way of dealing with these complexities has been to categorize feminism under various different ideological labels – explicitly embracing the 'hyphenation' Ruddick writes of – which arguably can offer 'orderly "frameworks" to manage some of its complexities', yet also carries the danger of creating too much opposition between different types of feminism and fragmenting it still further (Carroll and Hall 1993: 12–13). Zalewski suggests that the 'proliferation of feminisms over the last few decades has simply become too frustrating for some feminists' and that '[f]eminism seemed so much simpler a few decades ago!' (2000: 2–3). Earlier I mentioned Smith's description of essentialism as being like a wet bar of soap – hard to grasp yet sliding all over the place (2001: 33) – and this analogy could also be applied to efforts to neatly categorize or 'hyphenate' different types of feminism and assign specific feminist thinkers or activists to these categories. Placing rigid boundaries around notions of 'liberal feminism', 'radical feminism', 'cultural/difference feminism', 'pacifist feminism', 'socialist feminism', 'critical feminism', 'postmodern feminism' and so on is a difficult task and one that is not always ultimately helpful.[4] Theoretically, many perspectives spill over into one another; practically, many activists defy such limiting boxes. However, when discussing centrally important themes relating to women, peace and war, there are distinctly different feminist perspectives and therefore distinctly different feminist calls to action. Accordingly, in this book I do employ some of the different categories of feminism mentioned here, to ease the discussion, but I do so in full awareness of attendant problems.

Given the diversity of feminism discussed above, it should be no surprise that a recurring question in feminist scholarship is what actually constitutes 'feminist social research' and whether or not there is a distinctly feminist approach. As in all discussion of the practice of research, significant here are the concepts of epistemology, methodology, and method. In both traditional and feminist social science discourses discussions of the three are intertwined, and the issue is confused by the fact that either 'method' or 'methodology' is often used as an all-encompassing term referring to epistemology, methodology *and* research methods (Harding 1987b: 2; Stanley and Wise 1990: 26). Epistemology is a 'theory of knowledge', answering questions about who can be a 'knower', what tests a belief must pass to be legitimately considered 'knowledge', what sorts of things can be known, and so on (Stanley and Wise 1990: 26; Harding 1987b: 3). Methodology is 'a theory and analysis of how research does or should proceed' (Harding 1987b: 3), and includes 'how research questions might best be addressed and the criteria against which research findings might be evaluated' (Maynard 1994: 14). Finally, method (in this context) refers to specific evidence-gathering techniques. This part of the chapter outlines some of the feminist debates on issues of epistemology, methodology and methods. Largely I report and reflect on my own approach to the research for this book throughout the discussion, rather than addressing this in a separate quarantined section.

Feminist critiques of traditional epistemologies

There are now a range of different feminist epistemologies,[5] with competing background assumptions and approaches. It is beyond the scope of this book to do these epistemologies justice; accordingly, here I merely present and comment on some of the most significant feminist challenges. Feminists have argued that science and history are written from the point of view of men of the dominant class and 'race' and that traditional[6] epistemologies 'systematically exclude the possibility that women could be "knowers" or *agents* of knowledge'. Feminists, therefore, suggest other theories of knowledge that legitimate women as 'knowers' (Harding 1987b: 3, emphasis in original) and are sceptical about the possibility of universal accounts of knowledge which ignore the social context (and status) of knowers (Alcoff and Potter 1993: 1). Feminists have challenged the supposed disinterestedness and universality of traditional science which is based on the Enlightenment idea that reason, employed scientifically, could provide an objective, reliable and universal foundation for knowledge (Maynard 1994: 18). Stanley and Wise argue that '*all* knowledge, necessarily, results from the conditions of its production, is contextually located, and irrevocably bears the marks of its origins in the minds and intellectual practices of those … who give voice to it' (1990: 39, emphasis in original). They also challenge dichotomous understandings of the research–theory relationship: that is, either deductivism (associated with positivism) or inductivism. Theory within deductivism precedes experience and research; experience and research are predicated upon theory, to test theoretical hypotheses. In contrast, inductivism views theory as being derived from research experience. Stanley and Wise assert that in fact 'neither model has experiential validity as an actual description of how research is conducted and knowledge produced', and they propose that feminist research should not adhere strictly to either of these dichotomous models (ibid.: 22). This is significant, and actually most social science researchers today acknowledge that the ideal-type way that both deductivism and inductivism are often presented is inaccurate and over-simplified.

Related to this is the critique of positivism, wherein the observer is neutral, detached, and makes value-free observations of social events. The positivist view entails distance between researcher and researched and assumes that the researcher can objectively see and interpret the lives and meanings of their subjects. One of the main challenges feminist epistemologies present to mainstream science is a critique of such assumptions. Wolf argues that there are three main areas of feminist criticism of positivism: '(1) philosophical critiques of positivism and its pretense of value-free science, (2) moral critiques of objectification and exploitation of subjects, and (3) practical critiques of the way positivism opposes the interest of the researcher and the researched.' Feminists, in general, argue for an approach that focuses on the research *process* and uses the researcher's viewpoint as part of this process (1996: 4–5). The 'textbook' view of positivism equates it with science and the deductive approach, strongly emphasizing the supposed objectivity of method and value-neutrality of the researcher as assuring the reliability and validity of the knowledge produced. However, Maynard notes that some argue this is too rigid an understanding of how positivism operates. Developments in the fields of the sociology of knowledge and in the philosophy and sociology of science suggest that this picture of positivism is not how science actually works in practice (1994: 12–13).

Most feminist researchers are committed to 'a rejection of scientist "objectivity", in favour of a situated researching subject, seeking to make women's experiences, the social construction of gender ... and the research process itself explicit and visible' (Byrne and Lentin 2000a: 32). Smith argues that the methods and ethic of objectivity aim at separating the knower from what they know. Criticizing this, she says '[t]he only way of knowing a socially constructed world is knowing it from within. We can never stand outside it' (1987: 88, 91). Related is Stanley's notion of 'alienated knowledge', a Marxist influenced idea whereby the 'scientist' academic mode renders invisible the *process* of knowledge construction and the labour involved in research. This means that *how* things are known becomes invisible, resulting in 'alienated knowledge', which she categorizes as 'a product apparently complete, bearing no apparent trace of the conditions of its production and the social relations that gave rise to this' (1990a: 11). Feminist social science, she says, has a foot in both the academic mode and its production of alienated knowledge, and in the feminist insistence on breaking down dichotomies between knowers and known, objects and subjects. Feminism from outside the academic mode has asserted the need for useful knowledge, 'committed understanding as a form of praxis ("understand the world and then change it")', and unalienated knowledge: 'that which concretely and analytically locates the product of the academic feminist labour process within a concrete analysis of the process of production itself' (ibid.: 11–12).

Nevertheless, there is dispute over where the critique of objectivity takes us. Harding questions the notion that objectivity is incompatible with socially situated knowledge (1991) while Randall suggests that feminist researchers rightly argue that objectivity is impossible, but criticizes the fact that often this claim goes alongside 'rejection of scientific "rigour" altogether' (1991: 521). Randall disputes the judgement that rationality is innately masculine; locating herself as a feminist empiricist, she argues that '[t]he cultural and standpoint feminist rejection of "male" rationality and epistemology and as a consequence of "scientific method" is understandable but unwise'. Although the notion of objectivity is problematic, we still 'cannot afford to abandon these essential intellectual tools' (ibid.: 521–3). For Randall,

> [g]ood social science ... should recognize that it can never be fully 'objective'; it should acknowledge the limited extent to which the so-called 'hard' scientific methods can be usefully applied to the study of human society, but even when they are inapplicable seek to be scientific in the more modest sense of being logical and systematic in its method of reasoning.
>
> (Ibid.: 524)

Feminist methodologies

Maynard suggests that there is no one methodological approach or research practice that is specific to feminism, which is unsurprising since feminism embraces a variety of positions (1994: 18). Nevertheless, Byrne and Lentin argue that '[f]eminist research methodologies stress gender as a basic theoretical concept, a deconstruction of the power relationship between researcher and researched, a political commitment to the emancipation of women, and models of research and practice which privilege participation, representation, interpretation and reflexivity' (2000a: 4). However they also point out that '[w]hile we continuously strive to follow principles of reflexivity, collaboration and emancipatory commitment to political change, anyone who has ever engaged in research knows it is a far messier process' (ibid.: 50–1). Complicating this further is Patai's contention that feminist researchers face 'dual allegiances': we have obligations to our academic disciplines and institutions; however, 'if we take feminism seriously, it commits us to a transformative politics' (1991: 138–9). Similarly, Edwards and Ribbens view feminist researchers as being 'on the margins between different social worlds' (1998: 2).

Orthodoxies, ethics and inequalities

One of the feminist methodological contributions, arguably now a feminist 'orthodoxy', has been to emphasize women's experiences in research and analysis. Feminists argue that since traditional social science has based itself in the experiences of men of the dominant classes and 'races'/ethnicities, it has only asked questions about social life that appear problematic or interesting for men thus situated. Feminist challenges to this illustrate 'that the questions that are asked – and, even more significantly, those that are not asked – are at least as determinative of the adequacy of our total picture as are any answers that we can discover' and, therefore, feminist research bases its approach and research questions in *women's* experiences and these experiences are treated as important resources for social analysis (Harding 1987b: 6–7). However Kelly *et al.* (1994) maintain that whereas in the 1970s experience was seen as a necessary starting point for feminist research, it came in the 1980s to be seen as 'an end in itself'. Thus,

> [e]xperience/identity is ... deemed to be equivalent to ... politics, as if critical awareness and understanding are inscribed on a person through forms of oppression, with an implicit or explicit presumption that such awareness is inaccessible to those who have not 'lived' such experiences.
>
> (Kelly *et al.* 1994: 29–30)

Challenging this, they argue that for a 'critical consciousness' and 'committed understanding' to develop to challenge domination, it must be possible to develop an inclusive feminism which encompasses differences between women, 'where what we share is a politics within which experiences can be located, explained and struggled with/against' (ibid.: 30).

Maynard notes that an emphasis on experience can be problematic in other ways. 'Raw', unmediated experience does not exist; poststructuralism has shown how 'the very act of speaking about experience is to culturally and discursively constitute it' and, accordingly, some feminists have suggested that what we should do is just let women 'speak for themselves' (1994: 23). Maynard points out that this ignores

> the fact that *all* feminist work is theoretically grounded; whatever perspective is adopted, feminism provides a theoretical framework concerned with gender divisions, women's oppression or patriarchal control which informs our understanding of the social world. It is disingenuous to imply otherwise. No feminist study can be politically neutral, completely inductive or solely based in grounded theory.
>
> (Ibid., emphasis in original)

Furthermore, I would stress that there is no way to unproblematically 'let women speak' in an academic project. As researchers we always have to make choices about what we present and what we leave out, what quotes we choose and which we reject. Also, although women's experience can be an important starting point for the production of feminist knowledge, '[f]eminism has an obligation to go beyond citing experience in order to make connections which may not be visible from the purely experiential level alone'; in other words, we need to use our theory to make sense of experience (Maynard 1994: 23–4).

Another feminist orthodoxy, that feminist research is 'by' women, 'for' women, and 'on' women (ibid.: 16), is now more contentious than it used to be. The notion that for research to be feminist it must be carried out by women could be contested on numerous grounds. Personally, I side with those who argue that feminist research does not necessarily have to be done by women but it must be done by *feminists* – of any type and whether women or men. Kelly *et al.* (1994) maintain that the notion that feminist research is 'on' women is important, yet 'if our concern is to understand women's oppression we need to target our attention on the ways it is structured and reproduced.... Studying women's lives as a feminist means that male dominance, masculinity and men are always part of the research' (1994: 29, 32–3). Finally, it has been asserted that if we begin inquiry with problematics generated from women's experiences, we are led to designing research *for* women; that is, the goal 'is to provide for women explanations of social phenomena that they want and need.... Traditional social research has been *for men*' (Harding 1987b: 8, emphasis in original). This notion that feminist research is 'for women' implies that it will in some way help or empower the research subjects – and, perhaps, the researcher.

The suggestion that feminist research should be 'empowering' or 'emancipatory' for research participants is, therefore, another orthodoxy of feminist approaches to research methodologies (Kelly *et al.* 1994: 36–7). Kelly *et al.*

maintain this idea has often been accepted uncritically, with little attention paid to exactly what is meant by it and how it is to be achieved; further, realistically, in the vast majority of cases participating in a research project is unlikely to transform the conditions of women's lives (ibid.). Randall, too, notes that often it is not possible to help the women involved in our research projects and sometimes it may be patronizing to try (1991: 521). It may even cause further harm if participants have their 'consciousness raised' through the experience, without channels of subsequent and empowering action being available to them (Maynard 1994: 17). Thus, we should not be naïve about how feminist research may be potentially transformatory in regard to facilitating social change and empowering participants (Maynard and Purvis 1994: 7). I have to support these critiques of naïve and potentially patronizing assumptions about empowering feminist research. My own experience suggests that in fact it may be much more likely to be life-changing for the researcher than for the researched, which leads us into a brief discussion of ethics in research.

Patai asks 'is it possible – not in theory, but in the actual conditions of the real world today – to write about the oppressed without becoming one of the oppressors?' She argues it is not, at least not in an absolute sense. She asserts that utilizing others for one's own ends, and the possibility of exploitation, are built into most research projects with human beings (1991: 139, 142). Wolf suggests that confronting the exploitative aspects of research has led to crisis for feminist fieldworkers: '[n]aming the exploitation inherent in research relationships meant having to explicitly acknowledge that serious power differentials exist between the researcher and her subjects' (1996: 19). Lal maintains that the researcher is often placed in an overtly powerful position vis-à-vis the researched; this is inevitable because social science research 'unavoidably reflects the social world in which it and we are situated' (1996: 193, 196–7). Patai poses the perennially troubling question of whether or not contributing to knowledge justifies utilizing another person for one's own purposes, and whether or not the researcher–researched relationship should be ended along with the research (1991: 143). There are clearly no easy resolutions to the above issues; my fieldwork in Sri Lanka and Ireland served only to make me more uneasy and less resolved, as may become clear later on.

One proposal for dealing with the inequality in the researcher–researched relationship has been the notion of 'returning the research', which is also problematic. How and to whom do we return it, and in what form? There are numerous problems with returning a text to participants for feedback: issues of distance when you have researched people far away; issues of language and translation; of illiteracy; problems with mail services to remote areas; and potential political risks in mailing certain texts (Wolf 1996: 33). There is also another issue here – ultimately, in the usual course of things our research is much more important to us as researchers than it is to our participants. (These issues are returned to in a later sub-section when I discuss my own attempts to 'return the research'.) In fact, Patai maintains that sometimes our desire to 'involve the researched in all stages of the project runs the risk … of subtly translating into the researcher's own demand for affirmation and validation' (1991: 147). Encouragingly, however, she concludes that '[t]he fact that doing research across race, class, and culture is a messy business is no reason to contemplate only our difficulties and ourselves struggling with them'; indeed, 'too much ignorance exists in the world to allow us to await perfect research methods before proceeding' (ibid.: 150).

Reflexivity and identity: 'situating' the researcher

Byrne and Lentin argue that 'the flowering of personal criticism in the 1980s is a consequence of a (postmodern, post-colonial) disillusionment with meta-narratives and theories' and 'the increasing use of the personal and the passionate in conducting social research is also the reflexive response ... to tendencies in academic social sciences to return to scientism and positivism' (2000a: 32). The notion of reflexivity has attained vital importance in contemporary feminist approaches to social research. Reflexivity 'can mean reflecting upon, critically examining and exploring analytically the nature of the research process', or it may mean understanding the 'intellectual autobiography' of the researcher (Maynard 1994: 16). Haggis argues that '[d]oing feminist research demands that my participation and presence – my voice – within my research project must be explicitly admitted and included in the product of that research' (1990: 77). However many have pointed out that the process of reflexivity means the researcher also 'risks making herself more central to the discourse' (Edwards and Ribbens 1998: 3), thus it 'gives voice to the already-speaking author' (Lal 1996: 200).

Lal argues that we must 'be wary of the potential paralysis ... that ensues from the reflexive mode of analysis and concentrated attentiveness to the authorial strategies and powers of representations' and that '[w]e cannot allow reflexivity to become an end in itself – another academic fad that is pursued for its own sake' (1996: 207). Lal writes of 'a mere invoking of what has been called the "mantra" of self-positioning vis-à-vis the axes of race–sex–class–sexuality' (ibid.: 197). Similarly, Patai offers a blistering criticism:

> A currently popular strategy is that of 'situating' oneself by prior announcement: 'As a white working-class heterosexual...,' or 'As a black feminist activist....' Sometimes these tropes sound like apologies, more often they are deployed as badges. Either way, they give off their own aroma of fraud, for the underlying assumption seems to be that by such identification one has paid one's respects to 'difference' – owned up to bias, acknowledged privilege, or taken possession of oppression – and is now home free.
>
> (1991: 149)

Lal and Patai are highlighting the conceptual slippage that seems often to occur, from the rich notion of reflexivity to a shallow and static notion of identity. Lal acknowledges that the locations that shape a researcher's identity and notions of self influence their choices, access and methods in the research and the representation of research subjects (1996: 190). However, ironically, critiques of the universalism of feminist theory have resulted in this researcher trend to make 'obligatory pronouncements of their positioning into the analysis without ever actually contending with these differences *in* the analysis' (ibid.: 197, emphasis in original). Patai scathingly reminds us that the world 'will not get better because we have sensitively apologised for privilege; nor if, from the comfortable heights of the academy, we advertise our identification with the oppressed or compete for distinction as members of this or that oppressed group' (1991: 150).

Patai and Lal make some vital and thought-provoking points. However I would argue that true reflexivity can be seen as different from 'identity politics'. Reflexivity in the deeper sense has the potential to be much more than simply 'labelling' oneself in the text. I could assign various self-identity labels to myself now but how much would they really tell the reader? Assumptions would be made about the researcher/writer/me based upon a reader's own preconceived and socially situated notions of what these labels 'mean' about a person. The subtleties contained within each label are usually invisible and the choice of certain labels over others marginalizes other aspects of our lives and personalities. Surely I am more than the sum of my parts – or more than the conglomeration of labels I could give myself or others could assign to me? And by focusing on positionality labels like sex/gender, 'race'/ethnicity, religion, class, sexual orientation and so on, are we not also implicitly discounting the potential impact of our more individual personality characteristics on the research process in all its stages? How do I (or anyone else) know what kind of complex interaction of all my characteristics and social positionings goes into shaping my research? My point is not that my positioning and my (constantly shifting) sense of identity do not affect my research; on the contrary, it is that they affect my research in ways far too complex to be guessed at by myself or others. As Patai and Lal point out, assigning myself a few labels at the beginning of my work and then forgetting about the issue would not constitute meaningful reflexivity. We must continually strive to assess the relationship between ourselves and our research and pay constant attention to reflecting on the whole research project and *process*; this is the more valuable conceptualization of reflexivity, though much more difficult.

Subject representation, analysis and interpretation

Nordstrom compellingly argues that '[s]ilences – spheres where knowledge has been kept from public awareness – are undeniably political' (1998: 81). As already noted, in traditional social science research there was a huge silence about women's lives. Therefore, Lentin asserts, in privileging women's lived experiences we must view women's own accounts of their lives 'as primary documents' (1997a: 5). Edwards and Ribbens argue that academic conventions to attain credibility and authority in the academic setting 'risk silencing, mutilating or denigrating the voices of the subjects of our research' (1998: 16). Retaining the 'voices' of our research participants in written work is always difficult; as Haggis suggests, it is impossible to privilege one voice without risking 'slighting' another (1990: 76). On the other hand, awareness of how we exercise interpretive authority presents other dilemmas, as 'in our concern for representing the voices of others we may be constrained in developing our own voices as academics and authors' (Edwards and Ribbens 1998: 17).

Borland argues that gaining a narrator's commentary on a story can greatly assist the researcher's understanding of it, but not all narrators may be willing to analytically interpret their own stories (1991: 71). On the other hand, sometimes even when participants are given the chance to review how they have been represented or analysed in academic work ('returning the text', mentioned earlier), they are still unhappy. This, Sharoni argues, is often not about misrepresentation as much as it is about the uneasiness of participants with the overall arguments or theories that their words or actions are used to bolster (1995: 1–2). Interpretive authority is a complex and problematic issue. This may sometimes be an inescapable part of the nature of academic work. I believe all we can do is try to be as open to dialogue with our research participants and with other academics as possible, whilst remaining true to our considered interpretations. Borland notes that feminist researchers 'hold an explicitly political vision of the structural conditions that lead to particular social behaviours, a vision that our field collaborators, many of whom do not consider themselves feminists, may not recognize as valid' (1991: 64). Not all differences of perspective can or should be resolved in the written product, nor does Borland believe that our interpretations need to be validated by our research participants, for 'we bring our own knowledge, experience, and concerns to our material, and the result, we hope, is a richer, more textured understanding of its meaning' (ibid.: 73). Accordingly there are no easy answers to the question of how we might 'present our work in a way that grants the speaking woman interpretive respect without relinquishing our responsibility to provide our own interpretation of her experience' (ibid.: 64).

In the analysis of my own qualitative work, I follow the feminist argument that women's own representations and interpretations of their lives are a valuable (though not the only) resource. Using the example of Sharoni and others, I try to 'treat the daily experiences and struggles of ... women activists as locations where theorizing takes place. In other words ... women activists are treated as social and political theorists.' This approach, Sharoni suggests, stresses their political agency and de-marginalizes them (1995: 25). However this approach is used with caution; it does not mean that I take at face value everything told to me. Statements or suggestions that struck me as odd, or that were made by only one interviewee and seemed to be contradicted by others or by literature on the topic, were treated with more scepticism than ideas that recurred in various interviews and/or were supported by other literature.

I also gave my participants the option of commenting on my work as a way of monitoring the legitimacy of my representations of their narratives – though I knew we would not always agree on my overall conclusions. Most seemed interested in this offer; particularly in Northern Ireland, some women I interviewed had been interviewed in the past and had had negative experiences of interviewers either not doing this or, worse, saying they would and then not following through. However, as noted earlier, returning the research is far from easy. In Northern Ireland my main problem was getting feedback from those who wished to give it in line with the strict time constraints I was under on the completion of my dissertation. I was also a little unsure that all participants received what I sent since I often had to post them care of the organization I had contacted them through rather than to a personal address. In the case of Sri Lanka this was magnified enormously by problems of distance, unreliable postal service to areas not under government control (and possibly government-monitored post in other areas), and the language barrier. Some participants said sending the text in English would be fine, since they had translators but a few said that it would need to be in Tamil for them to read it, as they did not have access to a translator. In the end I found that given the extremely prohibitive cost of translation (a problem to which I could find no solution), for those participants I was simply unable to return the text. Only half of the republican participants in Northern Ireland responded with feedback and none of the loyalists nor any Tamil participants. I am unresolved as to the ethical implications this has. In the case of my interviewees in Ireland, their non-response may for the most part have been a perfectly valid conscious choice. In the case of my Tamil interviewees, however, this is much less assured – I am not even confident that they received the text – illustrating Patai's point (discussed earlier) that ethical research with human subjects is extremely difficult, if not impossible, to achieve. As for the question of how this may affect the conclusions I drew from the material, I am a little more optimistic. As discussed, Borland encouragingly suggests that our interpretations as researchers do not necessarily need to be validated by our participants, since we bring our own knowledge and experience to bear on the research process and hopefully produce richer and more balanced work.

Finally, a note on issues of validity and reliability. Maynard implies that questions of objectivity and value-neutrality are perhaps somewhat red herrings – it is the soundness of feminist research that matters most. Feminist research must be rigorous 'if it is to be regarded as intellectually compelling, politically persuasive, policy-relevant and meaningful to anyone other than feminists themselves' (1994: 24). I would add that this should be necessary if our research is to be regarded as worthwhile by other *feminists* as well. Requiring high standards of ourselves should be of at least as much importance as convincing the 'mainstream' of the worthiness of our research. Rigour, Maynard says, at a minimum 'involves being clear about one's theoretical assumptions, the nature of the research process, the criteria against which "good" knowledge can be judged and the strategies used for interpretation and analysis' (ibid.: 25). The issue of what constitutes valid and reliable feminist knowledge is a difficult and complex one, as in any research, and Maynard and Purvis argue that much of the debate has been carried out at the level of the abstract, the epistemological, which presents difficulties in adapting this to real-world practicalities of doing empirical research (1994: 5–6). In regard to qualitative research specifically, Edwards and Ribbens argue that it is, to some extent, 'a marginalized methodological discourse in that … researchers using this approach cannot escape addressing their position and foundations *vis-à-vis* quantitative and positivist methodologies and traditions'. Because of this, qualitative research 'almost inevitably appears "unconvincing" ... because dominant understandings of concepts of "validity", "reliability" and "representativeness" are posed within a numerical rather than a process framework' (1998: 3–4). Maynard and Purvis argue that 'reaching conclusions is a social process' (1994: 7) and interpretation is political and contested. Conclusions that seem reliable and valid to one researcher may well not to another. Accordingly, I believe we must focus on the soundness of our research *processes*, rather than merely the conclusions we draw, emphasizing reflexive, self-critical and transparent approaches in our research and interpretations.

Research methods

A major feature of much feminist research has been the favouring of the use of qualitative research methods over quantitative (though this position has more recently come to be questioned) and an important feature of feminist qualitative research has been an emphasis on the face-to-face, unstructured or semi-structured interview. The qualitative/quantitative debate is discussed briefly here. (Some would see this as an issue of methodology or epistemology, rather than methods, but the focus here is largely on methods (see Bryman 1984).) Various issues relating to interviews and fieldwork are then addressed, with particular attention paid to how I addressed these matters in this project.

The qualitative versus quantitative debate

Feminists who have advocated the use of qualitative rather than quantitative methods of research enquiry have based this in their critique of dominant research modes and, in particular, the epistemological challenge to positivism. Quantitative research methods, such as surveys and questionnaires, were seen as representing a '"masculinist" form of knowing', which emphasizes 'detachment of the researcher and the collection and measurement of "objective" social facts through a (supposedly) value-free form of data collection' (Maynard 1994: 11). In contrast, qualitative methods

> focus more on the subjective experiences and meanings of those being researched ... [and were] regarded as more appropriate to the kinds of knowledge that feminists wished to make available, as well as being more in keeping with the politics of doing research as a feminist.
>
> (Ibid.)

This anti-quantitative methods position was most important when feminist research was new; the emphasis on the importance of listening to and understanding women's self-descriptions and accounts led fairly naturally to a focus on qualitative methods. While the critique of the application of quantitative methods was an important step in feminist research at the time, it 'gradually developed into something of an unproblematized orthodoxy' whereby it was assumed that *only* qualitative methods were really appropriate in feminist research to generate useful knowledge (Maynard 1994: 12). A later view, which I support, suggests this is potentially problematic and limiting and notes that the polarizing of qualitative versus quantitative approaches is 'at odds with the critique of the inhibiting effect of dualistic categorization that has been mounted by some feminists in the debate on epistemology' (ibid.: 21).

Despite the assumption of a strong link between positivism and quantitative methods, many quantitative researchers recognize that 'producing figures involves as much of an act of social construction as any other kind of research' and, therefore, Maynard argues that positivism does not seem to be *intrinsic* to quantitative research, though many textbook discussions do not make a distinction between the two (1994: 13). When feminists reject quantification wholesale they neglect the contribution that research involving such methods has made to knowledge of women's experiences. Additionally, there is political potential in such work. Maynard notes, for example, that studies on domestic violence, on women's unequal pay situation, or on the feminization of poverty all require or benefit from enumeration (ibid.: 13–14; see also Byrne and Lentin 2000a: 8). So, just as the traditional social science interview was transformed to fit feminist practice, Kelly *et al.* suggest that perhaps we should explore somehow transforming the survey/questionnaire (1994: 35). Furthermore, many feminists are among the increasing body of social scientists who argue in favour of combining and comparing methods. Stanley argues that feminists should use any and every means available as 'there is no one set of methods or techniques, nor even a broad category of types of method ("qualitative"), which should be seen as distinctly feminist' (1990a: 12). I side with such scholars and argue for a plurality of methods whenever and wherever a research project would benefit from this, and assuming it is possible.

My own research for this project uses qualitative methods, utilizing in-depth interviews. This is not due to an ideological opposition to quantitative methods but is simply that the nature of this project lends itself better to a qualitative approach. The most important consideration is that 'the method adopted be that most appropriate to a specific set of research questions and the overall research context' (Maynard and Purvis 1994: 3). In this project I was trying to identify motivating factors for women enlisting in ethno-national militant movements as combatants, to come to an understanding of their experiences, and to reflect on what this may tell us in respect of theories of gender and nationalism and women's relationships to violence and non-violence, peace and war. This is not something that would be easy to do using quantitative methods. Furthermore, quantitative methods rely on large sample sizes which are difficult to obtain when it comes to secretive illegal organizations. Related to this is the fact that where total combatant numbers are a military secret and the identity of members is often secret as well, it would be impossible to use probability sampling to obtain a statistically representative sample – something which is essential for quantitative projects. The total population of female combatants in my case studies is unknowable; I used non-probability snowball sampling to obtain small samples.[7] In Sri Lanka this was 17 female LTTE members and ex-members over two field trips. I also carried out a number of other discussions and interviews with non-LTTE Tamils and also academics and NGO staff (Tamil, Sinhalese and Muslim) that inform my work in a less systematic way.[8] In Ireland (north and south) the republican sample was 11 ex-combatant women; I also had a less formal discussion with one male ex-combatant gatekeeper (the intermediaries a researcher approaches to help obtain access). With loyalists the sample in a strict sense was much smaller – only two of the 10 loyalist women I interviewed count as ex-combatants in the way I conceptualized 'combatant' earlier in this chapter, for reasons elaborated on in Chapter 4. Another two were active in an auxiliary role and were also wives of loyalist prisoners; another woman made petrol bombs at the beginning of the 'Troubles'; and one I believe to have been 'active' in some way but she was evasive about the extent of this. I also interviewed three other women from loyalist communities whose husbands were involved in paramilitaries (and were prisoners) and one who had no personal experience of paramilitaries. Finally, I also spoke less formally to four male loyalist ex-prisoner community worker gatekeepers. Though in quantitative research these would of course be unacceptably small samples, this is not the case in qualitative work, which is much more in-depth and focuses on richer understanding. Although I did not live with and immerse myself in the culture of the people I was studying for long periods of time (such as in anthropology), at least not in the case of Sri Lanka where I spent only four months in total, my work would fit within broader understandings of ethnography. The research material is deep, rich and detailed enough to justify the relatively small sample size and many more interviews would have been difficult to analyse and incorporate into the work in any meaningful way. Finally, my fieldwork relating to the two case studies is intended to spur further theoretical reflection, rather than to infer hard and fast generalizable rules.

Transforming the interview

As noted, the in-depth, face-to-face interview 'has become the paradigmatic "feminist method"' (Kelly *et al.* 1994: 34). Feminist social scientists have long attempted to practise a revision of the traditional interview technique, a technique which suggests: that rapport between interviewer and interviewee is necessary and good only in as much as to elicit the information required; that interviewers should remain detached from their research subjects; and that interviewers should not answer questions put to them by the interviewee. The emotionally detached form of interviewing treats the researched 'as the passive givers of information, with the researcher acting as a sponge soaking up the details provided' (Maynard 1994: 15). Feminist challenges to this approach argue that the interviewer–interviewee relationship should be non-hierarchical and that there should be a reciprocal, equal relationship between researcher and researched (Randall 1991: 517). There is an argument for 'a genuine, rather than an instrumental rapport', the claim being that this 'encourages a non-exploitative relationship, where the person being studied is not treated simply as a source of data' (Maynard 1994: 15–16). I personally do not believe that expecting or aiming for a close personal relationship with all the people I interviewed would be either reasonable or productive, nor do I believe that for rapport to be genuine it has to entail a deep and ongoing relationship. I tried to be as respectful of and attentive to my interviewees as whole people, rather than simply as interesting subjects, as possible, but I do not need to like or agree with all my interviewees, nor they me, to do good research.

More recently, some feminist researchers have revised the belief that interviews can be non-hierarchical. They argue that it is impossible for the researcher and the researched to really be on equal terms and that sometimes attempts to appear more equal can simply hide a deeper exploitation, with research subjects being convinced to open themselves up to researchers who ultimately maintain the power over how the information provided is used (Randall 1991: 518). Reports suggest some women enjoy being interviewed, whilst others find the experience intrusive and worry that they may be made vulnerable later through their participation (Maynard and Purvis 1994: 5). Of the frequent claim that the feminist interview process 'is empowering in that it "gives a voice" to those who might otherwise remain silent', Patai asks 'is it empowerment or is it appropriation?' Is it, in a sense, just a 'feel good' measure for the researcher? (1991: 145–7). I certainly do not accept the self-gratifying claim that my interviews were 'empowering' for interviewees on an individual level; indeed, I am very conscious of the fact that in most cases I gained much more from the experience than they did. I also agree that interviews are unlikely to ever be completely non-hierarchical or equal, but I disagree that in all cases and all contexts the power rests absolutely with the interviewer. In terms of the fieldwork overall there were innumerable points during the research for this project when I was extremely conscious of how reliant I was on both gatekeepers and interviewees to be able to carry out the project, and how quickly this could be pulled out from under me. In Sri Lanka I was constantly hyper-aware of my 'whiteness' and foreignness, as I felt under continual observation, and this in conjunction with my youth and inexperience as a researcher served to be pretty undermining. Some people I encountered obviously viewed me as in need of care and protection, and fussed over me almost as a surrogate daughter. While this can sometimes be hindering in a fieldwork context (see Henry 2007) there were also times when it was very useful to me and something I was grateful for; it did not, however, make me feel powerful. In terms of how participants and I responded to each other in the interview context, also, I certainly did not always feel that I was in a powerful position over my interviewees. I agree with Henry (ibid.) that the very presumption of researcher-power versus participant-powerlessness problematically assumes a fixed and static notion of power being something held by one person over another, neglecting the fluid and shifting nature of power relations between people. On the other hand, I certainly concede Patai's point that in terms of my overall location in respect to the whole project in comparison with that of my interviewees, I hold the last card in terms of how I represent the participants, and in terms of my socio-economic standing in the international system I am certainly more privileged than many of my participants in a structural sense, particularly though not exclusively my Sri Lankan participants. This is not the same thing, however, as personal, individual power relations and transactions within the research context.

Another issue in regard to interviews is the question of ways in which the gender, 'race' or ethnicity, social class and sexual orientation of researchers and the researched intersect (Phoenix 1994). This brings in the issue of 'matching' interviewer and interviewee along these lines – which, it has been claimed, produces 'better' interviews. The argument is that 'matching' helps to counteract the 'interviewer effect' (how the interviewer, and the interviewer–interviewee relationship, influence the 'data'), encourages rapport, and is less exploitative. Phoenix's position, which I concur with, is that social positions do 'enter into the interview situation but … they do not [do] so in any unitary or essential way' (ibid.: 49–50). Accordingly, the prescription of 'matching' is too simplistic. Phoenix argues that the complexity of the intersecting positioning of interviewers and interviewees makes it hard to know whether matching on particular characteristics will produce 'better' data than not matching (ibid.: 66–7). In the case of this project I was not matched with my interview subjects on anything other than gender and in some cases social class, and although I had a good rapport with most participants I certainly do not feel that being a woman interviewing other women meant there was an immediate bond. As I noted earlier, I do not believe it is possible to accurately tease out all the impacts and implications of my layers of identity and structural positioning in regard to that of my interviewees.

Anderson and Jack highlight some of the ways in which certain approaches to interviewing may either inhibit or encourage female interview subjects to share their narratives with the interviewer. Drawing on her fieldwork experience, Anderson reflects that the fact that she came from a similar background as the women she interviewed meant that she unconsciously slipped into the conventions of social discourse that she learned as a child, which had a negative effect because it meant that 'unwritten rules of conversation about appropriate questions and topics … kept me from encouraging women to make explicit the range of emotions surrounding the events and experiences they related' (Anderson and Jack 1991: 13). This lends support to the idea that 'matching' interviewer and interviewee does not necessarily elicit better responses. This issue of 'matching' is related to the wider research debate over 'insider' versus 'outsider' researchers, where there is disagreement over the relative advantages and disadvantages of studying one's 'own group' (an insider researcher) or a different group (an outsider researcher) (see Lee 1995; Wolf 1996; Lal 1996). There are reasonable points made on both sides of this debate, beyond my scope to discuss here, but for me the most interesting thing to arise from the debate is the destabilization of simplistic notions of what it means to be an 'insider' or an 'outsider' and the relationship this has to ideas about identity and subject positioning. Lal maintains that in the actual process of research, 'one is faced with the need to constantly negotiate *between* the positions of insider and outsider, rather than being fixedly assigned one or the other subject position' (1996: 193, emphasis in original), and that ultimately there are an indefinite number of insider–outsider border zones (ibid.: 196).

Anderson also argues that as part of the listening process we 'need to hear what women implied, suggested, and started to say but didn't. We need to interpret their pauses and, when it happens, their unwillingness or inability to respond' (Anderson and Jack 1991: 17). This is significant but very difficult. For example, one of the women I interviewed in Northern Ireland was unwilling to discuss the fact that she had small children when she was sent to prison, but never gave an explanation for this. I do not know whether the subject was just too painful for her to be prepared to speak of, or whether there were other factors here that I was unaware of, and I would be wary of making assumptions about what her refusal meant. Jack (a psychologist) also writes of attending to silences. She has found that often she is 'listening to how what she [the interviewee] says fits into what I think I already know'; she feels it is important to ask our interviewees what they mean by the words they use, and to ensure we 'attend to what is missing' (that is, listen for the silences in our interviews) (ibid.: 19). She discusses three ways of listening that she has found helpful. First, 'to listen to the person's *moral language*.' For example, 'I feel like I'm a failure' is a moral self-evaluative statement which 'allow[s] us to examine the relationship between self-concept and cultural norms ... [and] between how we are told to act and how we feel about ourselves when we do or do not act that way' (ibid.: 19–20). In Northern Ireland I found some of the women I interviewed appeared to demonstrate a lack of self-confidence in their own opinions and judgements: 'maybe I'm being stupid, but ...' was a recurring statement. A corollary of this was appearing to seek validation from me of their opinions: 'does that sound really dumb?' Second, Jack says, we should 'attend to the subject's *meta-statements*', which are 'places in the interview where people spontaneously stop, look back, and comment about their own thoughts or something just said'. These meta-statements, she argues, 'alert us to the individual's awareness of a discrepancy within the self – or between what is expected and what is being said.' In this way they tell us 'what categories the individual is using to monitor her thoughts, and allow observation of how the person socializes feelings or thoughts according to certain norms' (ibid.: 21–2). In Northern Ireland, one example of this I noticed on a few occasions was where ex-combatant republican women said something about wanting a society where all life is valued, then stopped and commented that they supposed that 'sounds strange coming from someone like me'. Finally, Jack suggests we 'attend to the *logic of the narrative*, noticing the internal consistency or contradictions in the person's statements about recurring themes and the way these themes relate to each other'. These are important as they often illustrate conflicting beliefs (ibid.: 22, all emphases in original).

In regard to how I carried out the interviews for this project, I used a semi-structured approach utilizing a combination of direct and open questions. I structured the interviews around a few topics and key questions and then saw where the discussion led, wanting to be open to ideas and to maximize the opportunities of participants for self-reflection. I had a basic interview schedule but the nature of the interview process and my own attitude to research meant that this was not used in a very strict sense. Each question was not necessarily asked in exactly the same way of each participant. The schedule was used more as a basic framework to work from, being adapted according to each interview. In some cases, a question I was intending to ask later was effectively pre-empted in a participant's response to an earlier question. In other cases, something a participant said initiated a new line of thought and questioning for me and, of course, the answer to one question from the schedule would often lead to supplementary probing.

Fieldwork matters

There are various issues that researchers frequently encounter in fieldwork situations generally (as opposed to the interview setting itself) pertinent to researching a violent socio-political conflict. Many researchers have found that they are welcomed in violent and socially divided contexts, occasionally because the researcher provides some security for the people under study (from government forces, for example) but more usually because the researcher is welcomed 'as someone who can provide them with an audience and a voice' (Lee 1995: 15). However, '[a]ccess to a research setting is never a given. What is open at one juncture can be closed at another time or in different circumstances', and sometimes access can become increasingly difficult as the conflict persists over a long period of time. Although locals may become used to the presence of researchers, 'they can just as easily find the attention of researchers increasingly burdensome, as is apparently happening in some areas of Northern Ireland' (ibid.: 16–17). Researchers wanting to study in these kinds of areas often face serious scrutiny of their background and intentions by police, security forces and paramilitary groups. I expected this in my research and was a little surprised to find this did not usually seem to be the case (to my knowledge). Only two paramilitary people (one in Sri Lanka and one in Northern Ireland) ever asked to see my student identity card, and I had no real problems with police or security forces.

As I mentioned earlier, to gain access to my sample I had to rely on the snowball technique, whereby gatekeepers I contacted put me in touch with some people, who then put me in touch with others. In the case of Sri Lanka I initially contacted a number of NGOs, particularly women's groups, which said they might be able to assist me, but ultimately this did not prove to be all that fruitful. Once I got to the north of Sri Lanka I found that the easiest way of accessing interviewees was to go directly through LTTE gatekeepers by presenting myself at their various Political Wing offices. Two interviews with ex-LTTE women, however, were obtained through Sinhalese local government officials working in an impoverished border area in the northeast, rather than through the LTTE, and another two ex-combatant interviews (carried out on my second visit) were obtained through a purely chance meeting. Gatekeepers largely seemed to take me at my word as to who I was and what I was doing and there was rarely a problem in gaining access to interviewees, except in Trincomalee where there seemed to be greater hesitation. The only reason I can think of to explain the difference in Trinco, aside from individual personalities, is that it is located in the east which is much more ethnically mixed than the north and even in terms of the east it has suffered particularly badly during the war, being a crucial strategic location. I wondered whether the LTTE in Trinco was in consequence more cautious and less open to outsiders there. In terms of access to the actual field (as opposed to access to interviewees), this was only possible because I travelled to the northeast during the ceasefire. On my first visit the ceasefire had only been in place for six months and the A9 highway north only recently re-opened, after being closed for many years as part of the government's embargo on the north. I had the great privilege of travelling to the northern conflict zone with an expatriate Tamil family who live in the UK and were returning home to Jaffna for the first time in almost 20 years, as so many Tamils were doing at this optimistic time. (I had been put in touch with this lovely family through my mother in New Zealand, who was a secondary school teacher and had taught the daughters of another branch of the family who migrated to New Zealand some years ago.) This journey was an experience in itself, with three different militarized checkpoints to go through in a process which took most of a day, given the queue of cars, trucks, motorcycles, and people on foot and bicycle which stretched for miles.

In the case of my interviews in Ireland it was ex-prisoner organizations, community groups and political parties that acted as my gatekeepers and interviews were mostly conducted on the premises of those organizations – though one was in a woman's home and four in cafés or hotel restaurants/bars. Again, gatekeepers did not usually appear suspicious of me but interviews did often take some time to be arranged (some were frustratingly postponed at the last minute on more than one occasion), and background checks on me may have been carried out without my knowledge. In one amusing, though slightly disturbing incident, it seemed that one republican ex-prisoner organization was confusing me with an Australian researcher who apparently wanted (unrealistically) to investigate women's involvement in the 'Engineering' branch of the IRA – that is, the bomb-making section. This had immediately caused her, and me by false association, to be 'red-flagged' by the IRA and her request for assistance was ignored. Thankfully this seemed to be resolved in my case after I forcefully reiterated a number of times that I had no specific interest in Engineering, nor any intention of trying to coax secret details out of ex-IRA women about their past activities.

A significant concern in fieldwork is the issue of researcher neutrality and lying to participants. Researchers are frequently challenged about where their own sympathies lie and often respond 'by proclaiming themselves to be neutral, explaining that they are present in the setting as an objective observer rather than an engaged participant'; however, '[c]omplete neutrality is probably impossible. It is unlikely that one's sympathies will be engaged to an equal degree by all the parties to the conflict' (Lee 1995: 23). I believe Lee is right, and researchers often face difficult choices, perhaps needing to find a balance between convincing participants of their neutrality and so gaining access, and their own private perspectives on the situation. This raises ethical issues around lying to one's participants to gain access. Is proclaiming neutrality when you are not completely neutral an unacceptable form of lying? What if that is the only way to be able to undertake the research? What if you are struggling within yourself to be as neutral as possible? What if you don't think you *should* be neutral? Should the research be abandoned as unethical? Lee comments that many people have argued that lying is permissible and necessary to gain access in highly stratified or unequal contexts, and also notes that some researchers have been 'radicalized by fieldwork in a conflict situation' and have subsequently given up neutrality as ethically inappropriate (ibid.: 23–4). Cockburn argues that '[t]here are ethics involved in ... wars and it is impossible for a researcher, even if she wants to, to position herself above and outside them' (1998: 3). I did try to remain as open-minded on the case study conflicts as possible, apart from the fact that being on the 'side of women' in some way is obviously a political judgement, but of course Lee and Cockburn are right; I am not as neutral as I strive to be and this has undoubtedly coloured my work. In regard to Sri Lanka I have more sympathy politically with Tamil nationalists than with the state, and in Northern Ireland more with republicans than with loyalists or with the British state (though my research and fieldwork with loyalists led to a much greater empathy for them than I previously had). The issue of violence to achieve those political goals is a separate matter for me, however, and although I may empathize with particular grievances or particular ideologies over others, where they lead to new forms of repression and abuse is where they lose me. In terms of being challenged about my sympathies, in Northern Ireland none of my interviewees asked me what my own view of the conflict was, which knowing the local cultural context I was not surprised by. One never asks outright what a person's religion or political views are in Northern Ireland; these things are assigned to you, assumed, read off you (sometimes erroneously) through various social and physical clues. In Sri Lanka, in contrast, a great many of my interviewees asked me – usually at the end of the interview – 'What do you think of our movement?' In these cases I answered, as honestly as I could, that I sympathized with their grievances but did not support violent means.

Another important concern when researching in socially divided contexts is the possibility of danger to the researcher. Lee distinguishes between two kinds of danger that may arise, which he calls 'the *ambient* and the *situational*.' Ambient danger is that which arises when the researcher faces dangers simply by virtue of being in a dangerous setting. Situational danger is that which arises 'when the researcher's presence or actions evoke aggression, hostility, or violence from those within the setting' (1995: 2–3, emphasis in original). There may also be risks of sexual harassment and assault (ibid.: 55–61), particularly (though not exclusively) for female researchers, which is an issue that is still not often discussed openly.

In my own fieldwork I rarely felt particularly unsafe, largely because my fieldwork in Sri Lanka was conducted during the ceasefire and in Northern Ireland post-Agreement. Northeastern Sri Lanka at the time of writing (2008) would be another matter. This does not, however, mean that either place was free from violence (thus ambient danger) during the time of my fieldwork but I largely felt able to manage and avoid it. Lee suggests that during research in a violent social context, the researcher, like locals and others in the setting, 'copes with ambient danger by developing a sensitivity to potentially hazardous situations and utilizing preventive strategies for avoiding them', which not only provides more safety for the researcher but can also offer one insights into how people living in the local culture cope (1995: 28). In Northern Ireland I think this was definitely the case for me. Because I was living there for a number of years doing my doctorate, I was much more intimately aware of what was potentially dangerous for me than I was in Sri Lanka. As well as living and studying there I also fell in love with a local man shortly after my arrival (still my partner today), who is from a Catholic-nationalist working-class background, and I became very rooted in the local setting. In some ways this had a contradictory impact. On the one hand I was more aware of how to recognize and avoid ambient danger than I was in Sri Lanka; on the other hand, my richer awareness of all potentialities meant that I felt more afraid (occasionally) while doing my interviews in Northern Ireland than I did in Sri Lanka, despite the fact that northeastern Sri Lanka was objectively more dangerous, even during the ceasefire, than Northern Ireland was at the time. I had absorbed the baseline fear and constant watchfulness of Northern Irish people (at least those from working-class urban areas, the most likely to be directly affected) who have lived through the 'Troubles'.

In Sri Lanka my greater ignorance of the local situation and my somewhat naïve doctoral student enthusiasm kept me from reflecting too much on potential danger during my first visit. I remember being terrified shortly before I departed for Sri Lanka, but this was much more to do with my anxieties about coping in a context where I was totally alone, did not speak the languages, and was not exactly sure how I was going to get around than it was about physical danger. I did not even have a system set up for periodically reporting in with my supervisor or partner, and once I was there I realized I could disappear off the planet and no one would even know for weeks. The one time I felt that ambient danger might be a problem was in eastern Sri Lanka on the first day of the peace negotiations in September 2002, when I was interviewing some LTTE members and had to travel from an area under state control to one under Tiger control. Although this was normally fine, on that particular day both the state forces and the Tigers were clearly nervous about the potential for trouble. Both sides were obviously and heavily armed and the state forces questioned me on the journey over, which they had not done previously. Similarly the Tiger office was patrolled by armed guards, which I never saw before or since at any of their political offices.

There was one occasion when situational danger was a problem. I was in eastern Sri Lanka, staying at a small run-down beach resort near Trincomalee and trying to get permission from the Tigers to visit one of their military camps (which I ultimately failed to do, not through lack of persistence). This entailed some days of waiting, eating, playing cards with tourists, talking to locals and swimming. One day I went swimming alone. The beach was deserted. While I was in the water I heard someone call out to me from the beach and turned to see a local man sitting on the beach near where I was swimming. He was masturbating. I turned away and kept swimming, hoping he would leave if I ignored him, but he kept calling to me. I ended up throwing a coconut at him after I got out of the water – sadly I was so upset I missed by a mile. Even six years later I find it hard to write about this, and indeed I never mentioned it in my PhD dissertation. I can see the absurdity and humour in the situation but it was also a deeply distressing and confusing experience, not just because of the incident itself but, even more so, the aftermath. I mentioned what happened to the owner of the resort and then found myself embroiled in a situation beyond my control – it turned out this had been a recurring problem and the resort owner, a Tamil, was afraid of losing business due to it. He had complained to the police about it in the past but they hadn't taken it seriously. He wanted me to complain to the police, as he said then they would do something – basically, because I was a foreign white woman. He and the police immediately blamed the problem on 'the refugees' down the road (a camp for internally displaced people (IDPs), mostly Tamil and Muslim). So I found myself enmeshed in an imbroglio involving the international political economy of tourism and its attendant neo-colonial elements, neo-colonial sexual politics, local inter- and intra-ethnic politics, and the position of IDPs (which is particularly difficult in the Trinco area (Alison 2004a; Smith 2003)).

Finally, the questions of sensitive research and confidentiality in the research process are important to consider in relation to potential harms. The potential harms to participants attached to a research project such as this one, which entails working with/on people who have been engaged in illegal activities and violent political conflict, are fairly self-evident. In avoiding such potential harms, the importance of maintaining anonymity of people, places or organizations is clearly particularly important (de Laine 2000: 72; Lee 1993: Ch. 9). Confidentiality of my participants was a serious concern for me with this research topic. I made all possible efforts to ensure their anonymity and protection, and transcribed my own interview tapes to ensure that I was the only person to have access to them. I changed the names of participants in my finished work and in my interview transcripts. There were a couple of exceptions where women insisted it was fine to use their real name, but I used only their first name and did not indicate in any way which names were real and which were pseudonyms. As Lee points out, however, this is usually not enough to disguise a participant's identity, as other personal features can often reveal this (Lee 1993: Ch. 9), so I also removed or generalized other identifiers in the final product whilst still being concerned to ensure that this did not distort my findings.

De Laine notes that sometimes participants come to tell a researcher too much, and 'can later have real regrets and even experience loss of self-esteem'

(2000: 79). Deciding what to disclose and what to conceal in the written research, then, is difficult and 'researchers must walk a tightrope' (Lee 1993: 206). Researchers are sometimes able 'to manipulate informants to reveal more than they intended through probing, which could constitute an invasion of privacy, or collect information that is inadvertently conveyed through non-verbal expressions' (de Laine 2000: 79). Overt observations and informed consent to participation in the research do not get around this problem; de Laine feels there can be real issues of betrayal and deception in many research projects, but especially in projects on highly sensitive topics (ibid.: 76). This can be particularly a problem in methodological approaches that emphasize the researcher forming close relationships in the field. As discussed earlier in the chapter, some feminist researchers promote this as positive while others point out it can lead to exploitative relations, ethical dilemmas and conflicts of interest. This is not only an issue 'in the field' but is also an ethical and methodological question pertaining to withdrawal from the field – a recurring feminist question is whether or not the researcher–researched relationship should continue after the research has ended. In my own work, as discussed earlier, I did not feel that forming close relationships with the subjects of my research was either appropriate or necessarily productive, nor entirely ethical; I agree with those feminist social scientists who suggest that maintaining some degree of respectful distance is warranted, in light of the potential for exploitation discussed above and the possibility that close relationships may lead to greater hesitation to challenge the views of participants or report anything negative in the research. Accordingly, although I had perfectly cordial (and indeed usually friendly) relations with my research participants, I did not maintain those relationships in any serious way after the research. When it was relevant I did share some reasonably personal information about myself with some research participants, which seemed to me only a fair exchange, but I did not perceive this as meaning that I was building a friendship with them. I liked some of my research participants immensely and could envisage real friendship with them, but ultimately it seemed to me that pursuing that would have made doing the research harder.

Conclusion: so what, then, is feminist research?

Despite the lack of a singular model of feminist research, there are recurrent themes such as 'the focus on women's experiences ... and the concern for ethical questions which guide research practices. Feminists are concerned with the role of the researcher in the research, and with countering ... scientistic philosophy and practice' (Maynard 1994: 21). Not all of these or other themes are restricted to feminism but 'the ways that they are treated (informed as they are by feminist theorizing about gender and feminist politics more generally), together with the manner in which they are combined, mean that it is possible to identify specific feminist research practices' (ibid.; see also Kelly *et al.* 1994: 46). Stanley suggests that a precondition of 'good research' is that it accounts for 'the conditions of its own production' – that is, it produces 'unalienated knowledge' – and that this should be a goal of all feminist work (1990a: 13). For many feminist researchers our work should also produce 'useful knowledge, knowledge which can be used by ourselves and others to "make a difference"' (Kelly *et al.* 1994: 28). Byrne and Lentin suggest that we should work against the establishment of new feminist orthodoxies, and argue that

> [i]t is not the method ... which makes research methodologies feminist, but rather the commitment to several feminist principles, as variably defined ... with prime attention given to the researcher–researched relationship and to the deconstruction of power relationships in the research process.
>
> (2000a: 3, 8)

Maynard questions whether the abstractions of epistemology (particularly though not exclusively postmodern discussions) can be translated into the concreteness and practicality of methods and methodology (1994: 22). This is a concern I deeply sympathize with as I struggle with my own development as a researcher. I agree with Stanley and Wise that feminist research should reject restrictive dichotomous ideal-type models of deductivism versus inductivism (1990: 22) and I believe in the importance of socially situated knowledge and critiques of traditional notions of objectivity. I also believe in the significance of starting from women's experiences and respecting the subjects/participants of research as 'knowers' and thinkers in their own right. I sympathize with many post-modern critiques both of traditional social science and of some feminist attempts to challenge this, but on the other hand the abstractions of postmodernism frequently leave me cold – and frustrated – as I wrestle with the intensely messy and inherently material world of empirical social research, trying to make sense of women's lives and the structures within which they are lived, with all their attendant ambiguities and contradictions.

Ultimately I suggest that my approach, focusing as it does on women's narratives and understandings of their experiences as combatants, has the potential both to shed more light on an under-researched topic and to do so utilizing the voices and beliefs of women who have been consistently ignored, by valuing their own accounts as 'primary documents'. This is attempted with full acknowledgement, however, of the fact that speaking about something is part of the process of constructing it for participants; it will be constructed differently with me than with someone else; and I have made choices about which stories and voices to share. I partially overcome the charge of unreflexive subjectivity or 'story-telling' by bringing into the analysis theoretical discussion on women, nationalism and violence. Naturally the emphasis on in-depth interviews and the privileging of women's accounts has both positive and negative likely results. While it allows for deeper and richer understanding of the motivations and experiences of women combatants, it relies significantly on their self-descriptions to do so. As we know, people sometimes lie to interviewers. More importantly and more frequently, people's self-understanding (according to psychologists) is often far from accurate. This is a difficulty for this project (and for other work with similar approaches) that can only be partially overcome by searching the research data for patterns in terms of women combatants' structural positioning, and recurrent themes or disparities, and by seeking out interviewee reflection and feedback on my interpretations. The project will, I hope, contribute to advancing our thinking on women's involvement in non-state military groupings in ethno-nationalist mobilizations, and to discussions about gendered agency in war; the focus is not on generalizing in a quantitative way beyond the two case studies of the research but the work should act as a spur for further development of theory and the prompting of new questions, both in relation to Sri Lanka and Northern Ireland and in regard to other similar conflicts. In any social science research, a good researcher should recognize that one can rarely hope to produce a definitive answer but simply more, and hopefully better, questions.

2 Overview of armed conflict in Sri Lanka and Northern Ireland

Sri Lanka and Northern Ireland are culturally and structurally different in a great many ways and their respective armed conflicts have also differed, though both are interesting in regard to the issue of female combatants. Despite their differences, there are a number of significant parallels between them. This chapter provides what can only be a broad overview of the history and progress of each of these two conflicts, then tries to draw together some of the comparative similarities and differences between them. I can only apologize to the people of both countries who have lived through and participated in these conflicts for the innumerable absences and generalizations that are inevitable in a half-chapter summary. You will notice, also, that this chapter is a largely ungendered narrative, where women's and men's differential experiences are not drawn out and gender structures are neglected. This was a pragmatic choice given the fact that such issues are addressed in Chapters 4, 5 and 6 and there would otherwise have been a substantial amount of repetition, but I pre-empt and fully accept criticism for this reluctant structural choice.

Conflict in Sri Lanka

Sri Lanka[1] is a small island with an ethnically diverse population currently estimated to be 19.3 million. Due to the war the last all-island census was in 1981 so exact current figures are unreliable. The 1981 census suggests 74 per cent Sinhalese,[2] 12.6 per cent Sri Lankan Tamil,[3] 5.6 per cent Indian Tamil, and 7.5 per cent Muslim.[4] There are also small minorities of Burghers (descended from colonizers and locals), Malays and descendants of other trading peoples from East Asia and the Middle East, and a tiny indigenous population of Veddas (Bush 2003: 35; Samuel 2001: 185). Sinhalese are predominantly Buddhist, with a Christian minority; Tamils are mostly Hindu, also with a Christian minority – Christians are about 7 per cent of the population overall (Bennett *et al.* 1995: 135). Outside the north and east Sinhalese are the majority of the population. Because of the war there are almost no Sinhalese living in the northern peninsula now but they make up about a third of the eastern population. Muslims are also almost non-existent in the north today, due to violence and forced evictions; they make up another third of the eastern population, with Tamils constituting the remaining third. There are significant socio-cultural and caste differences between Tamils in the north and in the east (for example, Jaffna Tamils have a matrilineal structure similar to that in Kerala while eastern Tamil systems are more like those of Tamil Nadu (Bush 2003: 50)) and class and caste differences within all Tamil and Sinhalese communities. Up to 70,000 people have died as a result of the conflict. In all, over 1.5 million Sri Lankans have been uprooted from their homes (UNHCR 2003a). During the conflict over 800,000 Tamils have been internally displaced within the country,[5] over 84,000 sought refuge in India and several hundred thousand more in other parts of the world, making up one of the largest IDP populations in the world and one of the Western world's largest groups of asylum seekers (UNHCR 2003b, 2004).

In the armed conflict, ethnically Tamil groups have been fighting against the state and Sinhalese and Muslim civilians, for an independent state in the north and east of Sri Lanka. Communal conflict was increasingly violent from the 1970s, leading to war from 1983. There have been at least five main militant Tamil separatist groups which have frequently fought amongst themselves but the Liberation Tigers of Tamil Eelam (LTTE, the Tigers or the Tamil Tigers) attained primacy in the late 1980s. The LTTE is a secular ethno-nationalist group which includes many Christians as well as Hindus. The Tamil groups, the LTTE in particular, have been well known internationally for their large numbers of female combatants and their use of suicide bombs. Muslims have largely remained uninvolved as combatants, with some exceptions, but have had a troubled and inconsistent relationship with Sri Lankan Tamils. Although the majority are Tamil-speakers, they came over time to perceive themselves (and are perceived by others) as a distinct ethnic as well as religious group (Ismail 1995). Another communal configuration affected by the conflict is the Vedda people, of whom there are only about 2,500 (Samath 2001). Veddas, too, are Tamil-speakers but have had their own identity, though it has been argued that currently the move is towards incorporation into a wider Tamil community (Wickramasinghe 2006: 265; Thangarajah 1995). Alongside the northeastern war, Sri Lanka has been wracked by two other periods of post-independence violence: the insurrections against the state by the Janatha Vimukthi Peramuna (JVP) in 1971[6] and 1987–9. The JVP was an authoritarian socialist group that appealed to Sinhala nationalism in an instrumental fashion (Chandraprema 1991: 21–2; Gunaratna 1990: 359).[7] Sri Lanka did not have a state military until 1971, when the government created one in response to the JVP uprising (Chenoy 1998: 103). The 1987–9 insurrection was the most violent period in the history of the southern areas of independent Sri Lanka – at least 40,000 people died, possibly many more (Chandraprema 1991: 312). The JVP reformed in 1998, claiming to be a democratic political party that will not use violence to achieve its aims, but remains highly Sinhala nationalist.

The first half of this chapter lays out some of the complicated background to civil war in Sri Lanka. I give a brief history of the island, attending to the contested nature of history and the use of history in nationalist projects. I go on to discuss the development of Sinhala and Tamil nationalisms post-colonialism then the development and growth of Tamil militancy; finally the course of the war and peace attempts. I focus on the war in the northeast, to the exclusion of further discussion of the JVP insurrections or (largely) the positions of other ethnic groups.

Pre-colonial Sri Lankan history

Sri Lanka has an ancient and complicated history which is highly politicized and contested; competing myths of the past have become hugely significant in contemporary nationalisms. The most prominent view of Sri Lanka's past is that held by many of the majority Sinhala-Buddhist population, according to which 'the Buddha himself entrusted the island's destiny to the Sinhala people' (Spencer 1990: 3). In response to Sinhalese constructions of the island's past, alternative Tamil historiographies have been constructed and propagated. The historiographies are opposed views but tend to share a representation of the past 'in terms of the interaction of two opposed entities, Sinhala and Tamil, who have always been as separate as they are today' (Nissan and Stirrat 1990: 21).

It is generally accepted that the Vedda people are the oldest remaining indigenous inhabitants, and that settlement of the island by Sinhala-speakers began in the fifth or sixth century BC. Much of the dominant Sinhalese perception of Sri Lanka's history is based on the Buddhist chronicle the *Mahāvamsa*, which relates the myth of Prince Vijaya (seen as the 'ancestor' of the Sinhalese) (Nissan and Stirrat 1990: 20; Roberts 2001b: 6–7). This myth has over time become entrenched as the 'colonization myth' about Sri Lanka and been used as a basis for Sinhala nationalism (Gunawardena 1990: 49; Jeganathan 1992: 19; Roberts 2001b: 5–12; Rajasingham-Senanayake 2001b). According to myth, from the third century BC to the ninth century AD a Sinhala-Buddhist civilization flourished which was constantly under pressure by south Indian Tamil-speaking Hindus. The Sinhala nationalist claim is that present-day Tamils are descendants of these invaders and their communities never (or rarely) formed separate political entities in the past (Nissan and Stirrat 1990: 20). The Vijaya myth remains crucial to Sinhala nationalist thinking today (Roberts 2001b: 5–12). In Tamil versions of Sri Lanka's history, one form claims that although Sinhalese were settled in the island before the arrival of Tamils, Tamils have lived there for as much as 2,000 years and have had autonomous political units. Another form claims the earlier inhabitants of the island were actually Tamils (Nissan and Stirrat 1990: 20; Roberts 2001b: 6; Nesiah 2001: 6–7). It is notable that Tamil myths of ancient origin, control of land and political units in the island developed much later than Sinhalese ones and in reaction to them; before this they did not feel the need to justify their position (Wickramasinghe 2006: 259). Whatever the 'truth' of earlier times, sixteenth- and seventeenth-century European colonial writings spoke of there living in the north and east

> people who spoke Tamil, called themselves Tamils, and were so called because the strangers recognized the similarity to the Tamil people of south

> India. They were ruled by independent or semi-independent kings who had a traditional rivalry with rulers in other parts of the island and who commonly spoke another language, Sinhala, though the use of both languages was common.
>
> (Hellmann-Rajanayagam 1990: 107–8)

Nissan and Stirrat dispute primordial explanations which assume Sri Lanka has always been dominated by two exclusive and conflicting 'nations', Sinhala-speaking Buddhists and Tamil-speaking Hindus, arguing that present-day political identities have largely been generated by the form (and formation) of the modern Sri Lankan state (1990: 21–2). They assert that

> [f]or long periods of time groups which would now be characterized in terms of the Sinhala–Tamil divide lived more or less at peace with one another. There were dynastic wars; but Sinhala–Tamil communal violence dates from after Independence. This is not to say that there were no differences between groups of people living in the island: the point is simply that differences of language, custom and religion were made into something new by the devices of a modern state.
>
> (Nissan and Stirrat 1990: 24; see also Nesiah 2001: 8)

Gunawardana asserts that originally it was through being ruled by the Sinhalese dynasty that ordinary people attained Sinhalese identity, rather than through blood; 'only by about the twelfth century ... [could] the Sinhala grouping ... [be] considered to be identical with the linguistic grouping' (1990: 64, 78). Even more complicated is the relationship between Sinhala and Buddhist identities, which seem never to have coincided exactly (ibid.: 78). So, 'prior to the nineteenth century the ideal congruence of race, language, religion and political territory assumed in nationalist discourse was not clear-cut' (Nissan and Stirrat 1990: 21–2). In premodern Sri Lanka ethnic, religious and linguistic differences were not used to exclude or include people in the polity and there appears to have been a certain mutability in regard to languages, religions and identities (ibid.: 26). A convincing case has been made for pre-colonial fluidity, ambiguity and hybridity of complex identities in the island (Rajasingham-Senanayake 2001b). Thus,

> there could not have been signs of incipient Sinhala–Tamil conflict as understood today because these categories did not bear the nationalist connotations that they now bear. The 'state' of the past and that of the present are very different; only the latter is associated with the idea of the 'nation', an idea which is too often projected back in time.
>
> (Nissan and Stirrat 1990: 26)

In other words, as argued in the introduction to this book, nationalism is a modern phenomenon and ideology that is intimately interconnected with the modern state form and cannot be mapped onto premodern kingdoms.

Colonialism in Sri Lanka

When Portuguese traders arrived in the early sixteenth century they found an island apparently divided into three major kingdoms: the Tamils of Jaffna, the lowland Sinhalese in Kotte and the highland Sinhalese in Kandy. They took control of the Jaffna and Kotte kingdoms but Kandy remained relatively independent (Wilson 1988: 30). From 1505 the coastal areas were ruled by the Portuguese; the Dutch succeeded them from 1656 until 1796 when the British took control; in 1802 Ceylon (as it was known) became a British Crown Colony. The British did not annex the interior Kandyan kingdom until 1815. In 1831 they began to bring the whole island under a single unified legislature and to centralize administration of the territory. From the 1840s the country was predominantly a plantation economy producing coffee, tea, rubber and coconuts. The plantations were mostly worked by indentured south Indian Tamil labourers brought over by the British (Nissan and Stirrat 1990; Wilson 1988). The expansion of plantation capitalism led to the development of a working class and a bourgeoisie by the late nineteenth century. Resistance to all colonial powers ranged from small-scale revolts to major uprisings (Jayawardena 1986: 115–16). In 1931 the country gained self-government and universal suffrage was introduced, making it the first Asian country to grant universal adult suffrage and one of the first to grant women suffrage (ibid.: 128). Sri Lanka attained full independence in 1948. It has a parliamentary form of government and, since 1978, an executive presidency.

Regardless of primordialist nationalist claims, it is clear that contemporary Sri Lankan nationalisms have a fairly recent history. Important to their development was the formation of racialist and racist ideas, attributable to the impact of developing European ideas of 'race' that British rule brought. The British maintained (eventually) that the different groupings in Sri Lanka were different 'races', with various combinations of language, religion, custom and clothing taken as racial markers. British policy in its colonies was very much influenced by new racial theories and the notion of 'Aryanism' (Nissan and Stirrat 1990: 27, 29–30), closely tied to the development of theories of linguistic affinity. In 1819 the term 'Aryan' was used by Friedrich Schlegel to describe a group of peoples whose languages were structurally related and spoke of a common origin of non-Semitic peoples of Europe and India. Although there was debate over whether or not Sinhala was an Aryan language, Max Müller's mid-nineteenth-century argument that it indeed *was* Aryan was influential, particularly among the Sinhala-speaking élite. By the end of the nineteenth century, linguistic groupings had become conflated with physical characteristics that were supposedly specific to those groupings as Aryan linguistic theory morphed into racial theory (partly thanks to Müller) and Sinhala and Tamil identities took on a racial dimension (Angell 1998). The view of Sinhala and Tamil as unrelated languages and the conceptual slippage of this into racial categories had an important impact on Sinhalese consciousness in particular (Wilson 1988: 27; Gunawardana 1990: 70). Aryan racial theory 'provided a section of the colonial peoples of south Asia with a prestigious "pedigree": it elevated them to the rank of the kinsmen of their rulers', and the term 'Aryan' had further appeal because of its link to the word Ārya, with Buddhist religious associations of nobility and spiritual advancement (Gunawardana 1990: 70–4).

The late eighteenth and early nineteenth centuries saw the beginnings of a revival of interest in Buddhism and presently Buddhist schools were started that had a more anti-colonial and nationalist-biased education than missionary schools. Subsequently, more directly political agitation began. From about 1890 the working class was calling for economic improvements and union rights and the emerging bourgeoisie demanded political reforms, equal opportunities and democratic rights from around 1900 (Jayawardena 1986: 122–5). The Buddhist revivalist movement[8] was in part about resistance to the old élite but was also an important part of resistance to the British; the stress on Buddhism was part of a wider cultural assertion that also involved 'race' and language (Nissan and Stirrat 1990: 31). Although Buddhist revivalism was initially part of anti-colonialism, it led to 'the reconstruction of a Sinhala-Buddhist identity with claims to political and ideological hegemony' (Samuel 2001: 186) and 'contributed the first wave of modern Sinhala nationalism' (Tennekoon 1990: 214).

British categorizations of 'race' and nationality were somewhat incoherent, inconsistent and variable over time (Rajasingham-Senanayake 2001b: 14–20) but by the end of the nineteenth century a number of distinct 'races' had been recognized by British authorities in Sri Lanka: Tamils (divided into 'Ceylon' and 'Indian'); Sinhalese (divided into 'Up Country' and 'Low Country'); 'Moors' (Muslims, divided into Ceylon and Coast); Veddas; Burghers (divided into Dutch and Portuguese); Malays; Eurasians and Europeans. Only a few of these racial categories came to be politically significant. 'Aryans' (Sinhalese) came to be opposed in the historiography in absolute terms to 'Dravidians' (Tamils): as '[l]anguage and race were conflated ... eventually the smaller "races" ... recognized by the British ... were subsumed into the Tamil–Sinhala divide' (Nissan and Stirrat 1990: 27, 30; also Rajasingham-Senanayake 2001b). The British administration organized national political representation on a 'racial' or communal basis, ignoring the social and cultural gaps between the élite of English-educated, wealthy Sri Lankans and the mass population (Spencer 1990: 8–9).

After the collapse of a short-lived coalition of English-speaking élites from different ethnic groups and religions who agitated for reform of the Constitution, between 1920 and 1930 ethnic groups competed over the share that each should have in the distribution of political seats (Wilson 1988: 6–8, 17). The principle of communal political representation had remained important for a hundred years but the 1931 Constitution and self-government removed this in favour of territorial electorates (Nissan and Stirrat 1990: 29). The Donoughmore Commission responsible for this Constitution recommended universal suffrage, which was not welcomed by most of the Tamil élite since universal suffrage in conjunction with territorial representation would mean institutionalizing a Sinhalese territorial majority. The leaders of the Muslims and the Kandyan Sinhalese were also unhappy with the reforms (Wilson 1988: 10–12) but other Sinhalese largely supported them (Nissan and Stirrat 1990: 33). The advent of universal suffrage did bring with it, as feared, majority Sinhalese rule through territorially constituted electorates. After the first general election in 1931 (boycotted by Tamils in the north) the new Sinhalese leadership showed no willingness to share power with minority ethnic groups (Wilson 1988: 15–16). Sinhalese leaders justified their actions by claiming they were trying to redress an imbalance they had experienced under colonialism – during the nineteenth century 'Tamils moved *en masse* not only into the colonial administration, but also into property and commercial enterprise in Colombo and the Western Province' (Wilson and Chandrakanthan 1998: 70–1). Sinhala nationalists claim Tamils were deliberately favoured under the British administration but this is hotly debated (Wilson 1988: 42), as is the extent of the imbalance.

Communalism was gaining support amongst Sinhalese, partly for economic reasons. In the 1920s and 1930s increasing economic crisis brought high unemployment levels and many Sinhalese blamed their unemployment on Indian Tamils and on the Sri Lankan Tamils who moved south for work. As communal tensions rose, nineteenth-century Sinhala and Tamil nationalist ideologies increased in influence and '[w]hat began as a series of claims by both Tamils and Sinhala against the British was transformed into claims directed against each other' (Nissan and Stirrat 1990: 33–4). In the lead-up to independence the Tamil élite, particularly the new Ceylon Tamil Congress, lobbied for 'fifty–fifty' communal representation within a centralized legislature (Wilson and Chandrakanthan 1998: 71–2). This would have had Sinhalese holding half the seats in the legislature with the other half reserved for minorities; the 1944 Soulbury Commission rejected this. By the 1947 Constitution and independence the following year a tradition of regional Tamil opposition to Colombo control had been established (Spencer 1990: 9). The Tamil leadership was not prepared to conceptualize itself as a provincial élite or minority interest group (Wilson and Chandrakanthan 1998: 71–2); the notion of Tamils as a separate nation with political claims to representation was already established.

Ultimately, in the late nineteenth and early twentieth centuries developing identities in Sri Lanka 'were primarily directed against, and mediated by, the British' and it was only after independence that 'the British were to be replaced by the Tamil as the "dangerous other" [for Sinhalese]' (Nissan and Stirrat 1990: 32). Contemporary Sinhala–Tamil conflict is, however, in large part the result of processes begun by British colonialism: the unification of the country; the introduction of a unitary bureaucratic structure; the import of Western ideas of 'race' and its relation to 'nation'; and the impact of mass media and state education. I do not accept primordialist claims to identity in Sri Lanka (or elsewhere) and I believe the narrative of how current identities developed is important. In my view what is most significant, however, is to recognize that primordialist claims (regardless of their 'truth') have been central to the development of nationalisms in Sri Lanka, particularly for Sinhalese.

Post-colonial nationalisms: Sinhala lions and Tamil tigers

This section of the chapter first discusses some of the most salient changes in the country after independence, many of which were both the result and consequently a further cause of the entrenchment of Sinhala nationalism and power. Subsequently contemporary Tamil nationalism is examined, before moving to discuss the rise of Tamil militancy.

Post-independence changes and the entrenchment of Sinhala nationalism

With independence, tensions arose among Sinhalese between a ruling élite and an 'indigenous' or 'rural' élite; that is, between the English-speaking, Westernized, Colombo-based class from which the MPs and bureaucrats of the time came and the Sinhala-speaking, non-Westernized class of village teachers, traders, monks, students, Ayurvedic physicians and so on. For the latter, 'Independence had meant little more ... than the replacement of the British by British-educated "brown sahibs"' (Nissan and Stirrat 1990: 34–5). Since independence the construction and reaffirmation of a predominantly Sinhala-Buddhist national identity, and the concomitant process of marginalization of minority identities, has contributed to the mobilization of Tamil nationalism.

> In the years of crisis there has been no overarching image of Sri Lankan national identity to hold Tamil sentiment back from the path to separatism; the only images available link the nation to one group, the Sinhala people, and one religion, Buddhism.
>
> (Spencer 1990: 9)

The Tamil nationalist movement in turn threatened Sinhalese hegemony and so stimulated a crisis of identity and security for Sinhalese (Tennekoon 1990: 205).

By independence, chauvinist Sinhala nationalism had begun and the Sinhalese élite was unwilling to accommodate other groups. Similarly, Tamil nationalism in its current shape was forming. Wilson asserts that the 1947 Constitution had an unexpressed consociational premise (1988: 34), but there was no explicit guarantee of minority rights (DeVotta 2002: 86) and the more positive recommendations of the Soulbury Commission (including specific weightings for the representation of ethnic minorities) were almost immediately eroded (Wilson 1988: 34). From the early 1950s, Sinhalese parliamentary representation increased at the expense of Tamils. In the early post-independence period the main Sinhalese-dominated political parties, the United National Party (UNP) and the Sri Lanka Freedom Party (SLFP), wrestled for power by using scapegoating and marginalization of Tamils as a form of intra-Sinhalese competition (P.L. de Silva 1999: 91). This ethnic outbidding where politicians play on and to their community's ethnic fears (DeVotta 2002) has been one of the major features of Sri Lankan politics since the mid-1950s, mostly among Sinhalese but also among Tamils and between Sinhalese and Tamils. It has been argued that the intra-group elements of political competition and violence in Sri Lanka post-independence and their interrelationship with inter-group elements are under-studied but are vital to understand the whole picture of ethnic conflict in the country (Bush 2003). Intra-group competition between the major political parties and ethnic outbidding combined with populist Sinhala nationalism resulted in some significantly discriminatory policies (beginning immediately with independence) and inter-communal violence, which will be briefly discussed here.

The Citizenship Act of 1948 and the Indian and Pakistani Residents (Citizenship) Act of 1949 disenfranchised Indian Tamils and made them aliens in their own country. The 1948 Act rendered one million people stateless and under the 1949 Act only 140,000 of them obtained citizenship (Schwarz 1983: 11). At independence Indian Tamils were around 11 per cent of the population; agreements with India meant about half were 'repatriated' as Indian citizens between 1964 and 1988 (Schrijvers 1999: 310; Bush 2003: Ch. 4). Sri Lankan Tamils did not view Indian Tamils as part of their ethnic community and the Sri Lankan Tamil élite did little to protest this manifest injustice.

Language policies have been extremely significant. During British colonialism and into independence the official language was English, giving disproportionate power to the cross-ethnic English-speaking élite. Sinhalese politicians who only a few years earlier opposed linguistic exclusion and favoured parity between Sinhala and Tamil had switched by the mid-1950s to supporting linguistic exclusion, in hysterical hyper-nationalist language (DeVotta 2002: 86–8). The 'mother-tongue' policy was enforced from 1953, meaning education was carried out in Sinhala for Sinhalese and Tamil for Tamils. In 1956 the socialist SLFP came to power with a 'Sinhala Only' policy, making Sinhala the sole official language (ibid.; Bush 2003: Ch. 5). These policies, Wilson argues, helped compartmentalize the two ethnic groups (1988: 44).

Related to the language issue is the matter of university entrance. Jaffna Tamils, in particular, had a history of disproportionate numbers doing well in examinations and attending university. From 1970 the government instituted a higher education policy known as 'standardization', where university admission was proportionate to numbers studying in each language; effectively this meant preference was given to Sinhala-medium students over Tamil-medium students (Wilson 1988: 46–7, 131; DeVotta 2002: 89). In 1973 the policy was changed to a regional population quota, which hasn't really helped. For example, whereas the Tamil-dominant Northern Province gained 27.5 per cent of the admissions to science courses on merit in 1969, under the regional quota system it dropped to 7 per cent in 1974 (Wilson 1988: 47).

Another important feature was the entrenchment of Buddhism. In the 1956 election, one of the pledges of subsequently elected Prime Minister S.W.R.D. Bandaranaike was to restore Buddhism to its 'rightful place'. Buddhism has never been made the state religion but a special recognition of it has been accorded: the 1972 Constitution 'gave Buddhism the "foremost place"' (Samuel 2001: 186; see also Wilson 1988: 52–3), retained in the 1978 Constitution. The growth of political Buddhism has been integrally linked to Sinhala nationalism. Buddhist leaders have been actively involved in politics and also with acts of violence (Liyanage 1998: 65). Certain actions of Tamil militants have served to harden Sinhala-Buddhist attitudes; for example, the 1998 LTTE suicide bombing of the Dalada Maligawa, the temple housing the Buddha's tooth relic. However there are also more moderate monks; the United Bikshu Congress, for example, from 1987 campaigned for devolution (ibid.: 67–8).

Employment and economic factors have also contributed significantly to ethnic tensions and the development of both Sinhala and Tamil nationalisms (see Gamage 1999; Hettige 1999; Winslow and Woost 2004). During the immediate post-independence period the economy suffered. There was a short-lived boom due to the Korean War and burgeoning industrialization by the late 1950s, along with universal free education for the rapidly expanding younger generation (Nissan and Stirrat 1990: 36; DeVotta 2002: 86). By the 1950s the population had nearly doubled since the 1930s, with fewer jobs to go around. There was an expanding middle class and increasing material aspirations, but without enough employment to satisfy this. The economy became highly politicized and one outcome 'was that Tamils were effectively excluded from the channels through which resources were distributed. … Tamils became steadily more and more alienated from the state' (Nissan and Stirrat 1990: 36). Sri Lankan Tamils had traditionally focused on government service jobs, as the Jaffna peninsula where most of them were from was arid and less fertile. Furthermore, due to coastal missionary contact a larger proportion spoke English than did the Sinhalese. Therefore there were disproportionate numbers of Tamils in the public services and the professions, which was used by Sinhala nationalists to claim it was time to redress the balance. Since the 1960s Sinhalese have had the preponderant share of public service jobs. As a result of the language and education policies mentioned above, Tamil-medium graduates became disadvantaged in the employment market and Tamils experienced increasing relative deprivation.

In the early 1950s, Prime Minister Senanayake began a process of land settlement in Tamil-dominated areas, providing a further source of grievance. Irrigation projects were started and thousands of Sinhalese were settled in what came to be called 'colonization schemes'. These re-settlement schemes profoundly altered the demographic patterns of predominantly Tamil areas and represented a decline in Tamil voting strength (Nissan and Stirrat 1990: 37), and helped foster the Tamil concern with the notion of 'homelands' (Spencer 1990: 10).

A significant source of tension between Tamil civilians and the state (and another stimulus to Tamil militancy) has been the repressive Prevention of Terrorism Act 1979 (PTA), made part of normal law in 1982 (Piyadasa 1988: 52; Wilson 1988: 164; Nissan and Stirrat 1990: 37). The PTA permits suspects to be held for 18 months without trial and implicitly sanctions the use of torture. It 'virtually remov[ed] all limits on what the police and military could do to Tamils, [thus] it multiplied the occasions which persuaded young people to rebel and take to arms' (Piyadasa 1988: 99). Torture in custody, including rape, as well as 'disappearances' and extrajudicial executions, have become a ubiquitous part of life for Sri Lankan Tamils and this seems to be an ever-increasing horror (Amnesty International 2002, 1999; Human Rights Watch 2008).

Finally, Sinhala nationalism erupted into violence against civilian Tamils in the riots of 1956, 1958, 1977, 1981 and 1983. The violence of 1956 and 1958 ignited over language policies and access to land and involved Sinhalese and Sri Lankan Tamils (Wilson 1988: 107–8; Nissan and Stirrat 1990: 36). The 1977 riot was in reaction to the Tamil United Liberation Front (TULF) election victory in the north, the first Tamil group to call for an independent state. This marked the first time that Indian Tamils were targeted along with Sri Lankan Tamils and was also the first time the state (in the form of the police) was actively involved in the rioting and violence (Nissan and Stirrat 1990: 37–8). The severe violence of 1981 surrounded elections for the new District Development Councils, set up that year by the UNP government (Sathananthan 1998: 63). In the lead-up to the elections the People's Liberation Organization of Tamil Eelam (PLOTE) carried out acts of relatively small-scale political violence (Narayan Swamy 1994: 73). On the Sinhala-state side, violence was instigated by government ministers; the police, MPs and deputy ministers were even organizers and leaders in some attacks, resulting in rapes and murders (Piyadasa 1988: 47; Nissan and Stirrat 1990: 38).

The violence of 1983 was particularly brutal and may have been orchestrated with government involvement.[9] It was particularly instrumental in stimulating reactive militant Tamil nationalism. Before the riots began at the end of July tensions were already increasing between Sinhalese and Tamils, and between the state military and Tamil civilians. Earlier that year the government's Sixth Amendment to the 1978 Constitution deprived the majority of Sri Lankan Tamil MPs of their parliamentary seats by requiring them to take an oath to the 1978 Unitary Constitution (the TULF MPs had been elected on a mandate to create a separate state of Tamil Eelam) (Wilson 1988: 99–100). In July, Amnesty International published a damning report on Sri Lanka and the use of torture by the armed forces and police, to which the government reacted 'hysterically' (Piyadasa 1988: 84–5). On 25 July, groups of Sinhalese committed acts of violence and vandalism on Tamil-owned dwellings and businesses in Colombo and other areas, in full view of police and government officials, killing large numbers of Tamils and creating a massive internal refugee crisis (ibid.: 89–91; Narayan Swamy 1994: 94).[10] The violence seemed to be in response to the LTTE killing 13 soldiers in Jaffna, which was itself revenge for the army killing two LTTE guerrillas (Piyadasa 1988: 87–8; Narayan Swamy 1994: 87–90; Gunaratna 1987: 32; DeVotta 2002: 90). Despite the fact that numerous ordinary Sinhalese tried to help Tamil victims of the violence, 'Tamil-Sinhalese ties ... had finally suffered a near irreparable damage' (Narayan Swamy 1994: 95). The 1983 violence is generally taken as signalling the beginning of civil war.

Tamil nationalism: from federalism to secession

Soon after independence, Tamil calls for federalism were articulated. The Federal Party (FP) emerged in the wake of intra-Tamil political élite wranglings over the issue of cooperation between Tamils and Sinhalese at the élite and middle-class level, especially in government.[11] Samuel Chelvanayakam's Federal Party, standing for a federal constitution with the Northern and Eastern Provinces as states of a federal union, soon gained in popularity over the All Ceylon Tamil Congress (ACTC) (Wilson 1988: 37–8). In the 1952 and 1956 general elections the FP called for a federal constitution in a unified state (ibid.: 84). The 1956 election saw the victory of the centre-left coalition People's United Front, headed by the SLFP, which used anti-Tamil ethnic outbidding to win majoritarian support (DeVotta 2002: 86–7; P.L. de Silva 1999: 91; Bush 2003: Ch. 5). In the past, eastern Tamils had been suspicious of Jaffna Tamils; after 1956, 'faced with the common danger of Sinhalese linguistic domination and state-sponsored colonization of their traditional territories with Sinhalese settlers, the Eastern Province Tamils closed their ranks and joined with the Northern Province Tamils' (Wilson 1988: 104), though this relationship has continued to be contested. In this period, the FP was also involved in an attempt to formulate a Tamil nationalism incorporating all Tamil-*speakers* – in other words, including Indian Tamils and Muslims – but ultimately this was largely a failure (Nesiah 2001: 15–16). Wickramasinghe notes that this is one of the differences between Sri Lanka and India – in Sri Lanka, being a Tamil-speaker is not equated with being a Tamil. As previously noted, Tamil-speaking Muslims came to have a distinct identity, and there are significant divides between Sri Lankan and Indian Tamils in the island, despite these differences being 'founded on perceptions more than on history or culture' (2006: 254–5).

In response to the new language policies and perceived discrimination the FP staged a series of non-violent protest campaigns (*satyagraha*) from the mid-1950s to the mid-1960s; women were prominent here (Maunaguru 1995: 160). The 1956 anti-Tamil violence was primarily a response to the first *satyagraha*. With the threat of another, in 1957 a compromise was reached with the Bandaranaike–Chelvanayakam Pact providing for recognition of Tamil as the language of a national minority, for the use of Tamil for administrative purposes in the Northern and Eastern Provinces, and for regional councils with various powers (DeVotta 2002: 87). Banadaranaike also promised to consider revising the Citizenship Act. However militant Buddhists objected to the Pact and agitated violently,[12] supported by the UNP opposition, and Tamils demonstrated against the use of Sinhala characters on car registration plates. All this led to the anti-Tamil riots of 1958 and the Pact was never implemented (ibid.: 87–8; Schwarz 1983: 9–10). The government declared a temporary state of emergency, proscribed the FP and placed its MPs in preventive detention. In August the Tamil Language (Special Provisions) Act was brought in but was rejected by Tamil parties and a group of Tamil academics (Wilson 1988: 111).

In 1960 the People's United Front was again elected, led by Sirimavo Bandaranaike (the world's first female prime minister). Another *satyagraha* in 1961 obstructed government offices in the two Tamil provinces, receiving wide Tamil support. The FP inaugurated a postal service with its own stamps and made plans to form a police force. In April a state of emergency was again declared; again the FP was proscribed and its leading members placed in preventive detention (Wilson 1988: 112–15). The Ceylon Workers' Congress (CWC) subsequently participated in the FP's activities, which was significant as up to that point Indian Tamil political groups had been ambivalent on the federal question, as most Indian Tamils did not live in the areas that would become Tamil states. Thus, 1961 saw the first indications of the formation of a united Tamil leadership. The last of the FP's strategies was the 'Tamil Only' letter-writing campaign of 1964, when Tamils corresponded and conducted business with the state solely in Tamil. After this, Tamil agitation largely began turning violent (ibid.: 114–15). A UNP government came to power in 1965 and in 1966 it issued regulations to implement the Tamil Language Act, based on the 1965 Senanayake–Chelvanayakam Pact, but these were never enforced. In 1968 the FP resigned from government. Tamil was not made a national language until the 1978 Constitution and was not declared an official language alongside Sinhala until the Thirteenth Amendment to the Constitution in 1987.

After the People's United Front came to power again and brought in 'standardization', 'Tamil secessionism became an active phenomenon' (Wilson 1988: 86). The 1972 Constitution forbade parliament from allowing devolution or federalism, reinforced the 'Sinhala Only' basis of administration, gave Buddhism a special position, and removed some minority safeguards (Sathananthan 1998: 60–1; Schwarz 1983: 5–6).[13] Its immediate effect was the formation of the Tamil United Front (TUF) and the beginning of demands for independence. The TUF brought together previously competing Tamil nationalists and signified the first unified step towards pushing for secession (P.L. de Silva 1999: 93).

In 1975–6, the TULF was formed from the TUF and other organizations representing Sri Lankan Tamils, Indian Tamils and Tamil-speaking Muslims (P.L. de Silva 1999: 93; Wilson 1988: 88–9, 84). They proposed the establishment of a sovereign state of Tamil Eelam[14] and declared Sri Lankan Tamils 'a nation distinct and apart from the Sinhalese' (Narayan Swamy 1994: 31–2). This made it the first Tamil organization to demand an independent state and the first time Sri Lankan Tamils cut their ties with those living outside its proposed boundaries. (Nissan and Stirrat note that 'the boundaries of "ancient Tamil Eelam" follow the administrative boundaries of the colonial era with uncanny exactness' (1990: 29).) With the formation of the TULF and the 1977 death of 'cautionary voice' Chelvanayakam, young Sri Lankan Tamils became committed to the use of force. In the 1977 general election, led by Amirthalingam the TULF obtained a mandate from Tamils to support the establishment of a separate, sovereign state of Tamil Eelam and became the largest opposition party, gaining more seats than the SLFP (Wilson 1988: 89–91, 160) and increasingly supporting militant means (P.L. de Silva 1999: 92–3). The Tamil independence claim was supported with reference to the independent kingdom of Jaffna in the sixteenth century and to the early nineteenth century, when the colony was administered as three separate units (Hellmann-Rajanayagam 1990: 117–18).

As mentioned earlier, economic policies have also been a factor (see Winslow and Woost 2004 for various perspectives). The squeezing out of Tamils from civil service employment was an important source of resentment from the 1950s and from the late 1970s free-market economics became a new source of resentment and stimulus to violent Tamil nationalism. When the UNP government that came to power in 1977 brought in free-market economic policies and relaxed import controls the market was flooded with cheap imported foods, having a negative effect on Jaffna farmers, many of whom believed this was a deliberate plot. Another badly affected Tamil segment was the fishing community. After 1983 the government professed concern about the movement of Tamil arms and fighters, and banned fishing along long stretches of coastline. Tamils who ignored this were (and still are) sometimes attacked and killed by the navy and thousands of families were deprived of livelihoods. All this helped foster Tamil nationalist mobilization (Bose 1994: 107–8).

In summary, Samuel argues that the current conflict is 'predominantly a reaction to the failure of post-independence governments to establish a political framework that is able to reflect the ethnic plurality of Sri Lankan society and to ensure respect for the democratic rights of all citizens' but also 'encompasses a complexity of issues ranging from identity to socio-economic and political grievances and discrimination' (2001: 186). The acts of discrimination and other structural and ideological changes discussed here led Tamil political parties to demand some degree of regional autonomy and power-sharing, but they were ignored. Continuing acts of discrimination and violence led in turn to an escalation of Tamil demands. In the 1960s this was for a federal state and from the 1970s it was for a fully independent state. The combination of these factors gave rise to the development of a militant Tamil movement and an armed struggle for independence.

The growth of Tamil militancy

Tamil armed struggle, small at the time, began in about 1972 (P.L. de Silva 1999: 97) when small guerrilla groups appeared in the north, focusing attacks on representatives of the state – police, soldiers, government officials and government property. Tamils perceived as 'collaborators' were also attacked. The government responded with significant counter-terror. After 1977 the LTTE (as it would become in 1978), along with other militant Tamil groups, took up the secessionist demand. After the election and violent Sinhalese reaction militant groups increased their activities. The riots and lack of parliamentary progress contributed to Tamil youth looking towards the militant movements in the late 1970s (Hoole *et al.* 1990: 75) and from this period the violence on both sides became increasingly organized. The Tamil militant organizations were proscribed in May 1978 through legislation that was replaced the following year with the more draconian PTA. A state of emergency was declared in the Jaffna peninsula and the army cracked down, arresting, torturing and killing hundreds.[15] The University of Jaffna at this time became a focal point for leadership and ideological direction – many students became involved with the militants and several staff members were sympathizers – but Hoole *et al.* claim that as authoritarian leadership, internal killings and internecine warfare between the groups developed in the mid-1980s, the students who had joined in the early period became disillusioned and by 1985 many of them were leaving the organizations (1990: 75–7). With the marked escalation of violence and growth of the militant groups in 1983, massacres and counter-massacres of civilians began in border areas between the two ethnic blocs (Spencer 1990: 2). With the 1983 riots and the government's fomenting of trouble in the east in 1984, a large number of youth from the Eastern Province also joined the militants (Hoole *et al.* 1990: 75–7). After the TULF MPs forfeited their parliamentary seats in 1983 the government strengthened the state of emergency in the north. Arbitrary detention and killings of Tamils by the security services became commonplace and thousands of young Tamil men were arrested or 'disappeared'.

As noted, the beginning of the civil war is generally taken as 1983. The membership of and public support for Tamil paramilitaries was minimal in the 1970s but the 1983 riots 'opened a floodgate' of young Tamils to these groups (Narayan Swamy 1994: 96). Whereas previously it had been hard to attract recruits and no group had more than about 50 members (ibid.: 104), with numerous Tamils arriving in the northeast from Colombo with tales of brutality, things changed (ibid.: 96–7). TULF parliamentarians initially played a supportive role towards the militants, particularly the LTTE (P.L. de Silva 1999: 94), but the party soon found itself outflanked and by the early 1980s it 'was satisfying neither Colombo nor the militants'. The TULF was increasingly unable to control the LTTE and in 1982 the party split; in 1989 Amirthalingam and another TULF MP were assassinated by the LTTE (Narayan Swamy 1994: 44). The long-standing leadership role in Tamil nationalist politics of the Colombo-based, wealthy middle- and upper-class professionals who made up the Tamil parliamentarians was eclipsed in only about 15 years. It has been noted that the proponents of political violence (at least in the LTTE) were a 'bunch of non-élite (in terms of power, prestige, connections and resources), rural (peninsula-based), non-*Vellala* Tamil paramilitaries (particularly from among the *Karayar* youth of Vadamarachchi)'. The Karayar is a traditionally mid-ranking, coastal Tamil caste; today, it is primarily Karayar people who make up the politico-military élite of the LTTE's inner-circle (P.L. de Silva 1999: 92–6; see also Bush 2003: 50–3).

In the 1980s there were five major Tamil paramilitaries with ideological (and arguably caste) differences and violent internecine feuds. The internecine relations in this period are significant but beyond the capacity of this book to address, so this is a sweeping summary. In the second half of the 1980s the LTTE moved to violently eradicate its various competitors, despite the defiance of brave lower-class women who protested against this violence (Hoole *et al.* 1990: 84, 92). The LTTE destroyed the Tamil Eelam Liberation Organization (TELO) and forcibly disbanded the Eelam People's Revolutionary Liberation Front (EPRLF), PLOTE, and the lesser group the Tamil Eelam Army (TEA), and forcibly amalgamated the Eelam Revolutionary Organization (EROS). By the end of 1990 the LTTE was militarily dominant in large areas of the northeast (ibid.: 94; P.L. de Silva 1999: 98–9).[16] Since this campaign many of the other

Tamil militant groups have become pro-government (though still Tamil nationalist) paramilitaries aiding state forces, as well as parliamentary parties (P.L. de Silva 1999: 99). The LTTE is now the only Tamil group still fighting the state for an independent Tamil Eelam, and is still led by Velupillai Prabhakaran.[17]

According to Gunaratna the LTTE has evolved to have 17 major departments in its political wing and 15 in its military wing (including Land Fighting, Sea Tigers, Air Tigers, Women's Military, Black Tigers (suicide), Intelligence and so forth) (2001: 4). Male and female units of the Tigers live and train separately but come together for military operations. After becoming dominant over the other militant groups the LTTE faced a personnel shortage and began encouraging child recruits in their early teens. By mid-1987 girls were being trained as well as boys (although it was the EPRLF that first recruited girls). The average age of the militants dropped from around 22 to around 14 or 16 (Hoole *et al.* 1990: 79). Cadres are extremely well equipped, well trained and highly disciplined and are forbidden alcohol, tobacco and sex (unless married). They have used more suicide bomb attacks than any other group in the world (Farrell 2002: 17; Zedalis 2004: 2) and are the most prolific users of female suicide bombers, who constitute 30–40 per cent of their suicide attacks (Zedalis 2004: 2). The LTTE constitution

> called for the establishment of a casteless Tamil society by armed struggle, warned members against tainting their loyalty to the LTTE with family ties or love affairs, promised a dissolution of the LTTE once a Tamil state was founded, and threatened death penalty for those who quit the group to join or form new groups.[18]
>
> (Narayan Swamy 1994: 59)

The LTTE and other Tamil groups have received training from other guerrilla groups (notably Palestinian), certain state organizations, and some British mercenaries (Gunaratna 1987: 52). It owns its own fleet of ships, is believed to have 'the most sophisticated finance and weapons procurement system of any guerilla group in the world' (Farrell 2002: 16; see also Gunaratna 1999), and is the only guerrilla or terrorist group to have assassinated two world leaders (Gunaratna 2001: 13). It currently has somewhere in the region of 12,000–18,000 active members, around a third of whom are women (at best estimate); each combatant wears a vial of cyanide so they can commit suicide if captured. The LTTE has invented new weapons, mostly projectiles and mines. In fact, it usually has better and more sophisticated weaponry than the Sri Lankan state military (Gunaratna 1999: 118; 1987: 47–8; 2001: 13) and it recently developed air capacity, launching its first ever confirmed air attack on a military base in 2007. The LTTE levies taxes and makes substantial money from businesses and trade in areas it controls but Gunaratna claims that since 1995 about 60 per cent of its war funds are generated overseas through the enormous international Tamil diaspora (1999: 120–1), though it seems this support may have waned since the 2002 ceasefire, judging by the evidence of extreme coercion for funds being put on members of the Tamil diaspora by the LTTE at the moment (Human Rights Watch 2006). The LTTE has also engaged in other very profitable ventures, investing in stock and money markets, real estate, restaurants around the world, farms and finance companies. Allegedly it also trades in gold, launders money and traffics narcotics (Gunaratna 1999: 120–1; 1987: 51) – this last is strenuously denied by Prabhakaran (Pirapaharan and Mazumdar 1986).

The ideology of the LTTE, as that of many of the Tamil militant groups, initially began with a strong socialist focus. A Marxist Sri Lankan Tamil living in London, Anton Balasingham, operated in the 1970s as a freelance ideologue for any Sri Lankan Tamil group that approached him. At the time he was living with an Australian woman, Adele, who would later become his wife and a Tamil militant who has been a role model for many female Tamil combatants. Balasingham authored the LTTE's first major theoretical work in 1979, *Towards Socialist Eelam*, and was soon brought into the organization in a more involved way. While Balasingham felt it was important to politicize people before taking up the gun, Prabhakaran felt violent action had to be undertaken first then people would follow. Narayan Swamy claims that Prabhakaran had a 'near total disinterest in Marxist politics and ideology' and was solely interested in military matters (1994: 67–9). Nonetheless, in an interview in 1986 he did state '[w]e want to establish a socialist society. Ours will be a unique socialist model, neither Soviet nor Chinese nor any other' (Pirapaharan and Mazumdar 1986). Balasingham was the LTTE's chief political strategist and negotiator, and head of LTTE peace delegations from 1985 until his health worsened in 2006. Adele Balasingham has also been involved in some peace talks as the delegation's secretary. Anton Balasingham died in December 2006; Adele remains committed to Tamil independence.

LTTE ideology soon made the transition to pure Tamil nationalism in its own use of ethnic outbidding, as it became clear that '[w]hipping up Tamil nationalism and fighting the Sri Lankan security forces appealed to sections of the Tamil community over ideological indoctrination' (Gunaratna 1999: 119). For the bulk of recruits who joined after 1983, Tamil nationalism was much more appealing than Marxist ideology and pragmatically was a bigger drawcard (Narayan Swamy 1994: 104–6). The LTTE was not slow to take a lesson from this and has become more strongly nationalist over the years of conflict, has basically abandoned any serious pretence to socialism, and is extremely authoritarian.[19] Prabhakaran asserts that '[w]e are not enemies of the Sinhala people, nor is our struggle against them.... We are fighting this war against a state and its armed forces determined to subjugate our people through the force of arms.' He claims '[w]e are a national liberation organisation. We are fighting for the emancipation of our people against racist tyranny, against military occupation, against state terror' and '[o]ur struggle has a concrete, legitimate political objective. Our struggle is based on the right to self-determination, a principal [*sic*] endorsed by the United Nations Charter. We are not terrorists.... We are freedom fighters' (LTTE 2001).

Civil war(s) and peace attempts

The period from July 1983 until the 1987 Indo-Sri Lanka Peace Accord (or until the collapse of this in 1990) is sometimes described as the first 'Eelam war'. The second 'Eelam war' was fought between 1990 and 1995 with a brief ceasefire in 1995; the third 'Eelam war' was from 1995 until the start of the ceasefire at the end of 2001. Writing this in 2008, it seems Sri Lanka is now into a fourth 'Eelam war'.

India's role, the Indo-Sri Lanka Peace Accord and the IPKF

The complexity of the dangerous and inconsistent approach of the Indian central government and Tamil Nadu state government towards the Sri Lankan conflict and Tamil militant groups is beyond the scope of this book; by necessity this is a very abridged account. During the 1970s Sri Lankan Tamil activists used Tamil Nadu as a safe haven, supported by the state but not the central government, and insurgent training camps were established in 1982. For reasons I won't go into (see Gunaratna 1999), from August 1983 Prime Minister Indira Gandhi covertly supported and aided the insurgency through India's Research and Analysis Wing (RAW, an organization similar to the CIA). The training camps expanded and some were also set up in north India, providing training for all the major Tamil paramilitaries. By mid-1987 over 20,000 insurgents had been given sanctuary, training, weapons and finance by the central government, the Tamil Nadu state government, or the insurgent groups themselves (ibid.: 117). Simultaneously RAW agents infiltrated Tamil militants to set the groups against one another, hoping to establish equilibrium; this failed miserably. Meanwhile, the Indian government was pressuring the Sri Lankan government to resolve the tension and offering assistance (Wilson 1988: 176–8). After an earlier attempt, in 1985 an Indian-brokered ceasefire was declared and talks were held between the Sri Lankan government and Tamil militants. The Tamil groups presented four demands: recognition of Tamils as a distinct nationality; recognition and guarantee of the territorial integrity of their 'traditional homelands'; the right of self-determination of the Tamil nation; and the recognition of the citizenship and fundamental rights of all Tamils who regard Sri Lanka as their home (ibid.: 183–6). These demands were rejected. Peace talks were attempted again in 1986, also failing (ibid.: 191; Samuel 2001: 187–8).

In the late 1980s the LTTE controlled the Jaffna peninsula and 1987 saw a major government offensive against Jaffna. When this failed the government (conceding a degree of political devolution) came to an agreement with India whereby it provided an Indian Peace Keeping Force (IPKF) to uphold a ceasefire. It has been argued that India, concerned about the flow of refugees into south India, forced the 1987 Indo-Sri Lanka Peace Accord on the Sri Lankan government and the LTTE (which did not sign it) (Samuel 2001: 188). With the Accord, assistance from RAW for Tamil militants ended yet assistance from Tamil Nadu state to the LTTE continued (Gunaratna 1999: 117). The

LTTE did not accept Indian involvement and within months was battling the IPKF, which was soon accused of involvement in killings, torture, disappearances and other human rights abuses of Tamil civilians as much as militants. Rape and molestation of women was frequent and brutal (Hoole *et al.*: 298–321). The LTTE fought off the IPKF and the troops left in 1990, along with many non-LTTE militant Tamils who had cooperated with the IPKF. The support of Tamil Nadu politicians for the LTTE remained firm after IPKF withdrawal, but has been shaken and less consistent since a female suicide bomber, Dhanu, killed former Prime Minister Rajiv Gandhi in 1991 (Gunaratna 1999: 118). It is widely accepted the LTTE was responsible, blaming Gandhi for the IPKF (ibid.: 134 n.19).

Post-IPKF: The second and third 'Eelam wars' and peace initiatives

When the IPKF left the Tigers were again in total control of the Jaffna peninsula. UNP President Premadasa brokered a ceasefire and opened negotiations but the LTTE broke this, starting the second 'Eelam war'; again thousands, primarily Tamils and Muslims, were displaced. Around one-tenth of the total Sri Lankan population was displaced during this period; in the east it was 90 per cent. During this time the LTTE forced all Muslims in the north (around 75,000 people) to leave (Schrijvers 1999: 311). The organization was also responsible for other human rights violations in the north, while the Sri Lankan Army (SLA) was responsible for human rights violations in the east – arresting, detaining and torturing Tamil men and women. In 1993 the LTTE assassinated President Premadasa (again using a female suicide bomber); this led to the election of Prime Minister (later President) Chandrika Kumaratunge on a platform of reform and peace, supported by a multi-ethnic electorate and winning an unprecedented 62 per cent of the vote (Samuel 2001: 187). After the elections renewed peace talks were held and in January 1995 there was a short-lived ceasefire but in April the LTTE dramatically broke this, signalling the beginning of the third 'Eelam war'.

In the 1995 talks the Tigers stated that although they maintained the objective of a separate state, they would consider a federal proposal. In their devolution proposals, the government declared Sri Lanka a 'Union of Regions' and proposed repealing Article 76 of the Constitution which forbade parliament from devolving its powers (Sathananthan 1998: 63). Meanwhile, the government's 'war for peace' strategy involved a simultaneous counter-insurgency campaign and military attempt to re-occupy Jaffna. This, and the subsequent bombing campaign against heavily populated Tamil areas and massive displacement of Tamils in the western part of the north, 'unleashed renewed waves of virulent resistance' led by the LTTE (Wilson and Chandrakanthan 1998: 75). At the end of 1995 the SLA took Jaffna city back, with the LTTE and most of the population fleeing. The Tigers regrouped in the northwestern and eastern jungles and in retaliation massacred Sinhalese civilians in border villages, suicide-bombed Colombo and launched attacks on military camps (Samuel 2001: 198–9). The

1995 devolution proposals were diluted in response to Sinhalese public opinion (Wilson and Chandrakanthan 1998: 75–6; Edrisinha 1998: 34; Sathananthan 1998: 63–4).

Wilson and Chandrakanthan argue for the existence of a de facto Tamil Eelam state, since the LTTE has in effect governed substantial areas of north and east Sri Lanka for extended periods of time since 1989 (1998: 74). In the north, they established a quasi-state from 1990 to 1995. Their administration dealt with central functions of government: the administration of justice, economic development and social provision. They resurrected a judiciary in 1992, published a 'code of law', and re-opened police stations. The Tigers also established the Tamil Eelam Economic Development Organization and the Tamil Eelam Bank, to stimulate small businesses and the rural sector. They re-established educational systems and provided facilities for displaced schoolchildren (ibid.: 74–5). Wilson and Chandrakanthan argue that 'steps were taken to undermine entrenched inequities within northern Tamil society based on caste and gender', including outlawing dowry and opening Hindu temples to previously excluded lower caste groups. The de facto state raised revenue through conventional methods. Allegedly, '[a]lthough lacking a formal electoral mandate, the LTTE administration enjoyed the active co-operation of a substantial proportion of the civilian population' (ibid.: 75). The 1995 re-taking of Jaffna brought down the de facto state here but it has remained in large sections of the Vanni area of the north and, until recently, some areas of the east.

Ceasefire 2002–8

In December 2001 the UNP, with Prime Minister Wickramasinghe, was elected with a mandate to facilitate Norwegian-brokered peace talks. A ceasefire was declared on 24 December, with a subsequent Memorandum of Understanding between the government and the LTTE in place from 23 February 2002, requiring both sides to adhere indefinitely to a ceasefire agreement (CFA). This was a precursor to direct talks and the government also eased the economic embargo on LTTE-held areas. Both the UNP and the People's Alliance parties endorsed the peace process; the JVP and Sinhala nationalist parties opposed it. There seemed at the time to be a recognition of the need for a political resolution to the conflict (Samuel 2001: 188) and a strong public desire to make the process work. Nevertheless, Sinhalese extremist parties such as the Sinhala Uramaya (formed in 2000) were rising in support (Roberts 2001b). During my first time in Sri Lanka there were a number of anti-peace protests in Colombo, particularly at the time of the first round of negotiations between the government and the LTTE in September 2002.

On the Tamil side, the Tigers insisted they be treated as the sole representative of Sri Lankan Tamils and hoped to run an interim administration in the northeast after negotiations with the government.[20] In December 2002 a federal proposal was announced by the government and the LTTE – the Tigers had dropped their demand for a separate state (Uyangoda 2001: 1–2; Uyangoda and Perera 2003: 280). An indication of the organization's economic plans was given by Prabhakaran when he cited his preference for an open economy (2002a), a clear shift in policy since earlier socialist days. Although it seemed outwardly committed to peace, the LTTE gave certain warning signals:

> The Tamil national question, which has assumed the character of a civil war, is essentially a political issue. We still hold a firm belief that this issue can be resolved by peaceful means.... [T]he Sinhalese political leadership is still buried in the swamp of racist ideology. That is why they have not developed the wisdom and understanding to deal with the Tamil question objectively and realistically.... The Sinhala people should realise that there can be no peace, ethnic harmony and economic prosperity in the island as long as the Tamil people are denied justice and their political aspirations are not fulfilled.
>
> (LTTE 2001)

Progress at peace talks was painfully slow and intermittent and there were violations of the CFA on both sides. There have been persistent charges levelled at the Tigers by Amnesty International, University Teachers for Human Rights (UTHR), UNICEF and Human Rights Watch that during the ceasefire they have been forcibly recruiting children (Amnesty International 2006; Human Rights Watch 2004; Samath 1997; UTHR various dates www.uthr.org/specialreport.htm). The LTTE denies the charges but is unconvincing. The UTHR also alleges that extortion and abductions by the LTTE continue in the northeast. Another important issue is the need for accommodation of the aspirations of Muslims. Given the Tamil–Muslim split in the 1990s, just resolution of this issue is essential for a lasting peace. Meanwhile, one of the most significant internal LTTE shifts in many years was the violent 2004 defection of its leading eastern commander, known as Colonel Karuna, and a large number of his followers. His real motivations are open to debate but the history of tensions and disputes between northern and eastern Tamils in general, and northern and eastern factions of the LTTE specifically, are significant and Karuna himself makes this clear (Buerk 2007). He also maintains that he was serious about the peace process and wanted to accept a federal solution but that Prabhakaran was never genuinely committed and was using the ceasefire to regroup. There is independent evidence for this regarding the LTTE but Karuna's attribution of noble goals to himself should be taken with a large grain of salt – allegedly he has since been assisting government forces in their fight against the LTTE, his troops have been involved in violence and intimidation, and they have recruited child soldiers (ibid.). Many of the child soldiers released from his unit have also been re-recruited by the main LTTE (Human Rights Watch 2004). Towards the end of 2007 Karuna was expelled from the Tamil Makkal Vidhuthalai Pullikal political party he had formed and he fled to the UK, where he was arrested for immigration offences and was sentenced in 2008 to nine months' imprisonment for identity fraud.

On the state side tensions between Prime Minister Wickramasinghe and President Kumaratunge and their respective parties escalated in 2003 and 2004, and peace talks were suspended. The December 2004 Asian tsunami further devastated already desperate communities, and although international agencies agreed that the best way to get aid into the northeast was by working with both the government and the LTTE, this proved difficult. In August 2005 the foreign minister Lakshman Kadirgamar (a Tamil opposed to separation and to the Tigers) was killed, apparently by the LTTE. Since the November 2005 elections, electing hardline President Rajapakse (Prime Minister from 2004), there has been increasing violence including renewed suicide bombs on buses and at state targets. Mid-2006 saw the worst fighting (up to that point) since the 2002 ceasefire, with outright battles between government forces and the Tigers. Renewed peace talks in Geneva in October 2006 singularly failed and throughout 2007 the state stepped up its war against the LTTE, particularly in the east where it claims to have retaken large chunks of Tiger-controlled territory.

Arguably, since at least mid-2006 Sri Lanka was in a state of undeclared war on both sides (Manoharan 2006). There is evidence that the LTTE has, certainly at least since the end of 2005, viewed the ceasefire as an opportunity to rearm, recruit and fundraise for a 'final war' (Human Rights Watch 2006), and the government's commitment to peace has been equally questionable. The splintering of the Tigers in the east is having ongoing ramifications. The death of Anton Balasingham at the end of 2006, followed by the Sri Lankan Air Force killing of LTTE political wing chief Thamilselvan during aerial bombing in November 2007, meant the loss of the two most prominent moderate voices in the LTTE within a year. The future is not currently bright. The real situation was effectively acknowledged when the government terminated the CFA in January 2008 and the Sri Lankan Monitoring Mission ceased to exist. The six years of official ceasefire in Sri Lanka 2002–8 were the longest absence of full-scale war in the northeast since war began in 1983. Sadly this has proved to be yet another interregnum between wars rather than the basis of lasting peace. In the current moment, with the bitter disappointment of the collapse of the hopes of the past six years, the loss of moderate voices on both sides of the conflict, and a return to horrific violence, the immediate future seems bleak.

Conflict in Northern Ireland

At the 2001 census the population of Northern Ireland[21] was just under 1.7 million, of which slightly over 53 per cent are of Protestant background and just under 44 per cent are of Catholic background (the numbers are lower when it comes to people professing to a practising religion, though much more so for Protestants than for Catholics).[22] From the outbreak of violence in 1969 until the 1994 ceasefires 3,400 people were killed and over 20,000 injured (Ruane and Todd 1996: 1). There have been deaths and injuries in Great Britain, the Republic of Ireland and continental Europe but people in Northern Ireland have been the primary victims. Nearly half the population (80 per cent in some areas) know someone injured or killed in the conflict, which has been over the constitutional status of Northern Ireland. Although the absolute number of fatalities is small when compared with other violent conflicts, when considered in the light of the tiny population of Northern Ireland as well as its long duration, using the local expression the 'Troubles' is a significant euphemism (O'Leary and McGarry 1996: 18).

Broadly, political conflict has taken place between British unionists and Irish nationalists, who largely come from the Protestant and the Catholic communities respectively. In Northern Ireland religion is a significant marker of ethnonational and political identity and also strongly informs and sustains these identities in a variety of ways, but is not the only element to them. The armed conflict is fought over ethno-political issues and encompasses complex interactions of multiple identities which cannot be reduced only to religion, though Mitchell has made a convincing case for the complicated (though variable) significance of religion in Northern Ireland and its mutually reinforcing relationship with politics and political identity (2006). The primary armed parties to the conflict have been republican paramilitaries, a variant of Irish nationalists who desire Northern Ireland to become part of an island-wide Irish republic; loyalist paramilitaries, a variant of British unionists who want Northern Ireland to remain part of the United Kingdom of Great Britain and Northern Ireland; and the British military forces.

This half of the chapter begins with a discussion of the history of Ireland and Northern Ireland after partition. As with Sri Lanka, although '[t]here are "historical" dimensions to the conflict ... many of its key characteristics and causes are modern rather than archaic' (O'Leary and McGarry 1996: 55). However, also as with Sri Lanka, history is highly politicized and used in nationalist projects. The chapter then moves to an examination of the competing nationalisms in contemporary Northern Ireland and the development of republican and loyalist paramilitaries. The last section charts the progress of the 'Troubles' since 1969: the 'long war' and the peace process.

Ireland before partition

Ireland was colonized by Anglo-Normans in the twelfth and thirteenth centuries, with a central administration established, but this was an uneven and insecure process. Intermittent plantation and conquest under Henry VIII and his children Edward VI, Mary and Elizabeth I resulted in Ireland being more thoroughly subjected to the English Crown. In terms of Northern Ireland, the most significant English policy was the plantation of Ulster under James I in the early 1600s. Ulster was the least anglicized region of the island and was colonized at the beginning of the seventeenth century after the defeat and exile of its last semi-independent Gaelic lords (O'Leary and McGarry 1996: 55–6, 64–6). The settlers profited from privileged access to official positions, Crown leases and direct land grants (Ruane and Todd 1996: 20). The territory that later became Northern Ireland encompasses the sites of these plantation settlements.

Ireland (or parts of it) was reconquered twice more in the seventeenth century: by Oliver Cromwell and by William of Orange. After Cromwell's brutal attack in 1649–52 the Protestant percentage of the population rapidly increased, as did their disproportionate share of land ownership (to 80 per cent by 1685 and 95 per cent a century later). A Catholic restoration of the English Crown failed when in 1688 King James II, the last Catholic monarch, was overthrown after a brief reign and the Dutch Prince William of Orange and his wife Mary were jointly offered the Crown by parliament, which led to a second conquest of the three kingdoms of the British Isles. Irish Catholic royalists captured most of Ulster but lost the Siege of Derry in 1689. On 12 July 1690 William's troops defeated James's in the Battle of the Boyne. Both the Siege of Derry and the Battle of the Boyne remain central symbolic events in Ulster Protestant mythology. Substantial immigration in the 1690s brought more settlers to Ulster, particularly from Scotland, and more land confiscation. From the 1690s Catholics were subjected to 'penal laws' excluding them from religious, political and social establishments and banning Catholic schools, burials and marriage. The penal laws remained in force until the late eighteenth century and were not repealed until 1829 (O'Leary and McGarry 1996: 67–70). The large population of Presbyterians in Ulster were also subject to discrimination by Anglicans and were excluded from religious and political establishments, but their legal discrimination was never as severe as that against Catholics and the last restrictions on them were removed in 1780 (Ruane and Todd 1996: 23).

Between the 1690s and 1800 the English Crown ruled Ireland indirectly through an Anglo-Irish Protestant élite with a parliament in Dublin, subordinate to Westminster. (Scotland entered into full parliamentary Union in 1707, creating Great Britain with England.) Agrarian violence was commonplace in the eighteenth century and had an ethno-religious character. After the French Revolution and the outbreak of war between Britain and revolutionary France in the 1790s the British needed to secure their western flank and so pushed a Catholic Relief Act through the Irish parliament that gave Catholics voting rights (with the same restricted property franchise applicable in the rest of the British Isles), but not the right to sit in parliament. The ideas of the Scottish Enlightenment and the French and American Revolutions were very attractive to some Presbyterian radicals and in 1791 they formed the United Irishmen, embracing Catholic emancipation and staging a failed rebellion in 1798, in the wake of which the Irish parliament was integrated into the Imperial Parliament of Great Britain and Ireland in the 1801 Act of Union. From 1801 the British controlled Ireland directly through the Union, with the Crown and ministers attempting to arbitrate conflicts between 'settlers' and 'natives'. However, 'Ireland was never treated as if it were just like England or the rest of Britain.' When it was formally integrated 'it was still governed differently from the rest of the kingdom, and marked off as a semi-colonial dependency' (O'Leary and McGarry 1996: 73).

O'Leary and McGarry argue that the formation of Northern Ireland was ultimately an expression of failed state- and nation-building in the British Isles. The legacies of colonialism led to 'no equality of opportunity for Catholics as the UK modernized' and Irish nationalists sought an independent Irish parliament through the Repeal of the Union movement in the 1830s and 1840s and the Home Rule movements after the 1870s. Both movements were blocked by British governments and by the Protestant settler population, which 'fertilized a more broad-based militant Irish republicanism which sought to create an independent Irish nation-state, if necessary through violence' (1996: 73–5). The Union faced small-scale nationalist/republican insurrections in 1803, 1848 and 1867. After the devastating 1845–9 Great Famine, Irish nationalist politics diverged onto two paths: militant Irish nationalism and parliamentary nationalism.

The third Home Rule bill was drafted in 1911 and was due to become law in 1914. In response to this the Ulster Unionist Council (UUC) prepared to establish a provisional government loyal to the Crown to be set up if the bill was passed. Unionists feared Home Rule would create a Catholic state and discriminate against Protestants (Bew 1994: Ch. 2; Hennessey 1997: 2–4). They also perceived Home Rule as threatening their Britishness and degrading their position within the UK. Since the 1886 Home Rule crisis they had 'exhibited a consciousness of themselves as both British and Irish. As such, unionists ... psychologically thought of themselves as belonging to a British nation, alongside the British-English, British-Scots and British-Welsh', and saw the 'British Isles' as the unit of their political nation, not Ireland (Hennessey 1996: 124–6; also McBride 1996: 9–10). In 1912 unionists formed and trained a large military group, the Ulster Volunteer Force (Ruane and Todd 1996: 47; Hennessey 1997: 4). Nationalists responded with the National Volunteers and its breakaway group the Irish Volunteers (Bew 1994: 112–13). In June 1914 an amendment to permit any Ulster county to vote itself out of Home Rule for a few years was introduced in the House of Lords, but the First World War began five days later. The Lords demanded the exclusion of all of Ulster from the bill and on 12 July the UUC declared itself the government of Ulster. Party political élites agreed to postpone the crisis because of the war; the Home Rule bill passed into law in September but its operation was delayed until the end of the war. Irish unionists now felt inhibited from using the threat of civil war by the fact that they would support Britain in the First World War regardless of the Home Rule situation; their bargaining power was thus decreased while that of nationalists was increased (ibid.: 118).

Partitioning the island: formation and development of Northern Ireland

Northern Ireland was formed through the partitioning of Ireland with the 1920 Government of Ireland Act, creating two jurisdictions and parliaments. Northern Ireland would be the northeastern counties of Antrim, Armagh, Down, Londonderry, Fermanagh and Tyrone (six of the nine counties of historic Ulster), separate from the remaining 26 counties. Northern Ireland was to have a two-chamber parliament with wide-ranging powers but Westminster retained control of the armed forces and foreign affairs. The creation of Northern Ireland was accompanied by widespread communal violence and intimidation, suffered disproportionately by

Catholics. At the same time the Irish Republican Army (IRA) was trying to undermine the new 'statelet'.[23] In the Anglo-Irish War/War of Independence the IRA carried out a campaign of guerrilla warfare, which unionists viewed as illustrating what they would face in a united Ireland. Nationalists saw the violence in Northern Ireland as a pogrom against Catholics (Hennessey 1997: 9–12). The armed Ulster Special Constabulary (USC) was established at the end of 1920 in response to the violence.[24] The USC was almost totally Protestant and became a symbol of repression for Catholics. Meanwhile, Protestants saw the USC as defending fellow Protestants from an IRA terror campaign.

The post-war settlement differed from pre-war expectations in three significant ways: a much more autonomous independent Irish state with dominion status was created; the partition arrangements were far more permanent than anyone had expected; and a Belfast parliament was formed at Stormont to run a devolved government, rather than direct rule from Westminster. The situation had been changed entirely during the First World War by the 1916 Easter Rising rebellion; the rise of Sinn Féin (a republican political party pushing for Irish independence) and its 1918 electoral victory; and the Irish War of Independence. In 1921 the British parliament accorded an Irish Free State to the 26 counties outside the new Northern Ireland, after the Anglo-Irish Treaty ended the War of Independence (Ruane and Todd 1996: 48; O'Leary and McGarry 1996: 96–101). Although Ulster unionists had not wanted Home Rule they soon saw the advantages of a Belfast parliament (O'Leary and McGarry 1996: 98–100). The Irish Civil War that broke out after the Treaty, between pro- and anti-Treaty nationalists, was not fought over the issue of Ulster. Both sides assumed the issue would be satisfied by the Boundary Commission established to examine the border, but this did not happen (Bew *et al.* 2002: 5).

Northern Ireland 'was a semi-state, a regime rather than a state.... None the less this "semi-state" was sufficient to build a system of hegemonic control [by unionists]' (O'Leary and McGarry 1996: 110–11). Since there were large numbers of Catholic and Protestant minorities on the 'wrong' sides of the new border it was assumed this would constrain each government into treating their respective minorities fairly, but this was not what happened (Bew *et al.* 2002: 3–4). Sectarian speeches by the unionist leadership became more commonplace from the late 1920s and early 1930s and Northern Irish Prime Minister James Craig spoke in 1934 of a 'Protestant parliament for a Protestant people', though the context of this (often forgotten) was the statement of a nationalist politician in the Irish Free State about having a Catholic state for a Catholic people (ibid.: 6–7). Kennedy-Pipe identifies three features characterizing Northern Ireland between 1920 and the mid-1960s: first, sovereignty over the region was (theoretically at least) contested by the British and Irish states but it was not fully integrated into either state. The dominance of Protestants created the second feature: political institutions lacked broad support across the two communities, with governing unionists making little effort to win nationalist support. The third feature was a disgruntled and disenfranchised Catholic minority, though largely this did not disturb the workings of the regime until the 1960s

(2000: 25–6). Meanwhile, as the Irish Free State advanced its state- and nation-building project its 'Gaelicisation … began a process of alienation by Ulster Unionists from their sense of Irishness and a greater reliance on their sense of Britishness' (Hennessey 1997: 74). The public power of the Catholic Church in the Free State further alienated them, as did the increasing republicanism of the state – the 1937 Constitution gave the Church a 'special position' and included a territorial claim to the whole island. In 1948 the Irish government announced it was severing all ties with the British Commonwealth and was to become the Republic of Ireland, increasing Ulster unionist insecurities (ibid.: 97–8).

In 1963 Terence O'Neill became Northern Ireland's Prime Minister, believing that the economic benefits of being in the Union could encourage Catholics to accept Northern Ireland's existence (Rose 1971: 288). He aimed for economic modernization, accepting the decline of the old staple industries, and wanted to expand the political middle ground. He wanted to reduce unemployment, develop economic cooperation with the government of the Republic and improve social services, believing the Ulster Unionist Party (UUP) could attract Catholic voters this way. He met the Republic's Taoiseach (Prime Minister) and thawed north–south relations (Mulholland 2000). Changes were also occurring in the Catholic community. There were social and economic shifts as a result of the development of the post-war British state and extension of the welfare state into Northern Ireland, though Bew *et al.* argue against an over-simplified notion that Catholic mobilization in the 1960s is attributable purely to an expanded Catholic middle class (2002: 146). They explain the mass popularity of mobilization with reference to changes in the social structure, whereby the relative position of the least privileged members of the Catholic community deteriorated during the Stormont period. While the unskilled section of the Protestant working class diminished as a proportion of the workforce, it increased in the Catholic working class (ibid.). External factors also figured; in the 1960s Northern Ireland was influenced by changing Anglo-Irish relations which grew out of the push for greater European integration (Meehan 2000; Arthur 1999).

Some Catholics were frustrated with the lack of real reform in the early 1960s and created pressure groups such as the Campaign for Social Justice (CSJ), which complained about political discrimination and discrimination in public housing allocation and pushed (in gendered language) for 'one man, one vote'. This referred to local government elections where there was still a property-based electoral system (abolished in the rest of the UK in 1945) – one person one vote did exist in Stormont and Westminster parliamentary elections (Hennessey 1997: 127–9). The property-based local government system applied to everyone but Catholics were disadvantaged because of their lower average socio-economic position. Whyte argues that allegations of gerrymandering of parliamentary constituencies to keep nationalists out of power were largely (though not completely) unfounded but that gerrymandering of local government boundaries is much more substantiated and is one of the clearest areas of discrimination (1983). Catholics were under-represented in the civil service and the judiciary and on statutory bodies; the pattern in public employment was generally that they were proportionately represented at manual labour levels but at any level above that they were seriously under-represented (ibid.). In regard to public housing allocation, it seems that overall discrimination here was much less widespread than in public employment, with exceptions in certain areas (ibid.).

Catholics have been economically disadvantaged as well as politically marginalized and the working class has been particularly affected. Unemployment is particularly a problem for working-class Catholic men and the decline of the construction industry further eroded their opportunities (Coulter 1999: 82–3). Protestant men tend to be over-represented in non-manual occupations while Catholic men are over-represented in manual, unskilled and low-paying occupations (McGarry and O'Leary 1995: 269–70). In 1971 Catholic men were 2.6 times more likely to be unemployed than Protestant men and in 1981 this had only dropped to 2.4 times (Hennessey 1997: 238). For women the ratio between unemployment rates has remained almost unchanged since the 1971 census; in 1991 Catholic women were almost twice as likely as Protestant women to be unemployed (Coulter 1999: 123). The Fair Employment Commission noted in 1995 that the overall gap had closed slightly but Catholics were still twice as likely to be unemployed (Hennessey 1997: 239–40).

In 1964 the British election of Wilson's Labour government raised Catholic political expectations, yet the government was unwilling to get involved. However there was mounting pressure for intervention from the Campaign for Democracy in Ulster (a group established by members of the British Labour Party, mostly of Irish descent) (Bew *et al.* 2002: 144). Meanwhile the IRA was waning with the end of its 1950s guerrilla border campaign[25] and the Nationalist Party was seen as having 'vacated its traditional role ... without finding a new one' (ibid.: 144–5). Around the same time the concept of an organized civil rights movement developed. Influenced by the international civil rights agenda of the 1960s, the Northern Ireland movement 'drew international attention and proved exceptionally damaging to the reputation of the Stormont regime' (Kennedy-Pipe 2000: 27). The Northern Ireland Civil Rights Association (NICRA – launched in 1967) and the broader civil rights movement were 'composed of those who, like the IRA, had revolutionary aims but were in a minority and those who, like the CSJ, were reformist, who were in the ascendancy' (Hennessey 1997: 137). By mid-1968 they had begun public protests, faced by loyalist counter-demonstrations led by the Reverend Ian Paisley.[26] Some loyalist groups were concerned about the direction of 'O'Neillism', even though his policies offered no structural reform of Northern Ireland, simply hoping that long-term economic improvements would mean Catholics would accept the existence of the 'statelet' (Hennessey 1997: 138). However Rose's 1968 Loyalty Survey found O'Neill's theory to be false. Rose argues this is because it was based on the presumption 'that individual aspirations are solely satisfied by the provision of private goods, i.e., personal economic benefits', whereas in fact the survey results imply 'a concern with collective wellbeing, that is, the wellbeing of the Catholic community' (1971: 300–1).

Competing nationalisms

In the seventeenth century peoples in Ireland were not divided into two blocs, Protestant and Catholic, and certainly not unionist and nationalist. Alongside religious differences (both Protestantism and Catholicism being internally diverse as well as divided between one another) there were also various groups that could be considered ethnic: Gaelic-Irish, Old English (Catholic descendants of late medieval Norman settlers), lowland Scots and English. Catholics and Protestants developed into single overarching communal groups slowly over the following centuries. Irish nationalism and unionism were products of the nineteenth century, during which two culturally and politically polarized communities emerged in Ireland (Ruane and Todd 1996). Later, '[p]artition created new bases for community formation, identity and solidarity' (ibid.: 83). Nationalism/republicanism and unionism/loyalism are the dominant political ideologies in Northern Ireland and are a fundamental source of conflict. Not all Catholics are nationalists and not all Protestants are unionists – though the following discussion suggests a higher correlation between being Protestant and being unionist than between being Catholic and being nationalist – but at least 80 per cent of the Northern Irish population vote for political parties that appeal to only one community (ibid.: 76–8).

Northern Catholics and nationalism/republicanism

Before partition Irish Catholics were a much more cohesive community at island-wide level than Irish Protestants. Although Ulster had a distinct regional identity for Catholics it also shared a common religious, political and cultural heritage with the rest of the island. Despite increased economic and social distancing between north and south after partition, an island-wide identity still existed; the final phase of forming a cohesive northern Catholic community (the mobilization in the late 1960s/early 1970s) included a reaffirmation of the unity of the nationalist community on the whole island. For Northern Catholics 'the building of a separate community was always ambivalent, conditional and strategic' (Ruane and Todd 1996: 52–3).

There are internal divisions in the northern Catholic community. Regular church attendance is high (86 per cent) but there are of course varying relationships with the church (Ruane and Todd 1996: 66), and divergent political attitudes and constitutional goals. The 2002 Northern Ireland Life and Times Survey showed 46 per cent of Catholics wanted reunification with the rest of Ireland, 22 per cent wanted to remain part of the UK, almost as many were undecided, and 9 per cent favoured an independent Northern Ireland (though other questions produced stronger apparent levels of support for reunification).[27] Overall, a united Ireland has often been a less popular option for Catholics in surveys than power-sharing in a devolved government (there has consistently been more Catholic support for integration with Britain than there is Protestant support for a united Ireland) (Whyte 1990: 80–1; Irwin 2002). Catholics also differ in their attitudes to political violence. Before the ceasefires support for violence appeared to be decreasing even among Sinn Féin (SF) supporters (Ruane and Todd 1996: 70), although Hayes and McAllister argue that there is a 'popular ambiguity ... towards the use of political violence' in both communities (2001: 901, 911). Survey data from 1998 showed 28 per cent of Catholics expressing some level of sympathy for republican paramilitaries (ibid.: 914). The two main political parties Catholics vote for are the Social Democratic and Labour Party (SDLP), which favours reunification in the long term and used to hold about two-thirds of the Catholic support (and is arguably seen as middle-class), and Sinn Féin, which wants more rapid reunification and used to have about a third of the Catholic vote. SF began slowly increasing in support in the 1980s as it changed its views on electoral competition and after the 1994 ceasefire its position relative to the SDLP significantly increased, until in 2001 it narrowly emerged, for the first time, as the largest nationalist party (Mitchell *et al.* 2001).

There is greater cultural than political unity among northern Catholics, with three basic ethno-national identities: Irish, Northern Irish, and British. There is some overlap of identities but less so than for Protestants. Surveys show 60 per cent identifying as Irish, 25 per cent as Northern Irish, 8 per cent as British and 2 per cent as Ulster (Ruane and Todd 1996: 71; Whyte 1990: 67–71). Class differences among Catholics have been less pronounced structurally and ideologically than among Protestants. State-sponsored fair employment policies and expansion of the state service sector created an expanded middle class, while recession further increased unemployment in Catholic working-class areas, but 'Catholic class divisions still lack the depth and intensity of Protestant ones and many of the new Catholic middle class are just one generation from the working class' (Ruane and Todd 1996: 73). The Catholic Church remains 'the single most important integrating social force', influencing all areas of communal life, and organizations fostering Gaelic-Irish culture also help integrate the community (ibid.: 74–6). The social and ritual elements of membership in the Church – the *practice* of religion as distinct from religious ideology or doctrine – seem to help construct a sense of community for Catholics more than for Protestants (Mitchell 2006: Ch. 5).

The two major clusters of political views in the Catholic community, 'nationalism' and 'republicanism', are both forms of Irish nationalism and largely map to the constitutional–militant divide between those who believe in pursuing their goals through political competition and change (constitutional nationalists) and those who believe in using armed struggle (republicans). Another divide, which does not map in the same way, is arguably between civic and ethnic Irish nationalism, in competition since the late eighteenth century. Many who have fought British rule in Ireland have claimed to be civic nationalists, including the contemporary leadership of the IRA and Sinn Féin (McGarry and O'Leary 1995: 14–15), but in reality civic and ethnic Irish nationalisms compete even within individual movements, perhaps illustrating Smith's argument (mentioned in the previous chapter) that civic nationalism is never entirely free from ethnic elements.

Irish republicanism is secular at the ideological level and 'asserts that all of those who live on the island of Ireland are members of the same national community'; problematically, however, 'Ulster Protestants have simply refused to accept that they are members of the Irish nation' (Coulter 1999: 226–7; see also English 1996). Republicans have often failed to take unionism seriously and their arguments for Ulster Protestants as co-nationals 'usually display a patronizing tone' (McGarry and O'Leary 1995: 48–50; also Coulter 1999: 230–1). The republican view of unionism as 'a fragile, propped-up or even artificial flower' has been seriously challenged by recent scholarship on unionism (English 1996) and republicans have begun to take unionism more seriously. The growing realisation that unionism is not just 'the bastard child of British imperialism' (Coulter 1999: 230) has meant republicans had to recognize that 'unionists were not going to disappear, or suddenly to lose their horror at the thought of being expelled from the UK' (English 2003: 313), and have had to acknowledge 'that the real obstacle to Irish unity lies in unionist objections rather than British intentions' (English 1996: 227).

Northern Protestants and unionism/loyalism

At the start of the twentieth century Protestants formed an island-wide community sharing political goals and loyalties and bound by religious, cultural and social ties yet were internally differentiated by religion, class and region. Ulster Protestants perceived themselves and were viewed as different from other Irish Protestants because of their strong Scottish and Presbyterian influence, demographic majority, participation in the industrial revolution and greater religious fundamentalism. In Protestant Ulster itself there were strong internal religious and class divisions (Ruane and Todd 1996: 49). After partition '[a]n institutionally and imaginatively cohesive Northern Protestant community crystallised', gaining a greater British focus with the experience of the Second World War and the post-war integration of Northern Ireland into the British welfare state (ibid.: 50). Protestant religious diversity remains significant and in contrast to Catholics less than half of Protestants overall attend church every week and at least 15 per cent never attend (ibid.: 54). Despite this lower level of (narrowly measured) religiosity, Mitchell argues that non-theological religious ideology continues to inform communal identification for Protestants more than for Catholics, and religious theology and doctrine are significant in constituting the meaning of group identity and politics for some Protestants (2006: Chs 6–7).

Most Protestants today are united in broad political aims to retain the Union and prevent its erosion but they differ in their reasons, motives and strategies (Cochrane 1997); historically, support for Britain and the Union was highly conditional (Miller 1978). Aside from the constitutional question there is significant political diversity and a number of different parties. Like Catholics, Protestants vary in their attitudes to political violence but 31 per cent expressed some level of sympathy for loyalist paramilitaries in 1998 data (Hayes and McAllister 2001: 913). The favoured institutional/constitutional preference for Protestants has varied enormously over the course of the 'Troubles' and is arguably 'strategic and situational' (Ruane and Todd 1996: 57), but it is clear from surveys carried out since the beginning of the 'Troubles' that only 1–4 per cent support a united Ireland and not many more would reluctantly accept it (Whyte 1990: 80). The 2002 Northern Ireland Life and Times Survey found 83 per cent of Protestants wanted Northern Ireland to remain part of the UK and only 3 per cent favoured unification with the rest of Ireland.[28] Within the Protestant community '[b]itter and periodically intense class conflict has long been endemic' (Ruane and Todd 1996: 61). After partition this was not fully mediated by the unionist state and class divisions widened. Since the 1994 ceasefires and particularly since the Good Friday Agreement (GFA) was signed, the more extremist Democratic Unionist Party (DUP) has closed in on the UUP and then passed it in terms of its electoral support (Mitchell *et al.* 2001), largely attributable to its anti-Agreement stance.

In contrast to Catholics, cultural differences are more marked than political differences for northern Protestants, with a consequent lack of consensus on ethno-national identity. There are four (not mutually exclusive) identities – Northern Irish, British, Ulster, and/or Irish Protestant – and there are various combinations and permutations of these. A British identity used to be seen as additional to other more local identities but in the recent period it has emerged as an alternative and even as a primary ethnic identity, though Ruane and Todd argue this is still a minority position and '[f]or the vast majority of Northern Protestants, the core community is the Protestants of Ulster or Northern Ireland' (1996: 57–9; see also Whyte 1990: 67–71). So there is some dispute about the nature of Protestant ethno-national identity, but a clear trend since the outbreak of the 'Troubles' has been a vastly decreased number of Protestants identifying as Irish. As with Catholics, despite internal diversity the Protestant community is held together by various integrative practices and networks. Communal solidarity and boundaries between the communities are maintained by structural and institutional mechanisms such as territorial segregation (particularly among the working class), extremely high rates of endogamy, separate educational systems and segregation in sports and youth clubs (Whyte 1990: 62–5).

The two major clusters of political views in the Protestant community are 'unionism' and 'loyalism'; both are regional forms of British unionism (Ulster unionism). It is possible to argue – and I do – that unionism 'is a type of nationalism, a variation of British nationalism, and it has both civic and ethnic dimensions, just like its Irish nationalist counterpart' (McGarry and O'Leary 1995: 92–3), but this is usually disputed by unionists (English 1996: 230). Certainly it is a less coherent and more ambiguous nationalism (as arguably most settler-state nationalisms are likely to be), though no less attached to its constitutional preference. Cochrane argues unionism

> contains diverse interest groups with little in common other than a commitment to the link with Britain. While this position remains relatively cohesive during periods of constitutional crisis when they can articulate what

> they do not want (namely a weakening of the link with Britain), the coherence of the ideology begins to disintegrate when unionists are forced to establish a consensus for political progress.
>
> (1997: 35, Ch. 2)

Devolutionist unionists assert that Northern Ireland needs extensive devolved self-government, even if only to protect unionists from British treachery, while integrationists argue for legal, political, electoral and administrative integration of Northern Ireland with the rest of the UK (McGarry and O'Leary 1995: 93). Overall, most unionists also argue that the 'instrumental advantages of the constitutional status quo are ... irrefutable' in regard to the political economy of Northern Ireland (Shirlow and Shuttleworth 1999: 31).

Todd's influential categorization of unionism differentiates between two traditions, Ulster British and Ulster loyalist, in terms of their different ideological structures. The Ulster British ideology has a primary 'imagined community' of 'Greater Britain', with a secondary regional identification with Northern Ireland, is primarily secular and has a middle-class bias. Ulster loyalist ideology has a primary 'imagined community' of Ulster Protestants and a secondary, conditional identification with Britain, has evangelical and secular working-class versions, and is loyal primarily to the monarchy and protection of Ulster Protestants. At the level of unionist politics, politicians have drawn on both ideologies (Todd 1987). Ordinary people commonly distinguish between 'unionists' and 'loyalists'. The way my loyalist interviewees explained it to me was that loyalists view themselves as part of a wider unionist 'family', but loyalists are loyal to the Crown (rather than to the British government or institutions) and are working class. Unionists are divided over their perceptions of Catholics and northern nationalists and their prescriptions for them. Unionists conventionally attribute the conflict to the Irish state and its nationalist irredentism, though this has been challenged by revisionists who point to 'an external "absence": the absence of a British commitment to make Northern Ireland ineffably British' (McGarry and O'Leary 1995: 95–6).

Development of paramilitarism

The October 1968 civil rights march in Derry and subsequent rioting and confrontations with the Royal Ulster Constabulary (RUC) were widely publicized, and, responding to British pressure, the unionist government issued a reform plan which for many in the civil rights movement was too little too late – meanwhile the reforms enraged unionists (Hennessey 1997: 142–4). In January 1969 a protest march ended in violent clashes with loyalists and off-duty B-Specials (the only remaining unit of the USC) at Burntollet Bridge, and violence in Derry. The Cameron Commission investigating concluded the RUC had used unnecessary force and had not protected the marchers; some police were guilty of assault, battery and malicious damage; and there had been organized interventions by followers of Paisley and Major Ronald Bunting that substantially increased the risk of violence (Cameron 1969: Ch. 14).

The worsening crisis and political tensions led to the dissolution of parliament and the 1969 general election, when the UUP split into pro-O'Neill and anti-O'Neill factions; ultimately O'Neill resigned (Mulholland 2000: 194–7). The election also saw the demise of the Nationalist Party, with new politicians such as John Hume emerging to dominate Catholic politics. It has been argued that as belligerence rose in both the Catholic and Protestant communities in the summer of 1969, 'leading [civil rights] figures of the previous year lost influence ... particularly in working-class districts.... As popular participation in public demonstrations increased, so did the unsought involvement of entire areas in violence'. In July and August no fewer than 1,505 of Belfast's 28,616 Catholic households were forced to leave their homes (Bew *et al.* 2002: 147–8). Estimates are that between 1969 and 1972 30,000–60,000 people were driven from their homes, 80 per cent of them Catholic and 20 per cent Protestant – at the time this was the largest enforced population movement in Western Europe since the Second World War (McKittrick 1994: 39). The civil rights clashes with the RUC, the eruption of violence on the streets and wholesale urban population movement into segregated Protestant and Catholic neighbourhoods led to local vigilantes forming and ultimately to paramilitary resurgence (Kennedy-Pipe 2000: 27).

Republican paramilitaries

The serious communal violence of 1969 led to a split in republicanism over the use of force and the left-leaning tendencies of the movement; in December those dissatisfied with the leftist turn of the IRA broke away to reorganize, electing a Provisional Executive and Army Council of seven (Bell 1989: 366). The new military wing came to be known as the Provisional IRA (PIRA or the Provisionals or, as they attained hegemony, just the IRA).[29] The political wing of republicanism, Sinn Féin, also split on the same lines (ibid.: 367–8). The Provisional Army Council's main priority was to defend Catholic areas from loyalists and the British army; as soon as it was feasible PIRA would move to retaliation, then an all-out offensive against the 'British occupation system' (Coogan 1995: 365 citing Mac Stiofáin 1974: 145–6).

Security force actions, particularly in the summer of 1970, soon turned many northern Catholics against the British army and PIRA gained increased support and recruits, largely young people from working-class Catholic strongholds. From 1971 they began targeting personnel of the British army, the Ulster Defence Regiment (UDR)[30] and the RUC (Coogan 1995: 376–7). The 'Official' IRA (OIRA, the Officials or, more commonly, the 'Stickies'), as those loyal to the original leadership became known, was also active but PIRA soon outstripped OIRA. In the first years of the 'Troubles' PIRA believed a united Ireland could be achieved by forcing British withdrawal from Northern Ireland, and conducted their campaign on the belief 'that victory lay just around the corner' (Guelke 1999: 38).

Three events of the early 1970s gained PIRA many new recruits: internment, Bloody Sunday, and the ceasefire of OIRA. The government responded to increasing IRA violence in 1971 with internment without trial for suspected 'terrorists' (ended in 1975), stimulating Catholic resentment. In 1972 the British army fired on a banned civil rights demonstration in Derry attended by nearly 10,000 people, killing 14 and wounding others in what is known as Bloody Sunday (see Pringle and Jacobson 2000), and '[a]s Derry mourned its dead, the IRA had more offers of help than they could handle' (Clarke and Johnston 2001: 67, Ch. 5). Subsequently OIRA ordered all British soldiers were to be shot on sight, but after outraged reactions to the May 1972 kidnap and murder of a young (Catholic) Royal Irish Ranger they declared indefinite ceasefire (ibid.: 73–4). Later, the 1981 hunger strikes of republican prisoners (discussed further later in this chapter) stimulated renewed support for republicanism and a new flow of recruits to PIRA and the growing Irish National Liberation Army (INLA), as did the tactics of the RUC in confronting protests (Ellison and Smyth 2000: 103). Stevenson notes the hunger strikes both increased the IRA's recruiting power in Northern Ireland and expanded it to the Republic (1996: 163). In my own research, many republican interviewees (including one from the Republic) cited the hunger strikes and attendant protests as either the arena through which they first became involved in republicanism generally, or as having had a direct impact on their decision to join the IRA.

Initially PIRA structure was modelled on the British army pattern of brigade, battalion and companies, and members were recruited from specific geographical areas, giving it a high profile in nationalist areas but making it vulnerable to intelligence-gathering (Coogan 1995: 377; Ellison and Smyth 2000: 93). After 1976 PIRA knew it had to adjust its strategy, which broadly coincided with leadership changes whereby northerners displaced southerners (Guelke 1999: 38; Feeney 2002: 320–1). In December 1977 a seized document showed that the military structure was to be replaced by a cell structure to improve the security of its active service units, and the IRA was gearing up for long-term armed struggle. The size of the military membership was to decrease and command to decentralize, with preparations made for a long, slow war of attrition (Coogan 1995: 464–7; Maloney 2002: 156–60; Guelke 1999: 38–9). The reorganization initially managed to stem security force successes and PIRA settled into the 'long war', but by the mid-1990s its finances had dwindled and traditional funding from Irish-Americans was drying up. This, with security force intelligence activities, arguably meant the IRA's campaign 'was falling to pieces' (Maloney 2002: 458–61).

There have been splits and internecine feuds within republican paramilitarism. The Irish Republican Socialist Party (IRSP) emerged as a result of a split in Official Sinn Féin; its more militant supporters formed the INLA in 1974, opposed to OIRA's permanent ceasefire (Holland and McDonald 1994; Coogan 1995: Ch. 32). The establishment of the IRSP and INLA led to a bitter feud and internecine warfare in 1975 with OIRA (Holland and McDonald 1994: Chs 2–3). In 1986 the INLA suffered its own split and feud, with a breakaway group forming the Irish People's Liberation Organization (IPLO) (ibid.: 279). PIRA violently moved against the IPLO in 1992, forcing it to disband (ibid.: 368).

OIRA has not been the only one to split. The 1996 internal dissent within PIRA over the ceasefire and delays in Sinn Féin being allowed into multi-party talks led to two new groups, Continuity IRA (CIRA) and the Real IRA (RIRA), both made up primarily of former members opposed to the peace process (McKittrick and McVea 2001: 219, 223).

Loyalist paramilitaries

The Ulster Volunteer Force (UVF) was founded in 1966 (promptly proscribed), structured along military lines. Its name reflects the fact that it views itself as the inheritor of the early twentieth-century UVF (Boulton 1973: 2), just as the present IRA views itself as the direct descendent of the earlier IRA. In the late 1960s the UVF comprised only a tiny group of working-class ex-servicemen from Belfast's Protestant Shankill Road, had little support, and remained largely dormant for the next few years. It did not grow in membership and violence until around 1970, when the increased violence and instability subsequent to the civil rights movement led to a heightened loyalist fear of republicanism (Bruce 1992a: 68; see also Bruce 1992b; Cusack and McDonald 1997) and after 1971 'recruits began queuing up to join' (Nelson: 1984: 174). Loyalist paramilitaries have seen themselves as counter-revolutionaries but what constitutes a revolutionary for them has been wide enough to include any politically active nationalist, and at times indiscriminate attacks on Catholics have been justified with the slogan 'any Catholic will do' (Guelke 1999: 32–4). Loyalist paramilitaries have also been categorized as 'pro-state terrorists' (Bruce 1992a, 1992b). The sectarian attacks on Catholics after 1971 by the UVF and the Ulster Defence Association (UDA) largely, it has been argued, were not due to conscious policy. Bruce maintains that there was 'no point at which leaders instructed their people "now" to kill Catholics'; rather, some volunteers just did (1992b: 51–4). From mid-1973 the UVF began to catch up with the UDA in terms of its campaign, retaliating to the IRA's campaign of pub bombings with its own and also with car bombs in the Republic (Bruce 1992b: 115; Hennessey 1997: 229).

In 1975 a UVF leadership coup led to replacement by a group of older and more experienced men who were slightly more political and insisted that random sectarian murder was to be replaced by attacks only on armed republican targets (Bruce 1992b: 129–34, 175), though this claim was seriously undermined by the brutal torture-killings committed by a group of UVF men known as the Shankill Butchers (ibid.: 173–81; Dillon 1989). With the reorganization and new tactics of the security forces from the late 1970s, increasingly efficient at imprisoning republican (and loyalist) paramilitaries, Protestant support for loyalist paramilitaries decreased as 'the sense of emergency declined' (Bruce 1992a: 70; 1992b: 135–8). Since 1979 the Progressive Unionist Party (PUP), comprised mainly of UVF members/ex-members and ex-prisoners, has been a sporadically active political party but has found it difficult to gain support beyond loyalist Belfast (Bruce 1992b: 147). Its electoral support has been marginal and since the 1998 Assembly elections has declined even further.[31] The

UVF has also split; in the late 1990s a small breakaway group, the Loyalist Volunteer Force (LVF), was formed by members opposed to the ceasefire, and carried out a number of sectarian killings (Guelke 1999: 49).

Although the UVF is older the UDA was, and remains, the largest of the loyalist paramilitaries and is 'overwhelmingly working-class' (Hennessey 1997: 203). It was established in 1971 by merging Protestant vigilante groups that sprang up in response to republican violence, along with some ex-UVF members and trade union activists (Bruce 1992b: 46–50). In 1972 it grew enormously and changed its structure to a more military one (though most members had full-time jobs and were not involved in the day-to-day organization) (ibid.: 59–60). The UDA/UFF (Ulster Freedom Fighters, essentially a military wing of the UDA) used shows of strength in the streets and random assassinations of Catholics; its campaign intensified after the first introduction of direct rule in 1972 (Guelke 1999: 46; Bruce 1992b: 54–6, 115).

After UDA leadership changes in the late 1970s, with a move towards politicization, the new leadership contained UDA violence to a lower level in the 1980s. However with another shift in the late 1980s, the incoming leadership 'was determined to demonstrate its effectiveness by matching the violence of the Provisional IRA blow for blow', resulting in a sharp increase in assassinations by the UFF in the early 1990s (Guelke 1999: 47).[32] As with the UVF, the UDA's reputation has been affected by torture-killings (Bruce 1992b: 182–3). From the late 1980s it has also been criticized for racketeering, extortion and drugs activities (ibid.: Ch. 10). Such activities have become increasingly widespread and more problematic for loyalist communities (BBC1 Northern Ireland 2003; Alison, forthcoming). The UDA has attempted political representation through various organizations, including the Ulster Loyalist Democratic Party (ULDP), later renamed the Ulster Democratic Party (UDP, now defunct), and to gain political influence through the think tank the Ulster Political Research Group (Bruce 1992b: Ch. 9).

The relationship between the UVF and UDA has often been significantly uneasy (Bruce 1992b: 114–17; Nelson 1984: 179) and has broken into violence on a number of occasions since 1974. Since the 1998 GFA, however, internecine loyalist warfare has vastly increased, both between the UVF and UDA in 2000 and within the UDA since 2002. Although the UDA has always suffered internal rivalries, possibly due to the fragmented and haphazard nature of its origins (Bruce 1992b: 66–7), the extent and intensity of post-Agreement intra-loyalist violence seems to be something new and has had serious consequences (Alison, forthcoming).

The 'Troubles': the 'long war' and the peace process

When Chichester-Clark succeeded O'Neill as Northern Ireland's Prime Minister in 1969, he also tried introducing reforms to reduce Catholic alienation from the state but his government instead faced alienating its supporters. The scale and intensity of communal violence in the summer of 1969, combined with the

RUC's inability to maintain order,[33] led to the arrival of the British army. Reforms introduced after the Cameron and Hunt Reports did not calm either unionist or nationalist anxieties. Chichester-Clark was forced to resign in 1971. Further reforms instigated by his successor, Faulkner, also met resistance from part of the unionist community (Hennessey 1997: 185–8; Kennedy-Pipe 2000: 27–8). Ultimately the old UUP fractured, resulting in the Alliance Party of Northern Ireland (APNI) (against violence and in favour of reconciliation), the DUP (dissatisfied with Stormont's reforms), unionist pressure group the Ulster Vanguard (strongly supported by loyalist paramilitaries) and the short-lived Vanguard Unionist Progressive Party. Meanwhile, the demise of the Nationalist Party led to a realignment of constitutional Catholic politics and the formation of the SDLP, which found that in some areas it had to co-exist or compete with the republicanism that had evolved since 1969 (Bew *et al.* 2002: 148). The SDLP agreed with many of the political views of PIRA but disagreed on violence, not accepting that Protestants could be bombed into a united Ireland (Hennessey 1997: 180–1).

Violence and politics

In the summer of 1971 the IRA campaign increased in violence. After internment was introduced and raids carried out by the British army, the IRA moved from selected bombings to a widespread campaign against economic targets and intensified attacks on the RUC and the UDR. The months after 1972's Bloody Sunday saw frequent bombs by OIRA and PIRA, in both Northern Ireland and England. With the deteriorating situation Conservative British Prime Minister Heath announced the imposition of direct rule from London in March 1972 and Faulkner resigned as Northern Ireland Prime Minister. A consultation paper shortly after direct rule was imposed stated that no UK government wished to hinder the realization of Irish unity *if* it occurred through consent, but also reinforced that Northern Ireland would remain part of the UK as long as a majority of its people wanted that (Kennedy-Pipe 2000: 29–30; Hennessey 1997: 214).

Meanwhile PIRA, encouraged by direct rule, held a truce and met with British ministers. The first Northern Ireland Secretary of State Whitelaw agreed to republican prisoners having 'special category' status (being allowed to wear civilian clothes and have more visits). Whitelaw saw this as a minor concession but PIRA viewed it as conceding that its prisoners were prisoners-of-war. Otherwise the meeting failed to produce results and the two-week ceasefire ended in July (Hennessey 1997: 210–11). A week later PIRA set off 26 bombs in Belfast in what became known as Bloody Friday. The immediate British response was to send the army to destroy the IRA's 'no-go' areas in Derry and Belfast (Clarke and Johnston 2001:77) (this was the only period PIRA came even close to running a mini quasi-state like the LTTE has run in substantial areas of northeastern Sri Lanka[34]) but the government realized any solution would require a long haul.

In 1973 the British government issued a White Paper calling for a Northern Ireland Assembly elected by proportional representation (in effect, unionist and nationalist power-sharing) and held talks at Sunningdale in England with Faulkner (UUP leader for a short while longer), the SDLP, the APNI and a Fine Gael–Labour coalition government from the Republic. In a joint communiqué the Irish government stated there could be no change in the status of Northern Ireland until a majority of the people desired such a change, and the British government stated that if in the future a majority wished to become part of a united Ireland, it would support that (Kennedy-Pipe 2000: 30). Feeling threatened, the United Ulster Unionist Council rejected the proposals. In 1974 the Ulster Workers' Council (UWC) held a general strike, paralysing Northern Ireland (Fraser 2000: 61), and the nascent power-sharing Assembly was prorogued.

There was an IRA ceasefire for most of 1975 and talks between the British government and Provisional Sinn Féin, but these failed and violence returned. The INLA was also active at this time but the main thrust of anti-state violence continued to come from PIRA. The collapse of power-sharing led to a long political stalemate and from 1975 Britain brought in policies to redefine the problem of Northern Ireland as one of criminal activity rather than political or constitutional struggle, refusing to call events in the region a war (Kennedy-Pipe 2000: 30–1). Counter-insurgency measures were put in place in the mid-1970s: the use of non-jury, single-judge courts in 'scheduled' (terrorist) offences (based on the 1972 Diplock Report); RUC interrogations and confessions (with persistent allegations of torture or inhumane treatment) and the admissibility of confessions obtained in this way; undercover operations and the use of informers (Ellison and Smyth 2000: 92–3). In 1974 the Prevention of Terrorism Act was brought in after the IRA bombs in Birmingham; this Act has been resented by nationalists and 'used by the state to gather information on large numbers of people, who ... have had no involvement in terrorist-type activities' (ibid.: 110). The period 1981–2 saw the 'supergrass trials', when mass arrests were made and dubious trials held on information given to the RUC by informers promised immunity from prosecution, reduced sentences or financial inducements (ibid.: 111–15). Alongside criminalization was the policy from 1977 of 'Ulsterization', designed to place the security burden on local forces such as the RUC and the UDR and allow a reduction in the number of British troops (Kennedy-Pipe 2000: 31).

Criminalization included the withdrawal of 'special category' status from paramilitary prisoners. After March 1976 new prisoners convicted of terrorist offences were classed as criminals with no special privileges; prisoners refused to accept this and refused to wear prison clothes (McKeown 2001: 51). Within two years hundreds of prisoners in Long Kesh/the Maze[35] had joined the first protestor, wearing only blankets – figures range from 250 (ibid.: 56), to 300 (Ellison and Smyth 2000: 100), to 400 (Crawford 1999: 54). About 20 loyalist prisoners also went 'on the blanket' in 1976–7 and for a few weeks in 1978 the majority of them were on it. For them this was contentious as they were trapped between hating their treatment by prison officers and wanting to resist, yet feeling there should be a residual loyalty to them as fellow Protestants and loyalists (ibid.: 54–6). The failure of the blanket protest led in 1978 to the beginning of what is known to republicans as the 'no-wash protest' and to the authorities as the 'dirty protest', when male republican prisoners in the Maze and female republican prisoners in Armagh refused to clean out their cells or wash (access to bathroom facilities in the Maze being dependent upon prisoners wearing prison uniforms), eventually smearing excrement (and menstrual blood, in the women's case) on the walls and being brutally beaten by prison guards as they were forcibly washed (McKeown 2001: 56–62). The republican movement outside the prisons was slow to offer support for the protests as the leadership viewed them 'as a distraction from the armed struggle, and feared that any attempt to mobilise mass protest would fail'. Their response was to attack prison officers outside (Ellison and Smyth 2000: 100).

After two and a half years of the no-wash protest some republican prisoners decided to go on hunger strike. There were two strikes, October–December 1980 (which included some female prisoners in Armagh) and March–October 1981.[36] Both were opposed by the PIRA leadership, the Catholic Church, political parties and many family members. However, the second hunger strike 'tapped a huge reservoir of support across the island. Demonstrations in support of the prisoners were the largest ever seen since the civil rights demonstrations of a decade earlier' (Ellison and Smyth 2000: 101). The PIRA and Sinn Féin leaderships believed the second hunger strike would fail as the first did and that another defeated strike would demoralize IRA volunteers and supporters. Nevertheless the prisoners continued, despite Gerry Adams writing to Bobby Sands, the most famous hunger striker, that '[w]e are tactically, strategically, physically and morally opposed to the hunger strike' (O'Malley 1990: 72). While imprisoned and on hunger strike Sands was elected to Westminster shortly before his death and another hunger striker, Kieran Doherty, along with blanketman Kevin Agnew, were elected to the Irish Dáil (ibid.: 74, 78). Ten men died, including three INLA members, and the second strike came to an end after pressure from the relatives of those remaining on strike. Although Thatcher's government still avoided using the term 'political status', the concessions given after the end of the strike came close to the original demands of the prisoners (Ellison and Smyth 2000: 102–3).

The reorganization into a cell structure and move to a lower intensity 'long war' from the late 1970s saved PIRA from military defeat, and the republican movement's political career was revived by the emotional trauma in the Catholic community caused by the 1981 hunger strike. The success of republican prisoner candidates in 1981 elections on both sides of the border convinced some Sinn Féin members of the benefits of electoral participation (Feeney 2002: 303). From the end of 1981 SF adopted the 'ballot box and Armalite'[37] strategy – that is, continuing armed struggle but pursuing electoral competition as well (ibid.: Ch. 9). (The continued armed struggle included the 1984 PIRA bomb attack on the Conservative Party conference in Brighton.) At Sinn Féin's 1986 Ard Fheis (annual conference), abstention from the Republic's legislature was abandoned. This was divisive and traditionalists left and established Republican Sinn Féin, though PIRA did not experience a corresponding split until later (ibid.: 331–3). The increasing support for SF following the hunger strikes was a threat to the SDLP and in response, constitutional nationalism throughout Ireland tried to reinvent its ideology through the New Ireland Forum throughout 1983–4, reaffirming the goal of a united Ireland pursued through consent and democratic political means but also recognizing that nationalists had underestimated the full extent of unionist identity (Arthur 2000: 202–3).

Moves towards peace

In 1985 the Anglo-Irish Agreement faced complete unionist opposition. All unionist Westminster MPs resigned their seats under the slogan 'Ulster says no' (Arthur 2000: 228–9). Mass demonstrations were held and a March 1986 'Day of Action' shut down much of Northern Ireland's commerce and industry, followed by weeks of rioting in Belfast and loyalist attacks on the RUC. A wider anti-Agreement civil disobedience campaign was carried out from May 1986 to November 1988 (Cochrane 1997: 179–80).[38] The Agreement also had consequences for Sinn Féin, since its popularity in the Republic suggested that partition was accepted (Kennedy-Pipe 2000: 33).

Subsequent to the failure of the Anglo-Irish Agreement there were a number of significant developments. Talks between the SDLP and SF in 1988 are generally seen as the beginning of the contemporary peace process, and had long-term implications. Respective leaders Hume and Adams continued secret talks in the following years, viewed by unionists (when they were revealed) as evidence of a 'pan-nationalist front' (Bloomfield 1998: 6–7). There was an inherent tension for republicans between armed struggle and seeking electoral victory (O'Doherty 1998). It was difficult for PIRA to give up its struggle let alone its arms, because of the perceived need to continue to defend the Catholic community against loyalist attacks. On the other hand, the problem for PIRA 'was that the political path being pursued by Sinn Féin deprived the bombing campaign of any sort of rationality' (Kennedy-Pipe 2000: 34). Simultaneously, SF leaders engaged in negotiations with the Irish government (ibid.; Maloney 2002: 461–5). An important gesture towards republicans from Britain came in a 1990 speech by Secretary of State Peter Brooke, stating Britain had 'no selfish strategic or economic interest in Northern Ireland', but 1991–2 negotiations involving the British and Irish governments and representatives of the UUP, the DUP, the SDLP and the APNI (discussions begun under Brooke and continued under his successor Sir Patrick Mayhew, coming to be known as the Brooke/Mayhew Talks) made no major progress (Bloomfield 1998: 51–2, 161). Meanwhile, secret communications between the British government and republicans had been going on for three years, unbeknownst to most people (Mallie and McKittrick 1996). After a 1993 statement by Hume and Adams, declaring that an internal Northern Ireland political solution with no Irish dimension was unacceptable, there was an increase in loyalist violence. After more British–Irish inter-governmental discussions the outcome was the Downing Street Declaration in December, the government stating it wanted to see peace established by agreement among all the people inhabiting the island, which could include a united Ireland provided that was supported by concurrent referenda in the north and south (Hennessey 2000: 80; 1997: 285–6).

These developments slowly led to an evolution in republican thinking and the first PIRA ceasefire in August 1994, followed by a loyalist ceasefire in October (Guelke 1999: 43, 47–8). The ceasefire was not enough to get Sinn Féin immediate entry to all-party talks but the two governments tried to find ways through the stalemate by establishing an international body chaired by former US Senator George Mitchell. The 1996 Mitchell Report suggested an approach whereby some decommissioning of weapons would take place *during* the process of all-party negotiations, rather than before (the British view) or after (SF's view). PIRA was opposed to this 'twin-track' approach and resentment grew, resulting in the end of the PIRA ceasefire in February with a massive bomb near Canary Wharf in London (Hennessey 2000: 100–1). This inevitably strained the loyalist ceasefire but it largely held for some months, though there was some serious loyalist violence during the summer Orange Order marches[39] (Guelke 1999: 48–9). The election of a Labour government in 1997 included a commitment to finding a solution to Northern Ireland. British Prime Minister Tony Blair actively sought outside intervention, enlisting the help of US President Clinton, who played an important role in convincing Gerry Adams and David Trimble (UUP leader since 1995), as well as Irish Taioseach Bertie Ahern, to try the latest experiment in power-sharing – the Good Friday Agreement (Kennedy-Pipe 2000: 36).

The Good Friday Agreement onwards

A 1997 change of policy by the new Labour government allowed Sinn Féin entry to the talks without first disarming, leading to the DUP and the United Kingdom Unionist Party withdrawing. The UUP judged, despite its pessimism, that 'it was better to be in than to be out' (Aughey 2000: 65) and this also seemed to be the mood of the electorate.[40] The Good Friday Agreement (also called the Belfast Agreement) was reached on 10 April 1998 and was endorsed at referenda in Northern Ireland (71 per cent in favour) and the Republic of Ireland (94 per cent in favour). Widely divergent interpretations of the GFA were put forward as to whether it was positive for unionists or for nationalists (Ruane 1999), and it has been argued that 'the Agreement is a constitutional and functional framework which solves neither the conflict nor its causes but shifts the contradictions to the political rather than military sphere' (O'Hearn *et al.* 1999: 10). Under the Agreement, Northern Ireland will remain part of the UK for so long as the majority there supports the Union, while Article 2 of the Irish Constitution was changed from its previous territorial claim to say simply that it is the entitlement of every person born in the island to be part of the Irish nation (Bew 2000: 42–3). The GFA is in part a Lijphart-style consociational devolutionist model (O'Leary 2001: 49; see Lijphart 1977) and also, in O'Leary's words, constitutes a

> tacit 'double protection model' laced with elements of co-sovereignty. The Agreement was designed to withstand major demographic and electoral change and … [i]n effect, it promises protection to Northern nationalists now on the same terms that will be given to Ulster unionists should they ever become a minority in a unified Ireland.
>
> (2001: 68)

There are three strands to the Agreement: Strand 1 refers to the local Assembly, Strand 2 to north–south cooperation within the island and Strand 3 to east–west (British–Irish) cooperation. The Agreement provides for a Northern Ireland Assembly of 108 members elected by proportional representation (d'Hondt procedure), with substantial domestic policy freedom but with foreign policy remaining at Westminster. The Executive authority of the Assembly entails a First Minister and Deputy First Minister (Bew 2000: 43–4). (Originally the First and Deputy First Ministers were elected by the Assembly on a cross-community basis, but the later St Andrews Agreement modified this so that now the largest party in each bloc nominates their respective Minister.) Sinn Féin members voted at their 1998 Ard Fheis to change their constitution to end abstentionism in regard to government in Northern Ireland, allowing their elected candidates to take up positions in the new Assembly.

So-called 'dissident' paramilitaries have presented serious problems for the stability of the Agreement by acting as 'spoilers' (those who utilize strategic and tactical use of violence to undermine peace (see Stedman 1997)). August 1998 saw the horrific bombing in the town of Omagh, the act of political violence throughout the whole of the 'Troubles' that resulted in the most fatalities (assumed to be the work of RIRA but in fact it seems to have been a joint operation with CIRA[41]); other republican and loyalist spoilers opposed to the peace process have also caused problems, though none on the scale of the Omagh bomb. Nevertheless, after many false starts governing powers were transferred to the Assembly in December 1999 though the Assembly would go on to be suspended many times, most notably from October 2002 to May 2007. Certain controversial aspects of the GFA generated more emotion than the three central strands, such as issues of policing, prisoners, the Irish language and the equality agenda.

The language issue remains unresolved. Commissions have been established to deal with equality, policing and human rights and a controversial programme of early release of paramilitary prisoners instituted: 450 people have been released: 196 loyalists, 242 republicans and 12 'non-aligned'.[42] Of the republicans, seven were women (personal communication with the Northern Ireland Office, 2003). Unionist attention focused negatively on provisions for the early release of prisoners and the reform of the RUC (Aughey 2000: 66). Under the GFA the Patten Commission was set up to investigate policing (Ellison and Smyth 2000: 177; Walker 2001). The Patten Report stressed the need for 'de-politicization' of policing, made it clear there was a serious problem with RUC accountability, and included a proposal that human rights issues be integrated into all training (Ellison and Smyth 2000: 184–8). Since then the name of the RUC (contentious for nationalists) has been changed to the Police Service of Northern Ireland (PSNI); new uniforms, badge and flag have been introduced, new training programmes instituted and recruitment of new officers is undertaken on a 50/50 basis (problematic due to low rates of Catholic applications). Since 2002 a strategy has been implemented aiming for community-centred policing utilizing District Policing Partnerships, involving more consultation with the public (Orde 2003). Serious reform of the notorious Special Branch was also recommended in the Report and in further investigations (ibid.) but progress has been slow. Most policing changes have been contentious for unionists, but not enough for republicans. Sinn Féin refused to support policing and did not take up its seats on the Policing Board until after their 2007 Ard Fheis voted, historically, to support policing.

One of the most significant issues for unionists in the deadlock leading to the almost five-year-long suspension of the Assembly was the question of PIRA decommissioning, but decommissioning of loyalist weapons and British state demilitarization in Northern Ireland has also been a concern for nationalists. PIRA disarmament did not progress as fast as unionists wished, but the Independent International Commission on Decommissioning (IICD) has witnessed four acts of PIRA decommissioning of weapons, including a final act in September 2005. It also witnessed one small act of decommissioning by the LVF in December 1998.[43] There have been no other witnessed acts of decommissioning by loyalist paramilitaries, but in May 2007 the UVF leadership publicly announced that the organization was standing down and that it had put all its weapons 'beyond reach' – declining to engage in a formal IICD decommissioning process. In November 2007 the UDA also announced that it was standing down its armed wing, the UFF, but had no current intention to decommission weapons, although like the UVF some leaders have met with the IICD. Meanwhile the British government scaled down the presence and role of state forces in Northern Ireland and Operation Banner, the British Army's 38-year operation in Northern Ireland, officially came to an end in August 2007. Unionist leaders were extremely reluctant to accept the IRA's decommissioning as evidence of a lasting commitment to non-violent political means, and expressed vocal disbelief that the IRA's final act of decommissioning in September 2005 really represented the sum total of their weapons, despite statements by the IICD (IICD 2006). As I have argued elsewhere (Alison, forthcoming), the United Nations Development Programme's argument that disarmament often has 'a symbolic and political importance beyond the sum of its parts' (UNDP 2002: 4) certainly applies to Northern Ireland. Brown and Hauswedell have made a convincing case that in Northern Ireland 'the symbolic value of guns surpasses their inherent military potential' and 'the issue of paramilitary arms … serv[ed] as the political foundation upon which both conflicting parties anchored their positions' (2002: 67, 4).

After the GFA, as noted earlier, the DUP overtook the UUP as the largest unionist political party (largely through ethnic outbidding appealing to Protestant fears about the GFA) and SF overtook the SDLP as the largest republican party, meaning a Northern Ireland Assembly would have to be run by the DUP and SF.

Although the DUP accepted its posts in the Executive even though it opposed the GFA, it remained obstructionist and refused to partner SF in government. In 2002 when the Assembly and the wider peace process became severely deadlocked over outstanding issues, as discussed above, the Assembly was suspended and direct rule from London reintroduced. Further political strife ensued. Current prospects, however, are more positive than they have been in some years. Following the IRA's final act of weapons decommissioning in 2005, negotiations between the political parties of Northern Ireland and the British and Irish governments at St Andrews in 2006,[44] subsequent political progress, and SF acceptance of policing, the devolved Northern Ireland Assembly was restored in May 2007 and has been in operation since then. For the first time the DUP was prepared to work with SF (though this has not been easy) and 2007 saw the remarkable spectacle of Ian Paisley as First Minister of Northern Ireland[45] with Martin McGuinness as Deputy First Minister – something many people in Northern Ireland thought was impossible. In 2008 the Assembly is very much still bedding down and despite 14 years of an absence of large-scale armed conflict (though persistence of smaller-scale but serious communal violence), the political situation remains unstable.

Comparative conclusion: similarity and difference

There are many immediately obvious differences between the conflicts in Sri Lanka and Northern Ireland in terms of background cultures and religions and levels of economic development. Their military conflicts have had some significant differences too. The LTTE uses a suicide bombing strategy frequently, and has developed over time to have the capacity to engage the SLA in conventional military battles as well as guerrilla attacks and tactics associated with terrorism. Neither republican nor loyalist paramilitaries in Northern Ireland use suicide attacks and no republican groups developed the capacity to engage the British military in conventional battle, though PIRA had much more sophisticated weaponry (and more weaponry) than loyalist groups. On both sides urban and rural guerrilla warfare and 'terrorist' tactics have been used.

Nevertheless, there are similarities in terms of processes of identity formation, nationalist patterns and demands, very long-standing armed conflict, and resistance to resolution. In both Sri Lanka and Northern Ireland the two overarching blocs of identity and political desire that are in contestation today have evolved slowly and unevenly over a number of years, incorporating numerous ambiguities, rather than existing in their current form for centuries. A past history of huge diversity and multiple overlapping identities in both places has been largely (though never completely) replaced by two opposed identities. This solidifying of identity, hardening of boundaries and plastering over of diversity is part of the project of ethnic nationalists everywhere, and in these two places (as elsewhere) this has been successful enough, in conjunction with material differences and inequalities, to lead to war.

The conflict in Sri Lanka is almost always acknowledged as an ethno-national one and described in ethnic terms. The marks and meanings of ethnicity, however, are variable and do not always conform to the nationalist projects. Very occasionally the conflict is represented as being between 'the Buddhist Sinhalese' and 'the Hindu Tamils'. This is patently inaccurate. Sinhala nationalism has come to be integrally related to a Buddhist identity, certainly, but this leaves ambiguous the identity and position of Christian Sinhalese. Past differences between 'lowland Sinhalese' and 'Kandyan Sinhalese' (which, arguably, were or under other circumstances could have become different ethnicities) have been successfully overcome to construct a Sinhala ethno-national identity, but religious diversity, it seems to me, has largely been repressed or marginalized rather than incorporated, due to the Buddhist 'special mission' (Horowitz 2000: Ch. 5) element of the Sinhalese myth of origin which is interlinked with their notion of prior occupation. For Tamils, Buddhist chauvinism has been a significant source of repression but religious diversity within their ethnicity – at least when it comes to Christianity – is more acknowledged and accepted within the Tamil nationalist project than the Sinhala. Many members of the LTTE (though of course this is not the only manifestation of Tamil nationalism) are Christian rather than Hindu. The LTTE is expressly secular, though devotion to the cause, the group and the leader, and worship of martyrs, come close to acting as a shared religion for members. At the same time, different religions are recognized and some of my interviewees said all different religious days are acknowledged within the movement, though members are not supposed to particularly favour religious days associated with their own background.

Unlike Sinhala ethno-nationalism, however, other forms of diversity have not been incorporated so effectively into Tamil nationalism. So-called 'Indian Tamils' are seen and treated as different; the Tamil ethnicity promulgated in Tamil nationalism in Sri Lanka is specifically *Sri Lankan* Tamil. At various points since independence and during the armed conflict Indian Tamils have seen and been seen to have common interests and somewhat shared identities with Sri Lankan Tamils, but this has always been ambiguous, negotiated, fluid and never consistent. Despite periodic attempts to emphasize shared language as the basis of ethnicity for Sri Lankan Tamils and to thus incorporate Muslim Tamil-speakers within Sri Lankan Tamil nationalism, this too has been inconsistent and largely unsuccessful. Although a few Muslims were involved with militant Tamil nationalism in the 1970s (primarily in the east I believe), generally by independence, and certainly in subsequent decades, Muslim identity in Sri Lanka had become a separate ethnic identity of its own. By the 1990s this difference was significant enough for the LTTE to violently expel Muslim civilians from the north and eliminate them from their ranks in the east (Gunaratna 2001: 6 and see McGilvray 1999). So, neither language nor religion map neatly or completely onto ethno-national communal groups here, illustrating the constructed and contingent nature of ethnicity everywhere.

The conflict in/over Northern Ireland is very occasionally presented as religious in nature, but this is far too simplistic. The core issues here are not only about religion, though religious discrimination, intolerances and identities play their part. Religion is the prime social marker of differentiation between the two overarching blocs and certainly it contributes enormously to how identities in Northern Ireland have come to be constituted, to the extent that religious labels are often used as a shorthand for identity even when religious belief is absent – for example, common statements I heard were along the lines of 'I'm Catholic by background community, but I'm not practising', or 'I'm Protestant I suppose, but I never go to church and I don't really believe in it'. There is an ethno-cultural divide here too, Gaelic-Irish versus Ulster-British, which is also important and politically controversial (witness the ongoing struggle between Sinn Féin and the DUP over an Irish language act, for example) and which has a not insignificant interaction with religious identities but does not reduce to this. In terms of the armed conflict, fundamentally the core issue is a political one of competing nationalisms in disagreement over appropriate state boundaries and configuration. These competing nationalisms largely (though, like Sri Lanka, *never* completely) map onto the religious and ethno-cultural divide: Catholic-Gaelic-Irish-nationalist versus Protestant-Ulster-British-unionist. Republicans traditionally present their struggle as being with the British state rather than with Ulster Protestants and argue their campaign is an anti-colonial nationalist one. Their nationalism is secular and largely civic at an ideological level (though certainly not always at ground level, where ideas of Gaelic culture and negative views of Protestants exist) and potentially includes Ulster Protestants – so long as they accept living in an Irish state. In this vein, they highlight the fact that anti-colonial Irish nationalisms of past centuries included or were led by Protestants. Loyalists see their struggle as being with disloyal insurrectionist Catholic nationalists who refuse to accept living in a British state. Their nationalism is arguably a more complicated and localized one and is almost never acknowledged as a form of nationalism by unionists.

Nevertheless the conflict in Northern Ireland, I and many others argue, *is* ethno-national in nature. While Mitchell's recent and potentially controversial intervention (2006) into the literature on Northern Ireland is a rich, fascinating and very well researched sociological study of the place and meaning of religion in Northern Ireland, and as I have mentioned earlier demonstrates the complexities of religion and its relationship to identity and to politics here in a way that few others have, I disagree with the argument that this means the conflict is not ethno-national in nature. I also think that to view it as an either/or situation masks complexities and ignores the fact that ethno-nationalism is a *process* rather than a fixed object, and is fundamentally a political project. The various cultural elements that are significant to a nationalist project – or, rather, are constructed and reinforced by certain nationalists as being significant, to the exclusion of other elements and the obfuscation of difference – vary between contexts, and between time periods. In Northern Ireland one of the most important constituent (and mutually reinforcing) elements of ethno-nationalism, as it has developed here, is religion. This is not at all the same thing as saying religion is merely a 'badge of identity'. Nor is it the same thing as saying this is a religious conflict. Nor does the fact that the Ulster Protestant 'ethnic' element of their nationalism is more ambiguous and unstable than that of Irish Catholics mean that it is not a nationalism. Ethnicity, and even more so ethno-national identity, is not a static *thing* one possesses but is a continual process of identification and differentiation, of interaction, contestation, resistance and negotiation. Finally, it seems to me there are two primary reasons that conflict in Northern Ireland is not always acknowledged as ethno-national in character. One is the fact, mentioned already, that unionists do not acknowledge their political project as being nationalist, largely due to the local association this has with Irish nationalism specifically. The other is the fact that both communities are white. Because of the history of the study of ethnicity and 'race', tied to anthropology and colonialism, we find it much harder to see, read, and talk about 'white' ethnicities. Ethnicity is something that attaches to everyone on the planet other than white people. When we consider theories and conceptualizations of ethnicity, this is patently ridiculous but it explains a lot about how Northern Ireland is read by some, both outsiders and insiders.

In both Sri Lanka and Northern Ireland the two overarching opposed identities which have developed in each place have roots in the nineteenth century but have evolved and changed. In both cases a history of British colonialism has been a hugely significant factor in both structural and communal identity terms. However one of the big differences between them is that Northern Ireland was a settler-colonial situation, while Sri Lanka was not. So conflict in Sri Lanka fits a classic 'post-colonial nationalisms' pattern, with nationalist identities drawing on identities and peoples who existed in the island before colonialism but becoming something new through the experience of colonialism, changing state structures and, just as importantly, de-colonization. The majority group which assumed control of the state at independence arguably then acted as 'internal colonizers' in their relationship to other groups on the island, stimulating resistance and new political identity mobilizations. In contrast, in Northern Ireland republicans argue that de-colonization of Ireland was never completed, because the island was partitioned and part of it retained within the UK. However in many respects Northern Ireland resembles the post-colonial nationalisms pattern too; in this case the majority community in the new 'statelet' are descendants of settler-colonials (which is *not* the same thing as being settlers themselves) but they, too, arguably acted as 'internal colonizers' within the new Northern Ireland.

In terms of respective competing political goals, clearly there are both similarities and differences. Militant Tamil nationalists want to secede from the existing state and become independent; Irish republicans also want to secede from the existing state, not to be independent but to be (re)attached to the Irish state. Sinhala nationalists and Ulster-British unionists share a determination to retain their respective unitary states; they differ, however, in that Sinhala nationalists are in control of their state while Ulster-British unionists have a much more ambiguous position within the UK as a whole, which is already acknowledged as a multi-national state and has devolved political arrangements in Scotland and Wales to prove it, quite apart from the Northern Ireland question.

A significant similarity between the two places is that all the communities in some ways share a sense of themselves as being the threatened minority; both places can be seen as double-minority models. Within Sri Lanka, Tamils are a minority and Sinhalese are a large majority. However Sinhalese are fearful of connections between Sri Lankan Tamils and the huge Tamil population of south India, and aware of themselves as a minority people within the wider context of the Indian subcontinent, contributing to their sense of threat. Within Northern Ireland, Irish Catholics are a minority (though today only just), and of course are a small minority within the UK state as a whole, while Ulster Protestants are a majority in Northern Ireland (though a small majority, and much smaller now than at partition). However Ulster Protestants are aware of their minority status within the island of Ireland as a whole, and conscious that in a unified Irish state their minority status would be clear, which significantly contributes to their sense of threat. Further contributing to this sense of threat and fear is their knowledge that the UK state no longer returns their loyalty with equal fervour. They are only too aware that the British government would cut Northern Ireland loose if it was thought this could be done without further serious violence, and that other British peoples do not quite view them as British in the same way as themselves, which also contributes to their ambiguous identity.

Sinhala and Tamil nationalisms in Sri Lanka, and Irish nationalism and Ulster-British unionism in Northern Ireland have not been purely reactive to each other, though that has certainly been important. In both places each process has been in part a response to ideologies, practices and structures begun in the colonial period and in part a result of the changes wrought after independence and partition respectively. Sinhala nationalism and Ulster-British unionism have been dialectical processes; expressions of nationalism at state level are both the product of and further fuel for nationalism at the mass level. The utility for groups wishing to gain or maintain state power of appealing to Sinhala nationalism in Sri Lanka and unionism in Northern Ireland (and the costs for Tamils and others in Sri Lanka and Catholics in Northern Ireland) are clear; ethnic outbidding has been significant in both places.

Since independence, the growth of violent Tamil nationalism has in large part been a response to perceived discriminatory policies instituted by the Sinhalese-dominated state, and to violence directed at Tamils by both state agents, such as the military and the police, and civilians in the anti-Tamil riots. It has also, however, made reference to past histories of autonomous political rule. Similarly, in Northern Ireland armed republicanism arose in part in response to perceived discrimination meted out by the unionist Stormont government, and to violence directed at Catholics by state agents like the RUC and the B-Specials, and later the British army, and Protestant civilians. It also, however, explicitly ties itself to a long history of anti-colonial Irish struggle and earlier manifestations of republicanism.

Both places, then, illustrate similar lessons for management of ethnic relations. Tamil nationalism in the early post-independence period was expressed through a discourse of rights, in response to perceived discrimination. Irish nationalism in the 1960s was also expressed through a discourse of rights in response to perceived discrimination. In both places these demands for rights were seen to be denied or change was not generous enough, contributing to more extreme demands. In both places a non-violent minority civil rights campaign was attempted first, met in each case with violence, also contributing to greater communal divisions and more extreme minority demands. On the other hand neither place is simply a case of foolhardy extremist state regimes refusing to accede to minority demands. Politicians want to stay in power and they are also supposed to be representatives of the people. There is a complicated relationship between state nationalism and the mass population which leads to moderates being squeezed out by extremists as ethnic outbidding becomes a way to attain or maintain political power – and this can happen on the minority side too. Once this has happened, as both cases show, the cycle is tough to break and bringing moderation back in is extremely difficult. Furthermore, both places illustrate that when an ethno-national armed conflict is extremely long-running, it takes on a dynamic of its own which produces new issues and new interests beyond the original sources of grievance, making resolution even more complicated.

3 Theorizing women-and-peace, nationalism and female combatants

Although the diversity of feminism makes it as a whole dynamic and creative and arguably constitutes one of its virtues, it also means that there is no all-inclusive singular feminist approach to issues of war and peace, or women's relation to and role in them. Western feminist discourses about woman's roles in war have contained 'starkly opposed views' (Carter 1998: 33). Liberal feminists advocate women's right to become front-line soldiers, while many feminist peace activists see war as a masculine enterprise. Feminist postmodernists are more interested in how the essentialist construction of femininity as peaceful came about. More nuanced feminist approaches to women's involvement in war and peace have been formed in recent years, particularly in regard to processes of nationalism. These feminist debates about women, feminism(s) and nationalism(s), much of which is informed by feminist literature from outside the white middle-class feminist realm, will be discussed in the second half of this chapter. In the first half of the chapter I focus on feminist debates about the relationship between women and peace.

Feminism(s) and peace

It has been persistently argued that in general Western cultures emphasize in politics, media, education and socialization, a 'dichotomy between "women's peace" and "men's war."' Women 'are expected to be inherently creative, nurturing, and peaceful, while men are bold, courageous warriors' (York 1998: 19). Many people, feminists and non-feminists, have assumed a connection between women and peace (women-and-peace), whether in terms of a greater interest in peace on the part of women, or their supposed peaceable feminine 'nature'. Cultural/difference feminists have argued that 'feminine traits' like cooperation, caring and nurturing have been devalued, but are actually superior to 'masculine traits' of individuality, violence and dominance; thus, we can bring about peace by revaluing these feminine traits. More recently a holistic argument has appeared, voiced particularly by ecofeminists, which asserts that all oppression (war, domestic violence, racism, environmental exploitation and so on) is interrelated and, consequently, all must be overcome to achieve social justice. Women are associated with the natural world and exploitation characterizes the relationship both between men and the earth and between men and women. It is also argued that women suffer war disproportionately and accordingly have a particular interest in peace for reasons of justice rather than biology or motherhood (ibid.: 22–4). Working for peace, therefore, can be a radical action rather than a feminine 'duty' for ecofeminists, though some ecofeminist lines of thought do express essentializing ideas about women and their putative relationship to nature (Mies and Shiva 1993). However by far the most predominant single argument for a special connection between women and peace has been the 'maternalist' or 'motherist' position, which maintains that war is antithetical to women's natural childbearing and childrearing role and, by extension, women should organize as mothers to oppose militarism and war. Accordingly, in this section I first discuss some feminist perspectives on women and peace, largely focusing on the debates over cultural feminism, before looking specifically at the arguments relating to motherhood. These debates have been primarily (though not exclusively) dominated in the academic realm by Western feminists, though ideas of Woman the Peacemaker or maternalist feminism have been used in women's peace groups and mothers' groups worldwide. I then discuss the debate on the relationship between military participation and attainment of full citizenship as it relates to women.

Is peace a women's issue?

Both within conservative political arenas and within feminism, debate has flourished over whether or not women have a 'feminine nature' and men a 'masculine nature', and whether differences are due to biology. Turpin notes a certain convergence between conservatives and some feminists in this area: conservatives claim women are more peaceful than men and have used this as a reason to try to keep women out of the military while still supporting war efforts in 'feminine' ways; some feminists also believe women are more peaceful but, therefore, feel that women should resist war and should be granted more power in world affairs, to make the world less violent (1998: 13). Other feminists, however, resist women-and-peace and men-and-war stereotypical linkages. These differing perspectives do not follow a neat chronologically linear pattern. As early as 1739 Lady Mary Wortley Montague argued that women were no less able than men to serve in the military, and there are examples from the eighteenth and nineteenth centuries of female combatants, assassins and bomb-makers beyond the singular individual (such as in the French Revolution, the Russian anti-Tsarist struggle of the 1870s and 1880s and in the Red Army during the post-revolutionary Russian Civil War) (Pierson 1987: 206–11). Nevertheless, feminist perspectives that construct women as peacemakers are still expressed today.

Berkman argues that in the decades preceding the First World War Europeans and Americans commonly held an image of 'woman as peacemaker', but that this image was actually relatively new. In earlier human history, 'woman's image might equally well incorporate two roles: that of warrior and that of mother or fertility goddess – giver of life'; it was in the nineteenth century that women came to be seen as naturally peaceful (1990: 142). Pierson, too, argues that it was during nineteenth-century European industrialization and the concomitant development and entrenchment of the ideology of 'separate spheres' for women, the 'cult of domesticity' and the glorification of motherhood, that 'the association of women with peace and the preservation of life gained credence, as did also its counterpart, the identification of war (indeed most killing) as a male enterprise' (1987: 211–12). In the late nineteenth century peace organizations in general, and specifically separate women's peace groups, began proliferating. In both mixed and women-only groups, 'women enjoyed more presence and influence on the peace movement in the nineteenth century than on any other reform movement, save perhaps Abolition [of slavery in the USA]' (Berkman 1990: 145). Even in this period women peace activists were divided in their approach to war. Some were absolute pacifists; some allowed defensive wars and wars of liberation; still others saw capitalism as the cause of all wars. Despite this, the pacifist and feminist/suffrage movements overlapped in theory and in membership. The divisions in feminist pacifism notwithstanding, prior to the First World War peace was 'viewed primarily as a woman's concern – a consensus reflecting the established gender conventions among white Americans and Europeans' (ibid.: 145–7). However as the First World War broke out and progressed, European and American feminist peace groups and suffrage unions split into pro- and anti-war groups, with anti-war factions making up the minority opinion (ibid.: 147; Pierson 1987: 214–16). Both factions were also divided among themselves. Pro-war groups were divided between those who reluctantly supported their government but wanted to mitigate the effects of war as much as possible, and those who were nationalist and militarist. Anti-war groups were divided between those who kept their pre-war beliefs about women's proclivity for peace, and those who could no longer believe this. Nevertheless, the trope of Woman the Peacemaker continued as a dominant cultural assumption throughout the interwar years (Berkman 1990: 149 and 156).

One of the most famous feminist pacifist writers from the early twentieth century, and one who relied upon essentialist assumptions, is Virginia Woolf. Her monograph *Three Guineas*, written between the two world wars, has since inspired many feminist pacifists. Woolf described women as 'outsiders' in their own country (England), because of their lack of economic, educational and legal rights. She suggested women should embrace this status and choose to become part of a 'Society of Outsiders', expressing nothing but indifference on the matter of war, as a way of stopping its continuation (1943 [orig. 1938]: 198–9). However, Woolf was an upper middle-class Englishwoman and did not recognize that the 'choice' of becoming an 'outsider', in the context of war, is one affected by class and ethnicity as well as other factors. She rejected the claims of men who said they were fighting to protect 'our country'; 'our' country has in fact, she said, 'treated me as a slave; it has denied me education or any share in its possessions'. Woolf belonged to the liberal internationalist feminist political position and famously wrote 'as a woman I have no country. As a woman I want no country. As a woman my country is the whole world' (ibid.: 197). The bitter crux of her argument is to say:

> Therefore if you insist upon fighting to protect me, or 'our' country, let it be understood, soberly and rationally between us, that you are fighting to gratify a sex instinct which I cannot share; to procure benefits which I have not shared and probably will not share; but not to gratify my instincts, or to protect either myself or my country.
>
> (Woolf 1943: 197)

One cannot dispute Berkman's assertion that the Woman the Peacemaker image survived twentieth-century feminism (1990: 157), and indeed it lives on in the twenty-first century. In recent decades it has been cultural feminism that is most centrally connected to notions of women as nurturers and peacemakers, arguing that 'women's psychosocial development prepares them to be connected caretakers. Men's psychosocial development prepares them to be individuated competitors. The prevalence of this masculine mentality leads to war. Therefore, war can be averted by promoting the female mentality' (York 1998: 21). Within cultural feminism there are differing opinions about how this situation arose – from the extreme (and much less common) view that the difference is biological, to the more moderate view that gender differences result from socialization.

The work of psychologist Carol Gilligan has been influential in the development of the ideas of cultural feminism. Her 1982 book *In a Different Voice* was the source of many of the ideas of feminists who argue that women are socially conditioned to think more than men about relationships between people and that their psychosocial development means they are more likely than men to be concerned with caring for others. During Gilligan's late 1970s research (an extension of, revision of and challenge to Kohlberg's theory of the development of moral judgement) she came to note two different modes of speaking about moral problems; women's 'voices' 'sounded distinct' to her. She found that when the men under study were asked to describe themselves, no particular person or relationship came into their self-descriptions. When the women were asked to describe themselves, however, they all described a relationship. Further,

> the standard of moral judgement that informs their assessment of self is a standard of relationship, an ethic of nurturance, responsibility, and care.... Similarly, morality is seen by these women as arising from the experience of connection and conceived as a problem of inclusion rather than one of balancing claims.
>
> (Gilligan 1982: 159–61)

Gilligan argues that this apparently distinct way that women approach moral reasoning has traditionally been seen as a flaw in women, with masculine moral reasoning assumed to be the superior, properly developed approach. She challenges this, maintaining that women's approach to moral reasoning is equally valid. However she appears wary of essentialism and maintains that this 'different voice'

> is characterized not by gender but theme. Its association with women is an empirical observation ... [b]ut this association is not absolute.... No claims are made about the origins of the differences described or their distribution in a wider population, across cultures, or through time.
>
> (Gilligan 1982: 1–2)

The work of Gilligan and others has been used by cultural feminists to bolster their position that 'masculine values' and ways of moral reasoning are valued and enshrined in Western society, while 'feminine values' and ways of moral reasoning are not. The supposedly feminine relational approach to moral reasoning makes violence and war less likely, they assume, because human relationships are less likely to be subordinated or neglected in the pursuit of abstract goals or principles (Salla 2001: 69–70). To reduce or eliminate war we need to revalue 'feminine values' of cooperation, nurturing and non-violence, as well as a feminine morality; to promote an ethic of care; and to put more women into political decision-making positions. This claim has been criticized by those who argue that it does not challenge 'the patriarchal dualism that constitutes the "self" by devaluing the "other" ' and that it 'ignores the roles women play in the service of war' (York 1998: 21). I would add that, critically, it also ignores the roles men have played in the service of peace. Furthermore, it has been argued that relational thinkers – women *or* men – are not likely to automatically be pacifist in the sense of rejecting the use of force from a principled position, 'since the value ascribed to human relationships makes it likely for ... [them] to take decisions to use force in cases where these relationships are under threat' (Salla 2001: 75–7). It can be argued that cultural feminism perpetuates an unhealthy dichotomy and implicitly accepts hierarchical thinking about gender; the hierarchy is simply inverted, with femininity valued over masculinity (York 1998: 21).[1] Promoting many of the values associated with femininity, and looking at the context-specific nature of moral problems is, I would agree, certainly important in trying to create more peaceful, non-violent societies. This needs to be done, however, without simply 'inverting the hierarchy' or falling back on essentialist and universalizing claims about 'woman'.

The cultural feminist argument about women and peace, while past its high-water mark, lingers within feminist and peace activism. In 1991 a statement made by some women's peace groups as part of anti-Gulf War activity was that '[w]omen have always been the true advocates of peace. We believe in living for a cause, not dying for it. If we had the power in our hands, we would sit at the negotiating table, and we would search for as long as it takes for a peaceful solution' (Papandreou 1997: 46). A well-known feminist activist, Betty Reardon, maintains that '[w]omen, whose experience of conflict has been long and varied, particularly as peacemakers in the family, see the best ways to resolve conflicts as those that help to meet at least some of the concerns of all conflicting parties' (1993: 145). Further, 'mothers of the world, who provide the care for most young children, are fundamental and formative peace educators' (ibid.: 143). Thus, our best hope for attaining a culture of peace lies with women's political participation (Reardon

1998: 289). Clearly drawing on Gilligan, Reardon asserts that 'research into women's ways of knowing, reasoning, and decision-making has demonstrated that, at least in Western countries, women's thinking is different from that of men' and 'this difference can shed new light on, and often produce unprecedented solutions to, some of the world's major problems' (1993: 141). Similarly, Vickers argues that 'in the global context … [women's] perspective makes it possible for them to see the inter-relationships between equality, development and peace … and enables them to become catalysts for peace and political change' (1993: 130).

A great many feminists, like myself, reject essentialist notions about womanhood and manhood and their associations with peace and war. Lentin maintains that '[f]eminist critique of militarism should exclude the essentialist category of "peace-loving woman"'; feminists need to show that their concerns about violence and militarism are 'political issues', not 'women's issues' (1997b: 67 and 72). Elshtain objects to the claim that women are to be 'the saviours of humanity, the avatars of pacific Motherhood', and to the binary contrasting of 'masculinism, patriarchy, violence, dis-order, with feminism, matriarchy, non-violence, harmonious order'. She feels that the simple inversion of 'feminine values' with 'masculine values', revaluing the former as superior to the latter, is a wrongheaded approach (1990: 265). Elshtain notes that in the West we have inherited a tradition that assumes an affinity between women and peace and between men and war; this tradition is culturally constructed and transmitted inter-generationally. During wartime, she suggests, actual men and women

> take on, in cultural memory and narrative, the personas of Just Warriors and Beautiful Souls. Man constructed as violent, whether eagerly and inevitably or reluctantly and tragically; woman as nonviolent, offering succor and compassion: these tropes on the social identities of men and women, past and present, do not denote what men and women *really* are in time of war, but function instead to re-create and secure women's location as noncombatants and men's as warriors.
>
> (Elshtain 1987: 4)

This, Elshtain argues, dangerously conceals those stories that do not fit. We have read women's violence out of the picture or viewed it as anomalous: '[f]emale fighters have surfaced throughout our history as stories of private transgression' (1987: 167, 174). She acknowledges that since the Second World War there have been enormous changes in Western societies in regard to expectations about social identities and roles for women and men, yet these changes may not have fundamentally altered our 'received webs of social meaning' in relation to men, women and war. Some feminists (and non-feminist women) demand the right to be 'Just Warriors' themselves but others deliberately utilize traditional ideas of women's connection to peace as a basis for anti-militarist action. As this reproduces the presumption of the 'Beautiful Soul', Elshtain suggests it paradoxically *entrenches* our notions of male and female identities in relation to collective violence (ibid.: 7–8).

Women who participate in political violence, war or state repression present a challenge to essentialist conceptions of 'womanhood' and shatter the illusion of feminine peacefulness. Writing in relation to South Africa, Goldblatt and Meintjes (who presented a report to the Truth and Reconciliation Commission) claim that '[u]nderstanding that women were capable of perpetrating violence enables us to see that women are not monolithic in their outlook as a group and are not bearers of certain essential qualities such as kindness and compassion' (1998: 45). Their findings about the violence carried out by women as agents of the apartheid South African state are horrific and include female prison warders participating in some of the worst forms of torture inflicted on female prisoners. Similarly, in relation to genocide Lentin argues that 'focusing exclusively on women as universal victims does not help the survivors of genocides and other catastrophes. Nor does it allow us to address women's participation as benefactors or perpetrators of genocidal processes' (1997a: 6).[2] Nevertheless, it has been noted that women's violence 'appears to be a phenomenon which feminists find difficult to face' (Mukta 2000: 163). Mukta argues that women in the Indian context who have not been much exposed to contemporary Western feminisms 'do not subscribe to the myth of women's innocence' and much contemporary Indian feminist work 'attempts to face up to the question of women-as-perpetrators (rather than as victims) of violence' (ibid.: 163–4). The implication of this is, as suggested here, that the assertion that women are more peaceful and less violent than men is primarily a Western construct with a specific historical and cultural background; its essentialist and universal claim is not valid.

Yuval-Davis stresses that women and men are not homogeneous entities in any context, yet the construction of men as warriors and women as linked to peace has been naturalized across social divisions. This construction of masculinity and femininity has, she claims, existed in Western ideas since Athens in the fifth century BC. The occasional images of women warriors that have appeared throughout history have usually retrospectively 'either enhanced the constructed unnaturalness of women as fighters, or been made in such a way as to collude with more generalized notions of femininity and masculinity in the society from which the women fighters have come' (1997: 93–4). Bennett *et al.* argue that the results of their 1993–4 oral testimony project on women and war show that we cannot assume that women are by nature more likely to work for peace and non-violence than men (1995: 20–1). Nevertheless, Mazurana and McKay comment that

> [w]ritings which portray women as intrinsically more peaceful are abundant throughout grassroots and some United Nations and academic documents. Indeed, much of the rationale for organizing women for peace, whether African, Asian, European, Latin American or North American, is based on beliefs that women are by nature – often because they are mothers – more caring, peaceful, and non-violent.
>
> (1999: 20)

Mazurana and McKay themselves, however, agree with Boulding's proposition (1990) that women may often be *socially conditioned* to display more peaceful qualities, but like Lentin and others they assert that relying on ideas of women's *inherent* peacefulness 'does not allow for adequate recognition of, or strategizing against, factors motivating women's violence'. They believe that groups acknowledging, addressing and seeking solutions to women's violence, as well as men's violence, are needed to properly strategize for peacebuilding (Mazurana and McKay 1999: 21).[3]

The contested issue of motherhood

The most persistent and recurring argument given for a special connection between women and peace is based in the 'maternalist' or 'motherist' position. Feminists employing this position often maintain that women are 'naturally' opposed to war and militarism because they create and nurture life. Therefore, having women in political power would create a world without war. In the early twentieth century feminists such as Olive Schreiner, who wrote in the context of the Boer War in South Africa, were to be found arguing that women, as mothers, have a greater appreciation of the value of human life than men (1978 [orig. 1911]). In a speech to a women's peace group in 1915, Anna Shaw famously proclaimed that 'looking into the face of ... one dead man we see two dead, the man and the life of the woman who gave him birth; the life she wrought into his life!' (cited in Ruddick 1990: 229). According to Pierson, during the First World War Swedish maternalist Ellen Key continued to believe that 'the motherliness of women' would be the salvation of the world, despite evidence of many women supporting the war and some even fighting in it. These women, she felt, were denying their 'woman's nature' and if they would only get back in touch with their inner nature and gain political power, war might be abolished (Pierson 1987: 216).

The belief in women's peacefulness stemming from motherhood persists in some feminist circles, though the waters are often a little muddied in regard to whether this is an argument from biology or from socialization (arguably more common).[4] As a resource for political activism, appeals to motherhood have been used in recent decades by many women's peace groups (not solely in Western countries) to protest against war: the women's peace camps at Greenham Common in the UK and Seneca Falls in the USA, the Materinskoe Serdise (Soviet mothers who publicized the deaths of their sons in Afghanistan), Another Mother for Peace (US women protestors during the Vietnam War), Women Strike for Peace (anti-nuclear activists in the USA in the early 1960s) (see Swerdlow 1982), the Mothers of the Plaza de Mayo in Argentina, the Mothers' Front in Sri Lanka, and others. However there is huge feminist disagreement about the nature, benefits and risks of 'motherhood as a space of public agency for women' (Mookherjee 2008: 37) and whether or not this is a good base from which to pursue resistance to militarism. Enloe maintains that as the Greenham Common and Mothers of the Plaza de Mayo peace movements progressed, dissension grew about 'the varieties of maternal values, about the patriarchal risks in relying on motherhood as a political idea, and about the limits of building a broad women's movement on a maternal role that not all women can or want to assume' (2000b: 260).

Possibly the most sophisticated contemporary argument for the maternalist position has been presented by Ruddick, who uses the 'practicalist' philosophical perspective to describe the relationship between mothering and thinking; that is, that 'distinctive ways of knowing and criteria of truth arise out of practices'. Thus, mothering children is a practice that produces a distinctive kind of thinking (1989: 13; 1990: 237). Ruddick argues there are three main 'demands' (requirements) constituting maternal work: children 'demand' that their lives are preserved, they 'demand' that their growth is fostered, and the social groups within which the mother and her child are situated 'demand' that she raise her child in a manner that they consider acceptable. To be a mother is to be committed to meeting these three demands through preservative love, nurturance, and training. Preservation is the pre-eminent demand, conceptually and historically; human children universally share prolonged dependence on adults and need protective care (1989: 17–18). Maternal practice, Ruddick maintains, requires that mothers think and make decisions and judgements about the relative weight of preservation, growth and acceptability. Maternal thinking, therefore, 'is one kind of disciplined reflection among many, each with identifying questions, methods, and aims' (ibid.: 24).

Ruddick is a social constructionist and she recognizes that maternal practice is not necessarily an automatic response of a woman to her child and that regardless of culture, 'maternal commitment is far more voluntary than people like to believe' (1989: 22); she also acknowledges that maternal thinking is itself often militarist. Nevertheless she asserts 'there is a peacefulness latent in maternal practice and … a transformed maternal thinking could make a distinctive contribution to peace politics' (ibid.: 136–7). When maternal thinking takes on the perspective of a feminist standpoint 'it reveals a contradiction between mothering and war. Mothering begins in birth and promises life; military thinking justifies organized, deliberate deaths.… Mothers protect children who are at risk; the military risks the children mothers protect.' Therefore, as a whole, maternal thinking conflicts with military thinking (ibid.: 148–50; also 1983: 480). She argues that 'mothers who acquire a feminist consciousness and engage in feminist politics are likely to become more effectively non-violent and antimilitarist' and that 'feminism actualizes the peacefulness latent in maternal practice' (1989: 242). She acknowledges that men are not always warlike and women are not always peaceful, yet argues that '[a]lthough mothers are not intrinsically peaceful, maternal practice is a "natural resource" for peace politics' (ibid.: 156). Therefore, a

> peacemaker's hope is a militarist's fear: that the rhetoric and passion of maternity can turn against the military cause that depends on it. Mothers have supported their boys and their leaders, but in the contradiction of maternal and military aims there is a dangerous source of resistance.
>
> (Ruddick 1989: 157)

Ruddick's work on 'maternal thinking' arising from maternal practice is intriguing and is much richer than can be conveyed here. However, her analysis effectively excludes many women: women who are not yet mothers, women who do not want to become mothers, women who are physically incapable of becoming mothers. Her attempt to include these women by saying that even women who are not themselves mothers are still connected to the mothering experience and to maternal thinking through their own mothers ('lessons from her mother's house' (1983: 479)) as well as sisters and friends who are mothers seems a tenuous claim to me, especially given her position that thinking arises from practice (which in itself is a claim I am perfectly prepared to accept). Having a friend who is a mother and being the daughter of a mother is not the same thing as the experience of being a mother oneself. As a social constructionist Ruddick does not argue that women are *innately* peaceful, yet overall her argument still strikes me as carrying a whiff of reductionism. She is most likely right to argue that distinctive 'ways of knowing' can develop from maternal practices, but I would stress that many elements of both maternal practice and 'ways of knowing' are specific to the context of the knower. Ruddick's framework does entail some universalizing of the experience of mothering (despite her attempts to get round or justify this), assuming a commonality in women's mothering experiences, regardless of context or culture, which is hard to sustain.

When Ruddick attempts to stretch her argument to claim 'maternal thinking' as the foundation of a feminist peace politics, her position becomes even shakier. I would argue that the experience of motherhood can only become a potential basis for peace when a mother's 'preservative love' is extended beyond her own children to the children of others, in particular to the children of her 'enemies'. As Carter points out, '[b]eing a mother does not necessarily lead to a hatred of war and an empathy with mothers on the enemy side. A mother has a gut concern for the safety of her own children; only if mother love becomes more generalized does it sustain a peace politics' (1998: 35). I agree in essence, although I would add that even Carter's implication that mothers *automatically* have a gut concern for the safety of their *own* children is possibly debatable. Finally, another concern with this part of Ruddick's argument is that it seems to prioritize the experience of mothering in the complex make-up of any woman's individual personal and political identity. Any person's identity has many different facets to it, including gender, ethnicity, age, sexual orientation, class, economic standing, political perspective, interests, talents and so on. To weight motherhood over other aspects of identity is potentially problematic.[5]

Many feminists challenge the notion that women are necessarily more peace-loving than men and especially challenge the idea that women are motivated to act peacefully as *mothers*, particularly when this is presented as stemming from innate biological differences. The idea that women's maternal instincts make them natural pacifists also correspondingly implies that men are naturally aggressive. Such essentialist and biologically deterministic claims, it has been asserted, ignore the role of culture and socialization in moulding personality and unhelpfully pit men against women. Since at least the 1990s feminism has become much more self-consciously aware of cultural, ethnic, class and other kinds of difference among women, both within and between countries, and many feminists would hesitate to make universal claims about women and war based on maternalism. Many feminists also challenge the maternalist position (even when it is based in social constructionist ideas) because it upholds a conservative ideal and does not encourage women to challenge traditional constructions of their appropriate roles (York 1998: 19–20). Smith asserts that mobilizing women *as women*, 'however progressive the cause, must run a strong risk of playing directly into the hands of gender traditionalism, especially if traditional gender concepts are the basis of the mobilizing appeal' (2001: 44–5).

A substantial challenge to maternalist claims to peace is presented by the reality that women have frequently been militarized into supporting particular wars – not *despite* their experiences as mothers but in fact by utilizing particular constructions of motherhood (Enloe 2000b: 244–60). Appeals to motherhood have been used both by state agents exhorting women to produce more sons for the military, such as in Croatia and Serbia in the 1990s (and earlier wars), or the Nazi pro-natalist policies towards women deemed 'superior' (and anti-natalist policies towards those deemed 'inferior') in the Second World War (Bock 1983), and by women's group themselves, such as the Mothers of Heroes and Martyrs in the Nicaraguan war against the Contras. Furthermore, Scheper-Hughes argues that some aspects of the mothering experience can in certain contexts both allow and direct women to readily sacrifice their children (and husbands) to war and death. In her anthropological research in the Brazilian shantytowns she found that many mothers exhibited a kind of 'accommodationist' maternal thinking. In the face of frequent experiences of child death the notion of acceptable, meaningful and inevitable death flourished – a notion which militaries and wars rely on (1992 Chs 7–8; 1998). Thus, sometimes the mothering experience can promote an accommodation to war and an acceptance of premature and violent death. Nonetheless I suggest we also need to be careful about how we make this argument, so that we do not read all mothers in war contexts as militarist or as being prepared to accept the loss of their children. Powers, discussing women's inter-ethnic peace activism in Israel-Palestine, mentions Palestinian mothers of 'martyrs' who are under social pressure or expectation to be happy and proud about their children's martyrdom, and the representation of them in this fashion in various media, when many resent this and mourn the loss of their children (2003: 28).

Scheper-Hughes claims women have just as often used the moral claims of motherhood to support war as they have to support peace. For women to use the thinking and practices of motherhood towards peacemaking rather than war-making requires 'intentional design, rather than … any natural predisposition' (1998: 233). Skjelsbæk (2001) maintains that essentialist claims conceptualizing motherhood as the antithesis of violence are hard to legitimize in light of women's comments presented in the Panos[6] oral testimony project on women and war, which indicate a variety of different constructions of femininity and motherhood in the three wars she looked at using the Panos research data: Croatia and

Bosnia, El Salvador and Vietnam. In Bosnia and Croatia, women's testimonies indicate that their children became their only source of optimism and reason to keep living and they sought to protect them by removing them from the conflict – though Skjelsbæk does not comment on what this means for women who became mothers to children conceived through the mass rapes here. In contrast, in El Salvador and Vietnam women sought to protect their children by supporting the war and participating in combat, viewing this as the way to ensure a future for their children. Therefore, '[o]n the basis of these observations, we cannot conclude that the actions of motherhood are essentially peaceful.... [They] may have a violent or a peaceful outcome, all depending on the context of the actions of mothering' (ibid.: 63–4).

Military participation and citizenship

As well as feminist disagreements over the existence or nature of a relationship between women and peace there is another significant related division among Western feminists that needs attention: the debate over the relationship between military participation and citizenship, and women's place in this. Feminists have noted that participation of women in the military can sometimes have economic, promotional and political rewards (Yuval-Davis 1997: 105), which are often related to conceptions of citizenship. Debates over citizenship and the military have a long history. Mary Wollstonecraft, writing *A Vindication of the Rights of Woman* in 1792, conceived of equality between the sexes in active citizenship as being possible to achieve through a gendered division of labour whereby men served in the military and women served their state as mothers. More recent feminist discussions have focused on whether or not women should or need to share in military service to be considered citizens equally with men. Many liberal feminists argue that claims to full equality of rights require women to accept the same duties of citizenship as men, and historically one of the primary duties of citizenship in Western states has been participation in the state's military. 'Ancient Greece provided the model of the male citizen who made the city possible by taking up arms on its behalf' and by the time of the Renaissance 'military commitment was integral to civil identification', a conception of citizenship which had no room for women (Kerber 1990: 92; also Yuval-Davis 1997: 96; Elshtain 1987: Part I).

This association of military activities with civil identification and the exclusion of women can be further understood with reference to the public/private spheres idea, which constitutes part of classical social contract political theories whereby those in the 'state of nature' exchange their insecurity for protection by the state. In her critique of social contract theories, Pateman argues that these divide civil society into two exclusive domains, public and private or 'civil' and 'natural', with women located in the private/natural sphere. However, '[t]he private sphere is typically presupposed as a necessary, natural foundation for civil, i.e., public life, but treated as irrelevant to the concerns of political theorists and political activists' (1988: 11). Pateman notes that in social contract theories, after the original contract (which is in fact a *sexual-social* contract) the term 'civil' changes to no longer refer to the *whole* of civil society, but only to one part of it – the public sphere – because '[o]nce the original contract is entered into, the relevant dichotomy is between the private sphere and the civil, public sphere – a dichotomy that reflects the order of sexual difference' (ibid.). Since military activity became so strongly associated with the civil/public sphere and thus with citizenship, there was no room for women in either military service or in citizenship. In fact, women have long been viewed as that (property?) which the (male) citizen fights to protect. Liberal feminists, therefore, argue that one of the reasons for women's lack of political power has been that in many countries military service is a prerequisite for high political office.

This conception of citizenship resonates with the familiar idea that equal rights demand equal responsibilities and has been described as 'martial citizenship' (D'Amico 2000: 107; Feinman 1998: 134) or 'armed civic virtue' (Elshtain 1987: Part I). D'Amico notes that although most states do not require all their citizens to be soldiers, willingness and obligation to fight and 'sacrifice' for one's country are the characteristics of this type of citizenship (2000: 107). Given the 'martial citizenship' model, some Western liberal feminists believe that military participation is a way to 'earn' full political and social equality for women (Ruddick 1983). (In the United States, the National Organization of Women opposed the military draft but argued if there *was* a draft women should be subject to it the same as men.) Grant notes that women play an increasingly important role in the militaries of several states and are reaching higher ranks than before. Warfare and related processes and decisions are, she asserts, 'no longer the exclusive domains of men'. Her view is that this is 'a quiet triumph for feminism', as women now have access 'to one of the last bastions of male dominance', and that the 'advancement of women in the military is one of the main achievements of the women's movement for equal opportunity'. She also views the phenomenon as changing the relationship between women and the state, since some women now participate in the state's war mechanism (1992: 83 and 93).

In contrast to liberal feminists, others (particularly critical and radical feminists) criticize this idea that women can or should gain full equality through the right and duty to fight, maintaining that militaries are fundamentally sexist, exceptionally masculine institutions which use derision of all things 'feminine' or 'effeminate' as part of their indoctrination.[7] It has been argued that female soldiers are often at as much risk (or more) of rape and/or sexual harassment from (male) soldiers on their own side as on the enemy side, and the greater participation of women in the military will not easily or quickly transform such institutions (Vickers 1993: 18–19; Carter 1998: 34).[8] A 2003 US survey found 30 per cent of the female veterans surveyed reported having suffered rape or rape attempt(s) during their service in the US military and over 75 per cent reported some kind of sexual harassment (Jeffreys 2007: 20). A 1992–3 study found 90 per cent of surveyed female veterans of the Gulf War reported suffering some kind of sexual harassment (including rape) in the US military (Benedict 2007).[9] An Israeli Defence Force study similarly showed 81 per cent of Israeli women soldiers saying they have experienced some kind of sexual harassment, including 7 per cent reporting sexual assault, 8 per cent being threatened into 'consenting', and 52 per cent experiencing unwanted touching (Mazali 2003). Given the endemic under-reporting of rape and sexual harassment in all contexts (most likely compounded when the militaries themselves carry out the research) the true numbers are likely to be even higher. If this is in any way representative of the common experience of women in state militaries it paints an extremely bleak picture. Critical feminists are wary of the dangers of the 'warrior mystique' and the image of the woman warrior, as they believe it promotes negative aggressive masculine values. The woman warrior image allows women 'to be militarized but not empowered'; the fascination of liberal feminists with this warrior image is dangerous as the military simply reflects the racism, sexism and heterosexism of wider society. Women's growing numbers in the military does not and will not change the fundamentally gendered structure of the institution. Rather, the increasing numbers of women 'helps legitimize the institution by giving it an egalitarian façade' (D'Amico 1998: 120–2). For Cockburn, the culture and character of armed forces do not generally become more 'feminine' as a result of women's participation and '[i]f they did they would no longer fulfil their current function' (2001: 21). At a fundamental level, for many feminists the military 'requires masculinity to function', as opposed to simply being historically a masculinized institution; it is 'fundamental to what militaries are for and necessary for their operation' (Jeffreys 2007: 18). For these activists and scholars the liberal feminist position on women and the military is wrongheaded and untenable.

Aside from those feminists who are either completely in favour of or completely against women's greater participation in militaries, for most feminists (including myself) the issue of women in the military is confusing, deeply troubling, and the source of conflicting feelings. In spite of her own positive comments on women in militaries even Grant recognizes that the issue of female combatants is not straightforward. Is women's participation as combatants really a feminist victory, she asks, 'if it ultimately funnels into the same tragic waste?' (1992: 90–1). It has been noted that the idea of previously excluded groups (such as women) 'earning equality' or attaining full citizenship through military service is problematic and that not all citizens are simultaneously soldiers, even in extremely militarized societies (D'Amico 2000: 116; Yuval-Davis 1997: 96–7). Sometimes even those who *are* soldiers are not treated as full citizens, as African-Americans discovered when they returned from the Korean War to a still-segregated America (D'Amico 2000: 116). Furthermore, Yuval-Davis argues that women's incorporation in substantial numbers into contemporary Western militaries (especially that of the USA) has been part of the general professionalization of the military. In the US, women began to be encouraged to join after the national draft was stopped. Women's recruitment, 'rather than enhancing their citizenship, was aimed at transforming the military service from a citizenship duty into a "job" ' (1997: 98).

Some feminists have deep-seated suspicions of and dislike for militaries, yet reluctantly conclude that as Western models of citizenship now stand, women do have an obligation to serve in their armed forces. Feminist peace activist Ilene Feinman now argues that '[u]ntil and unless we as a nation [the USA] move beyond martial politics, women have just as strong a set of rights and responsibilities to bear martial service as do men' (1998: 138).[10] Similarly, Elshtain states that '[a]lthough I do not favor the draft ... I have reluctantly come to the position that women should be granted no automatic exemption from this feature of civic life. Involuntary, unreflective pacifism is no pacifism at all' (1987: 243–4).[11] Yuval-Davis asserts

> I do not see, as many feminists do, the necessary connection between women 'fulfilling their patriotic duty' and their entitlement to full citizenship rights. However, I do feel that citizenship, as full membership in the community, does and should involve responsibilities and duties which might involve a national draft in a specific historical context, and that being excluded from the military, like being excluded from night shifts and other so-called dangerous jobs in the civil labour market, has been paternalistic and often to the detriment of the social positioning of women.
>
> (1997: 114–15)

D'Amico maintains that access to military service is important, not to 'prove' certain groups to be 'worthy' of citizenship, but because of what the 'right to serve' represents in terms of potentially changing societal structures and practices – military service is thus a means to an end. What we really need, she says, is actually 'a fundamental [demilitarized] revision of the concept of citizenship' (2000: 117); feminists 'can and must deconstruct the "warrior mystique" and build in its place a positive concept of citizenship and equality' (1998: 124–5). Similarly, Feinman argues that feminist antimilitarists must 'insist that the debates over women's roles be more than questions of equal opportunity/responsibility but that they be questions regarding the very construction of democratic citizenship and the further realization of citizenship activated through social justice and peace' (1998: 138).

Regardless of the question of citizenship, ultimately D'Amico sees women's military participation as potentially subversive towards the military's gender hierarchy, suggesting that 'as more women enter, their presence challenges the gendered dichotomy of "man as warrior"/"woman as pacifist" ' and maintaining that critique from the inside has more effect than critique from the outside (2000: 113 and 116). More controversially, the argument has even occasionally been made that filling the ranks of militaries with women (particularly conscripted women) will mean filling the ranks with 'peaceful soldiers', thus transforming the institution into a 'peaceful army' of 'reluctant soldiers' who will use the minimum of force necessary to win (Ruddick 1983). These are heartening thoughts but for myself I do not think that women or men who work in military institutions are *automatically* more able to effectively critique the system from the inside than one does from the outside; military institutions rely heavily on obedience and loyalty and tend not to train their recruits in the power of critique. Second, the 'peaceful soldiers' argument relies on notions of women's greater peacefulness which I have already challenged. Whether the presence of women will eventually and ultimately have a subversive and positive effect on militaries, or whether militaries will only ever have a repressive and negative effect on women, remains to be seen. It is certainly deeply questionable to unreservedly celebrate women's incorporation into military structures that are repressive, violent, highly masculinized and designed to kill other humans. More attention needs to be paid to context and to military women's actual lived experiences.

In this vein, I also suggest that always speaking in universal terms about 'the military' and how it impacts upon and is impacted on by women can be problematic. As noted earlier, the argument is often made that 'the military' is bad for women in a variety of ways and in particular is a source of sexual violence; further, that it necessarily entails a particular form of masculinity which is anti-feminine and abusive towards women. Up to a point, I do not deny this. Certainly there is ample empirical evidence of various militaries being the source of repression and enormous violence against female soldiers. In regard to the issue of military masculinity, as I have argued elsewhere (2007: 75–6) an expectation of a certain level of aggression (tied to expectations of physical strength and sexual performance) does seem to be a relatively enduring element of hegemonic masculinity[12] whilst an expectation of non-aggression is an enduring element of (hegemonic?) femininity, though these expectations are not entirely universal and do not always reflect the actual lived reality of real men and women. This expectation of masculine aggression is tied to socially sanctioned institutionalized uses of violence, with the military as the ultimate exemplar of masculinity. Hooper has suggested that '[s]oldiering ... has historically been an important practice constitutive of masculinity' (2001: 47) and Goldstein has shown that connections between masculinity and being a warrior are widely cross-cultural (though not universal), across historical periods (2001: 266). Segal argues that despite women being capable of aggression and violence most societies at least implicitly condemn female aggressiveness. Socially approved institutionalized uses of force or violence remain largely performed by men in jobs associated with masculinity – the military, police, prison officers (1990: 266–8).

However Segal suggests, notably, that we could *reverse* the assumed causal link between masculinity and violence.[13]

> The idea that what is at stake here is state violence in the hands of men (rather than, as many feminists believe, male violence in the hands of the state) is supported by reports of women's use of force and violence when they are placed in jobs [or other positions of power] analogous to men's.
>
> (Segal 1990: 268)

Furthermore, I assert that not all military groups are exactly the same in their gender constructs, their ideologies, their training, and their treatment of female soldiers. This is addressed more specifically in the second half of this chapter; what I want to say here is that although militaries (state and non-state) vary, they do share a universal function: organized, collective killing in the furtherance of political goals, broadly defined. What is actually required to fulfil this function at ground level, however, is in my opinion not masculinity per se but the trained willingness of soldiers to kill, which entails a certain level of aggression (and militaries require this to be *controllable* aggression), desensitization towards violence, and the formation of strong in-group solidarity and out-group enemy images. The first two of these elements have in many societies at various points in time been associated with masculinity rather than femininity (though not all societies at all times) but they do not inherently *need* to be. What I'm saying is that violence can potentially be decoupled from masculinity but it cannot be decoupled from militaries or from war. Let me be very clear here. I am not actually trying to promote aggression or militarized violence but I *am* suggesting that it is not inconceivable for militaries to be less hyper-masculine but still functional. Whether this is a goal we support is of course another matter and brings us full circle back to the fraught question of feminism's (and women's) relationship to pacifism and peace activism.

Gender, nationalism(s) and armed conflict

In recent decades feminist scholars have pointed out the fact that in the vast mainstream literature on nations and nationalism, gender has rarely been taken as significant. '[D]espite a general interest in the differential participation of various social groups in nationalist projects' this literature has 'engaged but little with the differential integration of women and men into the national project' (Walby 1996: 235). Even Enloe, one of the seminal feminist scholars in the related area of gender and militarization, is disarmingly (and charmingly) honest about her own much earlier gender-blindness when studying nationalist mobilizations (1993: 230–1). Since the early to mid-1980s, however, there has been a growing body of work examining the gendered nature of ethnic and national processes; what happens to constructions of femininity and masculinity during times of ethnic or national crisis; and how women have participated in nationalist movements, which has generally been hidden or marginalized. Nevertheless, despite the efforts of the feminist academics who have been working in this area and the related area of gender and world politics/international relations[14] the majority of texts on nationalism still do not take gender seriously. When these texts have tried to incorporate feminist literature this has usually been in the form of 'tacking on' gender, for example having one chapter in a collection on nationalism that looks at 'gender' or 'women' (almost never men or masculinity), rather than gender being integrated into the overall work. The centrality of gender to all nationalist structures and discourses, and how nationalist movements are carried out is still not recognized. As Yuval-Davis puts it, 'constructions of nationhood usually involve specific notions of both "manhood" and "womanhood"' (1997: 1). In fact, Moghadam claims 'laws and discourses pertaining to gender are central to the self-definition of political groups and, indeed, signal the political and cultural projects of movements and regimes' (1994a: 2).

Feminist interrogations of dominant theories of nationalism and of how nationalist movements have been played out emphasize the interdependent nature of gender, ethnic, national and class relations. Feminist theories about women's involvement in nationalist struggles highlight the often troubled relationship between nationalism and feminism and pinpoint the ways that women's reproductive role is utilized both symbolically and practically. The differential ways that women are affected by and affect nationalist projects are explored; the centrality of particular constructions of gender to nationalist movements is uncovered; and the specific context of each nationalist struggle is always emphasized. In this second half of the chapter I first discuss some of these feminist approaches to analysing women's participation in nationalist movements, then go on to more specifically examine the contested nature of the relationship between feminism(s) and nationalism(s). Women's participation as combatants is then addressed with some suggestions made about women, nationalism, military participation and agency, to be borne in mind as we move on in the next chapters to my empirical research on female combatants in Sri Lanka and Northern Ireland.

Feminist approaches to women in nationalist movements

In an influential intervention, Anthias and Yuval-Davis posited that in general there are five major ways that women tend to participate in ethnic and national processes:

a as biological reproducers of members of ethnic collectivities;
b as reproducers of the boundaries of ethnic/national groups;
c as participating centrally in the ideological reproduction of the collectivity and as transmitters of its culture;
d as signifiers of ethnic/national differences – as a focus and symbol in ideological discourses used in the construction, reproduction and transformation of ethnic/national categories;
e as participants in national, economic, political and military struggles.

(Anthias and Yuval-Davis 1989: 7)

Peterson points out that women are not homogeneous nor necessarily united and they are no less affected than men by the social hierarchies structuring a society. The various ways in which different women are 'located' or 'situated' in respect of divisions of power, violence, labour and resources will shape the allegiances they have in the context of nationalism. Unsurprisingly, there is no automatic relationship between the interests of women and national interests (1998: 45–6). Peterson also emphasizes that it is important to understand that the 'power relations of reproduction' are fundamentally political, despite reproduction's historical relegation to the 'private' and non-political sphere (ibid.: 42).[15] Walby discusses the Anthias and Yuval-Davis framework, arguing that the gendered division of labour needs to be more specifically included (1996: 237–8). She also states that '[i]t appears that Anthias and Yuval-Davis argue that women are just as committed to the national/ethnic project as men, but they sometimes do it in different ways', whereas she maintains that: '[s]ometimes women may support a different national project from that of men. There is a struggle to define what constitutes *the* national project, and women are, typically, heard less than men in this' (ibid.: 244–5; also Tétreault 1994b: 427). Walby argues that '[t]he national project may differentially affect women and men (and subgroups of these) and hence engender different degrees of enthusiasm' (1996: 238). These are all important points but I do not think that Anthias or Yuval-Davis would dispute them. Their point, as I take it, is to emphasize women's varied agency in nationalist movements and to not dismiss women as passive victims who simply have nationalism thrust upon them by men. Walby also (cautiously) suggests that women's political activities are usually more local and less nationalist than men's, and that women, when found in electoral politics at all, are more visible in local rather than national government (ibid.: 248). I am sceptical about the implication that women are 'less nationalist' than men. Which women? Which men? Such a generalized statement does not reflect the reality for many women in conflict situations. Furthermore the fact that women are often 'more visible' in local rather than national politics and governmental structures is not necessarily an expression of a lesser national interest on the part of women. This could also be accounted for by reference to the opportunities commonly available (or unavailable, more to the point) to women. Local government is not as prestigious or generally considered as important as national government. Therefore it is likely to be easier for women to gain access to local structures than to national structures.

Yuval-Davis notes that there have been many attempts to classify the different kinds of nationalist movements that have arisen in the last 200 years. Many focus on the specific goals and character of movements – she draws here on Anthony D. Smith's differentiation between 'ethnic-genealogical' and 'civic-territorial' nationalist movements (discussed in the introduction to this book) and on the German typology differentiating between *Staatnation* (civic nationalism or state-nations) and *Kulturnation* (cultural nationalism or nation-states) (Smith 1971; 1986). Some recent approaches, which Yuval-Davis calls 'new nationalism', promote 'civic nationalism' (*Staatnation*) as 'good nationalism' in contrast to and as a solution to the exclusionary nature of 'ethnic nationalism' (*Kulturnation*). However she argues that there can be no easy separation of specific nationalist movements into one or other of these types of nationalism, or into 'good' or 'bad' nationalism. Further, she asserts that since citizenship has itself been exclusionary, it 'cannot be the polar negation of ethnic exclusion'. She asserts that 'nationalist projects are usually multiplex, although often one version is much more hegemonic than others at different historical moments', therefore we need to treat 'types' of nationalist projects not as concrete classifications but as different dimensions of nationalist ideologies or projects, which are combined in various ways in specific cases (1997: 20–1). The three major dimensions (rather than types) of nationalist projects that she differentiates between are: constructions of nations based on genealogical and biological notions of origin (*Volknation*); those based on notions of culture, a symbolic heritage stemming from language/religion/customs/traditions as the 'essence' of 'the nation'

(*Kulturnation*); and those based on notions of citizenship as determining national boundaries (*Staatnation*). She argues that in each of these dimensions different aspects of gender relations are significant. Essentially, she relates *Volknation* to nationalist projects that strongly emphasize women as biological reproducers of the nation. Projects where this element dominates usually construct the most exclusionary and homogeneous visions of the nation. *Kulturnation* she relates to nationalist projects that emphasize women as social and cultural reproducers of the nation and as markers of its boundaries. Where this dimension is dominant, nationalist projects usually allow for assimilation but with a low tolerance for diversity. In regard to *Staatnation* she explores gender relations, citizenship and difference. Where this dimension is dominant in nationalist projects there is often more space for inclusion and diversity, yet as noted above and discussed earlier she also stresses the potential for citizenship to function as an exclusionary tool (ibid.: 21). Thus, the roles that women play in nationalist movements are affected by the specific nature and context of each movement. Arguably, in nationalist movements with a strong *Volknation* element women are usually likely to be strongly dissuaded from participating as combatants; in *Kulturnation*-type movements how acceptable female combatants are will depend on the specific cultural traditions that are celebrated by the movement; and in nationalist movements emphasizing the *Staatnation* element there may be a higher degree of accommodation of female combatants but this is by no means assured since the vision of citizenship that is being conceptualized is significant and variable.

Significantly, Coulter notes that women played important roles in anti-colonial nationalist movements in the late nineteenth and early twentieth centuries and that all over the colonized world the extent of women's political activity was different (and greater) from that of women in imperialist countries. She attributes this to 'the space created by the existence of mass nationalist movements, the widespread rejection of existing political institutions and culture, and the different family relationships which existed in colonial countries' (1993: 3). She believes that women were enabled to participate in large part because of the different experiences of the family and religion in colonial countries compared to that of colonizing European countries. She maintains that religion acts as a bridge between family and community, particularly in contexts where the community is denied expression as a civic entity, so religious beliefs and imagery are often significant in resistance movements in these contexts. She also maintains that women in colonial countries had different relationships to the family from those of women in colonizing countries. For women in Western Europe at the end of the eighteenth century society was based on a family structure sanctioning women's subordination to men, while in colonial countries (including Ireland, the focus of her work) public and civic life was 'dominated by an outsider, who forcibly occupied that space' so that 'public space became alien for *all* the native inhabitants'. In contrast, in the family one's own language, customs and opinions could be expressed. The family 'was an inviolate space, the one place where the occupier could not enter – at least, not without doing violence to his own rhetoric on the sanctity of the family' (ibid.: 7–10, emphasis added to 'all'). In regard to Ireland specifically, Coulter says 'the family could become the crucible of rebellion' and writes of the Irish tradition of 'political families' (ibid.: 10).[16] She asserts that '[g]iven the necessity for internal solidarity within families with a tradition of rebellion, the distinction between male and female roles could become blurred' and relations within the family more democratic than in civic society, compounded by the impact of widespread emigration of married men and the fact that colonized men usually did not get to perform masculinity (with its associations of public/civic power) in the same way as colonizing men (ibid.: 11–12). Chatterjee makes a very similar argument in regard to India about the separation of the social space into 'world' and 'home', where the 'outer' world (public) is typically the Westernized domain of the material and of men, while the 'inner' home (private) is the spiritual domain and the repository of national culture, represented by women. The inner/spiritual/female social space is protected and defended in the anti-colonial nationalist project from the colonizing West (1993, 1991).

Coulter and Chatterjee both present an extremely interesting case but, while it may be convincing in the cases of Ireland and India, I find it less persuasive as a blanket argument (as Coulter seems in danger of trying to make it), extended to colonized peoples in general. In many places the occupier did *deliberate* violence to the notion of the sanctity of the family. In Australia, for example, governmental policy from the late nineteenth century up until the 1960s was responsible for vast numbers of Koori (indigenous) and mixed-'race' children being forcibly removed from their families and placed either with white Australian families or in state children's homes. This was cloaked in rhetoric of it being for the good of the children, their families, and indigenous people in general. This policy has had a lasting effect, not simply in terms of personal trauma on the part of the children and their families but also in terms of contributing to the deterioration of indigenous family structures.[17] Similarly, in the United States until around the 1960s many Native American children were forcibly removed from their families and placed in repressive and brutal mission schools for years, to 'civilize' them. Again, this has contributed to changes in Native American family and social structures.[18] Perhaps the reasoning behind the forcible destruction of indigenous family structures by colonizers was based on exactly the kind of logic Coulter expresses – that these structures potentially provided the basis for resistance – but my point here is simply that, contrary to her assertion, the family was quite clearly *not* always 'an inviolate space'.

Moghadam, like others, argues that how women are represented in nationalist movements differs according to context. Within some projects, women are linked to progress and modernization. In others, they are viewed as central to cultural rejuvenation or religious orthodoxy. Therefore, '[r]epresentations of women assume political significance.... Women's behaviour and appearance – and the acceptable range of their activities – come to be defined by, and are frequently subject to, the political or cultural objectives of political movements, states, and leaderships' (1994a: 2). She differentiates between two models of revolutionary movement and constructions of national identity: a modernizing type that includes ideas of the equality and emancipation of women that she calls the Women's Emancipation model; and a form that views cultural identity and integrity as heavily dependent on women's 'proper' behaviour, which she calls the Women-in-the-Family model (1993: 71–2). Kandiyoti highlights the fact that there can be clashes between such models and a 'patriarchal backlash' directed at women associated with modernizing or liberating movements (1991: 433).

Moghadam discusses Anderson's proposition that nationalism is more akin to kinship and religion than it is to ideology. She maintains that nationalism *was* an ideology in 'Third World' countries in the early part of the twentieth century and in Latin America in the nineteenth century, but agrees that more recent nationalist movements have become less like ideology and more like kinship. She makes the simple yet arresting suggestion that Anderson's argument

> helps explain why, in so many contemporary political movements, women are assigned the role of bearers of cultural values, carriers of traditions, and symbols of the community. If the nation is an extended family writ large, then women's role is to carry out the tasks of nurturance and reproduction. If the nation is defined as a religious entity, then the appropriate models of womanhood are to be found in scripture.
>
> (Moghadam 1994a: 3–4)

Aside from anything else this suggestion highlights the surprising fact that seminal scholars of ethnicity and nationalism such as Anderson, Anthony D. Smith and Horowitz all discuss ethno-nationalism in terms of 'kinship' yet none of them seem to notice that which is immediately and glaringly obvious to most feminist scholars: that because of women's primary role in biological and socio-cultural reproduction, the kinship analogy *must* have implications for gender roles and relations in general and women's experiences specifically. Moreover, correspondingly, gender *must* be an integral determinant of how nationalist movements are constructed and played out. Gender is not simply a minor feature of personal identity to be tacked on to studies of nationalism.[19]

Finally, one way to approach nationalism(s) is to distinguish between dominant/state nationalisms; settler-state nationalisms; anti-colonial nationalisms; post-colonial nationalisms; and ethno-nationalisms (Pettman 1996: 48). Others, however, draw a broader distinction between institutionalized state nationalisms and 'liberatory' nationalisms (both may contain ethnic and civic elements). Abdo, who writes on the Israeli–Palestinian conflict, argues that 'it is necessary to distinguish, theoretically and politically, between an oppressive state national ideology and the ideology of a national liberation struggle' (1994: 151). Drawing on Abdo's work Sharoni, another scholar of the Israeli–Palestinian conflict, also makes this distinction (1995: 36–7). Both forms involve assumptions about masculinity, femininity and gender relations – explicit or implicit – yet there are often important differences between their gendered assumptions. Ultimately, the suggestion here is that 'liberatory', anti-state nationalisms may be more likely to be receptive to feminism and/or women's movements than institutionalized state nationalisms. However this is very far from being assured in specific contexts. Both forms still tend to construct and socialize men as protectors and liberators, while constructing and socializing women as reproducers of the nation and as in need of protection (ibid.: 37–8). Arguably, for women of the dominant ethno-national group there are compensations for their unequal status as women in the form of privileges accrued through their status as members of the powerful ethno-national group – a position which would be threatened by their challenging the gender conservatism of their institutionalized state nationalism. In contrast, for women of the marginalized group issues of ethnic or 'racial' inequality are fundamentally important, thus within their 'liberatory' anti-state nationalisms they have to make strategic choices about when to push gender issues (Mangaliso 1997; Sharoni 2001; Coulter 1993). This distinction between institutionalized state nationalism and liberatory anti-state nationalism is important to bear in mind in relation to the two countries under particular study in this book, Sri Lanka and Northern Ireland.

The thorny relationship between feminism(s) and nationalism(s)

It should already be clear that neither all women nor all feminists have empathized with Virginia Woolf's proclamation, noted earlier, that 'as a woman I have no country. As a woman I want no country. As a woman my country is the whole world' (1943: 197). In fact for many women, including many feminists, national identity and national*ism* are extremely important. However nationalist movements do not automatically come with principles of women's autonomy and liberation attached. It is often quite the opposite – these principles are sometimes 'regarded as inimical to the integrity and identity of the national group' (Moghadam 1994a: 2). Further, 'women and men within nascent national communities often struggle with each other over *whose* experiences – of humiliation, of insecurity, of solidarity – will define the community in its new national manifestation' (Enloe 1993: 232–3). In Enloe's words, 'nationalism typically has sprung from masculinized memory, masculinized humiliation and masculinized hope' (2000a: 44). Many have wondered, therefore, whether nationalism and feminism are compatible. Cockburn's answer is that this depends on what *kinds* of nationalism(s) and feminism(s) we are discussing, as both are plural movements (1998: 41).

The above answer is, it must be stressed, a fairly recent one for Western feminists; in the past the answer would have been a resounding 'no'. In the West, 'second-wave' feminism has historically taken a Virginia Woolf approach and been irrevocably opposed to nationalism, seeing it as conservative and as inherently bad for women and for the advancement of women's rights and status. Yuval-Davis describes the relationship in the 1970s and 1980s between 'second-wave' Western feminists and women of the 'Third World' as 'a dialogue of the deaf.' She argues that

> [f]or western feminists, as members of a hegemonic collectivity, their membership in the collectivity and its implications for their positioning was

> often rendered invisible, while Third World women acutely experienced their being part of a subjugated collectivity and often did not see autonomous space for themselves to organize as feminists.
>
> (Yuval Davis 1997: 117)

Furthermore, she asserts, Western feminists frequently had an oppositional relationship to their national collectivities. Many were centrally involved in anti-government political movements (such as the movements for civil rights and against the Vietnam War), which 'created in both sides very different assumptions concerning relationships between individual women and their collectivities'. At the same time, 'Third World' feminists often felt that Western feminists 'froze' them into 'archetypal victims' in their writings on such things as female genital mutilation and *sati*, ignoring 'some of the trade-offs that the continued existence of certain practices might have had on the lives of women in these societies' (Yuval-Davis 1997: 117; see Kandiyoti 1988).

In 1986 a book was published which contributed to changing this 'dialogue of the deaf' and had an ongoing ripple effect in the study of feminism and nationalism: Jayawardena's *Feminism and Nationalism in the Third World*. As Yuval-Davis points out, this book was important because it constructed feminist and nationalist social movements 'as interrelated in a way that very few, if any, feminist scholars had done before' and 'signalled a possible break in this deadlock between "the feminists" and "the nationalists"', illustrating that 'loyalty to one's national liberation movement does not necessarily mean that women do not fight within it for the improvement and transformation of the position of women in their societies' yet also pointing out that feminism 'has not been a specifically western phenomenon' (1997: 117–18). This book, and subsequent developments in the literature, forced many Western feminists to look at the phenomenon of nationalism with new eyes. At the same time some nationalists have come to view feminism differently as there has also been, Yuval-Davis argues, a 'growing realization of women in the liberation or post-liberation movements that "national liberation" usually not only did not guarantee women's rights in the nation but also that women were often confronted with new oppressions in the name of "custom and tradition"' (1998: 32). Further, the rise of 'minority' feminisms within the West and the new visibility of 'Third World' feminisms from outside the West, plus the increasing impact of postmodernism and poststructuralism in Western academia, have led to a push for a feminist understanding of difference among women, the inclusion of the concerns of non-white, non-middle-class and non-Western women, and the recognition of the plurality of feminism(s) (1997: 118). Although some feminists (both from within and from without the West) do still stress a belief in a universal commonality and common interests between women everywhere, it is impossible to deny that overall feminism as a whole has undergone some major changes. As Cockburn argues, '[i]t has taken time for authoritative Western feminism to respond to critiques and abandon their universalizing discourse. But the more they have done so, the more feminism has matured and pluralized' (1998: 44).

Jayawardena's book is historical, examining nationalist movements in Asia (she includes the Middle East) in the late nineteenth and early twentieth centuries. She explains that many in the 'Third World' are not aware that their own countries have a history of feminism or of women's emancipation movements that were supported both by women and men (1986: ix). In the 'Third World', it

> has variously been alleged by traditionalists, political conservatives and even certain leftists, that feminism is a product of 'decadent' Western capitalism; that it is based on a foreign culture of no relevance to women in the 'Third World'; that it is the ideology of women of the local bourgeoisie; and that it alienates or diverts women from their culture, religion and family responsibilities on the one hand, and from the revolutionary struggles for national liberation and socialism on the other.
>
> (Jayawardena 1986: 2)

In the West, there has also been a Eurocentric assumption that feminism has been a purely Western European and North American phenomenon and is not indigenous to Asia or Africa; 'Third World' feminist movements have been assumed to be imitations of Western models. Jayawardena takes issue with all of this, arguing that 'feminism, like socialism, has no particular ethnic identity' and that it 'was *not* imposed on the Third World by the West, but rather ... historical circumstances produced important material and ideological changes that affected women' (allowing, however, that the impact of imperialism and Western thought contributed to these historical circumstances) (Jayawardena 1986: ix, 2). Jayawardena's argument is that in most Asian anti-colonial movements of the period she examines, 'struggles for women's emancipation were an essential and integral part of national resistance movements' where 'the "woman question" forcefully made its appearance during the early 20th century' (ibid.: 8). The women's emancipation movements she analyses were 'acted out against a background of nationalist struggles aimed at achieving political independence, asserting a national identity, and modernizing society' (ibid.: 3). In this period, she argues, the most significant development in Asian feminism was the emergence of autonomous women's organizations as well as cross-class associations of women linked to nationalist political groups. She notes, however, that despite advances in women's legal and political equality in Asia, the women's movement of this period 'failed to make any impression on women's subordination within the patriarchal structures of family and society. Feminist consciousness did not develop, except in rare exceptions, to the point of questioning traditional patriarchal structures' (ibid.: 24).

Drawing on Jayawardena's work, Cockburn notes that positive examples of feminist–nationalist connections are more common in anti-colonial and liberatory nationalist movements than in other kinds. However, she cautions that

> [e]ven in liberatory national movements women are driven to a double militancy, organizing 'in and against' the movement to give a contrary spin to its prevailing gender relations. If women in the movement organize in the

> interests of women as women, and more so if they form anti-militarist and cross-ethnic women's projects, they are quickly cast as traitors.
>
> (Cockburn 1998: 42)

She also argues that as anti-imperialist movements gain power they usually lose whatever socialist and progressive gender ideology they may have had in the earlier stages (ibid.). Furthermore, she suggests that just as it is important to distinguish between different kinds of national movements, it is equally important to distinguish between different kinds of feminism. She notes that the majority trend in feminism stresses the socially constituted nature of gender identities, yet there is a feminist minority who remain essentialist, giving 'woman' a primordial meaning and describing her as 'someone "naturally" different from (and better than) men. This is an ideology every bit as immobilizing and divisive as essentialist constructions of the nation' (ibid.: 43–4). Tétreault comments, as others have, that '[a]lthough women have participated in revolutionary movements in all societies, not all of these movements addressed directly the problems of women in pre-revolutionary society or attempted to resolve these problems in post-revolutionary political and social constitutions and institutions' (1994a: 18). She notes that there is a hypothesis that 'state formation necessarily results in the repression of women' and argues that '[i]f this is correct, revolutionary transformation cannot liberate women unless it also constrains state power' (ibid.: 21). The logical extension of this would be that 'all revolutions against state based regimes have the potential to liberate women from men as well as to liberate men from one another.' However since 'revolutions also result in the strengthening of state institutions, the continued subordination of women and other previously exploited social groups after revolutionary transformation may be structurally favored' (ibid.: 19). Here Tétreault is picking up on the fundamental contradiction inherent in most nationalist projects: that these movements are focused on the overthrow of, or independence from, a particular state that is perceived as unjust or illegitimate, yet the goal is almost always state-centred in some way – whether the ultimate aim is to achieve a new, independent state, to be incorporated into another state, or to attain autonomy within an existing state.

An example of nationalism that did not fundamentally critique the nature of the state, according to Coulter, can be seen in the formation of independent Ireland. Coulter argues that most of the men concerned with Irish independence did not challenge the actual economic and social base the state rested on – their concern, she suggests, was simply to replace the British state with a sovereign Irish replica. Since Irish women were already largely excluded from the British-run state before the 1916 Easter Rising, 'any replica of the British state would equally fail to allow them to play their full role in public life' (1993: 22). However she neglects the fact that some of the leaders of the 1916 Rising, such as James Connolly and Constance Markiewicz (a woman), were socialists (challenging the economic basis of the state) and in favour of women's equality (challenging the social and political basis of the state). Nonetheless, it is certainly true that the attainment of the Irish Free State did not result in the advances for women that many had hoped for. The only important deviation from the British state model was the adoption of a written Constitution that spelt out the rights of citizens, which in 1921 gave the vote and equal civil rights to all adult women. Aside from this, Coulter argues, ultimately the Constitution and accompanying discriminatory legislation worked against women's involvement in public life. Worse, the later 1937 Constitution was more conservative than its predecessor and underpinned further discriminatory measures against women. By the end of the Second World War 'most of those women who had devoted decades of their lives to the creation of a different society and political system in Ireland had virtually disappeared [from public life]' (ibid.: 23–4, 27). Coulter's argument is that the colonial experience 'created a socially broad and varied oppositional response, with space in it for women. This space disappeared when that oppositional movement developed into the parties which now competed for, and alternated in, power within that [independent] state' (ibid.: 28).

Tétreault suggests that women's participation in revolutions underpins the legitimacy of post-revolutionary calls for women's liberation. Drawing on martial citizenship and the idea of military service as an avenue for achieving political equality for disadvantaged groups, she says a 'parallel argument could be made about the legitimacy of group demands after a revolution: what any group gets is at least in part a function of what that group is perceived to have earned by the blood of its members' (1994a: 19). I have already addressed some of the problems with martial citizenship in a previous part of this chapter. To be fair to Tétreault she does recognize that military service does not automatically lead to political equality: '[p]aying your dues does not necessarily guarantee permanent membership as an autonomous actor in a post-revolutionary society and political economy' (1994b: 434–5). In fact, it has even been argued that it is an 'almost universal phenomenon of successful national liberation movements ... that they renege on promises made to their female members during the struggle' (Miller 1998: 194; see also Afshar 2003). Tétreault claims that women's entitlements can be erased structurally by the new regime but they also 'disappear through gender-selective forgetting of revolutionary experiences' which 'erodes the legitimacy of women's claims to equality'. As an example, she reports that the Museum of the Revolution in Hanoi does not represent what she knows to be the case of women's pivotal involvement in the Vietnamese revolution (1994b: 434–5). Wilford also raises the issue of 'forgetting' after revolutionary and nationalist struggles as part of a regression in women's situation. Like Coulter, he gives the example of independent Ireland and the later 'forgetting' of the women of the 1916 Easter Rising, embodied in the 1937 Constitution (1998: 3–4). I suggest, however, that 'women's entitlements' are not erased solely or primarily through gender-selective forgetting of women's military participation, though this is certainly significant; I attribute this more to the problems inherent in the martial citizenship model. Female combatants are often presented as a necessary but temporary heroic sacrifice on the part of these 'exceptional' women, rather than as representing a fundamental shift in societal gender roles and relations.

Despite what is often a profoundly difficult task of pursuing both a nationalist and a feminist agenda, there are feminist nationalists everywhere. West takes a global perspective and states that feminist nationalist activists 'on both a grassroots and élite level work today for the identification with their national group, ... sense of place ... or kinship – while simultaneously fighting for what they define as the rights of women within their cultural contexts.' She claims that 'feminist nationalist movements are struggling to define and reconceptualize their relationship to states, nations, and social movements as activists central to the debate, not as passive recipients.' Feminist nationalists juggle competing demands of women's rights and national struggles. One demand may surface at a particular time as the most pressing, while the other remains in the background, but they are not mutually exclusive or binary (1997a: xiii). West defines feminist nationalist movements as social movements that concurrently seek rights for women and rights for nationalists within varied social, economic and political contexts. She posits three 'ideal types' of such movements: national liberation social movements; movements against neo-colonialism; and identity-rights movements that wage struggles that are internal to their societies. She acknowledges, however, that some movements incorporate elements of more than one of these ideal types (ibid.: xxx–xxxi).[20] In contrast, Moghadam argues that in comparison to the anti-colonial movements in Asia, nowadays 'feminists and nationalists view each other with suspicion if not hostility, and nationalism is no longer assumed to be a progressive force for change', suggesting this may be due to the changing nature of nationalism and definitely to the evolution of feminism (1994a: 3–4).

I personally would suggest that nationalist movements today are frequently more ethno-nationalist than earlier movements, more ethnically and/or religiously exclusionist, less progressive and less concerned with equality for all people than the more ethnically, religiously and socially pluralist anti-colonial nationalist movements of the late nineteenth and early twentieth centuries (which often emphasized the civil, political and economic rights of mass populations against repressive rulers). This *may* make contemporary nationalist movements less likely, in general, to be willing to accommodate feminist perspectives and aims. However although I agree with Moghadam, Cockburn and Jayawardena, for reasons given above, that the feminist-nationalist connection appears to have been more positive for women in historical anti-colonial nationalist movements than in contemporary nationalist movements, I do not believe that 'the alliance between nationalism and feminism has dissolved' (Moghadam 1994a: 5–6). As West's collection (1997b) suggests, women around the world have continued to forge their own unique conceptions of feminist nationalism and these debates are ongoing. Although the relationship is always problematic, feminism cannot ignore nationalism or dismiss it as always an impediment to women's rights; nor can nationalist movements always manage to subordinate women's claims to nationalist claims. The relationship between feminism(s) and nationalism(s) varies enormously according to context and historical period. We certainly cannot assume a universally positive relationship but neither should we assume universal hostility.[21]

Female combatants

Enloe argues that

> [a]ccepting a priori the assumption that women are best thought of as victims in any nationalist mobilization that has turned violent dulls the analytical curiosity. Ultimately, this dulled curiosity produces explanations that are naïve in their descriptions of power and camouflage men as ungendered actors.
> (1998: 53)

There is a tendency, Turshen maintains, to reduce war to ideas of blanket male guilt and blanket female suffering: '[i]n writing of armed conflict, it is tempting to portray men as the perpetrators of war, women as benign bystanders or victims. After all, men do most of the soldiering, most women are civilians' (1998: 1). In contrast, she and the authors in her edited collection (Turshen and Twagiramariya 1998) 'wish to emphasize the knowledge and active participation of women because men have so often denied women's agency in political contests' (Turshen 1998: 6). As she and many others have pointed out, women have participated as combatants or military support personnel in a great many wars, particularly in nationalist and inter-communal conflicts. Though still small, there is beginning to be a rich body of work looking at female combatants in various intra-state and/or unconventional conflicts; not all of these conflicts are nationalist nor does all of this literature engage with theories of nationalism, and it is beyond the scope of this work to address all these particular conflicts. The focus here is on theoretical points about women, nationalism, agency and military participation that can be drawn out from this and the preceding discussions and used to help analyse the cases of Sri Lanka and Northern Ireland and ethno-national conflict more generally. Sri Lanka and Northern Ireland are excluded from this discussion as they are addressed in depth in subsequent chapters.

The editors of *Arms to Fight, Arms to Protect* (Bennett *et al.* 1995), the result of an extensive Panos oral history project on women in conflict situations around the world, maintain that the stories of the women they interviewed illustrate that whether or not women support a war, and the extent and type of their participation in it, depends on their perceptions of the type of war it is. They suggest that where it is viewed as 'a struggle for some perceived justice or liberation involving the mass of society, or as a legitimate defence of home and community, women tend to be just as much in favour of the war as men'. In contrast, when women see a war as 'a struggle between men over things to which they do not in any case have access (political power or economic resources), [they are] ... rarely supporters of the conflict' (ibid.: 20). For example, the Ugandan women they interviewed generally saw the war as a senseless greedy battle between men concerned with getting rich by force, and did not support it. In Tigray, in contrast, all the women they interviewed had participated in the struggle against the Ethiopian government and 'saw themselves as fighting for political justice and social progress – including equality for themselves.... [T]hey felt pride in their suffering and their achievements.' Nevertheless, their interviews suggested that even when women strongly identify with a cause or community, they usually participate as combatants only when their families or homes come under attack (ibid.: 4–5), which is something requiring further investigation. Others have found that the goals of the movement/military group are significant in and of themselves in terms of levels of women's combat participation. González-Pérez (2006) argues in regard to Latin America that 'domestic' guerrilla organizations (acting within their own state or social structure against perceived forces of oppression) attract higher levels of female combatants than 'international' ones (working against external actors, neo-colonialism, global capitalism and so forth). She maintains that since 'domestic' movements are interested in restructuring the national society there is room in this project to address gender structures as well, which can lead to higher rates of women's participation, whereas 'international' movements are not focused on changing internal societal structures and are more likely to be gender-conservative.

The empirical findings of the Panos project mirror the recurring contention that in contrast to conventional wars, in contemporary wars there is no clear war front/home front boundary, which has an impact on women and their roles in and experiences of war (Turshen 1998; Afshar 2003). Many contemporary conflicts 'privatize violence and engage an array of state and non-state actors. As more and more civilians are drawn into conflicts, the conventional separation of male belligerents and inhabitants no longer prevails.' Concomitantly the binary stereotype of active/aggressive men and passive/pacifist women breaks down; particularly in contemporary civil wars and wars of liberation, women are also combatants (Turshen 1998: 1). Miller's point in regard to societal transition periods in general is also relevant here. He notes that women are more active in the public sphere during transition periods and suggests that part of the reason is that women, their children and families are more directly negatively affected by transitions and they may act partially out of desperation, especially with men absent through violence or intimidation (1998: 201). Further, he refers to Saint-Germain's assessment that '[i]ronically, it was in many cases the invasion of the private sphere by government authorities that provoked women to enter ... the public sphere' (1994: 274).[22] This may also be the case for some women in nationalist conflicts who enter the public sphere as combatants. For example, it has been argued that when the 1967 occupation of the West Bank and Gaza Strip brought Israeli troops into Palestinian communities and homes, 'women had no choice but to confront the Israeli military authorities' in a variety of ways, including a minority as fighters (Holt 2003: 228–9; also Afshar 2003: 181).

As discussed earlier in the chapter, it is often pointed out that women have so far not easily been integrated into most state militaries, which supposedly make 'boys' into 'men' (Yuval-Davis 1997: 101) and involve women-hating and homophobia as part of the training of male recruits, with rape and sexual harassment of female soldiers being common. Yuval-Davis suggests that, in contrast, in national liberation armies with less formal hierarchical and organizational frameworks, 'a strong common ideological stance might help to transcend some of these tensions, especially where women's emancipation is seen to symbolize the emancipation of the people as a whole' (ibid.). She suggests that incorporating women into militaries in nationalist movements conveys the message that women are (symbolically) equal members of the collectivity, and that *all* members of the collectivity are symbolically incorporated into the military (ibid.: 98; see also Afshar 2003: 179–80). However, liberation armies differ in how they incorporate women. Moghadam's distinction between 'modernizing' revolutionary movements that use women as symbols of liberation and those that use women as symbols of the traditions and national culture to be reclaimed (1993: 71–2, discussed earlier) has implications for women's involvement as combatants. In the former, 'women would be encouraged to participate actively in the military'; in the latter, 'women are virtually excluded from formal participation, and the nature of their supportive roles is highly controlled' (Yuval-Davis 1997: 103). I would slightly alter the second part of this claim, to say that women being seen as symbols of the reclaimed national culture and thus being excluded from military participation would only apply in particular contexts, where the national culture and tradition is one which is restrictive of women's roles and probably does not have a history of heroic myths of female national fighters and patriots.[23] This is not always the case, thus we must be careful to be attentive to specific context and history. Nevertheless, arguably

> [a]s long as the struggle of the powerless is to gain power rather than to transform power relations within the society, so-called 'national liberation' has often just brought further oppression to women and other disadvantaged groupings within the new social order. While armed struggle might sometimes be the only way open to fight against oppression and occupation, the ways this struggle is organized, its targets and social organization, are crucial.
> (Yuval-Davis 1997: 113)

Yuval-Davis notes that in some post-revolutionary societies, referring to Eritrea and South Africa, 'being part of the guerrilla fighters has earned women significant social and political authority.' However this is not always the case and she also points out that a reversal in the kind of women's participation in the military as well as a general reversal of women's rights and opportunities is common after war or national liberation (1997: 103–5). Indeed, with the benefit of a bit more hindsight the evidence on Eritrea is ambiguous at best (Campbell 2005) and it has been argued that there is a significant gap between reality and the rhetoric of sexual equality in the new South African Constitution (Mangaliso 1997). This post-conflict reversal trend is borne out by the evidence from many conflicts around the world where women have participated as combatants in national liberation movements. One of the best-known examples is the 1950s anti-colonial war in Algeria against the French where women were centrally involved, including as full-time combatants and urban guerrillas who planted bombs. It has been argued that the experiences of the *moudjahidates* (female combatants) during the war have been marginalized in post-war discourse and there has been a slow regression in the position of women (Bouatta 1994). As we saw in the preceding section, women's participation in many different roles in nationalist movements has never been a guarantee of their post-conflict greater rights or freedoms; this is no less the case when it comes to their participation as combatants. Initially this instinctively feels odd. Women combatants seem like such a strong challenge to traditional gender roles in many different societies and contexts that it seems reasonable to think this stretching or reshuffling of gender roles would later be extended into peacetime, yet this is often (usually?) not the case. As Wilford notes, 'fighting alongside men to achieve independence does not provide a guarantee of women's inclusion as equal citizens'; 'even where women have been active as warriors … they invariably are left holding the wrong end of the citizenship stick' (1998: 3, 15). Some argue that there is a 'purely instrumental agenda of nationalist policies that mobilize women when they are needed in the labour force or even at the front, only to return them to domesticity or to subordinate roles in the public sphere when the national emergency is over' (Kandiyoti 1991: 429).

As I have alluded to, part of the reason for this reneging on promises and forgetting of women's involvement, it seems to me, is that such gender role changes are often perceived as a necessary but *temporary* aberration in a time of national crisis and need, rather than as representing a fundamental societal change. Afshar argues that '[i]deologies do not change during wars; they are simply suspended' (2003: 185). Even in Israel, where women as well as men have been required to serve in the state military for many years now (a state military engaged in a nationalist conflict), it has been argued that '[c]ontrary to liberal feminist interpretations, the recruitment of Israeli women into the military has not been presented as a principle grounded in a struggle for gender equality, but rather as an inevitable necessity' (Sharoni 1995: 44–5). Sharoni claims that the state of Israel has tried to illustrate the seriousness of the conflict, to its own society and to the rest of the world, through images of female soldiers: the situation is so serious that 'even women' have to fight; things are so grave that the nation will make the ultimate sacrifice of risking the lives of women too (ibid.). In an interesting parallel, it has been suggested that the Russian government views the existence of Chechen women suicide bombers as signalling the absolute desperation of Chechen society and, therefore, the impossibility of negotiating a solution – thus justifying continued Russian counter-insurgency and military strategy in Chechnya (Sjoberg and Gentry 2007: 209). In Israel, contrasted to the ideological construction is the reality that despite the mandatory service law many more women are exempted from service than men; in fact, apparently only around 65 per cent of Israeli-Jewish women serve in the military. Further, official accounts show that around 70 per cent of Israeli women who do serve occupy traditional women's roles, 'as clerk-typists, folding parachutes, working in base kitchens, or serving entertainment to troops. The remainder are loaned out to various government ministries to cover shortages' (Sharoni 1995: 45–7). Furthermore, Segal asserts that despite their military service, Israeli 'girls and women are primarily expected to admire, create and preserve … [the] soldier culture, above all, in their role as mothers'. This manifests itself in media and popular entertainment images, educational curricula, and public and private pressure on women to have many children and shaming of those who do not (2008: 25). None of this is restricted to institutionalized state nationalist projects like that of Israel, though arguably 'liberatory' anti-state nationalist movements *may* have more potential to be open to deeper and wider-reaching change.

Another reason for reneging and forgetting is the fact that issues relating to women's emancipation, however this is conceptualized, are usually secondary priorities (if that!) for nationalist movements and other collective military mobilizations (such as ideologically based civil wars). As discussed in the previous section of this chapter, nationalist feminists have to engage in a 'double militancy' (Cockburn 1998: 42). Pettman points out that 'there is now considerable evidence that those causes that are marginalized in the struggle are likely to be marginalized in its victories, and especially in the consolidation and institutionalisation of victory in the state' (1996: 61). I suggest that one factor in the marginalization of feminist concerns during 'the struggle' is the nature of war itself – during 'hot' wars there is a continual crisis mode for those engaged in conflict in which there is little time (or there is *perceived* to be little time, or conservative elements argue there is little time) for serious, thoughtful analytical reflection, though in long-drawn-out wars there may be periods of relatively greater calm that provide some space for this. Ibáñez, writing about female combatants in the most recent civil war in El Salvador (1980–91), argues that 'the urgency of the combat zone left no room for reflections on gender'; the main priorities were political, economic and social changes and it was (wrongly) assumed that 'the rest' would follow in time (2001: 118–22).

Ibáñez writes of the 'contradictions' of the war experience for female combatants, particularly in regard to maternity in a society that places huge significance on motherhood: '[w]omen fighters … left their homes to become guerrillas and collaborated in destroying lives, while the generic construction of their identity continued to stress its link to maternity'. While these contradictions were not always clear during the course of the war, '[a]nalysing their actions in the present, away from the justifying context of the war, has increased their feelings of guilt and transgression' (Ibáñez 2001: 128). For some women guerrillas the contradiction was painfully clear even during the war, as sex was common but maternity was prohibited and women combatants were left with the sole responsibility of the many pregnancies that did result (ibid.: 121–2). These gender role contradictions were also visible in other Central American revolutions. Chinchilla argues that in the long wars in El Salvador and Guatemala, pregnancy seems to have been the main reason for women combatants 'falling behind' male counterparts; Nicaragua was rather different as it was a much shorter war. Although women were left with the full parental responsibility and were perceived as or saw themselves as having failed in their role as combatant, at the same time pregnant women were celebrated for 'bellies that give birth to more revolutionaries'. This produced conflicting messages for women combatants but '[t]here was little discussion in the revolutionary movements of alternative models of paternity and maternity or child rearing' (1997: 212–13). Accordingly, I suggest that whether or not female combatants are likely to have children during their active involvement will vary considerably according to context but this may often only be possible in circumstances where there are *other women* willing and available to take on the responsibilities of caring for the children of combatants. Male nationalists may be unlikely to support a fundamental reshaping of parental responsibilities to care for their children while their wives/partners go off to fight. Thus, the participation of some women as combatants frequently relies on the support of non-combatant women in their communities.

A factor which Chinchilla identifies as significant in all this is that when the Central American revolutions broke out there was 'a virtual vacuum of feminist theory or practice in the region, even of the upper- or middle-class variant' (1997: 204). Only a 'tiny handful' of women were conscious feminists before joining the revolutionary movement (in a variety of roles) and they were wary of pursuing the matter because of the Left's rejection of what they saw as bourgeois 'First World' feminism. Nevertheless, Chinchilla asserts, the historic shift in women's political involvement in this period did affect the consciousness of the women themselves and their families and close friends. One consequence of the participation of women specifically as combatants has been a 'symbolic and practical questioning of conservative frameworks regarding what women are and are not permitted to do' (ibid.: 207–8). Despite the failure of all three leftist movements to incorporate attention to gender and gender-specific demands, Chinchilla argues that 'women's participation in the revolution has unintentionally created the conditions for women's and explicitly feminist movements that are probably the most vital of any currently existing in Central America'; many women ex-combatants agree that it is their experience in the movements that has allowed them to critique the shortcomings of their movements in regard to gender (ibid.: 209).

Chinchilla identifies four themes of the movements that inhibited the achievement of greater equality and access to power for women: the lack of a gendered analysis of the revolutionary movement and the society it aimed to change; the role of masculinist culture in the supposedly 'genderless' vanguard party; the principle of absolute obedience to authority and self-sacrifice; and a weak understanding of the importance of democracy and the role of civil society in creating a new society (1997: 209–10). Even when women are present as combatants, their 'demands and access to power almost always suffer as the military aspect of struggles for fundamental social transformation take precedence over political struggle, negotiation, and dialogue' (ibid.: 216). Many of these features are also present in nationalist movements. Chinchilla concludes that 'participation, in and of itself, even participation in nontraditional gender roles, does not result in the transformation of gender ideology and culture'. Although participation 'is a crucible for such transformation', a parallel direct attack on gender ideology and practices is also a co-requisite. Feminism, too, is not the automatic result of women's involvement in non-traditional roles or of men's experiences with women doing things they were not expected to be able to do. For feminism to develop also requires 'direct challenges to gender ideologies and practices and giving women the autonomy, within mixed political organizations and outside of them, to share experiences with other women and collectively decide on leadership and priorities for demands' (ibid.: 215–16). Clearly, then, whether women's participation as combatants has any long-term effects on gender roles and opportunities available to women depends on the context, content and character of the nationalist movement and a significant issue here is the extent of the movement's commitment to gender equality and its openness to genuine challenge and debate.

Finally, some thoughts here about women's violence and agency. Like Mukta (2000) and others Jacobson *et al.* (2000) acknowledge that women, but also feminists specifically, have often avoided facing the issue of women who commit violence (though arguably the last decade has seen this begin to significantly change), but they maintain this reluctance among feminists 'must be seen in the light of well-founded fears that such investigations could be used to mask male violence'. They suggest we do need to tackle questions about women perpetrating violence but warn we must be wary of over-emphasizing women's violence at the expense of subsuming the more widespread problem of male violence (2000: 12–13). Similarly, Kelly asserts that the fact that women sometimes perpetrate violence 'does not … alter the fact that the use of violence – inter-personal, state-sanctioned and insurgent – remains a primarily masculine preserve, and that women who enter these terrains do so within a set of long-standing gendered meanings' (2000: 46). Discussing the concern about how focusing on women solely as victims of violence can constitute a denial of women as agents (actors capable of deliberate decision-making), she argues that on the other hand this perspective can lead to a disavowal of women's agency 'in resisting and coping with personal victimization but also through collective opposition to inter-personal violence and/or war'. She maintains that this restrictive notion of agency is unjust and dangerous; agency can come to be seen as only residing in the perpetration of violence. We need to move towards a deeper analysis of these issues, she suggests, 'without either valorising the use of violence or ignoring women's agency within victimisation' (ibid.: 46–7). Similarly, Coulter also reminds us that being a victim of violence does not mean that one has no agency (2008: 66). Coulter suggests that humanitarian discourse and conflict research often present a stark division between 'victims' and 'perpetrators' of violence, where there is a conceptual slippage from victimization to victim*hood*: 'a victim of a violent *event* becomes a victim as a *person*', concealing their other roles and experiences and, furthermore, presenting them as powerless and lacking in agency (ibid.: 65–6). The other side of this dichotomous construct of victim-non-agent versus perpetrator-agent is equally problematic, as being a perpetrator of violence becomes imagined to be synonymous with agency in a complete free-will kind of way, which clearly has relevance for the representation and analysis of female combatants (ibid.: 67).

The implications of these comments are thought-provoking. Narrating women who have suffered violent or abusive events in war as victims *as people* is disempowering, inaccurate, and constitutes further victimization. Presenting female combatants as free agents making totally independent and rational choices, on the other hand, is equally simplistic and can lead us into the trap Kelly identifies of reifying violence as the only kind of power and agency available. Clearly the lived realities of female combatants are much more complicated than this. No one, in fact, ever has 'pure' agency; we are all shaped and constrained (though never fully determined) by the structures and prevailing discourses of our societies and the events of our lives; the decisions we take are made within particular circumscribed contexts. Sjoberg and Gentry describe this as 'relational autonomy', recognizing an interdependence of all choice: although 'choices are not independent of the gendered social and political contexts of their local and global worlds, women's actions also cannot be seen as entirely outside of the realm of their choice and their agency'; 'actors act in a world of relational autonomy where choice exists but is dependent on social context' (2007: 17, 203). Arguably, however, most mainstream discourses about women who commit violence, both in war and non-war contexts, still largely resist affording these women any kind of agency, circumscribed/relational or otherwise, hence the interest of researchers like myself in challenging this.

It has been argued in relation to non-war contexts that violent women are usually presented in hegemonic discourses as either 'mad' (stemming from their hormones or biology, or as having suffered some tragedy causing the 'madness') or 'bad' (evil creatures and the antithesis of 'normal' women) (Berrington and Honkatukia 2002 citing Ballinger 1996, 2000). When it comes to women committing especially heinous acts of violence, and particularly when this is done to other women or to children, we want to erase all agency from them (they are really victims), or to show how they are not real women (they are unfeminine) or not really human (they are monstrous). Morrissey's truly, deeply horrifying yet brilliant study of the representation of women murderers (2003) has shown this so well – my own gut reaction to parts of her book arguably proving her point. As has been discussed in the first half of this chapter, violence is seen as unfeminine even by some feminists. The 'mad/bad' categorization 'presents violent women as rare exceptions; unnatural and deviant from other women' (Berrington and Honkatukia 2002: 54) – in fact, women are 'doubly deviant' (ibid.: 50). This is no less the case for women who engage in organized and/or collective political violence, though in regard to military women I think there is the added construct of 'feminist bitch' (arguably falling into the 'mad' category) and 'pathetic pawn'. These constructs still present these women as deviant. Sjoberg and Gentry stress that '[w]omen's violence is often discussed in terms of violent women's gender: *women* are not supposed to be violent' (2007: 2). As I have noted elsewhere, 'the mere fact that it is necessary to specify "female combatants" indicates their historical rarity and symbolic position as unconventional figures' (Alison 2004b: 447). As with non-war contexts of women's violence, in wars

> [w]omen who participate in violence that is not endorsed by state governments are not described as women with particular characteristics, but as less than women and as less than human. Women's violence must be specially accounted for, and is often explained as a flaw in women's femininity and a flaw in their humanity.
>
> (Sjoberg and Gentry 2007: 10–11)

For Sjoberg and Gentry, women who participate in non-state (proscribed) violence are frequently portrayed in one (or more) of three ways: as mothers (fulfilling biological destinies to belong and nurture, in a maternalism gone askew); as monsters (irrational, insane, damaged; neither women nor human any longer); or as whores (sexually depraved or men's sexual pawns). In this way, these violent women are freakish and/or biological mistakes, in which case 'our image of real women as peaceful remains intact, and violent women cannot be held accountable for their actions' (2007: 13). In other words, these narratives are constraining and oppressive for *all* women. They 'define what violent women are (less than women; less than human; crazy, sexualized or controlled) but they also define what all women are (peaceful, incapable of violence, and in the personal rather than the political sphere)' (ibid.: 222). I contend, therefore, that if we do not seriously address women's violence and militarism and the specific contexts within which these operate we leave these women to continue to be read as deviant, as different from ourselves, as victims (in identity rather than experience), and as apolitical. Women's violence and militarism *matter* and require much greater investigation than they have received so far. There are dangers, it seems, both in making women's violence invisible *and* in overemphasizing it.

4 Enlistment of women in paramilitary organizations in Sri Lanka and Northern Ireland

In this chapter I begin to examine women's participation as combatants in Sri Lanka and Northern Ireland. As stated in the introduction to this book my interest is in non-state military groups and so women's participation in the state militaries of the two countries (which has been both quantitatively and qualitatively different) is not addressed in any detail. In this chapter I focus on the reasons for women's participation as combatants in non-state military groups in these places, both the motivating factors of the organizations to open up military roles to women and, more extensively, the motivations of women themselves. There are many parallels between the Tamil nationalist women and Irish republican women, though many context-specific differences as well. Loyalist women in Northern Ireland exhibit some interesting differences as well as similarities, lending support to the utility of a distinction between institutionalized state nationalism and anti-state 'liberatory' nationalism (discussed in Chapter 3), and they have no exact parallel in Sri Lanka.

This chapter is integrally interlinked with Chapters 5 and 6 and I do not provide any extensive conclusions here or in the subsequent two chapters, reserving this for the final chapter of the book where I provide a comparative analysis of factors affecting women's involvement in political violence in these cases and their gendered experiences of paramilitaries, trying to draw out implications for other cases as part of a wider set of conclusions. The next two chapters move to examine gender relations and experiences of female combatants within the paramilitary organizations under discussion, and the question of feminism in relation to these nationalist movements and communities.

As discussed in the introduction to this book, I conducted two periods of fieldwork in Sri Lanka: August–September 2002 and June–July 2004. In Ireland fieldwork was conducted January–June 2003, with one further interview conducted in October 2003. (See Appendix for a list of interviews.) All LTTE interviewee names given are their 'movement names' rather than their real names, or pseudonyms in the case of ex-members. Almost all names of Northern Ireland interviewees are pseudonyms and bear no resemblance to their real names. Those few names that remain unchanged were at the request of the interviewees. I have not specified which names are real and which are pseudonyms; no attempt should be made to guess.

Sri Lanka

Women have participated in both the Sri Lankan state's armed forces and in the Tamil nationalist organizations. The Sri Lankan Army (SLA) has been recruiting women since 1979 but these women have only recently been trained for combat duty, though they have been posted to the northeast since 1995. It seems that in line with the opening up of state militaries to women that has occurred in other countries, the greater drive in recent years to recruit women is largely attributable to the increasing difficulty in fulfilling the perceived security needs of the state without women's involvement. Given that Sri Lanka has been at war for 25 years and the military has lost many troops in combat, has a significant problem with desertion and an insufficient number of volunteers to fill their places, the mobilization of women is unsurprising. However as with other state militaries, such as Israel (mentioned in Chapter 3), despite their combat training the primary roles of the female soldiers still seem largely to be supportive, civilian and administrative, enabling more male soldiers to be used in combat (de Alwis 1998b; Sebastian 1996; Hettiarachchi 2001). This does not, however, explain the motivations of women joining the Sri Lankan military, a subject on which there does not seem to have been any significant research (at least not published in English). A study on women in the Sri Lankan state military would provide an interesting counterpoint to the research on militant Tamil nationalist women, particularly in regard to the notion of institutionalized state nationalism and women's position within this, but this was beyond the scope of this book. In contrast to the state military, women have been pivotally involved as combatants in the Tamil groups. Ismail has noted that the cadres of the Liberation Tigers of Tamil Eelam (LTTE, the Tamil Tigers or the Tigers) have been frequently referred to as 'the boys' or 'our boys' by many Sri Lankan Tamils (1995: 6). This gendered appellation is interesting when reflected upon in light of the prominent role of women in the LTTE, particularly since the 1990s, and the lively debates about women's involvement that have been conducted both in academic circles and within Tamil communities.

During the two periods of fieldwork in Sri Lanka I interviewed 17 LTTE combatant and ex-combatant women. I also interviewed or spoke to around 20 non-combatant Tamil and Muslim women, but unfortunately due to spatial limitations I am unable to incorporate these interviews in any systematic way. I focus here on examining what the LTTE combatants and ex-combatants said about themselves and their reasons for enlisting. The ages of the 17 women ranged between 21 and 33 at the time of interview and their ages at the time of enlistment ranged between 13 and 22, although the majority were in the younger end of this range; nine of them were 16 or under. Seven of them enlisted in 1990 and two in 1991, after the brutal IPKF period and at a time when the Women's Front had fully established its own independent structures and expanded training to the east. The others enlisted between 1993 and 1998. All but one volunteered; one was conscripted. All had received at least the basic LTTE weapons training and only two had not fought in battle; the majority had fought in combat many times. Some were still soldiers in the Military Wing while others had moved into various political and administrative posts in the Political Wing, some in very senior roles. They come from a range of places in the northeast, covering the four main historic Tamil centres – Jaffna, the Vanni, Batticaloa and Trincomalee – but are not necessarily posted near their homes; the LTTE often has a practice of moving cadres around. All but four described their families as 'middle-class', though many have fallen on harder times due to displacement; the other four are from much more impoverished backgrounds. Regarding religion, 13 are Hindu and four are Christian: two are Roman Catholic and two have converted from Hinduism to an unspecified Christian denomination. Those still with the LTTE generally do not consider themselves to be practising their religion, since the organization takes an avowedly secular position and argues religion is not necessary, though it also recognizes all religious festivals and does not prevent its members from maintaining a religious belief. Four of the interviewees are no longer LTTE members, while 13 still are (or were at the time of interview). All except four of the interviewees (the ex-members) were necessarily selected by the LTTE, rather than through random sampling or even self-selection. The easiest way to gain access to interviewees was by approaching LTTE Political Wing offices, and contacting ex-members was much more difficult. There are, of course, potentially problematic aspects to this.

Women in the LTTE

Women have been active in all the Tamil nationalist groups but research on their military participation has focused on the LTTE because their presence as combatants in substantial numbers has primarily been a phenomenon of the 1990s, by which point the LTTE had attained primacy among the groups. Women's participation in the tiny militant nationalist organizations in a military capacity in the 1970s was not at all widespread but in the 1980s appeals were made by the various groups for women to join the struggle. The Eelam People's Revolutionary Liberation Front (EPRLF) was the first to begin recruiting women (Samarasinghe 1996: 213) and by the mid-1980s they were joining various Tamil groups – at first mostly the People's Liberation Organization of Tamil Eelam (PLOTE) and the EPRLF, which had 'sizable numbers', with fewer joining the LTTE. Later on there was a rapid growth in the number of women in the LTTE (Hoole *et al.* 1990: 326) and they have 'continued to aggressively recruit women into their fighting cadres' (Samarasinghe 1996: 214). Initially these women were involved in propaganda work, medical care, information/intelligence gathering, fundraising and recruitment, but they were soon given military training and participated in combat.

Bose and Liyanage (among others) posit that this shift was simply a practical response on the part of the organization to an insufficiency of male fighters, as the young male population was decimated through combat, arrest and the refugee flow as the civil war deepened (Bose 1994: 109; Liyanage 1999: 129). However it seems more likely that this strategic need on the part of the LTTE coincided with a demand for entry on the part of young Tamil women themselves. A UK-based Tamil woman who has spent time with the Tigers in the Vanni area maintains that women were among the flood of Tamil youth trying to join the various militant groups after the 1983 anti-Tamil riots. They were initially turned away by the LTTE as it did not at that time have a policy of accepting women but women were eventually accepted through their own persistence; the subsequent policy change that allowed them to be militarily trained and used in combat, rather than just in auxiliary roles, was because they themselves kept asking for this. According to her, Prabhakaran, leader of the LTTE, persuaded the other men, many of whom were more resistant to the idea, to accept and encourage women (personal communication). Adele Ann, too, argues that much of the impetus for women's combat role came from Tamil women themselves, accepted and encouraged by Prabhakaran, who, '[u]nlike many of his fellow cadres caught up in male chauvinist conceptions of women and their place in society ... was determined that women should have equal opportunity for participation in all aspects of the armed struggle' (1993: 7). As mentioned in Chapter 2, Ann (Balasingham) is the white Australian-born wife of Anton Balasingham, the LTTE's chief ideologue and negotiator until his death in 2006, and she was involved in the early years of women's military training. She asserts that:

> The emergent aspirations of Tamil women to join the armed struggle brought increasing pressure on the LTTE leadership to step up it[s] policy of inducting women into the armed struggle. Young women demanded their right to self-defence and their right to exercise their patriotic sentiments. The LTTE leadership, committed to the emancipation and equality of women, welcomed such demands and expanded it's [*sic*] military programme for training women.
>
> (Ann 1993: 6)

The Tigers quite obviously have had an ongoing strategic need for women since the civil war really got under way and its negative effects on the Tamil community and, in particular, young Tamil men increased. However this is unlikely to be enough on its own to explain the cultural shift of female soldiers, especially the fact that they are not restricted to auxiliary jobs which would be more in accordance with conventional notions of appropriate gender roles. As I have argued elsewhere, the change in LTTE policy seems to me to have been the result of (1) a strategic need for more fighters in the face of an increasing insufficiency of men; (2) the ideological need to demonstrate that the LTTE is an all-encompassing mass social movement; and (3) pressure from young Tamil women themselves (Alison 2004b). I have also pointed out that the LTTE is among those militant nationalist groups around the world which, while utilizing female combatants in a variety of roles, have not hesitated to draw on gendered cultural expectations of their appearance (traditional saris or loose dresses) and behaviour (non-violent, non-threatening) to gain access to targets as suicide bombers much more easily than Tamil men would be able to (ibid.). Stack-O'Connor makes the same point and argues this was one of the LTTE's motivating factors in allowing women into the organization in more than auxiliary roles, suggesting four considerations here that influenced the decision of the LTTE leadership: (1) tactical advantage over state forces (in relation to the point just discussed); (2) demographics (the short supply of men); (3) competition with other Tamil militant groups; and (4) women's demands for active combat roles (2007). Given what I have argued elsewhere and here I obviously agree; however I think Stack-O'Connor underplays the ideological value in female fighters for the LTTE, though she does allude to this (ibid.: 48). As discussed in Chapter 3, Yuval-Davis argues that incorporating women into nationalist military organizations is a way of symbolically showing women's equal status in the collectivity and, therefore, presenting the movement as being truly a mass social movement concerned with all members of society (1997: 98). The LTTE presents itself as a revolutionary movement seeking widespread change within Tamil society rather than only independence from the Sri Lankan state; the images it presents of women's equality and removal of caste discrimination are an integral part of this programme, though both are fundamentally viewed as dependent upon national liberation.

In Hindu mythology there are a number of fierce and strong female goddesses (even warrior goddesses), such as Kali and Durga, many of whom are also mother-figures. Arguably Hindu mythology does not uniformly present women as inherently gentle or peaceful creatures. Nonetheless, Ann asserts that 'Tamil literature does not emphasise the active participation of women in combat. Instead, it glorifies the motherhood aspect' (1990). Never before have Sri Lankan Tamil women fought in combat (Ann 1993: 8). As there was no pre-existing tradition of armed female fighters the LTTE has, Schalk says, developed this role by drawing on examples from other contemporary nationalist struggles such as those of the Palestinians, the Eritrean liberation movement and the ANC in South Africa. They have also clearly looked to the Indian National Army (INA) of Subhash Chandra Bose, which fought British colonialism in India in the 1940s and trained women for combat. The INA has been a main source of inspiration to organize Sri Lankan Tamil women on the battlefront, as well to use organized suicide bomb squads (also including women) (Schalk 1994, 1992). Some Tamil feminists also argued for women's military role in the early days and may have contributed to the first wave of female volunteers. Within the wider Tamil movement in the early 1980s a key person to introduce the issue of female fighters was Nirmalā Nittiyānanantan: a lecturer in English, sociologist, political scientist, feminist writer and translator into Tamil of books on liberation struggles in Latin America and Africa. She was imprisoned by the Sri Lankan authorities in the early 1980s but was helped to escape from jail and went into exile, where she came to reject the LTTE (Schalk 1994: 175). Her sister, Rajani Thiranagama, was also originally an LTTE supporter and helped stimulate female recruitment but later 'openly repudiated what the group had stood for' (Hoole *et al.* 1990: xiv). Until her murder in 1989[1] Thiranagama was one of the members of University Teachers for Human Rights, which is opposed to the LTTE and the use of violence. A third sister, Cumati Civamokan, also took up the question of women fighters in the Tamil liberation movements, though both Civamokan and Thiranagama eventually rejected the idea, deciding that the use of violence was part of male chauvinism and therefore 'counteracted the cause of women's emancipation' (Schalk 1994: 175).

Because the notion of female combatants was not well established in Tamil society, Ann says that when women first joined the LTTE, '[g]reat care was taken not to upset the cultural values of the society at large. First aid, cooking etc. were the overt functions.... As time went on, the birds of freedom began to participate in fighting also.' From quite an early period in women's involvement they engaged in active combat but the women's division also 'integrated and co-ordinated activity with women['s] organisations, trade unions, training centres, health centres, and primary education centres'. After the signing of the Indo-Sri Lanka Accord in 1987, the women's division was involved in propaganda work 'to eradicate the false sense of confidence that people had in India'. At the military level, according to Ann, the preliminary operation against the Indian Peace Keeping Force (IPKF) was by women cadres and the first Tiger casualty in the war against the IPKF was a woman (Ann 1990). In 1983 the LTTE founded a special section for women called the Vituthalai Pulikal Munani (Women's Front of the Liberation Tigers) but they did not begin battle training for another two years. A popular name for the women fighters is 'Birds of Independence', after a journal of this name put out by the first women to receive military training (Schalk 1994: 163; 1992). The first group of women were trained for combat in a military camp in Tamil Nadu (India) in 1985 (a potential cohort having been gathered together in 1984) and their first battle was against the Sri Lankan military in July 1986. In October 1987 Prabhakaran set up the first all-women training camp in Jaffna – completely organized and implemented by the existing women cadres – for the second and subsequent groups. In this period eastern Tamil women who wanted to participate in direct combat had to move to the northern camps for training. In the east, women cadres were engaged in extremely dangerous intelligence-gathering activities as underground guerrillas from the mid-1980s and particularly during the IPKF period, though they also received weapons training. The first eastern military training camp for women was established in August 1990, after the second 'Eelam war' began. Initially the LTTE's combatant women were organized in female guerrilla units headed by a male commander but by September 1989 the women had their own independent structure as the Women's Military Wing; since then the leadership is female and all the women's camps and units are headed by women (Ann 1993).

The Women's Military Wing, like the rest of the LTTE, is well organized, very disciplined and extremely effective. According to Liyanage the LTTE's naval force, the Sea Tigers, is largely female (1999: 216) and the suicide squad, known as the Black Tigers, also has a large number of women in it (Bose 1994: 108; Samarasinghe 1996: 216). Until June 1990 the proportion of female fighters in the LTTE was small but it then increased rapidly (Schalk 1994: 165–6). The number of female combatants is largely a military secret but in 1991 the Tigers stated a figure of 3,000 – apparently about 15–20 per cent of their core combat strength (Bose 1994: 108; Schalk 1994: 165–6). An unconfirmed rumour was also apparently spread by the Tigers in Jaffna that women represented 50 per cent of their fighters in December 1991. Schalk, however, claims this is 'wishful thinking on the part of the LTTE' (Schalk 1994: 166), again hinting at the ideological/symbolic value in women's military participation. Nonetheless, others still claim that the LTTE's women cadres make up 50 per cent or more of its fighting force (Samuel 2001: 195). The UK-based Tamil woman I mentioned previously suggested that women are about one-third of the LTTE's strength (personal communication). In 1997 an estimated number was still around 3,000 (Subramaniam 1997) while in 2002, 4,000 was an estimate (Bulathsinghala 2002b).

Motivations of female combatants for enlistment in the LTTE

It is generally known that the LTTE asks each Tamil family to contribute one member to the organization (Trawick 1999: 143), though I have heard that financial support is accepted instead. The issue of conscription notwithstanding, the majority of recruits seem to be voluntary. There are a range of different and often intersecting reasons why women have chosen to join the militants; most of these are likely to be common to female and male combatants, while others are gender-specific to women. There is rarely one single identifiable motivating factor in the women's decisions to enlist in the LTTE; more usually, a number of the factors that I have tried to identify and separate out here are interlocking in their effects.

TAMIL NATIONALISM

Bose argues that LTTE women, like LTTE men, are primarily motivated by 'nationalist fervour.' He suggests that by the time of the mid- to late-1980s drive for women to join the Tigers, 'Tamil nationalism, in its radical form, had been transformed into a mass phenomenon ... and women of the younger generation of Tamils were as alienated from the state, and as inspired by the vision of a liberated Eelam, as their male counterparts' (Bose 1994: 109, 111). This was largely borne out in my own research. Of the 16 women I interviewed who said they had voluntarily joined the LTTE, nine referred explicitly to nationalist ideas of freedom for the Tamil nation, self-determination, land and/or rights for Tamils (though this was not always expressed in terms of a determination for a fully independent state) as part of or as the main reason for them enlisting. Two others explicitly articulated nationalist ideas which they had come to view as important since joining the Tigers. It seemed to me that nationalism or nationalist ideology was a meta-reason for enlistment, beneath which there are other reasons, many of which intersect with or feed into nationalism and some of which are more personal or specific to the individual.

Krishna is from the Vanni but when I met her she was posted in the east as the Women's Political Wing Leader for Trincomalee District. She has been with the movement since 1990 when she enlisted at age 20. Krishna maintained that 'herein, there are three communities – Tamils, Sinhalese, Muslims.... Either you must be parallel to the Sinhalese and live together in harmony with the same status; if not, the Tamils must be separated and live happily with their own self-determination.' Furthermore, 'the north and east is the homeland of the Tamils, so they must govern themselves through themselves, with equal status with the Sinhalese.' Sailajah joined the LTTE in 1990 at age 21 and is also from the Vanni, but was posted in the east to the LTTE-controlled area of Kokadichcholai near Batticaloa as Cultural Affairs Leader when I interviewed her. Like Krishna, she said 'In the early days the north and east were a Tamil nation, therefore it must be given to the Tamils.' When I clarified what she meant by 'given to the Tamils' she said she wanted an independent state but argued (untruthfully, or at least incorrectly) that all Tamils wanted that, that this was not an individual opinion nor just an LTTE opinion. Prasanthi, who is from Trincomalee (though she was posted in the north for many years before returning) argued that

> There is discrimination between the races, so there must be no discrimination. But the language also, and cultural also; we have been penalized for being Tamil, and socially and economically as well we have been treated differently, discriminated against. So there must be no discrimination – that is equal rights.

Barathy, a soldier from the Jaffna peninsula, joined the LTTE in 1996 at the age of 16. She seemed to be a serious young woman who wanted to practise her English language skills on me, asserting in English that the 'Sri Lankan government did not respect our rights, they did not respect us, the Tamil people'. She felt that the Tamils must have freedom, by which she meant 'we have to have … a homeland for us, a separate homeland. We have … rights like Sinhalese and other Western countries.'

Thamilini, from the Jaffna peninsula, enlisted in 1990 at the age of 18. She is the overall Women's Political Wing Leader for the LTTE and is gracious and hospitable with visitors. Her view was that 'after we get the land, our people will be free'. She spoke about Sinhalese oppression since independence, Tamil language rights, and a 'freedom struggle' against the government, whom she blames for beginning the war. Furthermore:

> Not only people involved in war died but even the normal people who haven't been in the war died, so I thought instead of losing life for no reason let me fight for my country and give it; that will make me feel proud.… I want to make my life a meaningful life, … that's why I joined.

Thamilvily, also from the Jaffna peninsula, enlisted in 1995 at the age of 17. When I met her in 2002 she was the Women's Political Wing Leader for Jaffna District but on my return in 2004 I was told that she had been promoted to Thamilini's second-in-command. She is a tall, strong, friendly woman with a striking face and ready smile, as well as a seemingly irrepressible amount of physical energy, finding it hard to sit still. She claimed that

> We have witnessed the adverse effects of shelling and military action; we have seen people die and be injured. When we ask why, we see it is that we

> are not free and are at the mercy of the military. This is common to all Tamil people. So I joined the LTTE.

In the context of the ceasefire which was in its early months at the time of the interview, Thamilvily also said

> Everyone ... in this country needs peace, especially the Tamil people need peace because since 1948, since independence, they have been discriminated against ... and it should be peace with dignity and self-respect, which recognizes our nationhood and which gives us fair autonomy and fair share in the government.

Furthermore,

> Our political goals and path leading to the goals should be determined by us, not anybody else. So you know, we are ... a national ethnic group, and we are ... entitled to a homeland. That has not yet been accepted by all parties.... Sinhala parties must accept the fact that we are entitled to, we have a right to a traditional, our traditional homeland. So what we mean by self-determination is as a national ethnic group we are entitled to our home.

For Geetha, who enlisted at the age of 16 in 1993, poverty was the primary motivating factor but her experiences with the Tigers and the loss of two sisters in battle increased her sense of nationalism:

> Initially as I was young, I did not know much about the motive of the LTTE and joined it in order to support my family. But as time passed by, I learnt the motive and hence wanted to fight for the cause. After I lost my two sisters, this spirit got strengthened further and I wanted to fight for it.... I support the LTTE struggle as it is for a good cause of separate Tamil Eelam.

For Kailaivily, desperation as a result of displacement was her motivation for enlisting but since being with the Tigers she has clearly become committed to nationalist ideas:

> We all fought only to live. We did not want to get fired on like dogs by the enemies and also we did not want to surrender to the army and work under them. We wanted to live on our own. We should have our own government and leader elected by us. In the way to achieve a society and a living for us, we lost some lives and we accept that. There are obstacles like these in our way to freedom. But we are ready to face them.... Right now we have not got our own nation. Still, Sri Lankan government wants to play communal politics. We are determined to have our own nation. Our main aim now is to have a separate nation for us.

SUFFERING AND OPPRESSION: FAMILY LOSS, DISPLACEMENT AND COMMUNAL TRAUMA

One motivation to enlist, intimately intertwined with nationalist ideology, is the experience and perception of Tamil suffering, oppression and injustice. Sometimes this is related to a personal or family experience; sometimes it has been received as part of the Tamil narrative of oppression and suffering, borne out by the experiences of one's friends and neighbours. Ann argues that '[g]rowing national oppression ... brought about a situation where Tamil women took to arms' (1990). Thus, '[c]onstant exposure to oppression has had a profound effect on the life and thinking of young Tamil women' (Ann 1993: ii). She claims that the women cadres were often 'from families affected cruelly by the war. In some cases, personal experience was the motivating factor' (1990). Other research has found evidence to back this up. In an interview with Trawick, Sita made it clear that she and many other combatants were motivated to join the LTTE because of their anger at the deaths of loved ones at the hands of the Sri Lankan military and police. An older brother of hers was killed by the STF in 1985 and another brother was killed at Vantarmullar University in 1990. After the 'troubles' of 1990 she and her sister joined the LTTE. She clearly emphasized that it was the death of her brothers that prompted her decision: 'my brothers were killed, and out of rage, I joined the movement'; 'I wanted to die as my brothers died' (Trawick 1999: 151–3, 157).

Direct personal or family loss as a motivation for some cadres to join the movement was substantiated in my own research, though a sense of communal Tamil suffering seemed to be even more significant. Four women mentioned the death of an immediate family member. Banuka's father was killed by the Sri Lankan Army in 1990 (she is from the Vanni area) and she gave this as a major reason for enlisting, speaking of a loss of safety and security. She joined in 1993, at the age of 16, and later became the Women's Political Wing Leader for Batticaloa-Amparai District. She is a slight woman with a beautiful smile but a clear air of authority. Malarville, from Batticaloa, experienced the killing of her father by the SLA in 1987 when she was about 11, which affected her deeply. She told me that after she lost her father, her 'mental situation' was very bad and she could not immediately think of joining the LTTE, but three years later she did. She specifically stated that the death of her father was one of the main reasons she joined. She lost one leg in combat in 1993 and now works in the Political Wing in Batticaloa-Amparai District. Thamilnila's father was killed in a boat massacre in Jaffna in 1985 (allegedly perpetrated by the Sri Lankan navy in plain clothes), when she was a child. When I asked why she joined the LTTE, the first thing she said was 'One thing that affected me was I was deprived of a parent, of my father, and that was causing me agitation.' However she did not actually join until 1998, at the age of 18. She is a photographer for the LTTE and has been to the battlefield documenting the fight, not as a soldier, though of course she has had the basic military training. She is a tiny woman with a huge bright smile who looks much younger than her age, with an air of innocence and fragility even after four years in the LTTE. I could not picture her trying to survive combat and take photographs of the chaos. Thamilachi's brother died as an LTTE martyr in 1990. Her family was supporting the LTTE by sheltering and assisting cadres; she noted that 'we were already convinced about the justness of the struggle', but her brother's death hastened her own decision to join, which she did in 1991 at the age of 21. She reported that before this she had been involved in student movements since she was a teenager, helping people affected by the war and displacement. She was working towards her A Levels when her brother died and said that at that time the LTTE encouraged students to continue their education and did not ask students to join, but 'what I felt was there was a void, there was a certain vacuum that has got to be filled, a vacuum created by my brother's death, that has to be filled'.

Six of the women mentioned that their families had been displaced and this was clearly a contributory factor for many in their decision to enlist. Malarville's family was displaced from Batticaloa; after the death of her father she gave not being able to live in her own home and having 'no security' as reasons she joined. Thamilvily's family was displaced to the Vanni in 1995 after her village in Jaffna was bombed and she told me (in English) that 'all our people is dying and is wounding. Bad situation. My feeling is: not accept.' Like Thamilvily, Barathy's family was displaced when the army retook much of the Jaffna peninsula in 1995 and she enlisted the following year. When asked why she joined the Tigers she mentioned the displacement and the occupation of Jaffna, the subsequent lack of food and the deaths of fellow students through aerial bombing. Thamilnila's family was also displaced and she gave this as the secondary reason she joined the LTTE, after the death of her father. Sudarvili's family, also from the Jaffna peninsula, was displaced more than once. While on the move during one displacement she witnessed a horrific massacre, which also contributed to her desire to stop the insecurity and suffering her community was experiencing by joining the LTTE. She said that 'we feel this is the only way, to keep fighting against the military and safeguard the people'. She joined in 1998 at the age of 19 and has fought in combat since 1999. Kalaivily was also displaced with her family from Jaffna city in 1995, to an IDP camp in the Vanni. Like many LTTE members she is from the *Karayar* caste (fishing people) and her family was not able to fish after they were displaced. She had been a primary school teacher in Jaffna but was unable to continue this in the Vanni. Her family survived in the Vanni by doing agricultural labour for others, and after a year she joined the LTTE at the age of 22.

> Leading a life in [the] Vanni was very difficult when we came there. Daily basic necessities could not be met. There were diseases such as malaria was spreading. We did not even get medicine. We did not get basic items such as kerosene and oil for cooking. We thought that getting our land back is the best solution to get rid of poverty.

Ten cadres I interviewed spoke of their areas coming under attack by the military during the war, their anger over the suffering of people in their communities, and/or witnessing violence, and gave this as a partial or primary reason for enlisting. Sudarvili heard many stories about the St Peter's Church bombing and other incidents, and also witnessed a massacre, stating that

> our people have been suffering.... The common places and the churches and the kovils [Hindu temples] was bombed by the government, without any reason.... [W]e don't have anybody to save us, and what we feel is if we have someone to safeguard us then there won't be any problem. Because of the occupation of the army we have been forced to take the arms in our hands.

Prasanthi said that at the time she joined (at the age of 14 in 1990) Trincomalee was always being attacked by the military; the family of one of her classmates was killed, she saw people being cut and thrown into fires, and people being dragged off buses and killed. Thamilini witnessed suffering and violence all around her and used to see dead bodies every day. One of her classmates was killed in an Air Force bomb attack. Thamilachi said that

> the time I joined, about 1990, was perhaps the worst in this ongoing war.... And we had seen with our own eyes children who had been orphaned, parents who had lost their children. And there was no question of these children getting minimum education.... So what we saw, at that juncture, only convinced us that something must be done, there was an urgent need to do something.

For Thamilvily,

> in 1995 I was there during [a] bomb blast, where I saw a lot of people suffering for their lives, some without legs, hands; children helpless without their mother.... On personally seeing that has made some changes within myself. I already had a feeling to fight for my nation; this event has made me join [the LTTE].

EDUCATIONAL DISRUPTION AND RESTRICTIONS

Given the importance accorded in the literature on Sri Lankan Tamil nationalism to the scheme known as 'standardization', which has effectively discriminated against Tamils in university entrance, I was expecting this to be given by some of the interviewees as a motivating factor for joining the LTTE. In the Panos oral testimony project the standardization system is mentioned as one reason for young Tamils (female and male) to take up arms.[2] However what was revealed in my own research was that in recent years, perhaps more significant than the standardization system (Thamilini was the only woman to specifically mention this) has been the general disruption to all levels of education caused by the war, particularly linked to experiences of displacement. If one is prevented from even completing high school it is impossible to get access to tertiary education for this reason – without even factoring in the impact of standardization.

Eight of the interviewees discussed disruption to education (either their own or more generally) as a result of displacement and war, and the importance of education. Four of these women specifically included educational disruption as part of the reason they joined. Sudarvili said (in English) 'I wanted to continue my studies, but I was unable to continue my studies by the army operations. Again and again we were displaced.... When I was studying AL [Advanced Level], I was unable to take exam, so I decided to join our movement.' She does not want this disruption to education to happen to future generations and wanted to help stop this. Thamilini was also studying for A Levels when she joined the movement at the age of 18, and wanted to go on to university. Her A Levels were in 1990 and the war situation was so bad at that time that it was extremely difficult to study. More generally, Banuka said 'Only when we have a peaceful country, we can study safely and have freedom to do our own things; without that we cannot do our schooling safely.'

POVERTY

It is sometimes assumed that people who join guerrilla or 'terrorist' organizations in various parts of the world must come from impoverished and uneducated backgrounds. This is by no means always the case. In regard to the LTTE, though class categories do not necessarily translate well to the Sri Lankan context (particularly with the added context of caste) it seemed to me that most of the interviewees identified as or roughly translated to lower middle-class. Not all of them were prepared to talk about caste and, in retrospect, I did not ask about this as much as I should have. It seemed clear that many of them had middle-class aspirations to education and professional employment; aspirations which were thwarted by the various impacts of the war. Many came from families whose fortunes and social standing had dropped due to displacement and other war outcomes. It seemed to me that these disjunctures between past and present, between aspiration and reality, were at least as significant, or more so, as outright poverty. However four of the interviewees did come from family backgrounds of extreme poverty and I admit that poverty may be a more significant factor than it appeared to be in my work and that the LTTE may have strategic publicity reasons for wishing to downplay this, perhaps feeling it diminishes their ideological basis. It may be no coincidence that none of the four interviews with women who come from quite destitute backgrounds was arranged through the LTTE. (One of these women was conscripted; she is discussed in a later section.)

Shanthi joined the Tigers at the age of 15, in 1991. She is from an impoverished family in a northeastern border village that has suffered frequent attacks from all sides in the conflict. The interview was arranged on my 2002 trip through a Sinhalese woman who runs a women's group in the area and who works for a local government organization trying to improve the desperate economic situation in the area. Interpretation was extremely difficult with this interview, dealing with three languages without a professional interpreter (English to Sinhala, Sinhala to Tamil and vice versa). I was not able to access any of her own words and I know there is so much of her story I do not understand. From what I could gather, at the age of ten Shanthi was withdrawn from school and sent to live with a family in Jaffna, to be raised as their daughter; her biological family was financially unable to care for all their children. However after five years the family she lived with moved to India and left her behind (I was not able to establish how this came about). Alone at 15 with little connection to her biological family, afraid of the SLA and the police and with no means of support, she joined the LTTE. She fought in battle five times, being so seriously wounded in 1996 that she has been advised not to marry since having children would paralyse or kill her (her body is riddled with shrapnel). After her injury she joined the Political Wing and as a reward for her cleverness in battle she was made the LTTE area leader for a village on the Jaffna peninsula. After nine years in the movement she wrote to her biological mother (who had been unaware that she was in the LTTE) and her mother travelled to Jaffna, tracked her down and insisted she come back to her village. Shanthi struck me as bored, frustrated and restless; she has had no job since returning to the village and appeared to miss the sense of purpose and family she had with the Tigers. She seemed to be waiting: waiting for a job, waiting for peace, waiting for the LTTE to come and make everything better in the village.

When I returned to Sri Lanka in 2004 I was only able to revisit the north, as the east was too dangerous at the time. On this visit I spent most of my time in the LTTE-controlled Kilinochchi area in the Vanni. While on a visit to Jaffna I met, quite by chance, two women who were ex-members of the LTTE and I arranged to interview them when we had all returned to Kilinochchi a few days later. Geetha, from the Vanni area, described her family as very poor and one of her brothers is severely physically disabled. She attended school only until the age of 14, when she left to work in the fields to try and support her family. Two years later she joined the LTTE. She identified economic reasons as being why she enlisted and said 'our families are looked after by the LTTE'. Her older brother had joined the Tigers in 1990 but was allowed to leave in 1993 to help support the family, at which point Geetha enlisted instead. Her two younger sisters also enlisted, one in 1994 and one in 1999; both have been killed – one was killed in battle in front of Geetha in 1996. She fought in many battles and in 1998 was injured; she still has a piece of shell in her head, which cannot be removed and gives her recurrent headaches. She left the LTTE at the end of 1999, with permission, to help care for her mother (her father left in 1998), and reported that the Tigers gave her some money to help with her family.

Thangachi seems to come from an even more impoverished family in the Vanni area. She attended school only until the age of 13, in 1994, when she joined the LTTE. Her grandparents were from a washermen caste, one of the lower 'service castes'. Her parents are illiterate and unable to work due to health problems. Her father was badly beaten by the IPKF, leading to clots in his stomach. He now has cancer (which she attributes to the same cause). Her mother suffers from a rare skin disease which means she cannot go out in daylight. The family has barely been able to survive. 'Since I was from a poor family, I could not wear better clothes. I was dirty and ugly. I got beatings from my school teacher that I was dirty.... I was not going to school neat and clean like other children.' One older sister joined the LTTE, two years before her, and was killed in 1999. Her younger twin sisters have also since joined, in 2000. Thangachi said that she was worried she would be a burden on her parents, and she believed that if she joined the LTTE her family would be taken care of – though she reported that in fact this did not happen, other than a small amount of compensation when her sister was killed. Nationalism and/or political consciousness were no part of her motivation for enlisting in the movement: 'I did not join LTTE because of any of these reasons. It was only poverty which forced me to join.' When I asked why she had thought joining the LTTE would improve her family's impoverished situation, she replied:

> I was a child. I did not realize those things. I thought that if I join LTTE I would lead a better life. We were struggling even to get food. If I join LTTE, at least these basic needs of mine would be taken care of. Moreover, if I join LTTE, I would be able to grow better, I would be able to study something and learn something. When I joined, they made me study. But, after joining LTTE, worries about my family started. I was getting good food. They took care of me very well. But, worries about my family grew everyday. I could not study well.

She was 16 when she first fought in battle and after only about a year she was severely injured in her leg, which has left her with a lasting disability hindering her mobility. After this she performed menial labour tasks for the Tigers until she deserted in 2000. Although she has since been threatened, she believes they are no longer looking for her. She is now the sole earner providing for her family. Thangachi's visible desperation was moving; she cried at a number of points during the interview and said 'I never reveal my history to others.... I am telling for the first time to you [crying]. I am happy that someone listened to me patiently.'

SEXUAL VIOLENCE AGAINST WOMEN

It seems clear that as well as motivational factors common to both women and men, there are some reasons for taking up arms that are gender-specific to women. Ann claims that in regard to women's recruitment, the presence of the IPKF 'was a water shed. The Indian army was brutal and male chauvinist. The rapes, and molesting made a bitter impact' (1990). Bose agrees, saying the IPKF presence in the northeast from 1987 to 1990 'was marked by hundreds of rapes and assaults on women by Indian soldiers, yet another instance of the violence of the state abetting oppositional strategies of social mobilisation' (1994: 109). Sexual violence was not confined only to the IPKF period, however; sexual violence against Tamil women by Sinhalese military members and police is also an ongoing problem. Subramaniam reports on a letter sent from a young female LTTE recruit to her brother in Colombo, a member of a formerly militant group. She castigates him and other ex-militant Tamil groups as 'traitors to our cause'. The young woman asserts 'I want to do something. Staying at home and getting widowed at some stage or waiting to be sexually abused by Sinhalese soldiers is no life' (1997).

This idea that the fear and reality of rape are sometimes a factor motivating women to join the Tamil militants seems to be borne out. When I raised the issue of sexual violence against women by the IPKF and the Sri Lankan state forces (or this came up independently on the part of interviewees), ten of the women discussed this as a reason for women in general to join the LTTE and fear of or anger about this was part of their own reasoning for four of them. None reported having suffered sexual violence themselves but they may well not have felt comfortable discussing this. Thamilachi and Shanthi both reported that although this was not part of their own decision to enlist they had met many female cadres who had suffered sexual violence, were very angry and had joined for that reason: 'I must ... tell you there are a lot of young women who were affected during the IPKF days and who have been raped at the hands of the Sri Lanka forces, and they are in the movement. So they feel they are secure' (Thamilachi). Thamilachi also mentioned the infamous case of the rape and murder of schoolgirl Krishanthi, claiming that 'had she been in the movement she would have been safe'. These comments also illustrate the useful propaganda value that the LTTE has found in fostering fear of sexual violence and promoting the image of the LTTE as the protector and the safest place for women to be.

In the context of a question about whether she felt that being in the LTTE has been good for her, Barathy volunteered (in English) that 'particularly in the Jaffna peninsula, Tamil girls are raped by the Sri Lankan Army. I am a female; I have to liberate the Tamil women from the occupation. So I, we are, also fighting for the women's liberation.' When I then asked if fear of rape was part of her reason to join the Tigers, she answered 'Yes, it was part of the reason for joining. Everyone has to protect themselves.... And also I have to protect the Tamil people.' Similarly, Thamilini answered that the fear of sexual violence was a part of her motivation, because she felt that there was nobody who could protect her – she had to be able to safeguard herself. She maintained that only relatively few women and girls were actually raped or assaulted, but this created such a climate of fear that all girls and women were afraid of it. She also said that in normal society women are usually blamed for their own rape; she claimed that the LTTE does not do this and instead views sexual violence as an 'accident', meaning that it was not the victim's fault. Sailajah stated that from an early age she knew that women were 'suppressed' by the army, including through sexual violence, and one of her reasons for joining the LTTE was the desire to 'deliver the women' from this.

WOMEN'S EMANCIPATION/EQUALITY

As well as the fear of or anger about rape, it has been suggested that some women have joined the LTTE for a variety of reasons surrounding ideas of women's emancipation and increasing their life opportunities. All the Tamil militant groups have expressed some form of commitment to women's liberation within their commitment to national liberation. It has been argued that for the LTTE 'its female cadres are the ultimate symbol of women's liberation' (Subramaniam 1997) and women 'are said to achieve liberation from oppressive gender roles through active combat' (Trawick 1999: 141). It has even been suggested that 'in a society that continues to be fiercely male-dominated, the use of feminist ideas and terminology seems to have been a powerful magnet that attracted, and continues to attract, women to the organisation' (Subramaniam 1997). Bose suggests that it is possible 'that many women have joined the movement at least partly because they see their participation as a means of breaking taboos, and, in particular, destroying the stultifying straitjacket of conformity and subservience traditionally imposed upon them by a rigidly and self-righteously patriarchal society' (1994: 111). Ann maintains that the choice by a Tamil woman to join the LTTE 'tells society that they are not satisfied with the social status quo; it means they are young women capable of defying authority; it means they are women with independent thoughts; young women prepared to lift up their heads' (1993: 9). In joining the armed struggle Tamil women 'broke the shackles of social constraints, they ripped open the straight jacket of conservative images of women' (ibid.: 5–6). In joining the Tigers, Trawick notes also, '[w]omen are rewarded by freedom from constraints on physical mobility' (1999: 159). Schalk asserts that '[t]he main belief of the Tamil women fighters is that their participation in armed struggle will bring them advantages in future, in a society at peace. This is one of their principal motives for taking up arms.' Their fundamental objective is the independence of Tamil Eelam, so '[i]n their minds, these two objectives are connected: there will be no equality for women without an independent state' (1994: 163, see also 1992). My own research suggests that Schalk (and others) over-emphasize ideas of improving women's situation as being a 'principal motive' for women joining the movement, but certainly he is right that according to the ideology of the LTTE the only way for women to gain equality is through the nationalist movement (this is addressed further in the next chapter).

The majority of the women I interviewed said that they had not been aware of issues pertaining to women's social conditions, women's rights or equality before they joined the movement. However, all of them have had this awareness raised since being with the movement and many of them now seem to have a clear commitment to wanting to improve life for Tamil women (discussed in the next chapter). Five of the interviewees reported that they had had some ideas about social problems facing women before they joined the LTTE and a further two indicated they had had some vague ideas about this but were not really aware of or able to articulate this until they joined the Tigers. Four of these women indicated this as part of their reason for enlistment. When asked why she enlisted in the LTTE, Sailajah's first response was that she 'wanted to get freedom for the women … in the society'. After nationalist ideas of self-determination, Krishna also said that 'women are not equally treated'; she felt that if she joined she would be able to contribute towards changing this.

Sumathi is from the Jaffna peninsula but has been posted to the east since she enlisted at the age of 14, in 1990. She was in the Military Wing for four years before being transferred to the Political Wing, working in their publication division writing for the women's journal *Birds of Freedom*. When asked why she made the decision to enlist in the LTTE, alongside witnessing many people being killed and wanting to help achieve 'Tamil rights', Sumathi also said that when she was growing up at home there were some 'superstitions' surrounding female behaviour – that girls should not climb trees, go out alone or ride bicycles, for example – and she rebelliously 'wanted to break everything'. She stated that even at a young age she had had a desire to help 'deliver' women from their problems. Her family and others in the community tried to tell her when she was a child that there were no women cadres in the LTTE but she got to hear about them anyway and knew they were engaged in all the things she was prohibited from, 'doing all activities similar to men'; she felt 'they are doing everything, so why can't I?' When she finally met some women cadres with their weapons, she knew she wanted to join the movement. Sumathi is a solidly built woman with the look of what was called when I was a child a 'tomboy'. I could vividly picture her as a rebellious small girl railing against the restrictions of her life.

Sudarvili, a soldier, said of herself and other female cadres that despite societal expectations,

> we are able to see that the boys have joined the LTTE and are doing something, so we thought, if they can, why we can't do these things? The whole crowd is not thinking like that, few people are thinking that way, and the people who thought like that have joined the LTTE.

She asserted that 'through our struggle for liberation we are fighting for the women's liberation also.... [W]e will free the girls in this country, not only within the movement, outside also.' When I asked if she had had these ideas before joining the movement, she answered 'I had these ideas before, but most of the women cadres did not. I had a question why these girls were oppressed by these men.' She hoped to assist the struggle for women's liberation as well as Tamil national liberation but was unsure whether or not she could; once she joined she became convinced that she could do this within the movement.

NON-ENLISTMENT: CONSCRIPTION TO THE LTTE

The LTTE denies charges of using child soldiers, referring to its commitment of May 1998 to the Special Representative of the UN Secretary General for Children in Armed Conflict that it would not recruit children under the age of 17 and would not deploy them in combat under the age of 18. Of my 17 interviewees ten were under the age of 18 when they enlisted. Of these, nine were under 17 and six were under 16. Thangachi was the youngest at 13. The majority of those who were under the age of 18 when they enlisted did fight in combat before they were 18, but admittedly in all these cases this was well before 1998. Barathy said that normally the LTTE would only accept recruits at the age of 18 or over; she was accepted at 16 at the end of 1996 but only, she said, after she repeatedly begged them to take her. A number of times they returned her to her home but she kept going back until they accepted her. She said they would not, however, let her fight in combat until she was 18. This is a deeply contentious area and it is impossible to say how representative Barathy's experience is and to what extent there is variation between different LTTE districts and commanders. It is also difficult to tell to what degree the LTTE monitored this in terms of the cadres they selected for me to interview. The only two women I interviewed who joined after 1998 were 18 and 19 respectively at the time. It is possible that this was deliberate but I cannot tell either way. Regardless, there is too much (recent) evidence from human rights organizations and UNICEF of the continued LTTE recruitment of child soldiers, and indeed an upsurge in their recruitment drive during the 2002–8 ceasefire, for their denials to be believed (Human Rights Watch 2004; Keairns 2003, 2002).

It is true that a great many child soldiers – possibly the majority, at least prior to the 2002 ceasefire – have approached the LTTE themselves, wanting to join, as is the case for all but one of the women I interviewed who enlisted under the age of 18. On the other hand, the organization's relentless propaganda campaign has a lot to do with this. Many of the interviewees mentioned attending LTTE meetings and speaking with cadres, or having them talk at their schools, but identified themselves as having chosen to enlist rather than being forced. Thangachi, however, describes her mother's pain when her youngest daughters enlisted. She is convinced that the LTTE pressured them into it:

> My younger sisters were studying in school. There was a school day function. There, people from LTTE came and asked them about their family. My sisters told them that one elder sister was an LTTE cadre and died in war, and another sister is a cadre. So LTTE people [said] 'your elder sister died while fighting enemies for LTTE, her rifles are down now, both of you should join LTTE and continue fighting the enemies where she had left'.... Every day they used to canvass my sisters to join the LTTE. They used to talk to both of them daily and persuaded them to join. My younger sisters are twins. They are affectionate to each other. All activities, they used to do together.

Leaving aside the issues of children volunteering to enlist and others being pressured into it, it is also well substantiated that the LTTE does forcibly conscript children and that this has increased since the 2002 ceasefire (Human Rights Watch 2004). A fear of this was expressed by some Tamil mothers I met in the north. This is, of course, one of those issues that is used as political mileage. The Sri Lankan government and organizations opposed to the LTTE have made a consistent point of alleging, at both the national and international level, that the LTTE conscripts children. The LTTE and its supporters deny this, saying the Tigers only want members who want to be there and are committed and that often families who claim their child has been conscripted, or ex-members, make these claims to try and protect themselves from the wrath of the Sri Lankan military and authorities. Non-combatant Tamils I spoke to were divided in opinion on conscription; some seemed to believe this was a lie made up to slander the image of the LTTE, while others (including some who support the LTTE on the whole), assert that it has happened and continues to happen.

Of the women I interviewed only one said she had been conscripted – unsurprisingly this interview was not arranged through the LTTE. I have called this woman Kavitha; she said her own name would be fine but I was concerned for her safety so I chose to assign her a different name instead. Kavitha lives in the same impoverished northeastern border village as Shanthi and the interview was arranged through the same Sinhalese local government woman; the same difficulties with interpretation also apply. Kavitha was 28 when I interviewed her and said she was forcibly conscripted by the LTTE from her Batticaloa boarding school in 1990, with a group of classmates, when she was 15. They kept her for ten months and she went through the weapons training, though was never in combat. When she became seriously ill she was released and sent home, after which she was immediately arrested for having been in the LTTE and was imprisoned for a year, being beaten and tortured with electrical currents for information about the organization. In 1991 her father disappeared; the family believe the SLA was responsible, as further retaliation for her having been with the Tigers. Three months after her release from prison she married, at the age of 18, and now has three children and is a Montessori teacher. There was so much about her story I wished I could ask – how did she feel about being married so soon after coming out of a situation of torture and imprisonment, for example? The interview context made any deep understanding impossible; all I got was the bare bones of her story. Alongside the considerable interpretation difficulties there was the added burden of the presence of her husband and a male friend. With them, interpreters, and the people who took me to meet Kavitha, there was a total of seven people in the room – not an ideal interview situation under any circumstances but certainly not for talking about paramilitary conscription and torture. Amazingly, as far as I was able to gather, Kavitha did not appear to bear a significant grudge towards either side. Despite her conscription she supports the LTTE's political agenda, though not their methods.

Northern Ireland

Women have participated in both republican and loyalist paramilitaries in Northern Ireland in a variety of roles but have been more active in military roles in republican groups than in loyalist ones. Porter suggests that 'the nominal claim to socialist credentials in republicanism provides an ideological space for egalitarianism. The conservative leanings in much [of] loyalism stultify gender equality' (1998: 44). Women have also been present in the Royal Ulster Constabulary (RUC), the Ulster Defence Regiment (UDR) and the British military, but since the focus of this work is on non-state military groupings women's roles in the various state forces are not covered here.[3] Sales suggests that the conflict in

Northern Ireland 'has presented new yet contradictory possibilities' for women. New opportunities opened up as women took on roles more usually performed by men, as men abandoned them through imprisonment, military activity or death. On the other hand, she says, men have also sometimes increased their efforts to control women and prevent their entry into the public sphere. She also points out that the changes wrought and new possibilities opened up have been different for nationalist and unionist women, because nationalists have been fighting for change while unionists have fought to defend the status quo (1997b: 70).

During my fieldwork in Ireland I interviewed 11 republican ex-combatant women and two loyalist ex-combatant women. I tried persistently to gain access to more female loyalist ex-combatants but ultimately had to concede defeat. I also interviewed two other loyalist women who were active in auxiliary roles (such as transporting and hiding weapons) and who were wives of male loyalist prisoners, one who made petrol bombs at the beginning of the 'Troubles', and one who may have been active but was evasive about the extent of her involvement. To try and round out the loyalist perspective a little I also interviewed three other women from loyalist communities whose husbands were involved in paramilitaries (and have been prisoners) and one who has had no personal experience of paramilitaries. Finally, I also spoke less formally to a number of community workers, many of whom were (male) ex-prisoners themselves. As discussed in the introduction to the book, interviews were arranged through a variety of gatekeepers at ex-prisoner organizations, community groups and political parties. Because in this case study I shared a language with the interviewees and came from a more similar cultural background, I did not face the interpretation problems I did in Sri Lanka. Many of the interviews were also longer than the ones in Sri Lanka, with women having a lot to say about their experiences and emotions. As a result, I had much greater access to the women's self-reflections and ended up with a wealth of rich interview material, much of which cannot be incorporated here due to spatial limitations.[4]

Women in republican paramilitaries

Sales argues that although the rights of women have been seen as 'at best, secondary to the national struggle', Irish nationalism's history of conflict with British state authority has nevertheless meant that Catholic women 'are more likely to have a tradition of rebellion and radicalism' with which they can identify than Protestant women are (1997b: 5). The experience of community resistance in the 1970s helped to politicize many nationalist women and bring them into political activity. Women in nationalist areas have played an active role in community protests since the civil rights movement and are still more active in political and community groups than Protestant women as a whole (ibid.). Republicanism has promoted active images of women as 'freedom fighters' and female paramilitary members have been celebrated in a number of republican street murals in nationalist areas.[5] Some female IRA volunteers active in the 'Troubles', such as Mairead Farrell and the Price sisters, came to be internationally known names. As mentioned in Chapter 2, republicans view themselves as being part of an unbroken political tradition going back to the 1798 United Irishmen rebellion. In terms of women's contemporary paramilitary involvement, then, it is probably relevant that women were significantly involved in all uprisings since (and including) 1798, though not in a direct military capacity in all of them. Unfortunately it is beyond the scope of this work to discuss women in these other uprisings/conflicts.[6] In terms of the Irish Republican Army (IRA) it has only been during the 'Troubles' that women have been allowed in as 'volunteers' (combatants). As with the LTTE in Sri Lanka, it has been suggested that this was 'the result of a combination of female insistence and male recognition of the necessity of having some militarily trained women' (Ward 1989: 259). Younger women joining Cumann na mBan (the women's auxiliary organization set up to support and fundraise for the IRA, including providing first aid and hiding weapons) began expressing disillusionment in the late 1960s with their subsidiary role and strongly argued for their integration into the IRA itself. Sympathetic male IRA officers eventually gave them military training but apparently this was at first carried out without the knowledge of the older Cumann na mBan women. When the Provisional movement formed it maintained Cumann na mBan but allowed women to be seconded into PIRA – militarily active but without status as full members – but with the later restructuring of the organization into cells women were accepted into PIRA on an equal basis with men (ibid.).

Trying to assess the numbers of women as a percentage of the IRA (or other paramilitary organizations) is very difficult and I have not come across any estimates; I have two figures which may or may not even remotely be indicative. A republican ex-prisoner organization in north Belfast, when I contacted them to arrange interviews, was in the process of compiling a list of republican 'POWs' from the Ardoyne who were convicted in the 1970s. Of 158 names there seemed to be about 17 women, which is close to 11 per cent. Women may have increased in numbers as the 'Troubles' wore on but again this is hard to know. As I noted in Chapter 2, of 242 republican prisoners released early under the terms of the Good Friday Agreement, seven were women (personal communication with the Northern Ireland Office, 2003), which represents less than 3 per cent. This seems to me to be too low to be reflective of actual numbers of republican paramilitary women and if this is the case, it raises questions about why women have been so negligibly represented in the ranks of early release prisoners. Is there some kind of discrimination going on here? Or were women less likely to be caught and arrested than men (certainly a belief that this would be the case was part of the rationale for both republican and loyalist women being the ones to transport weapons)? Or were republican women given lighter sentences than men for the same offences? Or were they statistically more likely to be convicted of lesser offences than men, and thus serve shorter sentences for this reason? (Anecdotally I suspect this is true; there were certainly many women convicted of conspiracy to cause explosions, and even more of possessing weapons or incendiary material, but I believe not as many were 'lifers' convicted of murder.)

The 11 republican women I interviewed are all former combatants and nine of them are ex-prisoners. One is still officially 'on the run' in the Irish Republic, after 30 years. One had been an INLA member while the others were all Provisional IRA members, though two of them are now opposed to the Provisional republican movement. All strongly identify as Irish and republican and the majority are proudly working-class – though two consider their backgrounds to have been 'poorer than working-class', as their parents were continuously unemployed, and two feel their backgrounds were bordering on middle-class, having been slightly wealthier than many other working-class Catholics. Seven grew up in urban nationalist areas of west and north Belfast, while four come from rural areas (one is from the Republic of Ireland). All conceptualize republicanism as entailing much more than simply removing partition; it includes establishing an entirely new Ireland that is, in their imaginings, an equal society where all groups are treated with respect. For most, though not quite all, this requires a socialist state. All come from Catholic backgrounds and most (though not all) identified their parents as being fairly strongly practising Catholic. Few of the women themselves, however, still practise. Three identified their Catholic faith as remaining extremely important to them and one still 'hang[s] onto that comfort of it', praying in hard times but admitting she does not attend mass regularly and feels it is merely a ritual she sits through with her mind on other matters. The other seven women all said they came to question and largely reject the Church (though this does not necessarily mean they no longer believe in God). Three of these women specifically identified disillusionment with the Church's attitude towards republicanism, republican prisoners, the hunger strikes, and conservative attitudes about women.

Motivations of female combatants for enlistment in republican paramilitaries

Most of the republican women I interviewed became 'active' in PIRA (only one woman was aligned to the INLA) in their late teens, though many had been involved in the broader republican movement in a variety of ways since their early teens. Four were in their mid- to late forties at the time of interview and had been involved in paramilitary activity in the earlier period of the 'Troubles'; one was in her late fifties and was involved in two separate periods, early in the 'Troubles' and then much later on as well. Six of the women were in their thirties at the time of interview and had been involved in paramilitary activity in the later period, the 1980s and 1990s. It should be noted that not all the women specifically admitted to membership in these organizations; generally most spoke in the republican code of 'republican involvement' and becoming 'more involved' rather than 'IRA/INLA membership'. This is because although most had served prison sentences for various republican-related offences they had not necessarily been convicted as part of this of being a member of a paramilitary organization and such an admission still potentially carries jail time. The IRA has a tradition of not admitting who is a member until/unless they die, when their 'volunteer' status is acknowledged and celebrated. The women's membership in these organizations was imputed by me and my description of them as members/ex-members should not be taken as evidence. This means, however, that many would or could not tell me the exact age they joined their organization as a combatant. A variety of different reasons for volunteering in a republican paramilitary were given to me or could be deduced from my interviews. As in Sri Lanka, both ideological/political and more practical or personal factors have operated and interlocked. The most recurring theme was that of community or family experiences of discrimination and injustice or harassment and violence. For two of the older women, the civil rights movement was highly significant. For many of the younger women, the prison protests and hunger strikes were the turning point.

REPUBLICAN NATIONALISM

A number of loyalists I spoke to accounted for the higher numbers of women in republican paramilitaries in comparison to loyalist paramilitaries by saying that they must come from 'republican families' – that is, families whose connection to the republican movement goes back several generations. In reality, my research does not suggest this is necessarily so and in fact a number of women stressed that their families never talked about politics in the house. Certainly there are a number of such 'republican families', who have produced both male and female combatants in the 'Troubles', but only three of the 11 women I interviewed fit this profile. Two others also expressed directly political motivations. Interestingly, James, a male republican ex-prisoner community worker I spoke to claimed that IRA women tended to be more politically aware than many of the men who joined. Men, according to him, were more likely to be sectarian or to join because it was seen to be the thing to do and all their friends were doing it. Women who joined, he maintained, were more likely to question why things were happening and to be more politically aware. As I did not interview male ex-combatants as well as female, my research cannot test this. Merely that the suggestion was made, however, is interesting. If true (as a generalization), perhaps this can be accounted for in light of the fact that it was less expected for women to join than for men to join, and they may have had more to lose, so may have been more likely to carefully consider the decision. If James is empirically incorrect, however, this says something about the republican representation of politically active women.

Bernadette has a long family history of involvement with the republican movement, going back to the struggle for Irish independence. Her grandmother was a close friend of Winifred Carney, who was involved in the 1916 Easter Rising and was one of the last women out of the General Post Office. Her family was openly political and republican and Bernadette was raised with strong republican beliefs from an early age. Mary, too, comes from a family with a history (on both sides) of republicanism going back to the independence movement. Her paternal grandfather was involved in the 1916 Rising and her maternal grandfather was a veteran of the War of Independence. Her father also 'flirted' with the IRA in his youth but was never 'active'. Her family always believed in 'breaking the link with England' and she said that 'growing up we were always conscious of the national question and the fact that we'd have considered it unresolved'. Teresa also comes from a family that is proudly republican and socialist and very political; her whole family are republicans. However she stressed that although she was raised in a political atmosphere this was not 'in a brainwashing way'; their parents' beliefs were not forced on the children. 'They probably woulda broke their hearts if we'd a been any different from them, but they would've accepted it.' When I asked how she first got involved in republicanism she replied 'Well, you know, I say this and it does be a cliché, but I was born into republicanism.' She was the only woman I interviewed who gave solely political or ideological reasons for joining the IRA. When she was almost 17, in the late 1960s, she decided to join 'the Army' (that is, the IRA). She acknowledges that at that time things had 'come to a head' and 'this place was in turmoil, so it was just a natural progression of things that I joined the Army.' However she maintains that she probably would have joined anyway, regardless of the situation.

> It was not personal experience and it was not emotion. I joined the Army to further what I believed in, and it was purely for political reasons and for the principles of it and the way that I thought it was best to achieve what I believed in. I've heard that people joined the republican movement because of Bloody Sunday, or whatever – no, there was nothing like that. I mean, it was something that I had thought long and hard about and, as I say, had things not come to a head here I think that's probably still where I would have ended up. It certainly wasn't a gut reaction to some certain incident. No, I thought very long and hard and I thought how best to achieve what I believed in, and I believed that that was the way forward.

Niamh said her immediate family was reasonably republican, though she did not mention an inter-generational connection. Her mother was quite staunchly republican but her father did not feel as strongly about it. Her brother was also involved and spent time in prison in the 1970s. Even before the 'Troubles' broke out, she says, 'I had a strong sense of my Irish nationality, about the fact that Ireland was partitioned, you know, and I felt very strongly that Ireland should be united.' For Eileen, although she does not come from a republican family, political motivations are also clearly intertwined with real life experiences. The hunger strike protests came together in her consciousness with the Irish literature and language she was studying at university and the cultural interests she had. She was always very proud of the Irish history of struggle against British domination.

> So then with the build up of what was going on with the men on the hunger strike, who were the same age as us, it felt 'oh here we are with England doing this again to Irish people', same as what they had done … goin' way back.… And with the conflict in the six counties it did come to the point where really it felt like, you know, Britain's just taken a step too far.… So to me it seemed … actually that the involvement of people like myself at

> that time was the right thing ethically to do and I almost couldn't understand why other people wouldn't want to do it.... It just felt to me that this was the right thing to do, you know, the right thing to do for that time, at that time in Irish history that was the appropriate response.

DISCRIMINATION, INJUSTICE, HARASSMENT AND VIOLENCE: FAMILY AND COMMUNAL EXPERIENCES

Nine of the 11 women spoke of witnessing or experiencing incidents of discrimination, injustice, harassment or violence, either towards their own families or, more commonly, the wider Northern Irish Catholic community, which led them to feel that armed struggle was the only solution. Bernadette spoke of the British army shooting tear gas canisters in through people's windows, houses being raided, and people being beaten in the streets by the security forces. She also knew people who were shot dead and stressed to me that north Belfast, the area she grew up in, had the dubious distinction of having the highest percentage of people killed during the 'Troubles'. She said 'from you were a child you seen it all happenin' and I just naturally progressed into the republican movement.' Caral, also from north Belfast, explained that for her republican ideology and history were not important; 'It was just somethin' that was stale and rusty and totally impersonal.' Rather, 'What was important was the then and now from the late '70s/early '80s.... I just had a terrible sense of injustice.' She experienced harassment in the street and on the way to school and had her house raided by the security forces:

> There was this assumption that if you weren't an active republican you were helpin' active republicans. And I just felt really embittered and I felt that there was absolutely no justice at all, no equality, no social justice, no political justice.

Niamh comes from west Belfast and was 11 when the 'Troubles' broke out. She commented that 'you're very impressionable at that age and so I was very conscious of what was goin' on and felt strongly about it.' Furthermore, her father was badly injured and permanently disabled during an explosion in the early 1970s, when loyalists threw a bomb into a Catholic bar. Niamh

> was very conscious of the injustice, discrimination that existed and this just came from like listenin' to stories, you know my mother and her sisters and all talkin' about how people couldn't get a job if you were Catholic, so that was in my background and that was what was part of me when the Troubles started.

Emma, also from west Belfast, spoke of being a child and seeing people in her area being randomly stopped and searched while they were simply walking down a street, and beginning to question why. She was also frightened as a teenager when a loyalist paramilitary planted a bomb outside a bar near her house. She remembers being turned down for a job in the civil service for which she had the qualifications and believes this was because she is Catholic. She initially joined the Provisional IRA but left and joined the INLA, as she felt that PIRA simply used volunteers but did not really care about them.

Clodagh, who is from a rural background and whose parents were unemployed, said 'I just seen a lot of injustice, you know, and it [joining the IRA] was probably the … only thing you could do, you know? Like it wasn't like there was big alternatives.' She went on to say that

> when we were young … the work was very scarce like and it was all Protestants were the middle class and had all the jobs – not that it really came down to jobs … but it was like everything, you can see it very clearly, you could see the discrimination and you can see the oppression and the harassment and it was I think everything.

Maria is the oldest of my republican interviewees, in her late fifties. She grew up in the Ardoyne area of north Belfast, left school at 15 and worked in various jobs until at 19 she entered into what proved to be a very unhappy marriage. In the early 1960s, looking for work she encountered blatant anti-Catholic discrimination when she was asked in interviews what religion she was and was informed, when she told them, that the company did not employ Catholics. At the time 'it was just I didn't understand it, I was apolitical, I didn't know anything about the politics' and she came out feeling 'god, wish I was a Protestant, I could have a good job'. She remembers going to an interview with a Protestant girl who was less qualified for the position than she was but Maria was turned down because she was Catholic. The other girl told her she should have said she was Protestant but even then Maria felt that would have been denying who she was. When the 'Troubles' broke out she also witnessed two separate incidents of the British army brutally beating someone with rifle butts and was a witness in court in both cases. In the first case, the *victim* of the beating got a sentence of nine months in prison for riotous behaviour 'and I became so incensed by that'. The second victim got a six-month suspended sentence. Within her own family, when the 'Troubles' first began Maria's sister was one of those forced to leave her home after it was attacked by loyalist mobs while the sister and her four small children were inside. The mob was predominantly made up of women and Maria recognized some of them because she worked with them in a factory. The RUC were standing nearby but would not take action, telling Maria there was nothing they could do. She said to the women from the factory 'I'll remember this'; they replied 'They shouldna lived here anyway, shouldna moved here.' During the 1970s and 1980s she lost five family members to loyalists and the security forces.

Mairead grew up on a Catholic housing estate at the bottom of the Shankill Road. When she was a child one of her older brothers was in prison and another on the run, although this was never discussed at home and she did not begin to question it until she was a teenager. Her parents were not by any means strong republicans and they never discussed politics in the house, not wanting their children to be influenced. One of her father's relatives was shot dead by the security forces when she was a child but this, too, was never discussed – in fact, she only recently discovered this. Mairead remembers being beaten up at the age of eight by boys from the Shankill, hearing children at her school talking of how their fathers had been killed by loyalists, having a neighbour who lost an eye to a plastic bullet shot in through her window, and beginning to question why these things were happening.

> All of a sudden you were opening your eyes and seeing all this stuff, you know, and then questionin' why British soldiers – because they were based in the area I lived in – why they were callin' you names and why were they there anyway?

This was not restricted to urban areas of Northern Ireland. Maeve, from a rural area, remembers seeing the British military patrolling the roads, stopping and harassing people. However, as she had grown up in this way she did not really begin to question the status quo until she was 14 or 15. She also experienced a family loss when her mother suffered a miscarriage at one point, which she attributes to being harassed and verbally abused by the army at their house. The 1987 Loughgall (County Armagh) killing of eight IRA volunteers by the SAS[7] when she was a teenager had a significant impact on her, as she attended wakes (traditional gatherings of family and friends of the deceased before a funeral) for the first time in her life.

> And I think really from that time onwards there was a lot of anger and you did start to take notice of things and you did start to question things, especially when you knew that those fellas coulda been captured, they didn't have to be shot.... And I think probably from then onwards I took it a step further.

Mary's family experienced multiple losses and grief as a result of the 'Troubles'. She grew up in a rural area, where her family lived a relatively comfortable life. Gradually, over the early 1970s, the older children became involved in the republican movement. Two of her brothers were prisoners (one later being killed by the security forces) and another died in a premature bomb explosion. When her closest brother was arrested she felt that she should step forward to 'fill the vacuum' and take his place, and her own involvement stems from that point, when she was 18. She herself went on the run in the mid-1970s and has lived in the Irish Republic ever since, unable to cross the border for fear of arrest. Her youngest brother, who never became in any way involved, was killed by loyalists in the early 1990s. A number of other family members have also been killed by loyalists during the conflict.

THE CIVIL RIGHTS MOVEMENT

Many of the republican women I interviewed were too young for the civil rights movement (or internment) to have been a significant influence on their decision to join the republican movement, but for two this was a formative time. Mary, who was in her mid-teens during the civil rights movement, said of herself and her brothers that

> we were old enough to appreciate the whole euphoria of the civil rights movement, set against not just the civil rights movement in Ireland but you had the civil rights movements in the States with Martin Luther King, you had the Paris students, you had all these sorts of things happening in the world. We were just a new breed. We were young, we were articulate, we were getting educated, and we weren't going to be second-class citizens anymore. And it was just a case of that, and one step led to another. And then of course, to people of my age Bloody Sunday had a huge impact, you know, it was very formative. It sort of made us feel that regardless of what you tried to do, it would always be the answer of 'beat the Paddies', give them nothing. And it was a natural progression from there on in, you know?

Maria was in her mid-twenties during the civil rights movement, which was a pivotal point in her life. When it began she was still apolitical and did not understand what it was all about.

> So I decided I wanted to know, and then I had this great thirst to know, and I started to read, I got books out of the library on what happened in 1922 and 1916 and how the country was divided, and so my Irishness if you like came to the fore and I felt this great sense of pride in that I had a wee bit of Irishness in me and I wanted to have more, you know? So I suppose you could say I self-educated myself.

After the 'Troubles' began she and her husband allowed their house to be used by the IRA for meetings and to hide weapons, explosive materials and money from bank robberies, and she went on anti-internment demonstrations.

> But everybody's door was open then.... It was like everybody was in favour of the IRA at that time, who were the only ones that were doin' anything to defend our area, because we were comin' under attack from loyalists every other night in the week and the cops and the B-Specials woulda come in and anybody that got in their way got blottered.

This use of her house led to the arrest of herself and her husband in the early 1970s, when items were found in the house during a raid. When she was allowed out on bail she took the children and went on the run in the Irish Republic for a few years before returning north under an assumed name, after leaving her husband.

Maria then lived a very 'quiet life' with her children in Belfast until the early 1980s, though still participating in protests and involved with Sinn Féin. In the 1980s she began using her theatre acting and make-up skills to disguise IRA operatives and became directly involved almost by chance – a young woman did not show up for an operation she was supposed to go on and Maria volunteered to take her place.

> So I went out and I did whatever I was asked to do and then I was asked would I do somethin' else, and I said 'let me think about it'. And I thought it over carefully and I thought 'yeah, it's time this war was over, it's time this war was brought to some form of conclusion. And if I was there in the beginning, hopefully I'll be there when it's over.' And so I did.

Maria is an example of the fact, as I argued in Chapter 3 and as others have shown, that contrary to the maternalist feminist position motherhood can be as much a basis for militarism as for pacifism. A factor in her decision to re-join was that one of her sons wanted to join the IRA after he reached the end of his endurance when his girlfriend was repeatedly sexually harassed by British soldiers. She was totally opposed to any of her children being involved and conceptualizes her own participation as being in large part about trying to create a better life for them.

> I said 'I am *not* gonna go and visit you in prison. I am *not* gonna bury you with a tricolour over you. *I'll* do anything that has to be done, I will *not* see any of you doin' anything. When I first joined the IRA in 1970 it was with the view that my kids would never go through or suffer the indignities that we had to suffer, and I am stickin' to that.' And I went and I joined the IRA again.

PRISON PROTESTS AND THE HUNGER STRIKES

Five women raised the campaigns around the prison protests and hunger strikes in the late 1970s/early 1980s as being defining moments for them. Eileen is a slightly different case from the other women I interviewed, in that she is from the Irish Republic rather than Northern Ireland and so did not have many of the personal experiences the other women did. She had been too young during the civil rights movement to be involved but watched demonstrations on television in great excitement. When the prison protests and demonstrations in support of republican prisoners began in the late 1970s, while she was a student in Dublin, she became heavily involved and then participated in the hunger strike campaigns. Dublin

> was a hotbed of political activity and it felt very much in the air that something very big was happening,... something hugely important was happening – it was reminiscent of 1916 and stuff like that, you felt anything could happen here. It was very much a historical moment, but a very painful one, people were wearing black armbands and so on – very depressing, you know, because people were dying.... So for people of that generation, a lot of us anyway, probably the people who were kind of hit by the recession

> more and more kind of clued in then to what was going on [this was very significant].... So I think it started off from that point and it sort of built up.

For Caral, too, the hunger strikes were a turning point. She grew up in a house where politics were not discussed, 'with parents who basically kept their heads down and expected me to do likewise', so the hunger strike campaigns were 'where I would have seen politics'. Women's involvement in the campaigns was highly significant for her:

> the way they mobilized and organized street campaigns and political campaigns, and the fact that I knew these women were in the IRA and Sinn Féin and they were human rights activists, they were just multi-faceted, multi-tasked, multi-skilled women, and that to me was the catalyst for wantin' to be a republican, wantin' to get involved.

She also became disillusioned with the Catholic Church because of its reaction to the hunger strikes, as did other women I spoke to, feeling that the Church did not stand behind the prisoners and was part of the establishment that was trying to criminalize them. Bernadette was also a teenager when the first hunger strike started and it had a significant impact on her. In fact, she was expelled from school a few weeks before her GCSE exams, for leading a walkout over the strike. Like Caral, Mairead's family did not discuss politics and the hunger strike campaigns were enormously important as a stimulus to her self-education, just as the civil rights movement was for Maria.

> One of the biggest influences in my life was the second hunger strike. Even at that point, as I said, we didn't discuss politics at home, so it was kind of like you were wondering what was goin' on here, you know, what would make someone do this?... Because you were seeing things on TV and you were wondering what was going on and you were even at that young age still gettin' a bit of harassment from Brits [British army] and Peelers [police] and stuff, you know, so that would've been a big influence in my life.

Women in loyalist paramilitaries

The much greater difficulty I experienced in trying to gain access to loyalist ex-combatant women should not be taken unproblematically to indicate that women have not been active as combatants in loyalist paramilitaries, though they certainly do seem to have been much less strongly involved than women in republican paramilitaries. I believe it also reflects the suspicion of the motives of researchers that is prevalent among people in the loyalist community, many of whom feel that 'outsiders' are hostile towards them and favour republicans. It also reflects the more conservative communal view of women – loyalist women are less likely to admit to paramilitary involvement than republican women in part because of more negative societal attitudes towards such involvement.

Tracey, a loyalist ex-combatant and ex-prisoner, suggested that loyalist paramilitary women are less likely to talk about their involvement and experiences than loyalist paramilitary men or republican paramilitary members (of either sex) because there is still a Protestant community attitude that women should not have been involved in violence. This view was also expressed by other loyalist women, such as Linda (a community worker married to an ex-prisoner), who feels that there is definitely more of a stigma attached to being a female loyalist ex-prisoner than a male ex-prisoner. Jackie, an ex-combatant who has never been imprisoned, feels that it is possible for women to earn respect *within* loyalist paramilitaries but that loyalist people 'on the outside' tend not to give 'active' loyalist women respect in the same way they do men. Furthermore, active loyalist women are not visible to the community in the same way the men are; she feels people would often assume that women such as her, seen associating with loyalist paramilitary men, were not active themselves but were in sexual relationships with the men: 'They probably just think you're a slapper, you're in with all the boys – you know that's the way they would look at it.'

Sales highlights the fact that while the active involvement of women in republican paramilitaries has been comparatively well known, and was a source of pride for many Sinn Féin women she spoke to, '[m]uch less is known about loyalist women paramilitaries ... who appear to have had less prominence [and independence] within the movement' (1997b: 71). Similarly, Coulter asserts that '[t]he militant tradition that exists among republican women would seem to have no equivalent within loyalist circles' (1999: 131). Sales points out that while republicans have promoted active images of women as 'freedom fighters', as well as utilizing images of women's suffering as a metaphor for Ireland's oppression, there has been

> no equivalent symbolic role for women in Protestantism.... The imagery of the Protestant community is masculine, whether it is bowler-hatted Orange men celebrating Protestantism's triumph at the Battle of the Boyne, the archetypal Protestant worker (the skilled male manual worker), the harsh fundamentalist rhetoric of Ian Paisley or the balaclava-hooded Loyalist paramilitaries.
>
> (Sales 1997a: 144)

Coulter notes that in stark contrast to the heroic images of female paramilitaries in republican street art (as well as women in other public roles), in the iconography of loyalist political murals in Northern Ireland the images are almost entirely masculine (indeed the only loyalist murals I ever saw featuring women were ones showing female members of the royal family and one romanticized image of eighteenth-century rural Ulster, complete with busty maiden).

> The principal subject of the loyalist mural is the hooded male paramilitary. Women virtually never appear in the work of loyalist street artists. On the rare occasions that women actually do feature ... they are typically presented

> as passive and vulnerable.... Even within the profoundly reactionary political context of Northern Ireland, loyalism would seem to represent a particularly patriarchal ideological formation.
>
> (Coulter 1999: 240–1)

A number of loyalists also suggested to me that one reason for the lower number of women in loyalist paramilitaries compared to republican paramilitaries is the Protestant reluctance to step outside the law (which we could understand with reference to the attachment to the state and, therefore, the state's law and coercive forces). Women who wanted to be involved had the option of joining state forces as well as paramilitaries – an option that nationalists did not have. Loyalist *men*, however, also had these options so this is not a full explanation; this only makes sense in conjunction with conservatism regarding women's roles and, crucially, a different ideology about what the struggle was all about – an anti-revolutionary ideology unlikely to challenge that conservatism. Peter, a loyalist ex-prisoner and community worker, made the point that loyalists and republicans were 'fighting two different wars'. Republicans viewed the conflict as a revolutionary war of resistance against the state, so there was a role for more people to play, including women. In contrast, 'loyalist paramilitaries were never about buildin' a revolutionary movement. They were ... involved in a low-intensity counter-terrorist war against republicans. Now, what role is there for women to play in that?' The implication, it seemed to me, was that since loyalism was much less of a cohesive movement than republicanism and was not a revolutionary movement, there was neither the same perceived ideological need for women's involvement nor the same strategic need (the state forces were also fighting republicans so loyalists did not need to carry this whole burden themselves). As Peter said,

> if you are buildin' a revolutionary movement then you have to be fightin' that revolution on all fronts, and one of them is on that gender front – I mean you've gotta link your revolutions, you've gotta be all embracin' and you link yourself to human rights issues and to gender issues,... which the republicans have done. Loyalists didn't need to, you know?

He also pointed out that 'loyalists would define themselves [by] what they're not, so you look at your enemy and everything he's for, you're against. So if republicans are embracing women's rights, then again ... [loyalists would] move against that.'

Loyalist women's paramilitary activities have primarily been in the realms of welfare work and support for male prisoners and their families (Sales 1997b: 71–2). In fact, although the Ulster Defence Association (UDA) had a women's branch in the early years of the 'Troubles', this was disbanded as early as 1974 after a number of its members murdered Ann Ogilby, a married Protestant woman who made prison visits to an unmarried male prisoner. Ogilby's murder was particularly brutal as it was a 'romper-room' killing: she was beaten to death while her six-year-old daughter was sent out to buy sweets (Fairweather *et al.* 1984: 283). Sales notes that this murder provoked widespread revulsion, even among UDA prisoners, and suggests that although punishment of women seen to transgress the gendered rules of society has been tolerated within the Protestant community, as it has within the Catholic community,[8] 'the fact that it was women, acting on their own initiative, who carried out this particularly brutal murder may have contributed to the condemnation' (1997b: 71). Nevertheless women have continued to be involved in loyalist paramilitaries (though not in independent structures) and in 1980 a Protestant woman claimed to Fairweather that of 13 people on the UDA's inner council, at that time three were women (Fairweather *et al.* 1984: 304). One of the interviewees, Joy, informed me, however, that women currently have no say in the workings of the inner council.

The scale and extent of women's presence and involvement in loyalist paramilitaries is very hard to gauge and access to women willing to talk about their involvement I found, as noted earlier, to be extremely difficult. A community worker told me that in the rural area she works in, of around 300 ex-paramilitary members (affiliated with the Ulster Volunteer Force (UVF)) she has contact with she knew only one woman who was directly involved (Tracey, whom I interviewed). A male worker at the same organization told me of two more – one had recently died and the other would not talk to me as only two people knew about her past involvement. The proportion is likely to have been slightly higher in urban Belfast but I have no reliable figures. Of the women I did manage to make contact with, all strongly identify as British, loyalist, and working-class. Most explained loyalism simply by referring to a commitment to the Crown and the British royal family and many stressed a working-class element to the identity. All come from Protestant backgrounds of various denominations but almost all said they rarely attend church these days, though many still identify with their religion (to varying extents). Six of the ten loyalist women I interviewed were connected to the UVF or the Red Hand Commandos (a linked group): four were involved themselves to a greater or lesser extent and two were married to paramilitary men. Three of the ten women were connected to the UDA: one was strongly involved, one was evasive about the extent of her involvement, and the other was married to a UDA man. The tenth woman had no personal connection to paramilitaries.

Motivations of women for involvement with loyalist paramilitaries

Only six of the loyalist women I interviewed were actually involved in some way in paramilitaries themselves; accordingly, these six women are discussed here. The remaining four come into discussion in the next chapter. Five of these six women were in their fifties or late forties at the time of interview, and in their late teens or early twenties when the 'Troubles' broke out. The sixth was in her early thirties when I interviewed her. As with republican and Tamil women there are intersecting reasons for their involvement in political violence; directly political motivations featured but communal experiences of violence was the most recurring factor. Involvement through male family members may be an element more common to loyalist women than to republicans but this (as so much to do with loyalist paramilitary women) requires further investigation. As previously noted, only two of these women (Tracey and Jackie) fit my conceptualization of 'combatant' but I have expanded my discussion a little more widely in the case of loyalists to include women involved in auxiliary activities, given the difficulties gaining access to loyalist combatant women.

LOYALIST NATIONALISM? DEFENCE OF COUNTRY

Tracey is a UVF ex-combatant and ex-prisoner. She is from a rural area and comes from a strongly Protestant, unionist, and working-class background. She left school at the age of 16 to work in a factory and was about 17 when she joined the UVF in the early 1970s. 'Way I looked at it back then, they [the UVF] were the only ones that was defendin' their people.' She felt disillusioned with the UDR, saying that people who joined it 'altogether changed'. Although she strongly identifies as British, she also reflects the ambivalent nature of loyalist identity by making an implicit distinction between Ulster and Britain (which is perfectly reasonable; Northern Ireland is part of the UK but it is not part of Great Britain). 'I felt that bein' in the security forces, the British government had then won, because I knew ones in the UDR and all and they were just like talkin' to somebody outta Britain.' That is, from her perspective the security forces were not tough enough on the IRA and she felt she could achieve more by being a paramilitary member than joining a state force, although she did attempt to join the UDR at one point, being rejected because 'my photo come up as a terrorist!' Tracey was approached by male members of the UVF and asked if she wanted to join: 'I definitely wanted to join the UVF but there was different ones then come and said to me, would I join? And I said I would.... I was the type of girl, I would've done anything for them.' She believes that she was almost the only woman who was actively involved in her branch of the UVF, though there were another few women who were involved in the welfare, first aid and fundraising end of things. Echoing women on the Shankill Road in Belfast who complained that the paramilitaries had changed since the 1970s and were now all about drug-trading and making money for themselves, Tracey said:

> I don't regret ever joinin' the UVF, because the friends that I had in the UVF *were* friends. Not like the ones today, and it's all drugs. It's all money now, but back then it wasn't. The whole thing has all changed.... [In my time] money wasn't involved at all, you done it for your country.

Alison was raised in the Church of Ireland but, like the majority of the loyalist women I spoke to, is no longer practising in the narrow sense of church attendance. She grew up in a very working-class family in a mixed area of Belfast but the family moved after the violence of 1969, eventually to the Shankill Road. Her father was imprisoned with a lengthy sentence when she was a child (for a loyalist paramilitary murder of a Catholic) and she and her sister worked in part-time jobs to help support the family. She left school at 15 and went straight into work in a factory, marrying at 17. Like Tracey, Alison feels strongly that in the early years of the 'Troubles', when she was involved, loyalists joined paramilitaries 'to be loyal to the Crown.... They were there fightin' a cause.' She says 'we came in along because we believed in it, so we did', whereas

> a lot of them joins now for a cause for themselves, it's not the same, it's completely different.... And the drugs situation has a lot to do with that.... I think that a lot of loyalists are loyal to their pockets,... they're not loyal to the Crown anymore or they're not loyal to their people, they're loyal to themselves and their LSD, the money.

She also believes that women were more involved in the loyalist paramilitaries in the early days of the conflict and are not so much now, since the gangsterism took hold. Alison became engaged in paramilitary support activities through her husband but she stressed that she believed in the cause as well, or else she would not have involved herself. She never officially joined the Red Hand Commandos (her husband's organization) or the UVF (her father's organization) but was actively involved in support roles, primarily moving weapons. She is supportive and proud of women who were actively involved during the 'Troubles', 'because we were fightin' a war, you know?... If you're out there defendin' your country, why, you know – is there a law to say that it's just men that can defend a country? I don't think so.'

COMMUNAL EXPERIENCES OF VIOLENCE AND DEFENCE OF FAMILY

Ann grew up in a very working-class family in an area around Conway Street, midway between the Shankill Road and the Falls Road. She was raised Presbyterian but does not attend church herself. She left school at 15 and went to work in a factory, leaving at 17 when she fell pregnant and got married. She was pregnant with her third child when the 'Troubles' broke out. Her husband was a UVF member and was interned for a year. The family moved to a house in a different area after the communal violence of 1970 – Protestants were leaving the area at that time, some being burnt out of their homes, and she objects to the fact that it is often presented as though only Catholic families were burnt out of Conway Street. Like Alison, Ann engaged in activities like weapons transportation and first aid, rather than a more combatant role. Although Ann's progression into UVF activity was through her husband she stressed that she herself *wanted* to be involved, responding to the situation on the streets and the effect on families in her community. She said

> what I seen startin' down there and what we got accused of and what the other side done, I mean it just made you bitter. I was young then, but ... when that happened [the outbreak of the 'Troubles' and communal violence] it did make you bitter, I have to say it did make you bitter.

Isabella, from a working-class Shankill Road background, has never joined a paramilitary organization herself (though some male relatives have been involved with the UVF) and her participation was in a very peripheral way at the start of the violence, when loyalist communities were gearing up to either defend their areas from IRA attacks or to launch attacks themselves. In the very early days of the 'Troubles' for a few weeks she made and stored petrol bombs in her backyard. She reported that she did not want to do this but there was communal pressure to assist: 'I cried and sayin' "this is terrible, this is awful, this is terrible". And you're tryin' to hide it from your kids.' When I asked why, in that case, she had made the bombs, Isabella replied

> cos everybody [was doing it] – all the neighbours. They woulda just said 'here' and there's the petrol, they showed you what to do and I sat in the backyard with other neighbours. But I wouldn't speak out to them'uns, it was to my husband I was sayin' 'this is terrible, this is terrible, when's this gonna end?' But I wouldn't to the neighbours.

Tracey felt that Protestant people in her rural area were being murdered by the IRA while the security forces, which she perceived as being hamstrung by the British government, were unable to prevent this. In the early 1970s a milkman neighbour and a number of her friends who were in the UDR or the RUC were killed by the Provisionals: 'That had an effect on me, because they were good friends of mine.... It made me even more bitter than what I was.... I felt, well they were shootin' my friends, why can't I do the same?'

Jackie, the youngest of my loyalist interviewees, is from the Protestant Waterside area of Derry and grew up working-class Presbyterian. She first got involved with the UDA when she was about 17, collecting money, arranging parcels and lifts to prison and so forth, until at around 20 or 21, in the 1990s, she 'took a bigger part in it, as the saying goes'. She has never been imprisoned so she gave no specific details about her involvement, but made it as clear as possible, without giving anything away, that she had been a combatant. Like Tracey (with regard to the UVF in her area), she reported there were almost no other 'active' UDA women in her area at the time of her involvement. She thought there were perhaps one or two others who were active but generally the women who were involved were engaged in the 'welfare' type activities she had started out doing. When I asked why she chose to get actively involved Jackie replied:

> You get angry, when you see things, d'you know what I mean? And the police aren't doin' enough, they don't do enough, and to be honest with you, at the end of the day you've gotta do things yourself. That's the only way I can explain anyway, that's the way I felt. You don't get the support that's needed here, to help things out, so basically you have to go and do it yourself.

When I asked what sorts of things she saw that made her feel this way, she spoke of friends whose parents had been shot by PIRA and said 'and it turns you bitter, very very bitter, it does, and I just got in. It's easy enough to, you know, kinda get there.' She was very clear that her objection is to the IRA and not to Catholics:

> Catholics don't bother me; it's Provos, do you know what I mean? I have a lot of friends whose families were harmed and that by them, you know, so, and you've gotta, you've gotta make a stand somewhere, d'you know what I mean? And I don't want the united Ireland.

She worked for eight years in a factory in the Cityside of Derry (predominantly Catholic) and came to meet her best friend there, a Catholic woman. 'So it's just not a religion thing, d'you know what I mean, definitely not, no.... It's not a Catholic–Protestant thing, it's definitely [political].'

Like Tracey, Joy is originally from a rural area though she now lives and works around the Shankill. She had some kind of past involvement with the UDA/UFF but would not elaborate on the extent of this, saying only that she had 'considerable input' during the height of the 'Troubles'. She, too, experienced loss and violence. Joy was the only woman I interviewed to be quite openly and unashamedly sectarian in her remarks, saying at one point 'If I saw a Catholic on fire I wouldn't spit on them to put them out.' Unlike my other loyalist interviewees, Joy's family was middle- to upper-class when she was a child, as her father was a businessman, but she reported that when she was 20 her father died as a result of a severe beating by the IRA. After his death the family lost the businesses. She herself was badly beaten by the IRA as a teenager, her mother was once assaulted and a cousin in the RUC was killed. Such experiences have clearly embittered her and led to her involvement with the UDA. They also led to her going back to secondary school and later to university to do higher degrees, as she wanted to be able to help others in the loyalist community and felt education was the way to do this. She stated 'I wasn't born to hate, I was taught to hate. And I was taught by the best because Sinn Féin/IRA taught me.' Nevertheless, she does not want to pass on her hate to her sons and would like the conflict to end with this generation, though she is not optimistic that this will be so.

Alison and Ann both made a connection between loyalist women's paramilitary involvement and protecting their families, which presents a challenge to the maternalist feminist argument. Alison stated

> I would be a person who would fight tooth and nail for my family. And if I thought anyone was gonna harm them in any shape or form, I wouldn't care what measures I had to go to ... I would do it.

Alison suggests that for many women the reason they became involved was that the conflict began touching the lives of their families, and draws a distinction between loyalist men's motivations for involvement and that of loyalist women. Her comments here also present an interesting contradiction with her assertion, mentioned previously, that women did and should be able to defend their country in the same way as men.

> It was affectin' their families, it was affectin' their husbands, it was affectin' their kids.... They were defendin' their families and that's why they did do it.... Because probably the man, in my opinion, they joined for to defend their country; women would've joined to defend their families.... Within the loyalist side, yeah, they would've joined it because they were defendin' their families and their homes.

MALE FAMILY MEMBERS

Both Ann and Alison initially became involved with the UVF (in Ann's case) and the Red Hand Commandos (in Alison's case) through their husbands' participation but both emphasized that they themselves believed in the justness of the loyalist cause and violent campaign. Ann seemed to want to make it clear firstly that husbands did not coerce their wives into assistance and secondly that she was not aberrant as a woman because of her involvement in such activity:

> Well, my husband was involved and they couldn't be involved without you knowin' some things, you know, and you were used just. Didn't have to be, if you didn't want to do it you didn't do it but, you know, you used to go up the road with your pram, the child sittin' in it, and 'hello' to the soldiers and they didn't know what you had under the pram! [weapons] But ... I mean, it wasn't on me own doin' it in them days, there was a right few of us.

Later, Ann was asked to actually join the UVF officially (which seems to have been reasonably unusual), and she did so.

> Nobody forced me.... As I say it wasn't all wives was in it but I think it was just like a chosen few at that time was asked.... Well I mean you were doin' the things anyway so why not, you know?

For Jackie there was no husband facilitating her involvement in the UDA (she is single) but she did speak about having a significant 'family connection' which both made her entry into the UDA easier and afforded her some protection in terms of how she was treated. Her parents had no paramilitary involvement but all her brothers and various cousins and uncles seem to have been involved as prominent members; she was known to the community (and to the police) as coming from a 'connected' family. Her descriptions of her parent's attitudes indicate a fairly ambiguous position towards loyalist political violence. In essence she suggested they were not happy about their children being involved in violence yet they do think loyalist paramilitary activity is necessary sometimes; they have certain limits about what is acceptable: 'people maybe just gettin' a beatin' for nothin' ... they don't like things like that, that was their views like. Mine were different. Nobody gets a beatin' for nothin'. You get it for somethin'.' Her narrative made it clear that her connection through her brothers definitely aided her entry into the UDA and some parts of her narrative indicated a certain inevitability about the progression of her activities, rather than a well-thought-out definite decision: 'Well I didn't think about it hard now, just kinda happened, you know.' At other points in her narrative, however, she is keen to make it clear that her participation was what she wanted and was independently chosen: 'I mean it's your own choice, nobody makes you do anything, you know. It was my choice to get involved.' Later on she added:

> But it's a decision you make for yourself. It's what's goin' on around you, what way it affects you personally, d'you know what I mean? If you feel you can maybe do somethin' about it well then that's fine. And we obviously did as a family, know what I mean?

POLITICAL ACTIVITY IN OPPOSITION TO THE CIVIL RIGHTS MOVEMENT

One final factor that I noted, though it appeared only in the case of Tracey, was the loyalist mobilization in opposition to the civil rights movement in the late 1960s. Tracey was raised Presbyterian but the family converted to Ian Paisley's Free Presbyterian Church of Ulster and she remained a staunch Paisley supporter at the time of interview (since then Paisley entered into government with Sinn Féin and lost some of his support base). Her father and all her brothers are Orangemen. However, her parents were never in favour of violence or the paramilitaries and she is the only member of her family to have been involved. Her path to active paramilitary participation paralleled that of many republican women. While they became politicized through demonstrations and public activity in the civil rights movement and, later, in support of the hunger strikers and the prison protests, Tracey's politicization came through being involved during her late teens in the Paisley-led counter-demonstrations *against* the civil rights movement. It would be interesting to know if there are other loyalist women for whom this was a stepping stone into paramilitary activity, and if the 1973 mobilization against the Sunningdale talks and the mid-1980s activity against the Anglo-Irish Agreement had similar effects.

5 Women's experiences in the LTTE in Sri Lanka

Gender relations and feminist nationalism

As outlined in the previous chapter, the LTTE has an explicitly expressed commitment to women's liberation within their commitment to national liberation and has also been actively recruiting women into its fighting ranks for over twenty years now, making it different in this respect from all the paramilitaries in Northern Ireland. This explicit ideological commitment and its backing by detailed and consistent actual policies has had a significant impact on the experiences of women cadres, though this has not always been as unambiguously positive as the organization would like us to believe.

Gender relations and experiences in the LTTE

The Women's Front of the LTTE has tried to publicize the unequal position of women in Tamil society. In the 1980s they made a drawing summarizing the situation of Tamil women, with the pressures on women symbolized as the hands and feet of black demons: law, religious concepts, no equal rights, superstitions, the societal institution of male chauvinism and dowry. The aims of the Front, formulated in 1991, were to secure the right to self-determination of the Tamil Eelam people and establish an independent democratic state of Tamil Eelam; to abolish oppressive caste discrimination and divisions and semi-feudal customs like dowry; to eliminate all discrimination against Tamil women and all other discrimination, and to secure social, political and economic equality; to ensure that Tamil women control their own lives; and to secure legal protection for women against sexual harassment, rape and domestic violence (Schalk 1994: 169, see also 1992). These are admirable and ambitious aims but it is clear that the independence struggle fundamentally frames the struggle for women's rights. This is apparent in all Prabhakaran's speeches on the matter as well as the views of the Women's Front; the Tamil struggle is prioritized and women's emancipation is seen as dependent upon the struggle. This is arguably problematic and this matter is returned to in the next section of this chapter; here, however, I explore some of the positive and negative aspects of the LTTE's utilization of female combatants.

As mentioned in the previous chapter, the LTTE leadership recognized the momentous social change entailed in their incorporation of women into combat roles in the 1980s and was concerned to carry this out in such a way as to minimize any potential backlash from wider Tamil society. The LTTE rank and file are, of course, also a part of Tamil society; it is not surprising, therefore, that not all male members of the organization were entirely prepared to accept female fighting comrades. The separate organization of men and women seems to have contributed to the successful integration of women into the LTTE because it fulfils Tamil cultural expectations prohibiting fraternization between young men and women, reduces the perceived problem of sexual relations between cadres, and gives young women the opportunity to develop skills and grow in confidence in a supportive environment. Thamilvily reflected these ideas when she explained that

> men and women train and live separately because the movement is very conscious of discipline. Society is not quite happy to have women join the movement, so to have men and women train together would raise eyebrows. It is better to have separate camps. Also, when girls first join they are shy and need coaxing – this is easier separately. Also there are problems specific to women. Also because the LTTE is so strong on discipline, they want to avoid questionable behaviour.

Discussing the 1990 expansion in the number of female LTTE members Adele Ann comments that male cadres were largely unprepared for this and struggled with the prospect of female soldiers being injured or killed.

> Traditional ideas about their own role in society as protectors of women dominated their consciousness and, as men, they felt and assumed responsibility for the women as women, rather than as highly motivated and trained comrades in arms. Nevertheless, in line with the LTTE policy of deploying women in combat on one side, and the firmly articulated aspirations of the women cadres to fight on the other side, the women cadres won their case and were fully deployed into the guerrilla war.
>
> (Ann 1993: 98)

Through subsequent experience fighting with women cadres the men, she says, came to accept and respect them. 'As mutual confidence and comradeship grew from the battle experience the gender distinctions in the allocations of responsibilities and military duties started to melt away' (ibid: 100). This was borne out in my research in the recollections of some of the women. Many (particularly those who joined well after 1990) said things like 'We were treated as equals and we did not have any difference between us. We were like brothers and sisters' (Geetha, enlisted 1993). Kalaivily (enlisted 1996) argued that 'Only when we prove our capabilities through our action, men will start believing in women. Now things have changed. Our leaders have got faith in women and their capabilities. They believe in us now.' Thamilachi enlisted in 1991 and was in the north in 1995–6 when the Sri Lankan Army launched its successful campaign to retake Jaffna from the LTTE. She described to me how many male LTTE cadres felt that staying in Jaffna under those circumstances would be too tough for the women cadres; it was terribly hard even for them and they did not think the women could cope. However the women, including herself, felt very strongly that it was their duty to stay and they were determined to prove themselves. She described days without food with only dirty puddles of water to drink from, but felt that the women proved their abilities and earned a lot of respect from their male comrades. However Trawick argued a few years after this campaign that '[i]n non-combat situations, ordinary gender relations obtain between combatants. Sexual hierarchies have not been erased overnight' (1999: 158). Thus, '[i]t is Tiger policy for male and female combatants to treat one another with respectful distance. The possibility of gender conflict is serious. Some of the men are conservative, and uncomfortable with the idea of sisters in trousers' (ibid.: 145). Thamilini maintained:

> When we do something then men get to know about our capabilities, but our country's attitude towards woman is different and men are always praised for doing harder and cleverer jobs, so on seeing women doing the work it will kindle the men's ego and ego tends to stop women's growth in this aspect, but on that situation we need to be courageous and patient.

Participation in the LTTE has brought about significant changes in the roles, actions and skills of the women cadres themselves and also seems to have radicalized many of them in regard to gender issues and ideas about 'women's liberation'. Vinothini (a woman involved with the LTTE but not as a fighter) spoke about the female combatants to the Panos oral testimony project:

> We have to appreciate their confidence and potential talent to stand equally with the men combatants in the field. This freedom struggle has brought many changes to the society – many young women are trying to come out from the slavery life which they were living so many years.... The first time I have seen Tamil women fighting equally with men in the battlefield they have proved that women are no longer a weaker sex.
>
> (Panos interviews)

Reflecting on the experiences of female combatant Sita, Trawick notes that she has gained 'a privileged degree of physical power and mobility' in the LTTE, operating motorbikes, tractors and guns (1999: 151). When asked if she has noticed mental or emotional changes in herself since joining the movement, Sita responded

> [i]f I were at home, I could not do all these things.... I see the suffering of the people and I have no fear about fighting and dying for them.... When people in the movement die, it is a useful death. If I died in the house, there would be nothing remarkable about that.... If we were in the house, we would be confined. But now we are like men, so there is no fear.
>
> (Trawick 1999: 153–4)

In terms of the women I interviewed, six discussed specific social restrictions on women such as not riding bicycles or climbing trees, not going out alone or at night, not going in the sea or on boats; they were all happy that within the LTTE they have had the opportunity to do these things that they were raised to believe were inappropriate or dangerous for women. Others described more generally the idea of Tamil women being 'suppressed' and stressed a new self-confidence they obtained through their LTTE experiences. Four women also raised dowry practices as a problem, which was a smaller number than I had expected given LTTE declarations on the evils of the dowry system. This may be attributable to the fact that the LTTE approach to dowry has changed in recent years. At the urging of Tiger women, the organization at first took a strong line against dowry as a social practice negatively affecting women but they later toned this down, after conversations with Tamil women who insisted that the dowry system benefits women if it is properly implemented (though this may be particular to the customary laws of Jaffna Tamils and less so for eastern Tamils). Nevertheless, this seems to still be a problem amongst impoverished Tamil communities. Thangaci reported that with intra-LTTE marriages there is no dowry but outside the movement it remains common; she could never marry because her bridegroom would ask for a dowry which her family could never pay.

Krishna and Banuka both mentioned that in contrast to their childhood of being prevented from riding bicycles, they can now ride motorbikes and drive armoured vehicles. Krishna described being told not to go into the sea, as it would 'take' her; now she can swim for long distances. She was also told that women should not go on boats as they will make the seas rough; now women cadres make up a large percentage of the LTTE's navy, the Sea Tigers. Thangaci stated:

> If I were in my house without joining the LTTE I would not have known about the world. Girls were suppressed and I would have been inside my home and I would have never got any awareness about the world. But now, even though I am not educated, I have got the confidence to go out anywhere and discuss things with anyone.

Similarly, Geetha also spoke about self-confidence:

> Before joining the LTTE I was afraid of darkness and when I was at home I never used to go out during night times. But after joining the LTTE I came to know that we girls are also no less and can do anything and everything. Earlier, I was a very shy-natured girl and feared mixing with people. But after joining the LTTE I got confident that I can also speak to anyone, mix with people, like for example I am talking to you people.

For her, though she has left the LTTE, she feels the experience

> was good for me and also the other girls who were with me. It is because of that, we are able to seek livelihood for ourselves by working in other jobs

> and are able to get jobs on our own. Our society does not encourage the mixing between boys and girls. As we were in the LTTE, we mixed well with boys as we were working together during war times and hence this helps in our working environment now [masonry and roofing].

When I asked Thamilini if being female made it a harder decision to join the LTTE, she reflected the frequently implied problem of the social construction of gender when she replied:

> I wanted to join, but that time I was not sure whether I can.... Because we had grown in some other way in our houses.... A girl, she is very soft person – we were treated like that. I knew that we have to go to the jungles and we have to fight and we must go alone in the night ... but a small suspicion was in my mind, whether I am capable of doing these things, because of the way I was brought up in my house.... But I was able to see the other military cadres, the girls, who were doing all sorts of things. So then I thought, if *they* can do, why I can't do these things?

She went on to say that

> In our society, they have separated the work for the men and the women, so from the childhood the girl is brought up ... that you can't do certain things.... [A woman] feels that she can't take some decision on behalf of her, so she needs others to do that on behalf of her. Because she doesn't know herself. You know, we have been brought up in this LTTE movement that we have to take decisions for us; others can't take on behalf of us.

She added, 'Now I have the self-confidence, now I don't need anybody.... Now I won't allow any others to take decisions for my life. I have gained that belief here.' She feels that girls and their abilities should be respected by others and to get that respect girls 'must develop themselves and they must make others respect them'.

Only Thamilini independently mentioned alcoholism and domestic violence as problems facing women. This concerned me yet I also found it intriguing since many non-LTTE women told me that the organization opposes domestic violence and punishes offenders. It was suggested to me by a UK-based Tamil woman that these issues are now so well discussed and dealt with in the LTTE-controlled areas that the interviewees may have seen them as self-evident (personal communication). In LTTE-controlled areas victims of domestic violence can report this to local cadres, who deal with it through their de facto judicial system. Rajasingham-Senanayake was told by a young woman in an LTTE area that at the first complaint of domestic violence the abuser is given a warning, at the second he is fined, and at the third he may be put in an LTTE prison (2001a: 114). This policy is supported by all the Tamil women who spoke to me about it, including by women who in all other ways are opposed to the LTTE. When I raised the issue of domestic violence with some LTTE women in response to something they said about trying to help counsel troubled married couples to resolve their problems and stay together, they said they would never encourage a wife to stay with an abusive husband.

The war and recruitment of women into militant groups also produced changes in the lives of some non-militant Tamil women. Some started behaving unconventionally, for example by riding bicycles freely on the roads and wearing 'dresses that suited their physical movements' (Maunaguru 1995: 169). Such changes resulted in a backlash. In 1985, an unsigned handbill appeared in Jaffna that asserted various restrictions regarding women's dress and behaviour. All the local women's groups responded with counter-statements condemning this; however, while the LTTE women's wing was among those expressing condemnation, at the same time it 'emphatically stated that Tamil women should keep their ethnic identity in their dress and make-up', asserting that they should maintain the sari, long hair, and the *pottu* (a traditional Hindu mark on the forehead, in Sri Lanka now often worn also by Christian Tamil women as a mark of Tamil ethnicity rather than religion). An LTTE statement argued:

> It doesn't mean that we are enslaved if we dress according to our tradition.... Women should dress simply, and they should not attract men by their way of dressing.... We are engaged in a struggle for national liberation. But, the changes which have been taking place in our culture will only demean our society.
>
> (Maunaguru 1995: 169)

These particular dress restrictions or recommendations are not considered to apply to Tiger women themselves, who have their own restrictions. Women in the Military Wing wear a camouflage uniform (with trousers) while women in the Political Wing wear plain trousers and long shirts with a belt over the shirt. The shirt must cover their bottoms and the front zip of their trousers and button up to the base of the neck. While in training they must cut their hair short, for practical reasons, but later on they can choose to leave it short or to grow it out again. Most of the experienced LTTE women I met had grown it long again, in the local style, and wear it in braids pinned to their heads so it is not an encumbrance. Their defence to me of the fact that they encourage women outside the movement to wear traditional Tamil dress, yet wear the most non-traditional clothing imaginable themselves, was that they wear a uniform within the LTTE that suits the type of work they do. At home or in peacetime they would wear whatever suits the work they are doing and is appropriate – in other words, many said they would wear dresses or saris at home in peacetime, though many also freely admitted (usually smiling or laughing) that they find trousers much more comfortable.

In Colombo newspapers in 2002 I found rumours of an LTTE dress code for Tamil women in Jaffna, which implied that this issue had not disappeared. In my fieldwork I discovered that the pamphlets 'suggesting' 'appropriate clothing' for women had actually come out in the east and not in Jaffna, and for some non-LTTE women I spoke to in the east this was one of their main concerns about the movement at that time. I raised the issue with LTTE interviewees there and had an intriguing conversation with two of the women cadres in a Tiger-controlled area near Batticaloa. Essentially, their argument was that these are merely recommendations, not orders, and that they are for women's own protection. Sailajah told me that if women wear tight-fitting clothing it will sexually arouse men and 'create many problems'. Similarly, Sumathi said that women wearing immodest clothes 'are only creating problems for themselves'. I suggested that it is extremely dangerous to imply that women bring sexual violence upon themselves through what they wear; that all kinds of women wearing all kinds of clothes are raped; and that perhaps instead we should be focusing on changing the attitudes of men rather than policing women's bodies. They expressed agreement in principle but argued that it is very difficult to change men or tell them what to do; it is much easier to change women. When I asked about the stories I had been told by women in Batticaloa of male LTTE cadres cutting the skirts of women wearing 'immodest' outfits, Sailajah vehemently denied this and claimed it must have been other men trying to discredit the Tigers, as their cadres would never do that. Sumathi added that in earlier days they were 'stricter' on this issue (whatever that means exactly) but after they spoke to women in the community who told them that they felt the LTTE was restricting their freedom, they stopped compelling women to wear certain things.

In some of their other activities the LTTE is much more progressive on gender issues in their economic and social programmes for Tamil women, as part of their attempts to bring about wider social change. Many cadres emphasized to me the need to help Tamil women become free and independent, in particular economically independent. Barathy said that women should not have to depend on others; they need to 'live freely and independently' and earn money for their families. Sudarvili maintained that

> through our struggle for liberation we are fighting for the women's liberation also.... We want to ... free the girls in this country, not only within the movement, outside also. They must ... [come] to positions in which they can do the things which have been done by ... males in the country.

Krishna told me that women must be free; when I asked her what 'freedom' meant to her in this context she replied,

> here women do not come forward for anything, they have been asked to keep quiet and do the housework. So ... the future generation should not be like that, women must be free, socially and economically and they must have a place, equal rights with men.

Sudarvili mentioned that in particular young widows need to be able to be independent and live alone. The problems of widows, particularly young widows with children, were a recurring theme.

Many programmes and women's societies formed by the LTTE women's wing are aimed at encouraging and enabling women to engage in self-employment. Thamilvily told me about various projects they run in the Vanni for women, including 'a project where women are given training in auto-mechanics ... which has been a domain of men. And ... we have encouraged them to start an auto-repair shop of their own and they are doing it well.' However Banuka mentioned people speaking ill of women who attempt to go into self-employment as being a severe problem; various comments from women both inside and outside the LTTE also suggest that not all in wider Tamil society accept women engaging in non-traditional employment. Since leaving the LTTE and undertaking training at an LTTE-run technical training centre in the Vanni, both Thangaci and Geetha have worked as day labourers in a variety of activities, which have largely involved masonry and, in Geetha's case, roofing as well. Thangaci reported that in her community

> Sometimes they make fun out of us. Like, why are ladies doing this kind of jobs? Sometimes even my relatives used to ask me that, why I am doing this. I say, this is a work like any other job. I used to quote the leader Prabhakaran. He used to treat both men and women equally. Women also fight with the army. Similarly, this is also a job which women also can do.

Representations of female LTTE cadres

The concern over women's appropriate attire (a classic concern of nationalist movements), the disparity between women within and without the LTTE, and the difficulties entailed in balancing significant social change against more traditional community attitudes and expectations in the context of nationalist mobilization all tie into the issue of the representation and rationalization of women cadres. Maunaguru traces the different Sri Lankan Tamil constructions of appropriate Tamil nationalist femininity since the Federal Party political agitation of the 1950s and 1960s. She argues for the resurgence in this period of notions of *Veerathayar* ('Brave Mothers') (1995: 162),[1] based on myths from ancient Tamil heroic epics; Tamil women were exhorted to follow the example of the women in these poems. The caption of a photo of a women's procession to attend a Federal Party annual conference read: 'Tamil mothers of the past sent their sons to war against injustice; mothers of today have gathered their sons to wage a similar war.' This construction remains important within Tamil nationalism today, alongside newer ones. Appeals to the importance of motherhood have also been used in militant Tamil depictions of state family planning as a genocidal plot. Maunaguru reports that a poster campaign in Jaffna warned Tamil women not to be deceived by the state's family planning policy, alleging it 'was a conspiracy to control the demographic size of the Tamil population' (ibid.: 162–4). The Tigers banned family planning services from government health departments in the areas under their control and urged women to produce as many children as possible to increase the decimated nation and to sacrifice their sons and daughters for the good of the nation (Schrijvers 1999: 317). Interestingly, Schrijvers contends that one result of all this has been that 'unmarried mothers were no longer regarded as the ultimate stigma of their community, but they were encouraged to have their babies and then hand them over to the LTTE to be brought up as heroes for the nation' (ibid.: 317–18).

As outlined in the previous chapter, however, from the mid- to the late 1980s it became necessary for women to fight as well as to produce male fighters and almost all Tamil militant groups made appeals for women to enlist. One such 1984 appeal Maunaguru translates as:

> Women are half of our population and hence their participation in various levels of armed struggle is extremely necessary. Women are the internal revolutionary force in any national movement. The level of participation of women in the Eelam struggle including armed combats [*sic*] will prove the revolutionary potentialities of Tamil women.
>
> (1995: 163)

The change from 'brave mother' to 'woman warrior' in the construction of 'woman', Maunaguru contends, was a 'categorical shift' although the significance of motherhood was not abandoned. In fact, in the mid-1990s Maunaguru was arguing that a 'mother-warrior' construction of Tamil women had emerged, entailing gun-and-baby representations (nothing new in terms of revolutionary and national liberation movements elsewhere) (1995: 163–4; also Liyanage 1999: 129–30 and de Mel 2001: 215). The conjunction of warrior with motherhood, and the challenges and ambiguities this presents, seem to have made their way into popular culture representations of the Tigers as well. An Indian film, *The Terrorist* (Sivan 2000), follows a fictional female Tamil suicide bomber as she prepares for her mission of martyrdom. The character discovers partway through the film that she is pregnant from a one-off sexual encounter with a dying male combatant and spends the rest of the film agonizing over what to do. The implication seemed to me to be that she is faced with a nationalist dilemma: would she serve her people best by killing herself (and in the process assassinating an important political target), or by raising her Tamil child? It also at once exploits conventional notions about motherhood and femininity (her changed feelings when she discovers her pregnancy) and challenges them (the depiction of her as a committed and extremely able soldier). The film ends with the character deciding at the last possible moment not to complete her mission but one is left with unanswered questions about how her decision will be received by her commanders, how her pregnancy will be responded to by them, and how she will raise the child.

The mother-warrior conjunctive image is clearly in stark contrast to maternalist feminism (discussed in Chapter 3) which argues for motherhood as a basis for peace and non-violence – what Maunaguru calls the 'social mother'. In the context of worsening state repression in the northeast in the 1980s Tamil women organized themselves as mothers in groups such as the Mothers' Front and the Association of Mothers of Missing Youth, which 'operated to use their "motherhood" as a political force' (1995: 167). (There was also a parallel southern (Sinhalese) Mothers' Front, with the same attendant benefits and costs of using motherhood as a site of political protest (de Alwis 1998a).) While groups like the Mothers' Front in Sri Lanka and around the world show how the 'social mother' manifestation of maternalist feminism can be actualized, the mother-warrior (image and reality) illustrates that this is far from being an automatic link. In fact, it is a consciously constructed image or strategic tactic. The 'brave mother', the 'mother-warrior' and the 'social mother' are all different variations on how women's physical reproductive capabilities and their social nurturing role can be utilized in nationalist conflicts.

In conjunction with (yet also in contrast to) the Tamil mother-warrior construction that Maunaguru discusses, other scholars and commentators, beginning with Peter Schalk, have identified a construction of LTTE women as 'armed virgins' (Schalk 1992, 1994; Coomaraswamy 1997a, 1997b) or 'masculinized virgin warrior[s]' (de Alwis 1998b). Coomaraswamy and others view this extremely negatively as denying the women sexuality, sensuality and love and enforcing 'androgyny in a male sense – the masculine completely wiping out the feminine.... Is this liberation?' (Coomaraswamy 1997a). Schalk, however, sees it as strategically brilliant. He argues that the role of women fighters has been rationalized through reference to the classical Tamil concept of *karpu*, often translated as 'chastity'. This does not mean just refraining from engaging in what the culture considers to be illicit sexual relations; it also 'refers to a restraint in communication, especially with men'. *Karpu* 'means learning a behaviour of restraint that is especially important for virgins, married women and widows in their relations with men, but also more generally in all public behaviour' (1994: 177–8). Therefore, he argues,

> [t]he role of the fighting woman is thus implicitly rationalised with reference to an old classical societal value. This rationalisation creates a special type of woman, namely the armed virgin, a Tamil Saint Joan of Arc, who has no precedents in Tamil culture, but is a hybrid creation born of the conflict of introducing a new social role to an old culture.
>
> (Schalk 1994: 178)

The corresponding male version of *karpu* is the *tavan*, the ascetic who similarly restrains himself with regard to social relations; this 'is an honorific designation of a male LTTE fighter' (ibid.: 179). Ultimately, Schalk asserts, '[w]hoever created this role of the Tigress as a segregated armed virgin was a genius, because it made the martial actions of the Tigress acceptable to a popular understanding of decent female behaviour' (ibid.: 180). In other words, traditional social gendered expectations were utilized to make non-traditional female behaviour more acceptable. De Mel argues that

> [s]exuality is seen as a threat to discipline, and strictures come into place that 'police' both male and female sexual desire.... Such control is all the

> more important in an environment in which the usual social boundaries that segregate male and female have dissolved. What we have here is an exact replica of the sexual taboos that exist in the outside world, despite the militants' denunciation of those very norms.
>
> (2001: 219)

She goes on to say that

> [w]omen in these movements must subsume their own sexual desires to their role within the movement.... [T]he woman militant ... takes on, by choice, identities of abnegation and sacrifice rather than those of individual desire. This reflects, partly, her ideological commitment to the struggle, her understanding that life in existing society offers no real freedom for the individual; but it also signals an internalization of existing social codes. Curbing sexual desire within the movement would be an extension of, and no different from, the norms of conduct expected from her within her home and until her marriage.
>
> (Ibid.: 220)

The implication here, then, could be that the issue of sexuality illustrates how in a nationalist mobilization entailing a context of enormous gendered change, simultaneously social-sexual norms are reinforced which may be strategically useful for the movement; may be restrictive for both men and women, but transgression of which carries a particularly high cost for women; and acceptance of this may signal a Tamil nationalist 'patriarchal bargain' (see Kandiyoti 1988).

The reality of the 'armed virgins', however, is a little more nuanced. Certainly it is recognized that although marriage was originally forbidden for LTTE members of either sex this policy changed at some point, possibly after Prabhakaran himself married and had a family. Trawick notes that '[y]oung people fall in love and get married, subject to the permission of their elders within the organisation' (1999: 158), and claims that marriage between male and female members of the LTTE is permitted after each member has served in the movement for five years (ibid.: 145).[2] I found that female cadres reject the 'armed virgin' representation of themselves as being a misguided interpretation by outsiders rather than an LTTE ideal. Adele Ann (also known as Balasingham), too, has categorically denied that the organization promotes this construct (Balasingham 2001: 287–9). Certainly many of the women I interviewed were keen to refute this image of themselves and stressed that cadres could marry (with permission) after the appropriate age, which they told me was 23 for women and 28 for men. Nonetheless it is true that this in no way suggests that unmarried cadres would be likely to view premarital or extra-marital or, probably, homosexual sexual relations as acceptable, nor accepted by their leadership. However they are unhappy with the image presented of them as being without love and family life and dislike being the objects of pity for this reason. One of the interviewees, Sailajah, is married. Her marriage was arranged through an LTTE body that organizes marriages for members and her husband is an LTTE doctor. LTTE arranged marriages serve the purpose both of following local cultural practice and circumventing the problem of LTTE women not being seen as suitable wives by many outside the movement. I was also told a number of times about LTTE childcare centres in the Vanni, where children can be left when both parents are LTTE members. There is, however, a gender distinction in terms of marriages; some male cadres marry women in the movement but many marry women who are not involved, whereas female cadres generally seem only to marry men in the movement. Thamilini asserted in 2004, however, that the number of marriages where an LTTE woman had married a non-LTTE man had increased and was expected to go up further. From my interviews with both combatant and non-combatant Tamil women I received the strong impression that, as accepted as the LTTE women have come to be, people in the wider Tamil community do not view them as suitable wives. This may be because they are viewed as not being passive enough; another reason given was the idea that if the war broke out again the women would have to leave their families and go back to fight. For their part, female cadres expressed the idea that LTTE men tend to be more likely than non-LTTE men to understand them and not want to dominate them in the marriage. Kalaivily felt that she was ready for marriage but commented that

> outside women get adjusted to male cadres very easily. But for women like me, only a male cadre within the movement can understand me and my work nature. Only a person within the movement can understand a woman cadre. If I marry an outsider, I have to adjust to his lifestyle and he might not understand me and the nature of my work. Generally women prefer a male cadre within the movement, since he can understand her and her nature of work.

Once again, this reflects a divergence between LTTE women and 'normal' Tamil women (see also Stack-O'Connor 2007: 51–2), as well as arguably a similar divergence between LTTE men and 'normal' men.

Finally, the female fighters in the LTTE have a fearsome reputation and are often represented in the media and discussed amongst ordinary people (Tamil and Sinhalese) as being more violent and more terrifying than male Tigers. In interviews with a group of ex-prisoners of the LTTE, P.L. de Silva was told by the young men that 'they were absolutely terrified of the women cadres of the LTTE. The physical maltreatment meted out by the male cadres was a pale shadow to what the female cadres did' (de Silva 1995: 184). He also met men who lost control of their bowels at the thought of the female Tigers coming to torture them (personal communication). He suggests that one 'rather common' explanation of this is that 'female cadres have to be more tough, ruthless and less-sympathetic – in a word, more macho – in order to compete for status and recognition in a traditionally patriarchal context' (de Silva 1995: 184). Whether the women really are more violent than the men is, of course, hugely debatable (and difficult to establish empirically) but the very fact that such claims are made is interesting, signalling as it does the operation of the 'monster' narrative about politically violent women that I discussed in Chapter 3 (see Sjoberg and Gentry 2007).

Certainly the LTTE does expect its female cadres to act and present themselves as fierce and fearless warriors in the same way as is expected of male cadres; equality here is arguably about women emulating constructed/expected masculine qualities. Many of the women I interviewed related long recollections of battles they had fought in, what had happened and how they felt, frequently involving narratives of duty, sacrifice and self-abnegation. Some claimed they never felt fear during battle. Thamilachi described being under constant surprise attack by the SLA after they retook Jaffna in 1995–6, saying:

> But even in the face of such danger it never occurred to us that our life was in danger or we might be wounded or maimed or killed. Our instinct at once was to fight. We have to operate whatever weapons we had in our possession. Fear was just not there.

Geetha and Thangaci both reported being afraid but gave narratives that suggest that seeing people close to them killed made fear give way to anger and a renewed determination to fight. Thangaci said 'Yes, I was frightened. I was worried if something happens to me, who will take care of my parents?' She witnessed a number of friends in her combat unit die in battle and reported 'At that time, I felt that they are like my brothers and sisters; I should kill the opposition, and I should not leave the army.' When she returned from battle, however, she resumed being worried about her family. Geetha said 'Initially we used to be frightened but we got used to it as time passed by.' In one battle

> my sister was killed in front of my eyes and I became very tensed but I could not do anything at that time.... At that instant I thought that I could have died instead of her. But when I looked around many more women cadres had died, all of whom I regard as my sisters. So considering that fact, I still kept going.

Thamilini maintained that although cadres are afraid when they first enter battle, once they start fighting all other thoughts and fears of one's own death or injury disappear:

> we won't think about blood, think about dying or even think about our friends' death. The only thing that comes in our mind is we have been given an activity and we need to complete and achieve the activity.... Being in the LTTE and going to fight we know that people are trusting us, they are waiting for us, so we must take their load from them.

She did, however, describe how when the heat of battle is over and there is time for reflection, it is natural to grieve the loss of dead friends and mull over the events of the battle but argued that the focus on the goal of a separate state keeps them going. She related how her best friend was killed in battle in 1993 and her shock and grief over this, but said this is never enough to make her want to give up the fight. For Kalaivily, too, 'In the warfront it is a different world. We think and speak only about the target. We never think or discuss about anything else. No one of us will ever think about anything else.' She spoke about the value of each cadre's life, since they are outnumbered by the SLA, so that 'the things which come to our mind are, we have to rescue our fellow cadres quickly and save them as early as possible'. Furthermore, as with Geetha and Thangaci,

> These injuries and killings around us increases our anger towards the opposition. We suffer due to the thoughts of our cadres, the days we had spent together, and much more. However, we also make sure that we should never lose another life.

She went on to say:

> In our history, women are generally known for their soft nature. Women are full of mercy and kind hearted.... In our day-to-day normal life we still are treated like this. Also qualities such as love, affection, caring are all quite natural to us. But in the warfront we never think that we are women and we are soft by nature. These disappear from our mind. In the warfront we have only our aim in our mind, our aim to get an independent nation. We never think that we are killing someone. We think that we are doing our duty ... to get an independent nation.

Tamil nationalist feminism: the view from the LTTE and its critics

As explained in the previous chapter the majority of the women I interviewed said that they had not been aware of issues pertaining to women's social conditions, women's rights or equality before they joined the movement but all of them had this awareness raised within the movement, with the vast majority mentioning being taught about women's social oppression in LTTE political classes as well as their individual experiences contributing to this change. This does not seem to be entirely consistent for all cadres, however, since Shanthi said she did not receive classes of any kind aside from the military training. Kalaivily spoke of attending various kinds of training and classes, including on politics, history and leadership training but not specifically in relation to women's rights; she said 'I think that there is no training needed to be given on women's liberation or women's freedom. It is already prevailing in our movement.' She did, however, speak about the LTTE teaching the 'common people' about women's liberation and empowerment. Eleven of the 17 women appeared to now possess a genuine interest specifically in working towards improving the lives and opportunities of Tamil women, as illustrated in the first section of this chapter. Unsurprisingly their intellectual conceptualization of and ability to articulate on such issues varied from woman to woman but the depth of their commitment to women in their communities was unquestionable and humbling, if arguably also potentially autocratic in some contexts. I found it difficult to get interpreters to understand and translate the word 'feminist' or 'feminism' to the interviewees so was unable to assess whether or not they would identify with this label, but certainly the concept of working towards greater rights and freedoms for women was understood in a positive way and supported.

It seemed to me that the type of feminist ideas the women expressed were, while tied to their nationalism, largely of a liberal variant with some cultural specificities, where women and men are conceived of as essentially having the same potential capacities and qualities. What was often stressed was the idea that people vary in their abilities and talents and that each person should have the chance for their particular talents to be drawn out, but that this is about individual people rather than their sex. A few (in higher LTTE positions) also demonstrated awareness that cultural variation between countries is significant and that the problems women face are different in different places. Thamilini asserted that 'Even in the developed world … women will be facing some problems, but the problems are different for different countries. This depends on the country, life, development and the environment and culture; the problem varies.' She also spoke of the high rate of divorce in Western countries and argued that this had a negative impact on children and families as a whole. She said 'In our Tamil society, the relationship between the mother–father and children is very important and this relationship is very good between them'; she does not want Tamils to emulate the Western pattern and she is concerned about Tamil diaspora communities in other countries, whom she feels are struggling and are not integrated entirely in one culture or the other. In a similar vein Kalaivily also spoke of a mutual respect between husband and wife in Tamil culture and viewed the Western divorce rate as a negative thing. She also said:

> In Tamil culture things such as marriage, marriage rituals, dress, our way of worship, are different from other cultures. So women's liberation should be … [done] in an acceptable way to Tamil culture. We do not want to live a lifestyle like foreigners; our society is not willing to come out of this basic culture.… Women's empowerment must be well within our culture and be acceptable in general by our society.

She spoke of Tamil society raising girls to think that there are boundaries to the kinds of jobs they can do; that they are only fit for cooking and household work; expecting women to be at home by 6pm (and thus not being allowed to work at night); not being allowed to look at men while walking in public, and so on. In her view:

> These things suppress the natural qualities of women. Our aim is that there should be no such restrictions for women. Our movement has proved that women can do any job. So, we aim to empower women to overcome these problems and ensure freedom for them. We want women to believe in themselves and come out of these boundaries.

However once again she was keen to stress that there are cultural limits to change: 'In doing so, if there are changes to our basic culture such as the way women dress, it won't be acceptable.' All her comments imply the idea of the impetus for changes to the gendered order stemming from the LTTE and 'ordinary' people resisting some of them; there is no acknowledgement of the potential for Tamil society to set its own agenda for change independently of the LTTE (even if partially sparked by their actions) and the potential for LTTE resistance to this, as is arguably the case regarding the issue of women's appropriate clothing.

It remains the case that Tamil nationalism fundamentally frames and justifies LTTE feminism. Samuel views the female armed militants as one group of women who have rejected traditional notions of femininity but argues that '[f]or them the national liberation struggle is the paramount issue; women's subordination within it is not a question' (2001: 196). On the other hand, although feminism is certainly tied to nationalism and it is assumed that freedom for women will not/cannot/should not come *without* national freedom, at the same time not all the LTTE women seem to fall into the classic trap of believing that it will automatically come *with* national liberation either. Banuka said 'Even if we get the nation's freedom, unless there are equal rights for women in the fields of education and employment there won't be real freedom. So it is our responsibility to ensure women are getting their rights.'

Adele Ann, wife (now widow) of LTTE ideologue Anton Balasingham and an ideologue and soldier in her own right who has helped with the military training of LTTE women, expresses a set of ideas which have been described by Schalk as 'martial feminism' justifying military action against the Sri Lankan state. Her martial feminism is clearly indivisible from her commitment to Tamil nationalism; Schalk notes that she, like LTTE leader Velupillai Prabhakaran, 'insists on civil rights for women and on the taking up of arms, and connects the demand for civil rights for women with a demand for the liberation of the "homeland" from what is regarded as an illegitimate occupying force' (1994: 164–5). Ann talks of a dual oppression of Tamil women, arguing that

> [o]n the one hand, [Tamil] women … have borne the brunt of the national oppression stemming from chauvinist Sinhala policies. On the other hand, women have been subject to an internal form of social oppression rising out of male chauvinism. This form of oppression is reinforced by the conservative traditions and some of the cultural norms inherent in the Tamil community.
>
> (Ann 1990)

According to Prabhakaran himself, '[t]he historical storm of the liberation struggle is uprooting age old traditions that took root over a long period of time in our society.' Thus, '[t]he ideology of women liberation [*sic*] is a child born out of the womb of our liberation struggle' (Pirapaharan 1993); it 'is the fervent child that had its genesis in the matrix of our national liberation movement. Its rise and progress is an incomparably unique chapter in history.' The women's liberation movement is, he says, an integral part of the greater Tamil struggle (1996). He states that

> [o]ur women are seeking liberation from the structures of oppression deeply embedded in our society. This oppressive cultural system and practices have emanated from age old ideologies and superstitions. Tamil women are subjected to intolerable suffering as a consequence of male chauvinistic oppression, violence and from the social evils of casteism and dowry.
>
> (Pirapaharan 1992)

Prabhakaran suggests that some of these problems 'can be resolved if men and women recognize each other's liberty, equality and dignity and enter into a cordial relationship based [on] mutual understanding and share the responsibilities of family life and also contribute to the development of society' (ibid.). He asserts that

> [w]omen should be awakened from the darkness of an ideological world which makes them believe that their oppressive conditions are the result of their fate, of their actions of former births, of the moral laws enunciated for them, of the cultural configurations that determined their lives. Such ... [an] awakening is a necessary condition for their emancipation.
>
> (Pirapaharan 1992)

Prabhakaran is careful to state, however, that '[t]he struggle against male chauvinistic oppression is not a struggle against men. It is an ideological struggle against the ignorance of men.' Significantly, he implies that only women who are involved with the Tamil nationalist struggle can achieve liberation for women: '[i]t is only the women with a revolutionary consciousness who could become a revolutionary force. Only such a revolutionary force can destroy the shackles of oppression' (1992). Therefore, '[t]he Tamil Eelam revolutionary woman has transformed herself as a Tiger for the Liberation of our land and liberation of women. She, like a fire that burns injustices, has taken up arms. Our movement paved the way for this historical change' (1993). He claims that '[o]ur struggle shines as a superb paradigm of women's ability to accomplish anything' (1996).

Many feminists and other commentators have questioned the ideology of women's liberation that is expounded by the LTTE, being sceptical of Tamil nationalist ideology in relation to women and of the idea that participation in the militant groups can or has brought improvements for Tamil women as a whole. This is a contentious area, with some being absolute sceptics and others taking a more moderate position. Schalk suggests that although Prabhakaran's speeches on women's liberation are very radical in many ways, they are missing 'some statement to the effect that the common struggle of men and women is a training in and model for co-operation in a future society at peace' (1994: 168). Even Adele Ann noted, in an earlier phase of the war, that '[t]he overall impact made by the fighting girls on Tamil society is yet to be assessed. It is also too early to predict the future in relation to the position in Tamil society after the war is over' (1990). Samarasinghe argues that through women's participation in armed struggle in civil war they also 'become actors in the public arena'. The question is whether this public sphere activity is temporary and transitory, ending with the war, 'or whether the gains they made in times of war could be consolidated in terms of gender equity in times of peace'. She reminds us that 'women's participation in the public arena of the armed struggle is certainly no guarantee that women have finally penetrated into the public sphere of activities on a basis of gender equality' (1996: 213, 217). I would not dispute this; nevertheless the participation of women as soldiers and the expressed ideological commitment to women's equality in Tamil nationalism are significant socio-political changes that give feminist discourses an opening to try and stimulate debate. Maunaguru maintains that

> [a]ll major Tamil nationalist groups addressed the woman question as part of their political agendas. This was framed in a conventional Leftist format, which aimed at first eliminating the barriers for women to participate in the national liberation struggle. In addition, it was argued that women would be equal in a society that would eventually emerge out of the conflict. Even though this is an ideological commonplace, which did not recognize the specific oppression of women within the movement for national liberation, the acceptance of the concept of women's liberation, even in this very limited form, provided an important space for issues relating to gender, power and oppression to be debated by feminists.
>
> (1995: 164)

Women's wings of militant Tamil organizations and autonomous women's groups tried to use the opportunity created by nationalist lip-service to feminism to raise issues relating to the subordination of women and 'extended the discourse beyond the boundaries of ethnic repression' (Maunaguru 1995: 164–5). In the 1980s such groups focused mainly on economic relations, though they also began addressing sexual violence (Schrijvers 1999: 318). The focus on economic relations is not surprising, given the ideological commitment to socialism that the Tamil militant groups had at the time. The LTTE asserted that their vision of Eelam was of a socialist state with radical transformation of social attitudes to women and the EPRLF's women's wing expressed a materialist-feminist position that argued that the subordination of women arose from economic dependence linked with private ownership in society. Maunaguru contends that this 'fairly orthodox materialist-feminist ideological position', arguing that gender oppression is derived only from property and class relations, neglects 'debates on cultural traditions as reproductive sites for patriarchal relations' (1995: 165). On the other hand, the ideology of the EPRLF women's wing was arguably more radical in terms of gender relations than that of the LTTE, since it maintained that 'the liberation of women could not be automatically achieved through national liberation' and argued that 'women should consciously and constantly struggle against patriarchy in order to attain their own liberation while participating, simultaneously in the common struggle' (ibid.), while the LTTE leadership has been consistently careful to stress women's liberation solely *through* the national struggle.

In 1990 Hoole *et al.* asserted that the women's wings of Tamil militant groups, or at least of the LTTE, had failed to address issues surrounding sexual violence (1990: 324), though this does not seem entirely fair. Maunaguru argues that from the ideological space opened up by discussions on the 'woman question' in the militant Tamil nationalist groups came a new image of women: *Puthumai Pen* – 'New Woman'. This construction first emerged in Tamil poetry in early twentieth-century Indian nationalism and in the 1980s it began to be utilized by Sri Lankan Tamil women activists, who 'challenged the celebrated "traditional feminine," qualities of passivity and submissiveness'. For the 1986 International Women's Day, a joint march by various women's groups used the slogan: 'Let us forget the Four Virtues [modesty, charm, coyness and fear]/Let us own a fighting spirit' (Maunaguru 1995: 165–6). One feminist gain from this, Maunaguru says, was a new understanding of and activism around the issue of sexual violence against women, in the context of the numerous rapes and sexual harassment of women that occurred in the Tamil majority areas with a large military presence. In the past, rape had not been discussed as a social or political issue and instead was 'constructed as an isolated act that concerned only the individualized victim'. In the new context of a hostile military presence rape became an important political issue for nationalist militant groups. However while these groups saw rape as an instance of 'racial' oppression of the Tamil community, the women's activist groups viewed rape as an issue linked to gender and power and stressed its relationship to the general level of violence against women. Feminists stimulated 'discussions on the stigma attached to rape victims, the concept of chastity in Tamil culture, and the patriarchal interests underlying it'. Thus, Maunaguru asserts, the issue of sexual violence shows one way that 'Tamil women used the new context created by militant nationalism to articulate their interests as women'. Significantly, these women also linked constructions of 'woman warrior' with 'new woman', arguing 'that it was both tactically and politically wrong to separate or alienate gender interests from national interests' (ibid.: 166–7). Maunaguru argues, therefore, that the category of the new woman 'as a position of protest against patriarchy marked a new, liberatory moment in the struggle for gender equality'. This was possible because of the space created by previous struggles, especially the debate over the 'woman question' 'which took place in the context of militant, left-leaning Tamil nationalism' (ibid.: 172).

Bose argues that

> given the extreme conservatism that has historically been the hallmark of Sri Lankan Tamil society … it is difficult to disagree with the LTTE's assessment that the mass participation, in a variety of roles, of women constitutes 'the most remarkable feature of our national struggle'.
>
> (1994: 110, no citation for quote given)

Similarly, despite their criticism of the militant groups, Hoole *et al.* do maintain that whatever the experiences of women in armed liberation movements 'one cannot deny that this is a sweeping phase in the life of the whole community of women'. They comment that

> [o]ne cannot but be inspired when one sees the women of the LTTE, two by two, in the night, with their AKs slung over the shoulder, patrolling the entrances to Jaffna city. One cannot but admire the dedication and toughness of their training.
>
> (Hoole *et al.* 1990: 325–6)

In addition, Bose suggests that 'the high-profile participation of women has served to impart to the Tiger Movement a general, popular character that might otherwise have been absent from it' (1994: 111). This echoes Yuval-Davis's suggestion, discussed in Chapter 3, that incorporating women into militaries in nationalist movements conveys the notion that *all* members of the collectivity are symbolically incorporated into the military and the movement (1997: 98). Bose asserts, therefore, that

> [t]he liberating impact of Tiger struggles on the lives of young Tamil women thus should not be underestimated, especially if one remembers that this is a society where women have historically been totally excluded from the public arena. The confidence and poise of leading Tiger women is impressive indeed.
>
> (1994: 112)

This was also something I noticed during my fieldwork. Tiger women have an air of quiet assurance and confidence that is not necessarily obvious in other women; even the way they walk and carry themselves is different. In fact, this can be problematic for them in some contexts. Interviewee Geetha told me that the Sri Lankan Army observes Tamil women coming through checkpoints and looks at the way they walk. When she left the LTTE to return home she was stopped and questioned as they suspected, from her walk, that she had been in the LTTE. Luckily for her sake, she managed to convince them to let her go.

In the light of historical experience, however, Bose nonetheless suggests that it is 'probably more than prudent ... to sound a note of caution as well, lest one get too carried away'. He asserts that the changes within the Tamil social formation in regard to women and in other areas 'may not necessarily have been consciously *intended* by the leaders of the LTTE, though they have definitely been the concrete *result* of specific strategies of mass mobilisation pursued by these same leaders' (1994: 112, 115). Conversations with LTTE activists left him feeling that they welcome these societal changes, if only because they realize that to achieve the unified national movement required to bring about Eelam the movement must involve these social changes, though not all these changes are welcomed by all Tamils. In fact, the LTTE is itself a product of this social turbulence – much of its appeal and support comes from 'social categories such as the lower castes, the women, and the peasantry and fisherfolk, from its commitment to social justice and equality'. Despite this, he believes that overall these changes to the pre-existing Tamil social order are seen by the LTTE leadership as simply incidental to the ultimate goal of an independent state of Eelam which, he claims, is all the LTTE really cares about; 'their vision is not just limited but also myopic.' Social changes within the Tamil nation are welcomed and encouraged only 'so long as that process flows parallel to the national cause' (ibid.: 116). In regard to the changing status and roles of women this suggests, once again, an uneasy relationship between nationalism and feminism which needs constant negotiation.

Similarly, Samarasinghe argues that there are 'several tensions present between the articulated elements of women's emancipation and the reality of women's actual positioning within the revolutionary/militaristic praxis'. First, because of the common attribution of women's revolutionary role to the direction or command of the male leader of the LTTE, she views this role as more 'like a set of orders to be followed, rather than a spontaneous activation by society in general'. Second, as discussed in Chapter 3, in post-revolutionary states 'the priorities of governance and statehood change, and with that the agenda for women may also change. Evidence from other liberation movements illustrates that often times women are politely told to go back into the reproductive sphere and to the kitchen.' LTTE women do not, she suggests, seem to be creating a public space for women that can be carried through to peacetime. Third, '[b]y upholding the virtues of virginity and chastity for women in the LTTE, the boundaries of acceptable female behavioural norms are clearly marked.' Finally, on the one hand female soldiers are glorified by the LTTE and post-revolutionary gender equality is envisaged; on the other, leadership of the LTTE 'remains almost exclusively Tamil male' (1996: 217–19). There has been a rapid increase in female combatants but it is the male leadership that has made this space available to them, while continuing to uphold 'the gendered dimension of sexuality, which is a fundamental basis of patriarchy'. Thus, women's involvement in the Tigers has opened up a new space for them, 'but the boundaries of that space are determined not by them, but by the male leadership along lines of cultural and social norms of society'. The case of Tamil women in Sri Lanka, she says, shows that although women's roles become 'expanded and redefined during times of national liberation and struggle' and women become more visible, the question remains as to how much that redefinition is carried through to peacetime (ibid.: 219–21).

Although she makes some valid points, particularly in respect to the open question as to how much women's expanded roles will be carried through into peacetime, in other ways Samarasinghe is arguably too negative. Although the development of women's revolutionary role is often *attributed* to the command of the leader, in reality women themselves pushed hard for access to this role. Second, many LTTE women seem to be strongly involved in a wide range of women's development and community development programmes, although the extent to which these activities and programmes can be construed as 'feminist' does remain open to debate. Molyneux's influential categorization of women's gender interests into practical interests (those based on satisfying needs that arise from the sexual division of labour) and strategic interests (those which involve more potentially transformative aims towards social relations so as to fundamentally re-position women within society) may be useful here (1985).[3] She also categorizes women's collective action into different types based on where the authority to define women's goals and actions lies or stems from, of which the women's wing of the LTTE falls best into her categorization of directed collective action or directed mobilizations, where the women's organization or movement is subject to a higher institutional authority and, therefore, there is 'little, if any, room for genuine negotiation over goals' (1998: 229). Molyneux allows that there are different forms of directed action, some of which contain more explicit commitments to women's interests than others, and that there can be fluidity over time in the degree of direction involved (ibid.: 229–30). The nationalist feminism expressed by the LTTE does contain explicit commitments to Sri Lankan Tamil women's interests and arguably this includes elements of women's strategic interests, not just their practical interests; furthermore I would suggest that the jury is still out regarding exactly how much real room there is for a genuine debate and negotiation over gender goals, both within the LTTE and between the LTTE and the wider Tamil community. Third, the virtues of chastity and moral behaviour expected of female recruits are also expected of male recruits. Finally, the issue of the leadership of the LTTE is not nearly as clear-cut as Samarasinghe and others assert, which I will elaborate on here.

Hoole *et al.* assert that 'it would be a positive result if a few of those [female combatants] who come out, with a richness of experience and self-criticism, become a catalyst for the further advancement of the position of women in this land' and suggest that 'one would have expected tangible cracks in the ideology of Tamil society and some liberating experience for the women' (1990: 330, 323). They themselves are very pessimistic about what has actually been the reality but it is worth bearing in mind that their book was published in 1990, only five years after women first began joining the LTTE as combatants and right around the time that their numbers began to swell to more of a critical mass. One reason for the pessimism of many is the apparent or presumed lack of women in highly placed decision-making positions within the LTTE. Chandra de Silva maintains that there is no evidence of women's participation in policy-making, decision-making or planning at the highest levels of the LTTE (1999: 61–2; see also Liyanage 1999: 135). Samuel, also, asserts that despite their strong military involvement 'no woman was allowed into the patriarchal male echelons of political decisionmaking of the LTTE' (2001: 195). Finally, Coomaraswamy has famously said of LTTE women that

> [t]hey are not initiators of ideas, they are only implementers of policy made by someone else, by men.... They become cogs in the wheel of someone else's designs and plans.... They are the consumers, not the producers of the grand political project.
>
> (1997b: 9)

In contrast, Bose claimed in 1994 that '[t]hree of the LTTE's ten-member Central Committee, the movement's top decision-making body, are women' (1994: 108–9). During a 2002 interview Thamilini told me that there were (at that time) 12 members on the Central Committee, five of whom were women. At 42 per cent that is higher than the percentage of women members of national parliaments anywhere apart from Rwanda and Sweden (and the Welsh assembly at regional level) and is much higher than usual percentages of female Cabinet members in most national governments. Reportedly there are now also a number of women who are LTTE area leaders and administrators. There is also a separate women-only committee on women's development, with members drawn from various sections of the organization. Again this reflects tensions and ambiguities in terms of the level of autonomy that feminist or women's activities hold within the LTTE; the women's development committee was an idea of Prabhakaran, according to Thamilini, but on the other hand it meets and develops programmes autonomously. Kalaivily told me that there are female leaders at all levels below that of supremo Prabhakaran. When I asked her about the allegation that women are more represented in military activities than in decision-making (or in the peace negotiations), Thamilini argued that this was largely false bad press on the part of the Sri Lankan government and people like Radhika Coomaraswamy (who is, frankly, detested by the LTTE), though she did concede that in the past women were not so involved in the Political Wing but said that this is changing. She argued that since men have been involved in the LTTE and in the military activities for longer than women, they have had many more opportunities than women to rise to high political positions (military experience is largely a prerequisite for political office for the Tigers and all members of the Political Wing have at least had the basic military training). However women are not obstructed from political activities so once they have developed the necessary capabilities 'they will reach that position fast'. She argued that

> men have been brought up in a manner to lead the family and the opportunities for them to grow are very high.... In the females there are few people have been brought up like that, so the amount will be fewer, they [men] will be the majority in these things. But there are [female] leaders here [in the Political Wing] ... but ... they must bring others to this position. Through the training process – that's happening now.

Liyanage argues that the pattern of women's participation in the LTTE is similar to that of women's participation in liberation struggles in Algeria, China, Eritrea, Namibia, Nicaragua, Mozambique, Palestine and Zimbabwe. As in these movements, the LTTE

> recognised the importance of mobilising women and formed the women's front.... [However,] [s]imilar to most of these liberation movements, the LTTE has considered women's issues as secondary and their assumption

> has been that the emancipation of women will automatically be achieved by the victory of the struggle.
>
> (Liyanage 1999: 132)

In reality, the experience of these other struggles has shown that after war ceased, 'women were usually expected to assume their traditional roles or were largely limited to supportive positions in political and public life' (ibid.). Liyanage maintains that 'the LTTE movement has been projected and defined by men, particularly by Prabhakaran, executed by men and that women fight to fulfil men's nationalistic aspirations' (ibid.: 131). While I agree it seems likely that so far the main thrust of the LTTE project has been defined by men, I would not go as far as Liyanage does. It is worth re-emphasizing that women have 'nationalistic aspirations' as well and women in the LTTE view these as being of primary importance. It is also true that their specific nationalist aspirations may sometimes vary from those of men, as may their vision of an independent state. Schrijvers asserts that '[t]he feminist discourse is the only one in which women are defined in their own right, without being linked to the interests of nationalist and ethnic struggles' (1999: 328). I would contend, however, that this is equally problematic. Which feminist discourse does she mean? The LTTE women cadres and Women's Political Wing do express a form of feminism but clearly not the form Schrijvers is referring to. Also, it seems that she is implying that being a woman in one's 'own right' entails being somehow 'unethnicized', as though concepts of nation and nationalism are unimportant (or should be unimportant) if one is a woman. Many Western feminists in countries not affected by nationalism or political violence have been particularly guilty of assuming this; my experiences living in Northern Ireland and researching in Sri Lanka have forced me to challenge this. Women involved in nationalist struggles all over the world have shown that in their position, for many, the above assumption is not only untrue and impossible but also undesirable. Commitment to the perceived needs or interests of one's perceived nation or ethnic group is viewed as just as important, or more so, than one's needs or interests 'as a woman'. Similarly, the debate over whether LTTE women are agents or victims, liberated or subjugated, emancipated or oppressed strikes me as an unnecessary and unsophisticated binary. Ultimately, Rajasingham-Senanayake's phrase 'ambivalent empowerment' seems to me to fit best.

> The reality of LTTE women is probably somewhere in-between [this binary]. For while they may have broken out of the confines of their allotted domesticity and taken on new roles as fighters, it is indeed arguable that they are captive both to the patriarchal nationalist project of the LTTE leader Prabhakaran and the history and experience of oppression by the Sri Lankan military. However, to deny these Tamil nationalist women their agency because they are nationalist is to once again position them within the 'victim' complex, where the militant woman is denied her agency and perceived to be acting out a patriarchal plot.
>
> (2001a: 113)

6 Women's experiences in paramilitary organizations in Northern Ireland

Gender relations and feminist nationalism

Irish republicanism has expressed the notion (common to national liberation movements) of all members of society having their part to play in the struggle, which as discussed in Chapter 3 can have a significant impact in terms of the strategic and ideological benefit of incorporating women into nationalist militant groups, though how this plays out varies enormously. As noted in Chapter 4 republicanism, unlike loyalism, has certainly celebrated images of women as 'freedom fighters' in political street art and republican paramilitaries have allowed female combatants in much greater numbers than loyalist paramilitaries. Nevertheless, in contrast to the LTTE in Sri Lanka, the IRA and other republican paramilitaries in Northern Ireland did not develop specific policies dealing with the integration of women and do not seem to have actively or specifically targeted women in their recruitment. The republican interviewees' experiences of paramilitary gender relations varied primarily according to the time period of their involvement. It seems that there was a significant change in attitude over time on the part of some male members, though whether this was genuinely echoed by the leadership is harder to establish. On the whole the younger women I interviewed, active in the 1980s and 1990s, did not report experiencing a lack of respect or sexist attitudes from male comrades, nor any gendered division of labour aside from the fact that it was usually women who carried weapons away (a tactical decision since women were much less likely to be searched). Women involved in the early 1970s were more likely to report various incidents of sexism. In contrast, narratives of the loyalist women who were involved with paramilitaries suggest that there may have been little if any change over time for them and a high degree of resistance to women's paramilitary activities.

Gender relations and experiences in republican paramilitaries

The focus of discussion here is overwhelmingly on the Provisional IRA, since it was the dominant and largest republican paramilitary for most of the 'Troubles' and was the organization of all of the interviewees except Emma (INLA). The PIRA and the INLA share common organizational roots and collective nationalist myths and I would hypothesize that the respective experiences of female combatants have been similar; the greater socialist ideological commitment of the INLA does not seem to have led to a more explicit or different approach towards the question of women in the ranks. I have no information on the gender relations of or the numbers of women involved with the small republican paramilitaries currently still active, the so-called 'dissident republican' groups Continuity IRA and the Real IRA. It is notable, however, that on the occasions when CIRA has held press conferences or photo opportunities for local press there have frequently been female figures visibly present, and allegedly until a few years ago the third in command of the Real IRA was a woman, Bernadette Sands McKevitt, sister of Bobby Sands and married to alleged ex-leader of the RIRA Michael McKevitt.

In the early 1970s women had to struggle to be allowed into the PIRA itself rather than be restricted to the women's auxiliary, Cumann na mBan, and a male ex-prisoner told me that 'in the early days they [women] were treated as just a wee bit more than coffee makers'. When Teresa joined there were almost no other female volunteers anywhere in the country and her story indicates the individual nature of women's integration.

> When you first approached the movement you're told go and join Cumann na mBan and you said 'no, I don't want to join Cumann na mBan, I want to be a volunteer', and you basically had to fight your way. Of course it depended on who you approached – if you approached the right man and you kind of sussed out somebody who was a bit more forward lookin' than some of the older men [then it was possible].

Nevertheless, she reported that although she had to push significantly to be allowed in, once she *was*,

> I must say I had a wonderful experience with the men that I worked with. They accepted me totally. I was treated just as another volunteer, which is what I made very clear from the start, that I didn't expect or want any privileges because I was female. And they very much took me at my word, and I was very grateful for it.

However she did feel they were somewhat protective towards her and reflected that 'lookin' back I know they spoiled me in many ways, you know?' Like all the women, Teresa also stressed that her own experience should not necessarily be taken as representative of that of others.

> Now there would've been other people in the Army who would've been very dismissive of women bein' in the Army.... I had a very positive experience in the Army but that's not to say that there weren't men there who were Neanderthals, you know, thought 'what's a girl doin' in the Army?'

She believes that 'once we broke the ice it was easier, you know, once we had actually joined and the precedent had been set, it then became easier for women to become volunteers'. This does not, however, necessarily mean that once in the movement women were all treated equally. Teresa herself had some experiences of men demanding better weapons than the women when going on an operation which included female volunteers (indicating a certain conceptualization of masculinity whereby status derives from possessing and using guns) and knew of some men who refused to go on operations with women at all. She also indicated tension between female volunteers and Cumann na mBan.

> There was a great feelin' within the Cumann na mBan circles of, oh, you kind of thought you were better than them – but it wasn't a case of that, it was just a case of Cumann na mBan had its place and it was great work that they did but it was just that I didn't want to do that, I wanted to do somethin' else, I wanted to have more of an active role than a supportive role.

Mary, also involved in the very early years of the 'Troubles', argued that in those days

> there were very very few women who would've made it into the Army, but those of them who did make it into the Army in the early '70s would've been treated exactly as [the men]. The fact that they were brass-necked enough to get in there in the first place would have meant that they had the same responsibilities and duties.

On the other hand, her reflections suggest a divergence between the lack of a gendered division of labour and the attitudes of men.

> I was to an extent tolerated as a necessary evil and did indeed even have my uses but it is still essentially a male bastion and while I assumed a 'male' role to some extent I never seen any evidence that my male counterparts embraced or took on any of the more traditional female roles. This differs slightly where the male had spent some time in prison but essentially I feel the whole experience did not further the cause of female emancipation.

Like Teresa, Mary also indicated tensions with the older women in Cumann na mBan in this period.

> In the early '70s when I came to Dublin [on the run] the women's organization would've been quite standoffish from the couple of us women that weren't in the [Cumann na mBan] – I think the word 'hussy' would've been used, you know? [Laughter.] But I think that left, that stopped, you know as society itself progressed that stopped. I don't think that was an issue even in the late '70s.... It was just that first break had to be made, you know?

She remembers an incident

> when this particular [Cumann na mBan] woman was being obnoxious and giving out about being treated properly, and this woman [volunteer] was getting ready to go out for the night clubbing, and the OC made this woman [volunteer] stand guard all night on a training camp and was told 'that's equality for you dear'. Still in her finery!

However she also conceded that for their own part

> we [female volunteers] would've been scathing about them, you know? We would talk about them and their bandaids, you know, and their first aid kids. Yeah, we would've been just as chauvinistic. We didn't think so at the time, we thought we were super cool.

There were other republicans outside the immediate PIRA circle of people Mary worked with who were also less than pleased to see women in such active roles.

> It would be looked at differently in the north than it would in the south. I mean you'd get in the north, if needs must take all hands on deck and they'd be doing it, reacting to a situation. You take an old farmer there down in Kerry or Galway and you'd drive up to him and say 'right, I'm here', and the man would nearly have to sit down, he'd take a weak turn.... I remember even as late as 1980 ... and I was sent down till[1] Kerry to speak till a group, heart of republican Kerry. I got into the room and I looked round and there was a fine body of people in the hall, I mean the hall was packed, and it was just starting to get organized on the H-Block campaign, and I looked round and I said 'before I start, I've got one question to ask', I said, 'where are the women?' And they looked aghast at me and they said 'they're at home!' And I said 'next time, they'd better be here'. And I wasn't invited back I think.... That would never have happened in Belfast or Tyrone, d'you know, but this was Kerry.

On another occasion an H-Block committee member, who was not a member of the military side of the republican movement, told Mary that she should not lead a march in Dublin of (male) construction workers in support of the hunger strikers, because it would not do to have a woman lead the march.

> But actually, those were two incidents when I wasn't dealing with the strict military wing of the republican movement, I was dealing with outsiders. There was more equality within the military, and I would say that is probably because the soldiers respect [each other] – I've never thought of that!

There was also an incident when a neighbour of her family obviously snubbed her, while speaking to her parents and a brother who was also known to be involved in the movement. 'I was a fallen woman, nearly, you know?!' She feels there was a similar difference in her parents' attitude towards her involvement and their attitude towards her brothers' involvement, although they did not try and stop her activities. Her mother, she believes, resented her involvement, which in her opinion was tied up with 'an older woman's envy of a younger woman's freedom'. Similarly, Caral and Maeve, both involved in a later period of the 'Troubles', feel that their parents took their involvement and imprisonment harder because they were daughters rather than sons.

Maria was involved in supportive roles in the early days of the 'Troubles' and then very actively in the late 1980s to early 1990s, experiencing a significant difference in respect between the two time periods.

> In the early days I would say it didn't matter what you did, it was just 'thanks love', you know? 'Good for you', and like patronizing. But certainly the second time around I felt greatly respected. And I woulda been in charge of a job maybe … and I liked that,… I liked knowin' exactly what a job was about, where I was goin'.

Part of this, she feels, is due to the impact of male ex-prisoners, many of whom took some Women's Studies classes in prison and experienced some re-education in this area.

> I was almost revered at times and I couldn't believe it, you know, that I was gettin' this respect from men, and then we talked about Women's Studies and all and I thought 'god, so this is what the new men are like!' In sayin' that, mind you, there was still the ones who were still Mr Macho Man, you know? They tended to be the ones that hadn't been to prison and hadn't been educated in that way.

Niamh related similar experiences. In the early 1970s she joined Cumann na mBan as a teenager, having belonged to a junior organization before that. She carried weapons and performed other tasks for a number of years, being 'active' as a volunteer from the 1980s. In the earlier years 'it was very much a case where … men fired the guns and women generally carried the guns', though this was partly due to security concerns as women were less likely to be searched. Gendered expectations meant that women were perceived as less dangerous and they were less likely to be stopped and searched, even after it became commonly known that there were female IRA volunteers. Members of the British military previously stationed in Northern Ireland to whom I have spoken informally maintained that they knew that women were involved in such activities but that there was a significant risk of negative publicity attached to searching women's bodies. For Niamh, 'in later years and just in me own experience with people who have went to prison and come out, people who went to prison especially would be much more progressive in their attitudes towards feminism, towards equality'. Nonetheless, she still encountered some sexist attitudes. At one point she was arrested and held for interrogation (before the later time she was imprisoned) and afterwards she heard that a male volunteer had disparagingly said she would break and reveal information, which she felt he would not have said if she were a man. She remembers feeling very angry about the intimation.

As noted, the women who were active in the 1980s and 1990s all said that they were treated the same as male volunteers and that they felt respected by their comrades. This includes Emma, who was in the INLA rather than PIRA. However all stressed that they were speaking only from their own personal experience and that it was quite likely that others had had different experiences, which suggests a suspicion on their part that there was significant variation here. This may not be surprising given that the IRA has permitted female members but seemingly on an ad hoc basis rather than as a matter of explicit policy and recruitment. Stack-O'Connor suggests that the initiative of individuals (women who wanted to join and male leaders who encountered them) largely drove the integration of women into the IRA (2007: 52), finding in interviews with male IRA leaders that they had not received any explicit instructions about how to incorporate women into their units or what kinds of assignments to give them. Accordingly, what actually happened on the ground was determined by individual cell leaders (ibid.: 62n44) meaning, one would presume, there may have been greater variation than in the case of the LTTE.

Despite generally feeling that they were treated equally with men, like Teresa before them both Eileen and Mairead nonetheless believe that their male comrades were a little more protective towards them and a little more concerned for their safety, perhaps even unconsciously, than they were for other male members. Eileen also suggested that

> at the height of struggle people maybe were treated a little bit more equally in a sense, because there was so much to do and there was no point in saying well you go off and, you know, make the sandwiches while I – because there was too much stuff for people to do.

Interestingly, this echoes some of the comments from Algerian ex-*moudjahidates* (female combatants) about having experienced respect, equality and fraternity with male comrades while they were fighting the 1950s anti-colonial war against France – a situation they came to bitterly miss later (Bouatta 1994). Following what may be a pattern across time periods, in light of Mary's experiences and Eileen's comments, Mairead and Caral both indicated that there is perhaps more gender equality in the military side of the republican movement than in the political side in terms of how people are treated and issues are addressed. One of the few blatantly sexist incidents Mairead experienced was not in PIRA but was in Sinn Féin after her release from prison.

> I'm not going to say that there isn't people with sexist views in the movement; there is. I'm not going to say I've never experienced sexism. But it was in a different part of the movement that I experienced sexism – you know, where people just hadn't politicized themselves and were stuck in the past and then you were comin' in and you were young and you were female

> and, you know, they were just goin' like 'yeah stick the kettle on' and you were goin' like [said sarcastically] 'yeah, dead on, so I will'.

Finally, the issue of motherhood is significant here. Many active republican women over the course of the 'Troubles' have had children during their involvement, including four of the interviewees. Unlike the LTTE in Sri Lanka, neither PIRA nor the INLA had institutionalized childcare facilities for operatives and the impression I got was that the organizations made little effort to facilitate the involvement of women with children. It was expected that a man with children would have a wife to care for them while he was on an operation and it does not seem that much allowance was made for mothers, aside from giving them more prior notice than men about an operation so that they could organize childcare arrangements themselves. Maria had small children during the first, more auxiliary phase of her involvement in the early 1970s. However she chose to wait until her youngest child was a reasonable age before becoming 'active' and undertaking any operations that might have ended in her death or lengthy imprisonment. Her youngest child was 12 when she was imprisoned and was cared for by her older children. Emma had young children during her active involvement in the INLA and was reliant on other women to be able to carry out her activities – her sisters cared for the children while she was out or away. She was married but the relationship was strained and her husband was a fairly absent father as well as (I believe) being involved himself. Bernadette actually gave birth to her first child during her trial and was allowed to keep her baby with her in prison for the first year, after which she was forced to send the child out to be cared for by her mother-in-law. Her husband, also 'active', was not in prison at that time but their house was constantly being raided and he often had to move from place to place, so was not able to care for their child full-time. Finally, Caral's children were around one and two years old when she was imprisoned, which must have been extremely hard, but she was unwilling to discuss this and I am unsure who cared for them.

Republican women's imprisonment

All the republican women I interviewed except Emma and Mary are ex-prisoners, though the length of their time in jail varied considerably. Most of them were prisoners in the 1980s and/or 1990s and their experiences of jail were rather different from those of Teresa, who was imprisoned from the 1970s. For many, jail was an experience which politicized them further, especially in regard to ideas of feminism and women's rights.

Teresa had been 'active' for just over two years when she was arrested as a teenager in the early 1970s and was given a long sentence (though she did not serve the full term). Her last year in Armagh jail was the year the women without political status went on the no-wash protest[2]; as explained in Chapter 2, special category status was removed in 1976 for new prisoners. She herself had 'status' and was not involved with the no-wash protest; in fact she opposed it.

She argued that the women's situation in Armagh was not nearly as bad as that of the men in the Maze and said

> I think that there were some women in Armagh who were kind of of the impression that anything the men can do, we can do, and I don't really think that that's always a helpful situation, because in many ways I felt that the dirty protest in Armagh took away from the protest that was happenin' in Long Kesh [the Maze], because it was unnecessary in Armagh.

Obviously, women who were on the no-wash protest would have a very different perspective on the protest from Teresa but unfortunately I was not able to interview any women who had taken part. Teresa was disappointed at the level of political discussion in the prison.

> I found that very demoralisin' and that's when I first sort of realized that there were a lot of people in prison and really they didn't really have a very solid foundation of *why* they were in prison – they were caught up in things. I always had a very solid foundation of why I was in prison, I always knew why I was in prison, I didn't need to go through the experience to teach me why I was there.

By the 1980s, however, education in prison had become very significant for republican prisoners. This seems to have developed with the politicization of prisoners (male and female) that occurred from the late 1970s, after political status was withdrawn and the situation in the jails worsened. Teresa views it as a very positive development when the political programme from the Maze spread to the women's prisons (Armagh and then later Maghaberry) and women were encouraged to educate themselves and to discuss politics. This was certainly the case for most of the other ex-prisoners I interviewed, who were imprisoned later and were beneficiaries of this change – though they had to push very hard to maintain and increase these opportunities.

Niamh was arrested with an under-car bomb in the 1990s and was sentenced to 22 years, serving nine. At the time she first arrived in Maghaberry jail there were only seven other republican women there, vastly less than in the 1970s heyday though the numbers fluctuated at various times.

> And I suppose in a way goin' in in the later stages like that you're lucky because a lot of the battles had been fought and won by the other people who came before you. So what you actually go into in prison is a very supportive environment, you know, people there who've been there, some of them a long time, they know what you're feelin' so they know what to do to make it easier for you.

Nevertheless, although conditions were better than in the past there were still things to be fought for that many women mentioned to me – such as better access to the exercise yard and to different *forms* of exercise, better access to education and access to vocational training courses. For many of the women these matters were conceived of as feminist issues. The women had access to the exercise yard for only an hour a day usually, while in the male part of the prison the yard was attached to the wing and they could access this whenever they wanted. A battle ensued for a number of years, until eventually the women's yard was also attached to the wing. The women also had to push to have training facilities in the women's yard since, in Niamh's words, 'it was this attitude "women don't do weights, women don't use apparatus, women do aerobics and they jump up and down and they play volleyball"!' For her that was a feminist issue: 'When people are refusin' you things on the grounds of sex, you know, then it's a feminist issue.'

Education was also a problem since the classes were held in another building and with staff shortages the women could not always get access. Significantly, the issue of vocational training for men was contentious. Niamh notes that

> men could go to these workshops and do these kind of activities and they always assumed women don't wanna do that. They wouldn't ask you, they would just assume women don't wanna do that, women want a cookery class or a wee sewing class. So you were always battlin' against these prejudices.

All of Niamh's recollections suggest that the institution of prison was constantly reinforcing gendered expectations about what is appropriate for men and for women – in education, vocation, fitness, leisure activities and even in terms of ideas about physical privacy and men's and women's bodies (toilet facilities were different for women and men). For her, 'there were ways to fight a feminist issue probably every day of the week in jail'. Caral agreed: 'You had to fight to get woodwork or anything that was seen as non-conventional for women, or even vocational training for women, around what would've been seen as traditional male skills and trades.' Long-term prisoners, such as many of the women I interviewed, tended to do the Open University courses but there were a number of prisoners over the years who were in for much shorter sentences, usually for having allowed their house to be used by the IRA. Many of them did not want to do Open University courses, or were not imprisoned long enough to complete them, yet wanted something else. The women lobbied for vocational courses for women and eventually won. Niamh commented

> in the end it proved that successful that all the other women in the jail then got it as well and then everybody went, so even the people that were doin' the degrees, we all went to the workshops because it was good, we all made furniture and it was brilliant. So we proved them wrong.

As a result of this training Maria subsequently did a lot of the building and glazing work on the ex-prisoner centre where she now works, with the skills she gained in prison.

Bernadette, as mentioned earlier, cared for her baby in prison for the first year. When her baby was taken away 'oh it was heart-breakin', so it was. It was like a death.' Her prison experience was therefore very different from that of most of the women who were inside with her. She was arrested at 18, in the 1980s, but was released on bail and was not sentenced (to six years) and imprisoned in Armagh until the mid-1980s because the jails at that time were vastly overcrowded in the wake of the supergrass trials. While on bail she became pregnant. In prison she was kept isolated on a separate wing, away from the other republican women, and served three years. She still managed to connect with the other republican prisoners and spoke of a very close relationship with them. 'I mean they became your family, so they did.' Because of her situation she could not engage in education to the degree that other prisoners did and only managed a few months of studies, yet assisted others to participate:

> you supported each other cos you knew people fought and died hard for the education and all so if other people say couldn't get to a class for such a reason, then you helped them out to get to the class, you know?

Another gendered aspect of prison which became an issue for a number of women I interviewed was pornography. The republican women discovered that many of their male comrades used and defended the use of pornography in prison. Niamh explained that

> that started a whole debate goin'. And then people were writin' back and forward to each other, challengin' other people's opinions and defendin' their own opinions. And we were very angry about it all and enraged, so we did a project – a few of us got together and we did a project on it, designed a course on pornography.

She reflected that this issue shows

> that people can be progressive but it comes down to selfishness – I think their intellect would tell them how it does contribute to how women are treated, but for selfish reasons they just want to use it and they don't want to stop usin' it so then they just develop arguments why it's harmless – you know, 'no, but it just glorifies women's bodies' and all this kind of stuff.

Caral was angry that pornography went in relatively unhindered to male prisoners, while educational materials that the women wanted were sent to security for months on end. She asserts, I am sure quite accurately, that the prison authorities allowed pornography in because

> it was to contain them, keep them quiet. It was never an issue, but when it came to gettin' like educational materials and resources and things that

> would've developed you personally, it was seen more as a threat. And to me that was a feminist issue for us.

Republican women have often highlighted gender-specific ways in which Catholic women have been intimidated by the security forces, which includes sexual assault, harassment and strip-searching. Coulter claims that, as in other situations of armed conflict or political upheaval, rape has been used in Northern Ireland as a political weapon but the scale and role of this sexual violence is as yet unclear (1999: 134–5).[3] None of the interviewees raised the issue of rape. Strip-searching, however, was certainly an extremely significant gendered aspect of the prison experience for republican women. In 1992 in Maghaberry jail there was a mass forcible strip-search carried out on all republican inmates (which had not been done before in Maghaberry, though it was regularly used in Armagh since 1982 (McAuley 1989: 72–3)), which was ostensibly for 'security reasons'. All the women I interviewed who had been imprisoned at that time brought up the strip-search as their worst experience of imprisonment. In a typically Northern Irish ironic understatement, Clodagh commented 'so like that was probably an experience that you could very well do without'. Eileen, imprisoned between the mid-1980s and the late 1990s, suffered an even worse fate; while on remand she was subjected to hundreds of strip-searches in just one year. There is no way this could have possibly been justified on security grounds; it was a deliberate and gendered tactic of intimidation and was experienced, as an ex-prisoner has stated elsewhere, as 'psychological rape'.

For Eileen, women's equality became a driving force while she was in jail. Imprisoned in England, she felt that in English jails women were treated worse than men and campaigned on the fact that she and other women were imprisoned on a wing which had previously been closed down as unfit for men. Also, many of the 'ordinary' female prisoners she was inside with were mentally ill or had backgrounds of abuse and extremely low self-esteem and were treated very cruelly by prison authorities, including having unnecessary medical procedures performed on them. The fact that she was 'supported mainly by women, and English women too at that, who were wonderful' (women's groups demonstrated outside the prison in support of her campaign to improve conditions) was also significant for her.

Republican feminism: a disputed concept

The relationship between republicanism (or Irish nationalism more broadly) and feminism has been a complicated and difficult one, as is usually the case in a nationalist movement. Ward maintains that '[o]ver the past two centuries the relationship between Irish women and the nationalist movement has centred around a struggle for recognition and inclusion in the face of a male reluctance to accept female political agency' (1999: 219). She suggests that

> [t]hroughout the long history of women's involvement in the various phases of the struggle for national liberation, a tension has existed between those

> women who demanded equality of status (and who, on occasion, were more radical than the men in their conception of the political direction to be taken) and women who were content to perform unquestioningly whatever services were demanded of them.
>
> (Ward 1989: 248)

Ward notes that it was not until 1979, ten years after the 'Troubles' began, that 'Sinn Fein was forced to admit that "apart from a few articles in the Draft Charter of Rights and a short declaration made at a press conference in 1972, nothing has ever been said or written on the subject [of women]"' (1989: 255).[4] Wilford suggests that 'although the formal claim to socialist credentials espoused by Irish republicanism creates the ideological space for a commitment to gender equality, not all women in the contemporary republican movement are persuaded that this goal is a constituent element of its project' (1999: 197).

As Porter notes, feminists on the island of Ireland are divided over nationalism/republicanism.

> Some see no contradiction between simultaneously struggling for the liberation of a nation and for women. Others believe that women's issues need to be prioritized because if women themselves do not raise their needs, their oppression will be ignored. Some women are hostile, or indifferent, or confused as to the struggle for national freedom.
>
> (Porter 1998: 51)

Many of the issues significant to republican women which they conceive of as gendered or feminist issues have caused a great deal of division and dispute among the wider feminist movement in Northern Ireland (and in the Republic of Ireland and Great Britain). The forced strip-searching of republican women prisoners created a conflict amongst feminists. Republican feminists viewed this as a feminist issue, holding protests outside Armagh prison, and sought support from feminists in trade unions and in women's centres and organizations. As Rooney points out,

> [t]he call to unity on this clarified the nature of the conflict between rights feminist action and republican feminists. Women's rights feminism viewed the campaign as essentially a republican campaign and for that reason, and because such support would alienate unionist women, a number of women's organisations and groups refused support.
>
> (1995a: 44)

The campaign for political status and specifically the women's no-wash protest in Armagh was also divisive (Porter 1998: 51).

Rooney explains that republican feminists 'give priority to the national struggle and see a unity among women which transcends, rather than deals with, the political cleavage, as an evasion and avoidance of personal experience' (1995a: 44–5; see also Aretxaga 1997: Ch. 7). IRA volunteer Mairead Farrell is known to have said

> I'm oppressed as a woman but I am also oppressed because I'm Irish. Everyone in this country is oppressed and we can't successfully end our oppression as women until we first end the oppression of our country. But I don't think that's the end of it. It happened before where women took the back seat. But women today have gone through too much, no way will they allow that to happen.
>
> (McAuley 1989: 47)

Republican feminist Claire Hackett argues for the notion of self-determination with both a nationalist and feminist meaning and suggests:

> [i]n its republican meaning, national self-determination is not simply the question of Irish nationhood.... It is more. It includes the questions about the kind of society we want as a people and most crucially our ability to decide this ourselves. Self-determination in both feminist and republican meanings is a simple concept but a revolutionary one.
>
> (Hackett 1995: 111)

The women's movement in Northern Ireland has been consistently and continually hampered, stalled and divided over the national question. Groups that approach it head on are seen to be aligned with either nationalism or unionism and are thus rejected by women of the 'other', though they sometimes make tactical alliances across the divide on certain single issues. Groups that try to avoid it and come together 'as women' with common interests, leaving their nationalist hats at the door, ultimately implode over the national question (see Roulston 1997) which can never be avoided for long. Some feminists even maintain that republicanism is totally incompatible with feminism and that any woman calling herself a republican feminist is fooling herself (Coulter 1998: 161–2). This is a remarkably intolerant and narrow position and one that is challenged by the experiences and voices of many of the republican women I interviewed. I support Coulter's assertion that to simplistically present feminism and nationalism/republicanism as fundamentally incompatible 'hampers the development of feminist thinking, and ... means the very relevant experiences of women who have had to deal with the combined oppression of imperialism and patriarchy are not brought to bear on it' (ibid.: 165). She maintains that

> [t]he Eurocentrism of the dominant agenda within feminism has led to an ignoring of the traditions and real history of struggle of women in other countries and other cultures, a blindness to the reality of their struggle because it does not conform to what they view as the norm.
>
> (Coulter 1998: 168)

Some of the republican women I interviewed would not explicitly describe themselves as feminists – such as Maeve, who believes in equality but does not see why a person has to be feminist to believe in this. Similarly, Clodagh said she would rather call herself an 'equalist' than a feminist, feeling that some feminists 'go a wee bit too far'. On the whole, however, many women did accept the label 'feminist' or 'a bit of a feminist' or, if hesitant about the label, seemed committed to women's equality (in various conceptualizations) in their viewpoints. For many, as suggested earlier, the prison experience was significant in developing more nuanced feminist ideas (see also Aretxaga 1997: Chs 6–7). Like others, Niamh told me that republicans who went to jail tend to be 'more progressive' than those who did not, particularly in regard to feminism. 'Prison experience does seem to be a very positive one for the vast majority of republicans, they come out with more progressive ideas, with a better understanding of a lot of different issues.' She attributes this to the education republicans made use of in prison, both through formal courses such as Open University degrees and informal political discussions and sharing of experiences with other prisoners.

> You've got this amount of time where you can do things that's not possible outside – people don't have time outside, there's too many other things pullin' at you, in your life. In prison time is very very structured and disciplined and it's very easy to say 'we'll have a discussion from six o'clock to eight o'clock', cos there's nothin' else happenin'! So there was lots of time to talk to people, you talked a lot, you really were able to go into issues in great depth and really talk about things a lot.... So your views on republicanism, on where the struggle was goin', became much more sophisticated.

Niamh does now consider herself to be a feminist but reported that she was not really aware of issues of women's equality when she was growing up and that 'imprisonment probably would've been the time whenever I became most sort of clear about the way I feel about it'. For her,

> goin' to prison and bein' kind of in an environment where you face the issues [was important,] because when you're with women all the time you do tend to be focused on issues that relate to women. And you're hearin' stories all the time and so it just sharpens your focus on the inequalities and how women are treated and some of the awful lives that women have. So that came about because I was a republican, so I don't think it can be separated.

In contrast, Teresa hated being imprisoned with so many women and the experience did not seem to act as a catalyst for feminism in her case.

> I always thought there was nothin' worse than bein' stuck in a prison with loads of women. It was horrendous, cos it was so catty and bitchy and the stupidest things were fought over and I just thought it was so petty. And in many ways I kind of just opted out, you know, I thought 'I can't be bothered with this'.

She also has strong conventional beliefs about motherhood and argues that women should not be actively involved if they have children (she did not have children until after her active involvement ceased).

> I think, regardless of what we say, I think a mother's role is very important to a child, you know? I'm not tryin' to diminish a father's role and I do believe that that's very important but it is different, you know? ... I'm a great believer that you have to look after the revolution at home before you look after the wider revolution, and I have seen a lot of – there would be a lot of republicans who have spent long times imprisoned, and I mean I see they have children who are basically lost souls, you know they've been lost somewhere in all the turmoil, they got forgotten, and I think that that's very wrong.

She concedes, however, that this applies to children of both female and male ex-prisoners. She does not call herself a feminist 'because I don't feel the necessity to do that'. She asserts 'I don't believe that there are issues that are totally related to women, because I think that they're all intertwined. That's just my personal belief, you know? So I never approved of all that.'

Caral, on the other hand, does consider herself a (republican) feminist: 'I mean I would class myself as a republican but certainly I would class myself as a feminist too.' She was one of the few women I interviewed who mentioned having had a sense of gender inequalities before she went to jail or even before she became involved in republicanism.

> I even seen differences within my own community about this kind of hierarchical entitlement almost, you know that I seen a lot of women who were workin' really hard, holdin' down jobs or families and also political activists, and you just knew that they always got the raw deal. I wasn't able to articulate it or analyse it or anything, but I just knew it wasn't right.

Like others, however, it was prison that brought this into sharper focus for her.

> In jail, I mean the differences were probably like no other, because it was an all-female environment for a start and you began to put things that happened to you in a context.... And I knew like, for example, the mass strip of '92 happened because a new governor came in, seen that body of women who were republicans, who were organized, who were strong, and decided to use forcible strip-searching as a weapon against us.

Although she did not report experiencing any inequality within the armed side of the movement, 'because first and foremost you were a soldier and that was it', Caral maintains that in the wider movement

> there was a certain amount of denial about, you know, we're gonna build this utopia and we're gonna do A, B, C and D – well I never seen that. I seen the

> same women who were struggling, who were demanding equality within every aspect of their life – and they got it within the movement but they got it because they fought for it, not because it was the right thing to do.

Although she views Sinn Féin as the most progressive of the Northern Irish political parties, though 'certainly not where I would want it to be', she said

> to me it's the contradiction of fightin' a struggle for national liberation, and it's always been a big contradiction for me because yes, me and a fella will certainly take up arms to liberate A, B, C and D, but will the same comrade feel as strong about gettin' equality for women? No, not them at all. And that's a contradiction.

Caral went on to say that in jail she read about women in Nicaragua and El Salvador and their experiences of the contradictions for women in liberation struggles, and about women in the African National Congress in South Africa 'still fightin' for the conditions that were denied to them, you know, durin' apartheid and after apartheid, and it's still a struggle and it's a big contradiction for them, and I know it's the same for me as well'. At the time of interview she told me she votes for Sinn Féin in elections but chose not to become a member or to lobby for them because she is opposed to their stand on abortion[5] and because of the contradictions she perceives. Since then, however, she has been a Sinn Féin Member of Local (i.e. the Northern Ireland) Assembly (MLA).

Eileen's feminism, too, is intertwined with her republicanism and socialism. Echoing the sentiments of some of the LTTE women I interviewed in Sri Lanka, she implied a perception of feminism as abstracted when she said 'I'd like to think I was a bit more practising of a feminist'. She feels that her socialist republicanism and feminism have

> kind of developed into something that speaks to each other.... Within the socialist republic there has to be equality for women, otherwise it's not socialist. So these things sit together, you know, there's no equality without equality of the women [and other marginalized groups].

Bernadette, like some of the other women, revealed in her reflections a definite interest in issues pertaining to women's rights and equality, yet said 'I suppose I am [a feminist] without callin' myself one.... I don't suppose it's been something I've really sat down and thought about.... I don't feel as if I have to call myself one, put it that way.' Mairead highlighted the complicated relationships between republicanism and feminism and identity when she noted that

> I think other people would probably call me a feminist. I don't know. I don't think it's anything bad, you know I wouldn't be insulted, I would actually kind of probably be complimented if somebody called me a feminist, but I would call myself an Irish republican. And as bein' a republican I

see equality as part of that, so I probably have – yeah, I do actually have very strong feminist views though [laughter], so yeah I probably am a feminist but I probably wouldn't describe myself as such, which is kind of quite a mixed up idea, but there you go.

Mairead struck me as a reflective person and was prepared to think about the failings of republicanism as well as its positive aspects, noting 'you have to ask yourself why there's no visible gay republicans, if we're part of a liberation struggle and we're supposed to be so great on equality?'

In terms of the interviewees' perspectives on women in conventional electoral politics, all the republican women except Emma and Teresa feel that women should be more involved in this field in Northern Ireland; women have been and continue to be vastly under-represented (Ward 2000; Wilford and Galligan 1999; Wilford 1999). Both Emma and Teresa believe that politicians should simply be elected on merit and are not particularly interested in encouraging or assisting more women to become politicians. The other interviewees all feel that women should be more involved in politics and should be both encouraged and enabled to do so, for various reasons, many of which reflect a fairly cultural feminist perspective that women bring something different to the political arena from men. For some this is socially constituted; others seem to view it as more innate. Eileen thinks that women, from their own experiences of oppression, may bring a different perspective on equality to bear. Mary maintains that women, on the whole, have more commonsense than men. Clodagh feels women can be more understanding and Maeve believes that women will bring new ideas and understand and represent women's issues better than men. Niamh suggests that women have different approaches to problem-solving than men and more imaginative ways of looking at things, are more sympathetic and caring and can see the other's point of view better.

With three exceptions[6] the interviewees are predominantly Sinn Féin supporters and many of them are active party members; one has been a Sinn Féin councillor and one an MLA. In part the majority support for Sinn Féin amongst the interviewees merely inevitably reflects their republican commitments and the party's role as the political representative of the Provisional Republican movement, but with their interest in women's greater participation in conventional politics there are other reasons to support Sinn Féin. Sinn Féin has consistently had high numbers of female MLAs and local councillors, has included women in senior positions, details specific policies on various gendered issues affecting women, and has used a quota system for its National Executive (Ward 2000). With the 2007 Northern Ireland Assembly election Sinn Féin has the highest absolute number of female MLAs (eight) and ties with the Alliance Party (which holds a much smaller number of seats) for the highest percentage of female MLAs, at around 29 per cent. Of their five ministerial posts two are held by women (Caitríona Ruane, Minister for Education, and Michelle Gildernew, Minister for Agriculture and Rural Development). The difference between the nationalist bloc and the unionist bloc overall is striking; the SDLP currently barely lags behind Sinn Féin in its percentage of female MLAs (25 per cent) while on the unionist side the DUP, holding the most seats of any party in Northern Ireland, has only 8.3 per cent female MLAs and the UUP, incredibly, has none.[7] Nonetheless some of the interviewees demonstrated an awareness of structural and institutional barriers to women's participation in formal politics. Bernadette strongly believes in encouraging women to put themselves forward more and to engage in politics, and in providing resources to enable them to do so, saying 'I don't think the resources are provided for women, d'you know? You know, you don't have crèches up at Stormont, you don't have crèches in City Hall!'[8]

Gender relations and experiences in loyalist paramilitaries

The focus of discussion here is on loyalist paramilitaries in general rather than one specific organization, though more of the interviewees had connections with the UVF than with the UDA. I make no claim that this in any way represents a greater involvement of women with the UVF and its affiliated organizations than with the UDA; rather it reflects the context in which I was carrying out the research and the contacts I made. The narratives of the interviewees suggest that despite the quite different organizational histories and structures of the UVF and the UDA, the framing context of loyalist community gendered attitudes and political ambitions made for similar experiences of women in both organizations and similar resistance from men. All the loyalists I interviewed (female and male) who had been personally involved in some way with paramilitary organizations stated that in general there was a clear gendered division of labour in loyalist paramilitaries, with women being involved in support roles such as carrying weapons and providing first aid rather than planting bombs or close-quarter killing; very few women took more directly combative roles. It also seems that a fairly common pattern for loyalist women was to never officially join an organization but to be quite active in support roles through association with their husbands. Alison suggested that perhaps the men just never thought to ask women to join; it never occurred to her to raise the issue of membership, though she is clear that she would have accepted had this been offered. She maintained that the majority of those women who actually enlisted in loyalist paramilitaries would have done so with the backing and help of husbands but that 'there would be some male chauvinist pigs out there within the loyalist side thinkin' that women couldn't do just as good as a job as them'uns.' Alison also claimed that probably most loyalist women would not have wanted the same kinds of roles as men had, indicating conventional expectations of supportive female behaviour when she said 'from my experience and different bits and pieces that I would have done, I was just quite happy in exactly what I was doin' because it meant I was still doin' my bit, so I was. I was doin' my bit.'

After joining the UVF Ann had weapons, physical exercise and drill training and did 'certain things but [was] never involved the way the men were'. In one incident she had to dispose of a gun, with a soldier standing nearby, in the middle of a fraught situation where her female companion had been shot four times in the back when their car got caught in crossfire between the IRA and the British army. On numerous occasions she took weapons away for male UVF members after they had been on an operation, as it was riskier for men to carry guns since they were more likely to be searched. She went out with men who were going on an operation, to carry the weapons to and from a job, and said that if women were caught with guns the men would say that they forced them to carry them. 'Many's the time a fella just walked past you, you just opened your bag [for the weapon] and walked on, you know?' Her description of hiding guns in her baby's pram in order to transport them (related in Chapter 4) illustrates the way in which women like her could and did utilize traditional gender norms in order to carry out non-traditional activities. Ann also went to inform young women that their paramilitary husbands had been killed and took away any weapons left in the house, before the RUC arrived. As well as these activities she was also involved in first aid: 'I've nursed fellas where a bomb'd gone off in their hands.... I wasn't a nurse but we done what we could for them. Sometimes they didn't have to go to hospital, sometimes you couldn't do nothin', they had to.' She says of her involvement 'I was proud to be in it and was able to do the things that I done and most women that was in it with me were the same.'

At the time of her involvement Alison was very supportive of the paramilitaries and feels that 'the women were the backbone of the paramilitaries, years ago; the men couldna done it without the women, so they couldn't've. You know, moving guns and things – the *men* didn't do that, the women done that, so they did.' A number of times she travelled to Liverpool on the ferry and came back with grip bags full of guns. She remembers one time when there was 'trouble' going on in the Springmartin area of Belfast, she and other women put rifles up under their long coats and pushed their way through the army to get them to a safe house.

> It was easier for the women to do. But not only that, it took a dedicated woman to do it, it wasn't every wife that would've supported their husbands in that affair.... It took you to believe in it yourself. It wasn't just so much supportin' your husband, you have to believe in it, that what you were doin' was right – I'm not sayin' it *was* right but then, yeah, I did think it was all completely right to do.

Alison is remarkably honest about her past sectarian attitudes, saying that although she is still definitely opposed to a united Ireland 'I've become a bit [more] moderate now than what I was years ago.... Years ago, yes, I would've called myself a bigot; not now. I think times have changed, I think we've all moved on a lot since then.'

Like Ann and Alison, Tracey cleaned, stored and moved guns and drove vehicles on operations. However she also admitted to a more active involvement, involving planting bombs and shootings. She was imprisoned in the 1970s, serving five years in Armagh for possession of guns (after an initial murder charge was dropped) and told me that she drove the car for the men who carried out the murder. With an interesting moral logic she explained that when she joined the UVF she informed them she would never participate in armed robberies (one of the fundraising activities of paramilitaries on both side of the divide) as she viewed that as wrong; her interest was in removing IRA operatives. Tracey reported that when she first joined the UVF there were a number of male members who, because she was female, were 'very iffy, but they seen then that I was genuine enough like, I wouldna talked.' She noted 'I woulda said that most of the men didn't want women to be involved.' When asked why this was she replied 'I don't know. I don't know – the female's the weaker sex.... I always seem to be the odd one out.' Over time they came to accept her but she gave the impression that this acceptance had to be hard earned through proving that she was trustworthy by not revealing information when arrested. With some exceptions, men generally did not say things directly to her but a male paramilitary friend told her of some who had made remarks about not wanting her to be involved in operations.

> They don't think that's a woman's place. Like I was told one time I should be at home washing dishes. That's the place to keep a woman, chained to the kitchen sink! [Laughter.] Aye, dead on. I says 'get stuffed, wash them yourself!'

She recollected that 'I got an awful stick off men for, as they said, carryin' on the way I was doin'.... I was a girl, I should be sittin' knittin', washin' dishes and rearin' childer [children].' Men also seemed to assume that women were more likely to crack under interrogation and give away damning evidence – which, as noted in the section on republican women, was also an experience of Niamh. The week Tracey was in the army barracks being interrogated in relation to the incident she was later convicted for, she refused to admit anything or make a statement until after all the men arrested with her had made statements. She feels that this changed the way the men looked at her: 'No matter who I'm talkin' to ... they would give me anythin' if I asked for it.' She carries no bitterness towards the men who earlier doubted her, as she feels she proved them wrong and receives a lot of respect from them now.

As for Tracey, respect was also an important idea for Joy, with regards to UDA ex-prisoners in her case. A male ex-UVF member claimed to me that for women to advance within loyalist paramilitary ranks (in any of the organizations) they have to be sexually promiscuous with male paramilitary members. When I asked Joy about this she was irate and told me to tell him to come down to the Shankill and say that to her and she would 'send him away with a red face!' Any woman who 'went down that road', according to Joy, would lose all respect. 'Any bitch can lie down with any dog. It takes a woman to stand up and say "no".' The accusation of female promiscuity, then, can operate not only as a means of social control of women in general but also specifically as a way to contain the challenge to gender norms presented by militant/combatant women. In her work with ex-prisoners Joy feels she has to wear the 'hard bitch' mask or risk losing male respect and undermining her job. She would not socialize in the same area as people she works with and would never get drunk around them, believing again this would lose her respect. She also maintained (as did other loyalists I spoke to, male as well as female) that loyalist men often discourage women from getting education and feel threatened when their female partners are seen to have a better job than themselves (or any job, if they are unemployed).

Jackie, who as noted in Chapter 4 was extensively active with the UDA but was never imprisoned, also disputed the idea of women rising through the ranks by sleeping with men. In her view 'that's people looking in now, thinkin' that. You've gotta earn your respect, you know. And I've well and truly done that like.' When I asked if the sexual behaviour of paramilitary women and men would be looked at differently she replied that if a woman acted the way most paramilitary men do (extra-marital affairs and promiscuity) she would be viewed as a

> [s]lapper, mmm, she'd a been a slapper like, most definitely. And all the wee girlies like the [loyalist paramilitary] boys, if you know what I mean? Cos they are who they are. That's why they get away with it. It's like, they idolize them, if you know what I mean.

This idolatry does not operate in the same way for women who participate in the paramilitaries.

> No, no. Cos you're just, you're looked on as a hard woman, you know, not the way men are looked on as heroes; you're looked on as, you know, 'who does she think she is?' ... That's definitely different from men like. If you're a man you're set when you're in there; get what you want, when you want. It's not so good for a woman.

Jackie's views on whether or not she was respected as a UDA member again reflect gendered differences, particularly in the area of sexual behaviour.

> I wouldna said I was respected. Well I suppose by some people I was obviously cos if you can keep your mouth shut you do, you earn respect. But that would be the people on the inside [of the organization]. You get people on the outside, who don't know these things, and would look on you differently cos you're a female. They probably just think you're a slapper, you're in with all the boys – you know that's the way they would look at it.

Jackie narrated some very similar experiences regarding her reception by male members of the organization as Tracey found with the UVF. As explained in Chapter 4 Jackie chose to join the UDA independently, rather than becoming involved through a husband or male relative, but her strong male family connections to the organization seem to have been the primary reason for her somewhat grudging acceptance. She said 'They don't like girls there but deal with it, you know? ... I just feel like they don't think that you can do what's needed of you, d'you know what I mean, whereas they think a man can.' She attributes this to

> [j]ust the male ego, I think – it would be the same on any side, regardless of what – I just think it's just a male thing.... But sure we can all prove people wrong, that's the way I put it.... You do have to let them know that you're there for real.

Jackie stated that she wanted to be involved with the UDA because of her beliefs in 'the cause' yet conceded that without her male family connections she 'mightn't even have got involved', though she reiterated that it was her choice to enlist. She was clear that the reason she did not encounter any overt challenges to her presence and role from male members was the protection of her family connections, which meant that had anything happened to her there would have been a violent response from her family. 'I had that backin'.... It wouldna happened without anythin' happenin' vice versa so. But you can tell, you can honestly tell that they didn't like you bein' there, you know? But they just grin and bear it.'

Like Tracey, Jackie's narrative indicates the idea that she had to outperform male members to be taken seriously and accepted. She did not report feeling that she was given different jobs from male members but did say 'I always pushed anyway, d'you know what I mean, I wouldna had them say *anything*, that I wasn't up for it or I wasn't good enough or, you know?' Like Tracey, she thinks men believe women won't hold up under interrogation but strongly disagrees with this, contending that women can often hold on longer. Her own worst experience of interrogation was when she was held for three days and beaten. This, she said softly, was 'terrifyin', mhmm, terrifying. And I still didn't say nothin'. It's not pleasant like, there's nobody gonna sit there and tell you it is, definitely not – it's not an experience I would like to go through again.' She said she did not experience any sexual harassment as part of the interrogation but

> you do get beaten.... It's hard like, definitely it's hard.... You're numb anyway, d'you know what I mean? After so long you don't feel it anymore. It does hurt at the start like but after a while ... you just lose your feelin'.... They do hurt you like, they don't take you any easier cos you're a woman. Definitely not. In fact it probably makes them worse, cos they think you'll lose it easier than a man will.

For her, the main reason she managed to withstand the interrogation without revealing information seems to have been that she was more afraid of her own organization than of the state forces:

> What you were gettin' was nothin' to maybe what you mighta got [from your own paramilitary organization] had you said somethin', you know. You're better lettin' on you know nothin'.... For me that's what scared me anyway, what I would maybe get had I said somethin'.

This fear of the UDA extends to her current life. A few years ago she moved to Scotland for a number of years, having become disillusioned with the UDA's internal feuding, saying 'If they can't stand by one another well there's nothin' to fight for.' In Scotland she had no involvement with the UDA and established a new life for herself. After returning to Northern Ireland she has continued to try to stay out of old paramilitary circles but said that this meant 'you lose a lotta what you thought were friends'. She reflected that escaping a paramilitary past is difficult; 'It still carries with you.... You can't just shake it off, people know what you done, who you were.' She also said that 'it's easy to get in, not so easy to get out. Let's just put it like that and say no more.' Later, she said 'You just don't leave. No. You just don't walk out and leave. You still help out, you know, do the odd thing and that, but not to the extent I woulda done.' Again, her male family connections have offered protection; she believes that if her brothers had not remained active with the UDA and had also wanted to leave it might have been harder for her. Despite her years of service for the organization it has not been easy to put that life behind her, particularly as she is not an ex-prisoner. 'I mean I know if you do your time [in prison] like then it's maybe easier to get outta it, you know? You've done your time for them. But I didn't, I was never caught.'

Loyalist women's imprisonment

As noted earlier, Tracey is the only loyalist women I interviewed who has been imprisoned. Like female republican prisoners she experienced certain gender-specific torments, though never strip-searches. While being interrogated in the barracks she started menstruating and asked a policewoman for a sanitary towel; she was not brought one and was forced to sit for days in the barracks, menstruating, with nothing for it. During her time in Armagh women's prison Tracey was the only loyalist prisoner, with over 30 republican women prisoners (though she noted there were some women with UDA connections who were not in on 'scheduled'/terrorism-related convictions). While she was on remand

> It was hell. It was hell. But my personality – I'm very determined. And they [republican prisoners] tried to scald me w'water, tried to burn me w'an iron. Then the prison officers, they got word that they were gonna do me in, and they had to guard me.

After she was moved to the sentenced wing things settled down a bit. After some time, republicans 'were in lock-up because of the dirty protest at that time. So that got them out of my road.' In a later incident,

> a Provo [PIRA member] did swing for me, pushed me down the stairs ... and just by the luck of God I put my hand out and I grabbed her and I pulled her and I took her to the foot of the stairs with me, and I landed on top of her.

She laughed a lot of the harassment off to me but admitted that 'anybody that had a been weak-nerved definitely wouldna come through Armagh'. Her reflections on those republican women who came off the no-wash protest are interesting.

> Them ones that broke off the dirty protest, they weren't the same. When they were with me on remand they were soldiers but once they split away from the dirty protest they were nothin', you know? So they couldn't really say anythin' to you then.... That was failure, they weren't a soldier anymore.

Those women were then scorned by the other republican women and 'they woulda spoke to me then and things like that, but I never went outta my way to speak to them'.

Tracey's prison experience was largely profoundly different from that of most republican prisoners. While 'they had a community', she was isolated and completely alone and maintains that her strong Protestant faith was what got her through her time in jail. Her time was taken up with prison work, learning to knit, reading, a cookery class and a handicraft class. She did not take any more formal educational classes or do an Open University degree but told me that she had really wanted to go to the Irish language classes, simply to be able to understand what the republican women prisoners were saying. 'They were shoutin' over in Irish and I hadn't a clue what they were sayin', they coulda been callin' me anythin'.' However she says that she was prevented from this because the Price sisters, who had been transferred to Armagh from England the year after their hunger strike, refused to have her in the class. While she was obviously not involved in the mass prison protests carried out by republican inmates Tracey did occasionally launch her own one-woman protest to, as she saw it, be treated the same way as republicans. When Mairead Farrell, who was the republican commander on the wing Tracey was on, would give the order to republicans to refuse to be locked up Tracey too would refuse. 'I wouldn't please them to lock *me* up and not lock them up.... Why was I gettin' locked up when they weren't gettin' locked up?' She feels that she had to fight for her survival not only against republican inmates but also against prison officers. 'For they'd a kept me locked up and let them run the wing. I was different treated.'

After her release, Tracey went back to live with her mother and worked in a factory until her health deteriorated. She explained that 'the Protestant community, round where I live anyway, they are really not in for paramilitaries at all. But I was surprised to see how well they accepted me back into them.' Even a Catholic neighbour, who years before had reported her to the police because she suspected Tracey was involved in a bombing incident, is very friendly with her. 'And you know, I was surprised, because of what I had done and all the rest of it. I can't see me, if it had a been *her* done what *I* done, I can't see me even speakin' to her.' She feels there is a real stigma in much of the Protestant community, at least in her rural area, about being a loyalist ex-prisoner. This, presumably, at least partially accounts for the reluctance of loyalist women to speak about their experiences. For herself, she says

> I'm not ashamed of what I have done. In fact I'm proud of what I have done and I'm proud of my life as I have run it. I'm 49 years of age now and I don't regret one thing in it that I have done. And there's people that just don't want to talk about it, as if it's not there, as if it never happened.

She feels that her experiences in the UVF and in prison have meant that she now has more self-confidence and is 'not afraid to say what I believe.... And if I thought you done wrong, I'll just say it there and then.... And I think maybe I've learned that outta the UVF.' As is also the case with so many republican women ex-prisoners, she now devotes much of her energy towards helping other (loyalist) ex-prisoners.

> You know, I'll do anythin' for prisoners and I'm not happy unless I'm in prisoners' company and all. It's somethin' I feel we've all been through the same gate type of thing and I'm level with them, if you know what I mean.

Family ties: the impact of male imprisonment

Sales explains that loyalist women married to male prisoners have had to renegotiate their domestic roles and become more independent while their husbands were in jail (1997b: 72). Similarly, Joy noted that when men are released they want all their old power and responsibilities back but many women do not want to give these up; this was a recurring theme in my interviews with loyalist women. The stories of women were echoed from the male perspective by an ex-prisoner and community worker, who told me that when he was released from prison after 13 years he felt that his wife had become a different person, much more assertive and confident. He felt he was constantly being challenged by her and that she wanted to continue to make decisions in the way she had while he was in prison – before his imprisonment she was much more likely to acquiesce in his decisions.

Ann, while being involved herself, was also a prisoner's wife. While her husband was interned she received £8 a week from the UVF's welfare organization to help the family pay for the parcels they took to her husband each week. This did not cover the whole amount needed and like other women in her position she received social welfare payments and worked late nights in loyalist clubs as well, trying to make ends meet. Although Ann's husband was only inside for a year, this independence meant that

> when he come out I was able to answer a wee bit more and I knew more people than him then, actually, from workin' in the clubs and that, and he, I would've said he was a bit of a male chauvinist pig! He didn't like it too much like, I'm bein' honest, and then sure, I mean, after a couple of years I had to give the bar work and all up because he just didn't like me workin' in them.... I think he thought I was getting' on top of him really.... I was only 17 when I was married too – he was 21 like, but he was always kinda way the boss and made the decisions.

Alison was the daughter, wife *and* sister of loyalist prisoners, as well as having a cousin and an uncle in prison at one point too. As a child in the late 1960s when her father was in prison there was a strong stigma attached to being a paramilitary prisoner in loyalist communities, even in urban Belfast, and she faced a lot of taunting in school. 'It changed but there was a big stigma [then].' This stigma began to lessen over time, particularly in urban areas badly affected as the 'Troubles' worsened. Her husband was arrested when Alison was four months pregnant with their first child (they had been married for less than a year) and was imprisoned for five and a half years. Her husband and father were in different prisons at first so 'in them days your life was just spent round visitin' jails, so it was.' The stories of Alison and Ann paint a bleak picture of the strain of being a prisoner's wife, financial as well as emotional. Prisoners expected to get their 'parcel' of cigarettes, newspapers, clothes, food items and so on at every visit (which for internees or prisoners on remand was more than once a week). Alison said

> you always made sure that your husband had his parcel. Didn't matter [if] you were left sittin' without anything whatsoever, you made sure that his parcel was brought up to him, so you did.... Like I went away down then to six stone or somethin' in weight, but you made sure he had his parcel, so you did.

After her husband was released, the first six months to a year were a difficult readjustment for Alison and her husband, as well as for their son (see Spence 2002 and Hall 2000a on how children were affected by parental imprisonment).

> It was difficult because I was the provider, I made the rules in my house, I done everything, you know, and for a man to come back in then and try to take over – he still has never took over to this day like – but, for to try and take over, that was difficult. And I think especially the first six months of any man gettin' outta jail, in all families, I think it's hard. It's like buildin' a relationship up all over again, so it is. There was a lotta marriages broke up through men bein' in prison, so there was.

Despite the friction in the beginning, things settled down and over time 'we just learnt to appreciate each other that wee bit more and accept each [other]'. Ultimately, she feels their relationship became a much more equal one in terms of sharing decision-making than it might otherwise have been had he never been imprisoned.

Catherine, married at 18, lives in east Belfast and has three children. She was the main income-earner after her husband was released from prison for the final time; with his criminal record he found it very difficult to get work. Her husband even took over most of the child-rearing of their youngest daughter when Catherine obtained a good job in a community group. The first time her husband was arrested and convicted for an offence she was pregnant with their second child;

their third child was conceived after he was released, before he was imprisoned for another offence. Her view of his involvement in the UDA/UFF is that 'I knew what he was before I married him ... he has his beliefs and I have mine and I have to accept what his beliefs are. Don't agree with them sometimes but I have to let him get on with it.' She tried to protect her children from the impact of having a father in jail by making up stories about where he was and felt she could never tell her children's school about her situation, which she found extremely difficult.

Marion, who was a (UVF) prisoner's wife and now heads an ex-prisoner organization, presents a slightly different story from the women in Belfast. Although her experiences echo theirs in many respects – such as the financial difficulties when her husband was in jail, the problems of taking him his parcel every week, the stigma their daughter sometimes faced in school, the renegotiation of his relationships with both her and their daughter after he was released, her role as the main income-earner – she differs in that she had had no idea of his paramilitary involvement until he was arrested. She had known of his past involvement and indeed had broken off her relationship with him as a teenager when he was sent to prison the first time; the resumption of their relationship years later was strictly on the promise that he had given up his paramilitary involvement. She believes that her ignorance of his involvement was fairly common in the rural area they lived in as she knows many other wives in the same position (probably with the idea of protecting them), indicating a difference between urban and rural experiences in this respect. The nature of rural life, the far fewer numbers of paramilitary members in the area, and the greater community stigma meant that she was much more isolated as a prisoner's wife than the women in Belfast, where prisoners' wives and families almost formed a community of their own.

Linda, from east Belfast, is married to a man who was involved with the UVF (though he has not been imprisoned during their relationship) and his commitment to the UVF and the PUP has placed serious strains on the marriage. 'It comes first, before you do, d'you know what I mean?' She was never involved in the UVF herself (though she knew when something was going on with her husband or when there were guns in the house) but it seems that this is due more to the fact that no one ever asked her to be rather than to a total lack of desire on her part. In her younger years she was very militant-minded and supported the loyalist paramilitaries; her views have changed and she is now thankful she never became involved. During the 'Troubles' she felt that women should be more involved in the military side of things and told me that there were quite a few women who had wanted the UVF to set up a women's military wing. She could have joined her husband's unit but chose not to because her husband would have been her superior in rank and therefore in command over her; if a women's wing had been set up there would have been autonomous structures. She supported his activities at the time, however: 'If he had a stood ten men up agin a wall and shot them dead I woulda been standin' there beside him.'

Gender and loyalist feminism

Sales notes that while Irish nationalists have been struggling for change, unionists have been defending 'the present and the past'. Nationalism has, accordingly, 'provided more space for radical ideas, and women have been more visible in its politics – as spokespeople for their communities ... and also involved in paramilitary activity'. This has meant that for unionists,

> feminism is associated with 'the other side', and regarded as an object of suspicion.... Republican women have developed links with feminists in Britain and elsewhere, which have provided support in their struggle for a women's agenda. Protestants have been largely excluded from these sources of support and ideas. A feeling of betrayal and isolation does not provide a fertile ground for new ideas.
>
> (Sales 1997b: 70)

The 'public face' of the Protestant community remains overwhelmingly male in terms of political and church leaders, many of whom hold strongly anti-feminist views (Sales 1997b: 5). One of the most obvious public faces of unionism is the Orange Order and its annual parades. The Order is heavily male-dominated and female members belong to separate women's lodges, occupying a subordinate position. For women to march in the parades a women's lodge must be invited by a men's lodge – very few extend such an invitation. In general, women's role in the marches is as spectators. As Racioppi and O'Sullivan See argue, 'the marches constitute expressions of *masculine* loyalism' (2000: 13). Interestingly, some male loyalists seem to be aware – and somewhat defensive – about outside perceptions that the loyalist community has less progressive attitudes towards women than republicanism is sometimes seen to have. William, a community worker and ex-prisoner, contended that unionism is 'more honest' about its chauvinism towards women than republicanism is, which he feels tries to present women as being at the forefront of the movement yet really pushes them aside. Peter, also a community worker and ex-prisoner, expressed similar ideas.

Both Protestant churches and unionist political parties in Northern Ireland largely deny women 'legitimacy in the public sphere' and 'perpetuate a strongly male culture' (Sales 1997a: 145).[9] Ian Paisley, both a religious and political leader, has said 'I believe that the husband is the head of the wife and the home. I believe that the father should be prophet, priest and king in his home.' His wife, Eileen Paisley, has said that 'a woman must be on a pedestal to a man so men can look up to her and give her respect. But younger women, the extreme women's liberation, they want to do things that have always been the man's privilege' (Fairweather *et al.* 1984: 266, 278). There have been some shifts within unionist political parties over time and the language of equal opportunities has come to be incorporated into public policy statements. In 1987 Rhonda Paisley, daughter of Ian and Eileen, was appointed as the Democratic Unionist Party's (DUP) spokesperson for women's issues. In 1992 she criticized the male dominated nature of unionism and called for a radical rethink of women's involvement in unionist politics. However she later resigned as party spokesperson on this issue and was replaced by Iris Robinson, at the time a DUP councillor (now MP and MLA).[10] Robinson is extremely conservative on social matters[11] and despite her public position once described herself as 'a simple housewife' without 'any particular skills' (Sales 1997a: 146–7).[12] Sales suggests that '[t]he ties of Protestantism to Unionist hegemony have made it difficult for Protestant women to challenge the authority of "their" state and political leaders. Those who fight for their own interests are seen as "rocking the boat"' (ibid.: 140–1). Wilford maintains that within unionism 'the status of women ... has been an historically subordinate one. Its conservatism, expressed most obviously in terms of the determination to maintain the constitutional status quo, has spilled over into the realm of gender relations' (1999: 197). As Rooney asserts, '[t]he historical accommodation between republicanism and feminism, and the links between feminism and opposition or liberation politics ... pose a challenge to unionist ideology' (1995a: 44). Feminism is viewed as alien; for many feminists, Sales contends, such 'contradictions have been resolvable only through a renunciation of unionism, or through "avoidance" of broader political questions' (1997b: 200).

Most loyalist women I interviewed were reluctant to label themselves feminist yet expressed interesting ideas on gender. Tracey was clearly a determined woman who prefers the company of men, dislikes conventional expectations of femininity and, unusually in Northern Ireland, has never had any interest in having children. When I asked her whether she felt that being female had made her decision to join the UVF harder, given that there were so few women in loyalist paramilitaries, she replied 'no, I didn't worry that I was workin' with men. I would rather have had men actually, because I get on with men better. Always could'. After her release from prison she tried living with a male ex-prisoner, though generally she has no desire to marry or settle down with a partner, but the relationship ended over the fact that she was much more hardline in her religious and political beliefs than he was. She objects to men trying to dominate her in a romantic relationship and furthermore distrusts men's fidelity, which seems to partially stem from her experiences in the UVF where most men she knew were unfaithful to their wives. She noted that 'you're definitely looked down on here if you're not married, if you're not Mrs', and as mentioned earlier men in the UVF gave her the impression, explicitly or implicitly, that they thought she should be at home raising children. When I asked if she would consider herself to be a feminist, she replied

> I don't know. I suppose I would be a feminist, because I don't believe that a woman can't do that a man can do [*sic*], you know? ... And I don't see anything wrong with it like, because I still say that a woman can be as good as a man. Definitely. And I don't see why, [when] a woman's got her family ... don't see why she shouldn't go out to work when he can go out to work and she's the responsibility of lookin' after the childer.

Ann feels that her experiences with the UVF gave her more confidence than she had had before, as did having to cope on her own with the children when her husband was imprisoned. However she does not identify with the label 'feminist', saying

> it's the way you're brought up really. I like a man to open a door and, you know.... I mean I think of a feminist as somebody that hates men. You know, I just have that – maybe it's the wrong opinion, ok – the way we were brought up, I suppose young ones now say 'well we're not gonna be treated the way they were, my mummy or my granny' – I think they have a point, that they're not gonna be under no man's thumb, I say good luck to them, but I just wasn't brought up that way.

Alison has a similar opinion, saying she would not call herself a feminist and that to her feminism means being anti-men.

> I'm not anti-man, by no means. I do believe that a man and a woman's equal. Maybe not in everything, but I do believe that a man and a woman's equal. But I'm certainly not a feminist, no.... My sister would be a feminist, so she would, very much so. I'm not. I still like a man holdin' the door for me, you know, and lettin' you go first and gettin' up and givin' you a seat.... I very much like when it suits me, only when it suits me, my husband takin' over the role. But only when it suits me in my end of it. [Laughter.]

Both Ann and Alison have daughters whose attitudes to gender relations are rather different from their own and 'their husbands does their fair share of the housework and fair share of lookin' after the kids and their fair share of everything'.

For Jackie there is a certain ambivalence about the identity 'feminist' ('I suppose I am in a way like') but strongly feels that women's capabilities are equal to men's.

> I'll not be put down. I'll not be told I can't do anything because I'm female, d'you know what I mean? No matter how small it is, trivial.... If I was to say I could do somethin' and somebody says 'no you can't', well then I would do it just to prove them wrong, that way. That would annoy me, I would just have to prove them wrong, regardless of how simple it was or whatever. I'm quite strongminded like, definitely.

She does not, however, view this personality as being something she developed through her involvement with the UDA; rather, although she feels being in the UDA made her both mentally and physically stronger, this 'strongminded' quality was what enabled her to become involved with the UDA in the first place.

Isabella laughingly reported that her husband tells her she is a feminist. 'If anything goes wrong in a marriage I always blame the man.... Yes, I am a feminist....

To me, men always try to belittle women. Always. That's in my experience in my life.' Years ago, she says,

> clean home, the dinner on the table when he comes in from work, that's the way I lived. If the dinner wasn't ready you were panickin'. Cos that's the way I was brought up. But now, from the feud, I've a different opinion. If I don't want to do it I'll not do it, and you'll not make me!

Isabella's son's family were targeted in the 2000 UDA-UVF feud and narrowly escaped alive. This feud was very much present in the minds of the Shankill women I interviewed, three years on, and for some this had more of a personal impact than the 'Troubles' themselves. Isabella became involved with a community group set up by women after the feud to assist displaced families and her experiences in that group have been enormously empowering.

> It's made me stronger. It's made me more forward, as I always sat at the back of the room. Now I sit at the front. I wouldna dreamt five years ago, say even three years ago, of sittin' here talkin' to you. I'd a crawled into a hole.... Maybe it's because it happened to my own family. If it hadna happened to my own family personally, I probably would be still sittin' at the back of the room. I wouldn't have said boo to a mouse before this happened.

Like the republican women, many of the loyalist women are in favour of women's greater participation in conventional politics in Northern Ireland. Linda (who considers herself 'a *bit* of a feminist') feels that women are underestimated and should be able to have more prominent public roles; she also believes they are able to deal with a crisis better than men. Lily (who laughed when I asked if she considers herself a feminist and said 'I suppose I would be!') suggested women should be more involved in politics because 'they can sorta see things, you know, from other people's points of view'. Jackie supports women's participation because in her view 'women have stronger beliefs, stronger, I don't know, just – stronger ways of puttin' things across than the male.... [W]omen are stronger minded. If you get the right woman ... they're not all like that.' Tracey also feels women should be more involved and said 'I think that if a woman has the brains and all for it, to go for it and do it. Iris Robinson, the DUP, she's done it. If you've the brains and all and can stand up to them, do it.' When I questioned her support for the DUP, given their extremely conservative views on women's roles, she indicated that her support was not total or unconditional when she replied 'Well I just disagree with them and I would do me own thing.' Catherine does not consider herself a feminist yet feels women should be more involved in politics because 'women don't really have a lot of say and men don't really understand women's wants in their own communities'. Both Ann and Alison are Progressive Unionist Party (PUP) supporters and have been involved in various ways in supporting the party. Both express socialist ideas and a lot of class loyalty to the working class. As Alison said, 'We have more in common with the people of the Falls Road than we have to the Protestants of the Malone Road.'[13] Alison feels women should be more involved in formal politics, suggesting the different socially constructed roles of women and men when she said

> I think a woman knows more about the bread and butter issues of ordinary politics than what the men would do. What it's like to even hold down a job and have a young family at the same time, you know? Although the roles is changin' in this day and age, but even ... [so] a woman would be far more experienced at speakin' about that than what a man would ever be. And I think that's why they need to take more of a role. Although Maggie Thatcher never done very good whenever she was runnin' the country like!

Again like the republican women there were also indications of awareness of barriers to women's greater political participation, particularly women with children. Linda, a PUP supporter and former member/activist, found it difficult to balance her activities with home life and working. Although her husband supported her involvement up to a point, when it came to meetings she was expected to be the one either to arrange childcare or to miss the meeting, not him – illustrating the persistent inequity of access to conventional politics for women with childcare responsibilities.

7 Conclusions and reflections

Arguments for a special connection between women and peace (and men and war) based on cultural feminist and/or maternalist ideas are a focus of division among feminists. They are also empirically hard to sustain, as was illustrated in this book. Clearly there is an enormously varied range of feminist perspectives on women's relationship to peace and to military participation. To be a feminist (or a woman) is not a necessary or sufficient condition for being a pacifist, just as being a pacifist is by no means a necessary or sufficient condition for being a feminist. Political divisions between liberal feminists and feminist pacifists, theoretical disputes between cultural feminists and critical and postmodern feminists, and the failure of some feminists to confront fundamental questions about war and peace make this whole area extremely complex. The argument presented both by some feminists and by anti-feminists that universally women are less aggressive, more peaceful and less militaristic than men is one with which I fundamentally disagree and one that is challenged by the actual experiences of many women, particularly (though certainly not exclusively) female combatants.

Just as being a woman or a feminist is not a sufficient condition for being a pacifist, it is also not a sufficient condition for being anti-nationalist. For many women situated in contexts of nationalist mobilization their national identity and the nationalist struggle are more important, or as important, as their gender identity and struggles for women's rights. Women are intimately involved in national projects and mobilizations not just as symbols of the nation or as passive recipients of nationalist ideology but as nationalist (and anti-nationalist) actors themselves. Feminists, too, can be nationalists though there is a struggle to balance and reconcile what are often conflicting demands; the specific relationship between feminism(s) and nationalism(s) is highly variable according to political, social and cultural context and historical period.

That women are nationalist actors does not mean, however, that they are completely free agents making totally independent choices about their lives. As I argued in Chapter 3 the lived realities of female combatants (in this case) are much more complicated than this, as are the lived realities of male combatants. There is no such thing as 'pure' or 'complete' agency; we are all constrained and impacted upon by the structures and discourses of our societies and the events of our lives. In this 'relational autonomy' choice exists but is dependent on context;

we make choices but our choices 'are not independent of the gendered social and political contexts of ... local and global worlds' (Sjoberg and Gentry 2007: 17). Relational autonomy can be seen at work in the lives of the nationalist combatant and ex-combatant women under study here. Almost (though not quite) all the women interviewed in both countries emphasized that they *chose* to become involved with their paramilitary organization, that they *wanted* to be there; the desire to be seen as agents was clear and deserves respect. Nevertheless the contexts which shaped and constrained their decisions were also apparent, and at least implicitly acknowledged by most. Agency within the paramilitary organizations is arguably even more constrained, however, or at least more complicated and troubling. For de Mel:

> If, on the one hand, violence draws on the most noble of human qualities such as sacrifice for a collective good, on the other it 'expropriates agency' as it acts to silence both an individual and a majority, and speak on their behalf.
>
> (de Mel 2001: 205)

Therefore, she asks, '[h]ow should the woman combatant who participates in such an expropriation of agency, even as she transforms her own life through agentive moments *in* violence, be looked at?' (ibid.). This may be one of the most difficult questions to answer.

It is hoped that this book has contributed in some way to advancing our understanding of factors encouraging and enabling women to become combatants in nationalist conflicts; of their experiences in the specific cases of the LTTE in Sri Lanka and the republican movement and loyalist paramilitaries in Northern Ireland; and of conditions under which women's experiences as combatants may contribute to their developing a feminist perspective. More research, however, is necessary on the role of ex-combatant women in post-conflict reconstruction projects. Though there is a growing body of work examining gender and post-conflict reconstruction there seems to be little on the specific issue of female ex-combatants in this regard. My research has indicated that women may sometimes occupy more equal positions and have greater decision-making power in the military side of nationalist movements than in the political. This needs to be investigated and potential solutions found. As many have noted, although being part of guerrilla fighters can in some contexts 'earn' women a certain social and political authority this is by no means always the case, nor even the norm (Yuval-Davis 1997; Kandiyoti 1991; Pettman 1996; Wilford 1998). Ways of utilizing the confidence and abilities of ex-combatant women in projects to rebuild war-torn societies in more gender equal ways must be found, rather than re-marginalizing these women or expecting them, metaphorically and literally, to return to the kitchen. As Irish republican Maria said, 'I was part of the war and I want to be part of the solution.' She and others like her should be encouraged and assisted to do so.

This project had a number of research aims that have been explored throughout. How feminists, as the main scholars of women's experiences of war, tend to approach and analyse women's varied relationships to war, peace and nationalism was assessed in Chapter 3. What factors seem to impel and/or enable (some) women in nationalist conflicts to become combatants was investigated in Chapter 3 and specifically in regard to the case study conflicts in Chapter 4. What women experience as combatants in non-state military groups and whether these experiences are any sort of catalyst towards developing a feminist perspective was addressed in Chapters 5 and 6. The comparison of case studies of women's participation as combatants in paramilitaries in Sri Lanka and Northern Ireland has raised some interesting points in relation to these research areas. This concluding chapter brings some of these points together, looking specifically at factors affecting the enlistment of women in nationalist paramilitaries, their experiences of gender relations within their respective armed nationalist groups, and to what extent their participation as combatants seemed to be a catalyst for women developing a feminist perspective. First, however, the research project is reassessed.

Assessing the research methodology

As addressed in the introduction, this book used a qualitative feminist methodology relying strongly on in-depth semi-structured interviews. This had both positive and negative implications. While this approach gave me access to detailed data and personal experiences of participants, allowing me to explore in relative depth their self-reflections and conceptualizations about the issues I was researching, it also naturally meant that my focus was on a small sample of the total population of female combatants in each case. The nature of the topic also meant that knowing the total population and using random sampling was impossible and participants were accessed through the 'snowball' method. These factors largely do not make for generalization, though I believe it is still possible to identify tentative patterns which could be investigated in other cases.

I was an outsider in both Sri Lanka and Northern Ireland, though in the latter I was more of an insider-outsider than in the former, since I was living there and had greater access to and understanding of the background culture. This outsider status, particularly as someone from a small country not vested in either conflict, seemed to assist me in gaining access to participants and in setting them at ease. I did not seem, in either country, to be seen as someone likely to have a particular stake in the conflict and so was probably viewed less suspiciously. On the other hand if I had been seen as an insider in any of the three communities it is possible – though not certain – that those interviewees might have been more open with me. An interesting feature was that because I was viewed as an outsider in all three communities, interviewees sometimes presumed an ignorance on my part, which I did not possess, about the respective conflicts and their histories. Although this sometimes made for a recitation on their part of things I already knew, it was also useful in two ways. First, this meant in those cases I had a clearer idea of where they were coming from in their viewpoints and what they saw as significant. Second, when I would subsequently indicate my lack of ignorance through something I said or asked, I was met in those cases with a surprised positive response which seemed to lead to a greater ease on their part.

The fact that access to the research field can be open at one time and closed at another (Lee 1995: 16) was brought home to me in the course of this project. In Sri Lanka the field was relatively open during the first trip due to the recent ceasefire but the east was effectively closed on the second visit due to the recurrence of severe violence. In Northern Ireland the field was on the whole relatively open in terms of access to ex-combatants (or at least to ex-prisoners and at least to republicans). However I have heard suggestions that at that particular time, with the political situation tense and unstable and the Good Friday Agreement under threat, interviewees may have been less likely to be open about the extent of their involvement or their exact activities than they had been in the past. In terms of access to loyalist women I had particular difficulty with regard to the UDA. The time I was carrying out my fieldwork turned out to be an especially bad one in that respect because of the internal feud the UDA was experiencing at the time, centred then round Johnny Adair and his struggle for power against other UDA leaders. Since Adair's power base was in the lower Shankill, safe access to UDA members on the Shankill was difficult. Just as I had managed to organize a meeting with Adair's wife, Gina, and another woman, the feud reached new levels of violence when mainstream UDA leaders launched a major strike against Adair's faction and Gina and her family, along with other families in the lower Shankill, were forced to flee their homes and move to Great Britain. Just like that, the field was closed. As for east Belfast, the other area where I managed to make contact with UDA gatekeepers in the form of ex-prisoner groups, one female ex-prisoner who had been in the Ulster Freedom Fighters (the UDA's armed wing) agreed to speak to me. In a piece of tremendous bad luck, something went wrong at the ex-prisoner organization: twice they arranged a day and time for this woman to meet me; twice they failed to phone and tell me this. The woman, understandably, was extremely annoyed, particularly since she had arranged childcare both times so that she was able to meet me. Presumably she blamed me and she refused to rearrange an appointment. This was immensely frustrating but I could in no way blame her. In the end the only female UDA ex-combatant I did manage to interview was actually met through a male UVF ex-prisoner.

There are, inevitably, weaknesses in and exclusions from this project. As part of a women-centred approach I chose to interview female combatants only (though of course I spoke to male gatekeepers) but I recognize that this prohibited a deeper understanding of how the male hierarchies in these paramilitaries and nationalist movements operate, and the attitudes towards women these entail or prescribe or are based upon. The lack of examination of women in state militaries in the case studies means the research also suffers from the lack of a comparison with women's involvement in state nationalist mobilizations – and after all state militaries are the armed expression of state nationalism, a form of nationalism that can often be made dangerously invisible by virtue of its dominance. I also concede that the complex and contested role of religion in these cases, and the interplay of class with other factors, needs greater elaboration.

Significant factors in enlistment of female combatants

The distinction between institutionalized state nationalism and liberatory nationalism (Abdo 1994; Sharoni 1995, 2001) that was addressed in Chapter 3 seems to be a useful one; women do seem more likely to participate as combatants in armed movements based on a (self-defined) 'liberatory' nationalist ideology. In both the LTTE and the IRA there has been a higher presence of female combatants than in loyalist paramilitaries. Arguably this is due in part, as Yuval-Davis says (1997: 98), to the fact that the inclusion of women in these groups shows the nation that symbolically all members of the collectivity are involved in an important mass struggle. In asymmetric wars for liberatory nationalist movements to succeed in overthrowing a state with a larger and/or more heavily armed military than their own they may also simply *need* to include female combatants in more than auxiliary roles. Although in the Sri Lankan case the LTTE has at certain times been larger and better armed than the state forces it has still needed to replenish its fighting strength in response to the massive loss of Tamil combatants through death and emigration. This means that there is both an ideological and a strategic necessity for such movements to incorporate female combatants. In both the Tamil movement in Sri Lanka and the republican movement in Northern Ireland, after an initial phase of resistance to women's involvement as combatants paramilitary organizations began welcoming female recruits for all roles. This seems to have stemmed in each case from such practical and ideological necessities that are likely to apply to many armed nationalist movements, and these needs on the part of the paramilitaries combined in both cases with pressure from women themselves who wanted to participate in combat roles.

Women combatants may be more likely to be present in substantial numbers in militant movements that incorporate ideologies that have at least a rhetorical commitment to gender equality. However as the 1970s and 1980s socialist revolutionary movements in Latin America have shown, a shallow rhetorical commitment to women's rights far from guarantees post-war changes that are beneficial to women. Both the Tamil and Irish republican movements conceptualize themselves as being secular national liberation movements and both have at various points in time had some kind of commitment to socialist ideals. New, more public roles for women fit with both a socialist and a revolutionary ideology. As Moghadam has suggested, 'modernizing' revolutionary movements that use women as symbols of liberation are likely to encourage women to actively participate in the military (1993: 71–2). This has been only implicit in the Irish republican movement but very explicit in the LTTE. The Tigers have actively sought female recruits and the leadership has expressed clear ideas on the need to free women from oppression, including introducing changes to Tamil gender relations as part of a wider set of ideas about necessary changes in a new society. This may help account for the large numbers of female cadres. Although few of my LTTE interviewees joined specifically with ideas in mind about advancing women's liberation, the example of other women being prominently involved may have contributed as a subconscious factor in their decision. The reduction of old societal injunctions against women taking up arms was essential in providing the ideological and psychological space for more women, after the initial small number of female recruits, to imagine themselves in such roles.

Yuval-Davis's categorization of *Volknation*, *Kulturnation* and *Staatnation* dimensions to nationalist projects, and their implications for gender roles, are also useful. Projects with a strong *Volknation* element construct the nation based on genealogical and biological notions of origin and tend to emphasize women as biological reproducers. Those with a strong *Kulturnation* aspect construct the nation based on notions of shared culture and symbolic heritage and emphasize women as social and cultural reproducers and markers of the nation's boundaries. The *Staatnation* dimension relies on notions of citizenship as determining national boundaries and may be more inclusive and open to diversity, yet there is still much room for citizenship to function in exclusionary ways in regard to women and minority groups. In Chapter 3 I suggested that in nationalist movements with a strong *Volknation* element women are usually likely to be strongly dissuaded from participating as combatants. In movements emphasizing the *Kulturnation* dimension I proposed that how acceptable female combatants are will depend on the specific cultural traditions that are celebrated by the movement. Finally, nationalist movements emphasizing the *Staatnation* element may be more accommodating of women as combatants but this is by no means assured. In Irish republicanism the *Staatnation* dimension has dominated at the level of official ideology, always vying with a more exclusionary *Kulturnation* element in both ideology and the viewpoints of supporters. In the *Kulturnation* aspect of Irish republicanism some of the cultural traditions celebrated are ones in which women have (in the nationalist interpretation of them) held positions of power, acted in the public arena and even been fighters; since the nineteenth-century Gaelic revival movement nationalists have spoken of women having had a more equal position in Celtic society than in contemporary Irish life. The Tamil movement has probably been more strongly dominated by the *Kulturnation* dimension than by *Staatnation* or *Volknation* (though *Staatnation* comes into official ideology and *Volknation* comes into many personal views) but has managed to successfully blend old traditions with new ones to create an acceptance of female combatants, particularly through notions of purity, chastity, virginity and sacrifice.

In contrast to both Irish republican and Tamil paramilitaries, loyalist paramilitaries in Northern Ireland, as counter-revolutionary organizations, have on the whole been interested in maintaining the status quo rather than imagining a new society and have had more conservative views about appropriate roles for women and a hostility towards feminism or revolutionary ideas. The loyalist community has also, significantly, had the option of joining state forces rather than paramilitaries. Loyalism has had a stronger *Kulturnation* dimension than anything else but the culture and traditions celebrated and reified in this case are deeply masculine and conservative. These factors have meant that loyalist women have been much less likely to join paramilitaries than republican women in Northern Ireland or Tamil women in Sri Lanka and when they have become involved (whether officially enlisting or not) they have primarily acted in auxiliary roles. Loyalist paramilitaries have made use of women in auxiliary roles, in particular to move and hide weapons (as have republican groups) as a practical response to reality since women in Northern Ireland have been less likely to be suspected and searched by the security forces. On the whole these groups have not, however, extended this acceptance to a greater involvement of women in all roles in political violence, except in a small number of cases.

My research suggests that in both the LTTE and Irish republican paramilitaries there was usually an interplay between ideological and practical, experience-based motivations for women to enlist as combatants, which is likely to be a common pattern in nationalist conflicts. Though the vast majority of my participants who are or were members of the LTTE or the IRA expressed nationalist political goals appropriate to their respective movements, many were also responding to their lived realities. Turshen has argued that in contemporary civil wars and wars of liberation civilians are drawn into the conflict and the separation between civilians and (male) belligerents breaks down, as can the aggressive male/passive female binary (1998). The blurring of the conventional front line/home front boundary may thus contribute to a corresponding blurring of the male combatant/female nurturer boundary; the invasion of the private sphere by the state, or by the war more generally, can be a spur for women to enter the public sphere more, including as combatants. Women may be more likely to take up arms in intra-state conflicts where the war has impinged on the domestic sphere where women predominate, rather than in inter-state/international conflicts where the battle zone is distant. Indeed a recurring theme in the literature on Latin America, Palestine and Africa is that women become combatants in greater numbers in conflicts where the battle-zone impinges on the civilian home front. My research appears to support this as a factor in intra-state nationalist conflict. A clear motivating factor for women in all cases (LTTE, Irish republicans and loyalists) has been concern for their respective families and wider communities. In both Sri Lanka and Northern Ireland there exists a very strong sense of family, of community and of communal loyalty, which has deepened in both places through the experience of war. In regard to Northern Ireland, Porter argues that for both Catholics and Protestants it is women's 'traditional maternal role as guardian of the family' that prompted them to become politically active (including in paramilitaries) in the early 1970s, in response to events that threatened their families (1998: 45–6).

A maternal-type guardian role, however, is not necessarily restricted to one's own immediate family. Nationalist movements, it is often argued, construct the nation as the family writ large. The concern for family and the belief that taking up arms or engaging in political violence in more auxiliary forms was the best way to protect their families was also proffered to the respective 'imagined communities' (extended kin?) of all three groups. The communal experience for Tamils and Irish republicans of discrimination and injustice in employment and public service provision and, in Sri Lanka, in education contributed to paramilitary enlistment, as did arbitrary arrest, harassment and violence by the state security forces, including rape in Sri Lanka and sexual harassment in Northern Ireland. This communal experience did not always have to actually be experienced first-hand in the families of those who became combatants; the involvement in the northern struggle of people from the Republic of Ireland, for example, illustrates the wider communal concern. Nevertheless for many, personal experience *was* highly significant and many paramilitary members discussed in particular the death or arrest of loved ones, usually men. In a striking parallel between an Irish republican and a Tamil nationalist, Mary felt that she should 'fill the vacuum' when her closest brother was arrested and Thamilachi felt the same way when her brother was killed, describing this in almost identical terms to Mary: 'I felt … there was a certain vacuum that has got to be filled, a vacuum created by my brother's death.'

The loyalist community in Northern Ireland has not experienced the systemic injustice, harassment and violence from the state that republicans and Tamils have but *has* suffered violence from republican paramilitaries. The republican campaign against the security forces, overwhelmingly drawn from the Protestant (and usually loyalist) community, as well as sectarian attacks on Protestants by republican groups, were perceived by loyalists as attacks on their community, which felt militarily, politically and culturally under siege. Defence of one's immediate family seems to have been a primary motivating reason (certainly in the early years of the 'Troubles') for loyalist women to become involved in some kind of paramilitary activity, though whether this is a significant factor for loyalist women who became involved in more than auxiliary roles is less clear. Neither of the two loyalist women combatants I interviewed, involved in different time periods of the 'Troubles', have children or partners/husbands but my research cannot show if this is likely to be a pattern.

Loyalist women seem frequently (though not always) to have become involved in paramilitary activity through connection with a male family member, usually a husband, and some loyalists stressed to me that a married woman would have to have the support of her husband to be able to participate. In the republican movement more single than married women seem to have participated but among married volunteers, according to two of my republican interviewees, some were involved without the knowledge of their husbands. Another, however, felt that this would be difficult due to women having to invent excuses for frequent absences from the house, particularly if the couple had children. In Sri Lanka most female LTTE cadres are single but of those who are married, the vast majority are married to male members of the movement. The LTTE is of course distinct from both republican and loyalist paramilitaries in Northern Ireland in that rather than engaging in part-time urban and rural guerrilla warfare it has operated a more conventional military campaign as well as utilizing both urban and rural guerrilla warfare tactics; it has controlled large areas of land (and people) for extended periods of time; and participation in the organization is a full-time occupation, with cadres leaving their homes and families to live in LTTE camps. Under these circumstances, given cultural strictures on the importance of women's roles as wives and mothers, it seems to me unlikely that a woman already married to a man who is not himself part of the movement would be accepted into the LTTE. It seems more likely that any such woman would be told she could assist the movement in other ways, such as by sheltering cadres and producing children for the nation.

As I contended in Chapter 3, whether or not female combatants have children during their active involvement is likely to vary considerably according to context and may depend on the presence of other, non-combatant women in caring roles. In Sri Lanka most female cadres are unmarried and are not mothers. For those who do have children, however, there are LTTE-run childcare facilities (though I did not see these for myself), which I suspect are likely to be largely staffed by women. In Northern Ireland the participation of women who are mothers has been largely dependent on the availability of other women, usually female relatives, to provide childcare. Even when women's participation as combatants is accepted in principle, men have been generally unwilling to reshape parental roles and responsibilities. This indicates that motherhood and the lack of available childcare is likely to be a constraining factor on the participation of many women in military roles, as it still is on their participation in conventional politics. Nevertheless one very clear result of my research was a refutation of the maternalist feminist argument. As discussed in Chapter 3 the maternalist feminist argument is either that women are 'naturally' opposed to militarism and war because they can create and nurture life, or that the experience of motherhood produces a way of thinking that conflicts with military thinking and can lead women to anti-militarism and non-violence (Ruddick 1989). Others, however, have shown that in fact appeals to motherhood have been used just as often in the service of militarism as they have to promote peace and that in the context of war the experience of mothering can sometimes promote an accommodation of premature and violent death (Scheper-Hughes 1992, 1998). My research in Northern Ireland illustrated how the experience of motherhood can sometimes lead women to support the use of force and in fact to take up arms themselves; in their eyes, this is to protect their children or to create a better future for them in a more just world.[1] Women I spoke to in Northern Ireland (both republican and loyalist) who had children during their period of involvement often saw their actions in this light. Anecdotal evidence from Sri Lanka suggests the same may apply for the few Tamil mothers in the movement. The mother-warrior trope is clearly alive and well.

Gender relations within nationalist paramilitaries

The distinction between liberatory and institutionalized state nationalisms proved to be relevant in my research not only in terms of numbers of women participating as combatants but also in regard to the gender relations, particularly sexual division of labour, that operate within paramilitaries. Within the LTTE and the PIRA (and probably the INLA as well) there seems to have been little sexual division of labour in terms of tasks assigned. In both cases there appears to have been a change over time in respect of the way women have been treated in the paramilitaries. After their initial difficulty breaking into the organizations there seems to have been a period when women had experiences of men treating them with less respect, or feeling that women were not up to the tasks required of them. Later, after women's involvement had become more common – and as women had 'proven' their military capabilities – this was less of a problem. However Yuval-Davis's suggestion (1997: 101) that compared with state militaries a potentially less hierarchical nature of anti-state militaries/paramilitaries combines with a strong shared ideological position to contribute to transcending tensions between male and female soldiers and a better integration of women into the ranks does not entirely fit the cases under study here. The LTTE certainly does have a very strong shared ideology but at the same time it has historically been one of the most hierarchical and tightly organized of all such groups, while also being one of the most significant in terms of numbers of women involved in military roles and the explicit attention paid both to this and to wider issues of gender equality. In this case arguably the strong and cohesive ideology, which includes explicit commitment to women's rights, actually combined with the extremely hierarchical and disciplined nature of the organization of the LTTE to help the integration of female soldiers. In the IRA there is again a strong shared ideology and hierarchical organization (though not to the extent of the LTTE) but this shared ideology has not been as explicitly or consistently interested in women's rights. Although acceptance of female combatants improved in the IRA it seems that even with the passage of time there remained some male combatants who retained old gendered notions to the extent that they felt more protective towards female volunteers and acted accordingly, potentially endangering the success of operations. Similarly, the reception of female republican combatants by their communities also indicates certain ambiguities. Republicans spoke of the 'freedom fighter' image of their paramilitaries in the nationalist community and largely of being treated as heroes upon their release from jail, in the case of ex-prisoners, but a minority had experiences that suggest a gender-differentiated attitude still exists for some nationalists as they felt certain people had treated them slightly differently as *female* ex-prisoners or combatants.

In both the LTTE and the IRA a factor in the increased acceptance of women in the ranks seems to have been education. In the LTTE this was by the explicit design of the leadership. Cadres of both sexes participate in political education classes during their training and specific attention is paid to feminism and the question of women's position in society. In the IRA this seems to have been more of an organic process and, since it has on the whole been limited to education in prison (men taking Women's Studies courses and debating with female prisoners issues such as pornography, for example), it has not by any means influenced everyone. Thus, arguably nationalist movements that explicitly utilize education of their members on feminist issues are likely to result in a more equal and respectful treatment of female combatants than movements that do not.

In contrast to the IRA and the LTTE, in loyalist groups a clear sexual division of labour appears to have been very much the norm, with women generally being given auxiliary roles and few women participating fully as combatants. This does not seem to have shifted over time. Both Tracey (involved in the UVF in the early years of the 'Troubles') and Jackie (involved in the UDA in much later years), the only loyalist female combatants I was able to interview, seem to have had to 'prove' their abilities and trustworthiness by not making a statement when arrested and interrogated, and in Tracey's case by serving time in prison, in order to be afforded respect by male comrades. Tracey spoke of encountering some men in the UVF who said she should be at home washing dishes and raising children and indeed she feels that *most* men in the UVF were not in favour of women participating beyond an auxiliary capacity. Similarly, Jackie felt strongly that men in the UDA did not approve of women's participation in more than auxiliary roles and that it was her male family connections to the organization which protected her from more overt resistance. The loyalist women I interviewed who had participated in auxiliary roles expressed similar ideas, though some also said they thought that perhaps it just never occurred to the men that women might want to participate in more active roles and so never asked them to. It is more likely, however, that most loyalist men did not feel that it was appropriate for women to take on such roles and so did not ask them to. Significantly, for their part most women *did not push* for access to those roles; most were content to have 'done my wee bit'.

Doing their 'wee bit', of course, was frequently much more dangerous than such women self-deprecatingly imply, and involved exploiting local gendered norms in combination with British military gendered expectations and concerns about negative publicity in order to create a space in which such women could operate. Such gender norms intersect with power and punishment and their impact sometimes even extended to the prosecution of women, and not exclusively loyalist women. When republican Maria was finally arrested and prosecuted in the late 1970s for hiding weapons for the IRA a number of years before, the judge in the case commented that she had six children and since the time of the incident she had tried to make a new life for herself and had kept herself clean. The charges were dropped. On the other hand, this does not seem to have been the sole reason for the abandonment of the charges; the three men involved had been released due to their statements having been taken under duress after severe beatings. A more explicit example is the case of loyalist UVF-member Ann. In Chapter 6 I mentioned an incident in which Ann disposed of a gun after her female companion had been shot. When she appeared in court a year later in relation to the incident (a soldier had witnessed her disposing of the gun) she told the judge that she had been forced into the action. '[T]he judge looked at me … and he just says "go home and look after your children, never mind"…. I thought I was gonna get jailed!'

It is possible that part of the loyalist resistance to women's full participation in paramilitaries was due to the fact that women were known to be fully active in republican paramilitaries. As in any nationalist conflict, the opposing groups in Northern Ireland construct themselves in opposition to the other. Thus women's involvement as combatants may have been seen by loyalists as being too radical, too revolutionary, too much against the grain of prevailing gender relations, too feminist – and *too republican*. Their construction of themselves in opposition to republicans was illustrated in a recurring response to my question about why they thought women had been less heavily involved in loyalist paramilitaries in comparison with republican paramilitaries. As part of their response many women slightly spitefully maintained that republicans, including republican women, were always wanting to boast about themselves and get publicity, while loyalists were 'not in it for the glory'. While it is certainly true that the republican movement has used propaganda and publicity consciously, consistently and much more astutely than loyalists, my interviews with republican women did not at all lead me to accept the rest of this claim. Thus, the assertion may say more about the loyalist perspective towards the 'other' than it does about republicans. Traditional expectations about gender roles remain strong enough within loyalist communities that many loyalist women are extremely reluctant to discuss their involvement in paramilitaries – even with other loyalists, let alone with 'outsiders'.

Judging from the results of my research on Sri Lanka and Northern Ireland, in conjunction with existing research on other such conflicts, I therefore contend that the greater participation of female combatants in nationalist movements conceptualized by members as liberatory (such as the Tamil movement in Sri Lanka and the Irish republican movement) compared with their lesser involvement in institutionalized state nationalist or counter-revolutionary movements (like loyalist groups) is a recurring nationalist pattern. Furthermore, gender relations in the former have more potential for greater equality than in the latter. Significantly, education about gender inequalities (both formal and informal and both directed by the movement or undertaken independently by members) seems to have an important role to play in altering gender relations within nationalist movements. Organizations or movements aimed at upholding an oppressive status quo or containing those revolutionary movements that desire to disrupt this are, in most cases, likely to be more conservative than their opposition and to have correspondingly more conservative views on the appropriate roles of women. Such views may become hardened, rather than softened, as the conflict progresses and the perceived need to maintain cultural integrity and traditions (in which the appropriate place for women *always* figures) increases rather than decreases.

The question of feminism

One of the questions I was interested to investigate was whether or not women's experiences in paramilitaries in Sri Lanka and Northern Ireland were any kind of catalyst for developing a feminist perspective, as appears to have occurred to some extent in Latin America (Alegria 1987; Chinchilla 1997; Ibáñez 2001; Mason 1992; Montgomery 1982; Randall 1992; Urbina 1994). This seems, on the whole, likely not to be the case for most women who have been involved in loyalist paramilitaries, though I would be hesitant to state this too categorically given the extremely limited number of 'active' loyalist women I managed to interview. In contrast, for the majority of my LTTE participants their life with the movement seems definitely to have stimulated the development of feminist ideas. This has stemmed I believe in large part from the explicit emphasis of the movement on women's equality and feminism, which has created an ideological space that has been more than merely rhetorical, and the education on these matters discussed earlier, alongside their vastly changed life experiences. Although most female Tiger cadres did not join the movement with such ideas, many have certainly since developed them and now feel, as Sudarvili does, that they 'are fighting for the women's liberation also'. Irish republican women, who seem to have been equally or even less likely than Tamil women to have become involved because of pre-existing feminist ideas, again have often since become feminists or, if uncomfortable with the label, increasingly willing to express feminist-type ideas. For them, the most significant factor here seems to have been imprisonment. The experience of living in close quarters solely with other women for long periods of time, the informal education they received through their own political discussions (amongst themselves and with male republican prisoners) and through sharing of experiences, and the formal education undertaken while imprisoned have all contributed to many of them developing a heightened awareness of some of the difficulties facing women in society *and* within the republican movement.

Many republican women I interviewed are currently involved in various projects or jobs aimed at the betterment of their communities, including encouraging and enabling women's participation in public activities (though this can partly be attributed to the ways I gained access to them and may not be an entirely representative picture). Many were happy to describe themselves as feminists but in keeping with their status as republicans, others were sometimes reluctant to label themselves or to categorize their activities purely in this light (presumably not wanting it to seem that they were prioritizing the women's struggle over the national struggle) and preferred to speak of equality for all sections of society (which is arguably a concern for feminism at its best). Some indicated the internal tensions between republicanism and feminism. For the majority of republican women who accepted the label 'feminist', their consciousness was raised through their experiences in prison. In contrast, the majority of loyalist women were less willing to call themselves feminists, even if they mentioned ideas of believing in women's equality. This seemed to be partly attributable to the perception of many loyalist women that feminism is about 'hating men' as well as, arguably, to the tendency to associate feminism with Irish nationalism/republicanism. The Tamil nationalist women I interviewed who are still with the LTTE are engaged in a range of activities, from soldiers in the Military Wing through various political, social and economic activities in the Political Wing. This includes many projects specifically directed at improving women's lives. They seem unable, or unwilling, to conceptualize a life for themselves outside the LTTE (at least not that they told me about). When asked what they wanted to do in peacetime, should this ever come, the continual refrain was that there would be much work to do building the new nation and they wanted to be part of this so would continue working for the LTTE in a non-military capacity. They also seemed generally surprised, bemused or slightly scornful at the idea I proposed that reintegrating into a normal civilian life might be difficult for them. Their view is that they are still a part of the Tamil community and, therefore, there will be no such problems. This seems a significant underestimation of what is a perennial problem in other similar post-conflict settings. For the four women I interviewed who are no longer with the LTTE, ex-combatant life has not been easy. Three of the four had left the LTTE with permission (Kavitha, the conscript, apparently due to her poor health and disappointing performance; Shanthi and Geetha apparently due to their serious battle injuries) while one, Thangaci, had fled. This difference does not seem to have had a significant impact in terms of their post-LTTE lives; all four live in extreme poverty. Geetha reported being received with respect by her community because she had fought in the LTTE, but this has not eased her own adjustment. When I asked how she had experienced settling into civilian life she said

> I had great difficulty. It was difficult to adjust initially. While I was in the LTTE, we were at war most of the time and I almost lost all my kindness to humanity. But when I am at home, this kindness builds relationships and bonds. I have to be kind with my family members, neighbours and so on.

For nationalist combatants who are feminists, their feminism is inextricably intertwined with their respective nationalist commitments. This clearly presents challenges, significantly the question of how far women within the movements would be permitted to push a feminist agenda. What happens if some begin to raise feminist issues or concerns about women, or questions about masculine roles, that the leadership (still predominantly male in both cases) or other, non-feminist women in the movements perceive as contradicting the nationalist project? It may be significant here that this research revealed the suggestion that in both the LTTE and the Irish republican movement there has in some ways been more gender equality in the military side of things than in the political side, though in both cases this is being addressed and is improving. (For loyalists, both military and political aspects have remained largely inhospitable places both for women and for feminist demands.) This may be connected to the fact that in military matters the female recruits in the LTTE and the IRA have 'proven' themselves capable of living up to (or exceeding) the masculine standard, as well as to the deep bonding between fellow soldiers that can occur in the context of war. Nevertheless, the comradeship and respect largely accorded women in the military does not necessarily translate over to the political side of the respective movements.

For many nationalist women in conflicts around the world it has been in the post-conflict period, away from the immediacy and urgency of war, that the contradictions of being both a feminist and a nationalist became most apparent. Translating this into societal change is difficult. Furthermore, when 'liberatory' nationalist movements succeed and take political power they are not always open to feminist demands. Feminist nationalists need to forge alliances and engage in dialogue with non-nationalist, autonomous feminist groups as well as directly challenge the regressive aspects of their own nationalist movements. In as much as I could ascertain from the outside it seemed that LTTE women have not as yet begun to raise issues that challenge the movement's leadership or direction. With the 2002–8 Sri Lankan ceasefire in tatters and a peace settlement seeming further away than ever the question of what will happen in a peacetime context remains unanswered. Northern Ireland has had a peace agreement formally in place since 1998, though the devolved institutions have not been continuously operating since that time and some things are yet to be implemented. It is still not an easy place to be a feminist. It seems to be very difficult for women to raise feminist issues (or even to identify as feminist) within loyalist and unionist organizations, particularly the larger mainstream political parties, though the smaller UVF-aligned Progressive Unionist Party has a somewhat better record of at least encouraging women's participation in the party than the larger unionist parties.[2] The current situation for women in the republican movement is more positive yet still mixed. Republican feminists pursue a feminist agenda but for some the contradictions between feminism and nationalism are evident in the political side of the movement on issues such as abortion. Nevertheless, to dismiss nationalist feminists in Sri Lanka, Northern Ireland or anywhere else as irrelevant and ineffective, or even as non-feminist, is both insulting and unfair. The difficulty of pursuing feminist issues within a nationalist movement is one with which feminists within those movements must negotiate and struggle, with passion and courage, as they are doing now and have done in the past.

Possibly the most recurring theme in all my interviews (LTTE, republican and loyalist) was that of respect and, tied to this, of women proving themselves (to a *masculine standard*) to earn this respect. This I found immensely depressing. How many times in how many ways and in how many varied places, and at what cost, do we have to keep 'proving ourselves' worthy of respect? The fact that women succeed in the military in large part by taking on a masculine gender role and by denying or subsuming gender differences means that the movement's politics, no matter how liberatory it considers itself to be, will not *automatically* be genuinely or consistently interested in addressing systemic gender inequality in wider society. This requires a direct challenge to existing gender ideologies and practices and a chipping away at the often narrow concerns of nationalist movements. Although the very presence of women in non-traditional combat roles (at least in significant numbers) may be the drip of water which opens up a crack in the rock, to split it wide open requires a constant feminist assault.

Appendix
Interviewees/participants

Sri Lanka

Banuka, two interviews, September 2002, Kokadichcholai (interpreted)
Barathy, August 2002, Kilinochchi (in English with some interpretive assistance)
Geetha, June 2004, Kilinochchi (interpreted)
Kalaivily, June 2004, Jaffna (interpreted)
Kavitha, September 2002, anonymous border village in northeast (interpreted)
Krishna, September 2002, Trincomalee (interpreted)
Malarville, September 2002, Kokadichcholai (interpreted)
Prasanthi, September 2002, Trincomalee (interpreted)
Sailajah, September 2002, Kokadichcholai (interpreted)
Shanthi, September 2002, anonymous border village in northeast (interpreted)
Sudarvili, August 2002, Kilinochchi (interpreted with some parts in English)
Sumathi, September 2002, Kokadichcholai (interpreted)
Thamilachi, August 2002, Jaffna (interpreted)
Thamilini, two interviews August 2002 and June 2004, Kilinochchi (interpreted)
Thamilnila, August 2002, Jaffna (interpreted)
Thamilvily, two interviews August 2002, Jaffna (interpreted with some parts in English)
Thangachi, June 2004, Kilinochchi (interpreted)

Ireland

Alison, February 2003, Shankill Road area (Belfast)
Ann, February 2003, Shankill Road area (Belfast)
Bernadette, May 2003, north Belfast
Caral, April 2003, west Belfast
Catherine, February 2003, east Belfast
Clodagh, March 2003, rural Northern Ireland
Eileen, April 2003, Dublin
Emma, May 2003, west Belfast
Isabella, January 2003, Shankill Road area (Belfast)
Jackie, October 2003, Derry/Londonderry

James, June 2003, north Belfast
Joy, January 2003, Shankill Road area (Belfast)
Lily, February 2003, Shankill Road area (Belfast)
Linda, March 2003, Shankill Road area (Belfast)
Maeve, June 2003, rural Northern Ireland
Mairead, May 2003, north Belfast
Maria, May 2003, west Belfast
Marion, March 2003, Armagh
Mary, March 2003, Dublin
Niamh, March 2003, west Belfast
Peter, June 2002, rural Northern Ireland
Teresa, April 2003, Belfast
Tom, January 2003, Shankill Road area (Belfast)
Tracey, March 2003, Armagh
William, January 2003, Shankill Road area (Belfast)

Notes

1 Introduction

1 When I embarked on the first fieldtrip as a doctoral student I could not afford to hire professional interpreters. On the second trip I attempted to hire someone in Colombo to come with me but had no luck through my contacts; everyone seemed to be too afraid at the time to travel to the north.
2 Guelke notes that normally the term 'paramilitary' is 'used to refer to state security forces that lie between the civilian police and the military. In Northern Ireland, unusually, it is used to refer to non-governmental organisations that have used or threatened to use political violence' (1999: 31). The term 'paramilitary' is also sometimes used in regard to non-state Tamil militant/guerrilla groups in Sri Lanka. Accordingly, for convenience and consistency I use the term in this sense in regard to both case studies.
3 For a critique of Anderson's 'imagined community' notion see Chatterjee (1991).
4 Zalewski, for example, explicates the dangers of sometimes assuming too much difference (especially between so-called 'modernist' or 1970s feminisms and so-called 'postmodern' feminisms) or too little difference (especially between different types of 1970s feminisms) (2000: 4).
5 For example on feminist empiricism, see Harding (1987a, 1991) and Randall (1991). On feminist standpoint epistemology (and criticisms of it), see Harstock (1987), Harding (1987a, 1991), Crosby (1992), Randall (1991). On the related notion of epistemic privilege (and criticism of it), see Bar On (1993), Wolf (1996), Lal (1996). On feminist postmodernism (and criticisms), see Singer (1992), Flax (1992, 1987), Butler (1992), Maynard (1994), Harding (1987a), Wolf (1996).
6 'Traditional' (epistemologies, methodologies, methods, and so on) is used here to mean older, well-established, generally Enlightenment-based social science approaches and techniques; it is also generally assumed to mean non-feminist (though not *necessarily* anti-feminist).
7 Also known as 'network sampling' (Lee 1993: 65–9).
8 Sri Lanka Muslims are generally considered to be an ethnic group rather than purely a religious one.

2 Overview of armed conflict in Sri Lanka and Northern Ireland

1 'Sri Lanka' is generally used to refer to the country, to save confusion, even when discussing the colonial period when it was called 'Ceylon'. It has been argued that the change of name from Ceylon to Sri Lanka was done without the consent of Tamils (Wilson 1988: v). I use 'Sri Lanka' because that is how most people outside the country know it. The name was changed from Ceylon to Sri Lanka in 1972.
2 There is an inconsistency in the literature about when it is best to use 'Sinhalese' and when to use 'Sinhala', and some use the terms interchangeably. In accordance with

the pattern which seems to me most logical and most consistent in the literature, I use 'Sinhala' for the language and the variant of nationalism and 'Sinhalese' for the people, and try to be as consistent as possible with this.

3 Smith has suggested that as a result of the war, Sri Lankan Tamils now make up only 8 per cent of the population (2003: 3).

4 'Sri Lankan Tamils' are sometimes referred to as 'Ceylon Tamils'. 'Indian Tamils' are also known as 'hill country Tamils', 'plantation Tamils', or 'Up-Country Tamils'; they are the descendents of south Indians brought over as indentured labour by the British to work the plantations in the central hills in the mid-nineteenth century. 'Muslims' are considered a separate ethnic group, sometimes called 'Moors'. I use 'Sri Lankan Tamils', 'Indian Tamils' and 'Muslims' here. This is not intended as a political judgement and certainly the distinction between 'Sri Lankan' and 'Indian' Tamils does not imply any less of a right of 'Indian Tamils' to live in Sri Lanka.

5 See www.unhcr.lk/ for up to date information on IDPs.

6 For a detailed account of the 1971 insurrection, see Alles (1977).

7 Publicly, the JVP became extremely Sinhala-chauvinist over time, particularly after the July 1983 anti-Tamil riots when many members left the party because of their objections to this (Chandraprema 1991: 54–5). Privately, the JVP had various forms of involvement with certain Tamil militant groups in the northeast in the late 1980s (ibid.: 103, 180–2, 266; Narayan Swamy 1994: 27; Gunaratna 1987: 70).

8 To a lesser degree there were also Hindu and Muslim revival movements (Jayawardena 1986: 122).

9 Wilson states there have been suggestions but no hard evidence that members of the government and civil service were involved in planning the anti-Tamil riots (1988: 173).

10 Government figures acknowledge 384 deaths but independent observers believe the real figure is much higher (Schwarz 1983: 15). Some estimate that over 1,000 were killed and thousands more injured (Gunaratna 1987: 33); others put it as high as 2,000 deaths (Bennett *et al.* 1995: 135).

11 At the élite level there were, and continue to be, some numbers of Sri Lankan Tamils who move in the same circles in Colombo as élite Sinhalese. The intra-Tamil struggle over this issue was exemplified by the divisions within the ACTC, led by the supposedly 'collaborationist' Ganapathipillai Ponnambalam, which led to Chelvanayakam leaving the ACTC and forming the Federal Party (P.L. de Silva 1999: 91).

12 The Prime Minister was assassinated in 1959 by a Buddhist monk.

13 The 1978 Constitution retained the same provisions for the maintenance of the unitary state and retained Sinhala as the only official language, though adding that Sinhala and Tamil would both be national languages; among other things, the 1978 Constitution provides that where one language is used in a university, the other language must also be available for students previously educated in it. The Constitution was rejected by the TULF as it did not concede regional autonomy but the more moderate and anti-secessionist Indian Tamil CWC took a different stand and voted in favour of the new Constitution (Schwarz 1983: 5–7, 10–11).

14 The term 'Eelam' (or 'Ilam') is an old name for Sri Lanka. In the 1920s and 1930s the term 'Tamil Eelam' came into increasing usage, meaning the areas inhabited by Tamils and considered to be traditional homelands. The term was widely used in the late 1930s and is currently used in Tamil nationalism to mean 'belonging to the Tamils' (Hellmann-Rajanayagam 1990: 114).

15 This resulted in the flight to Tamil Nadu in India of some key militants – including Velupillai Prabhakaran, the now infamous leader of the LTTE.

16 There have been some significant differences between the north and east, particularly relating to caste, which cannot be gone into here. Hoole *et al.* argue that ideological and group differences between paramilitaries were less important in the east than in Jaffna. Ideas of their common suffering as eastern Tamils overrode those concerns and

the different groups often shared camps and meals. LTTE leaders in the east tried to resist Jaffna orders to eliminate the other groups, but ultimately failed (1990: 96–7).

17 Prabhakaran has been LTTE leader since 1981–2. 'Prabhakaran' seems to be one Anglicized spelling out of a variety. The Anglicized Tamil spelling seems to usually to be 'Pirapaharan' (though there are others); I use Prabhakaran for the sake of clarity, since that is how it is generally spelt in media reports, but in the bibliography, statements by Prabhakaran are listed under the name Pirapaharan since that is how they are presented by the LTTE.

18 The prohibition against marriage changed in the mid-1980s after Prabhakaran himself married and had children.

19 In his first major interview in the early 1980s, Prabhakaran admitted that the LTTE was opposed to multi-party democracy and that it 'believed in a single party state and would brook no opposition' (Narayan Swamy 1994: 199).

20 The Provincial Councils Act of 1987 established the north and east as one province, which has been controversial since the east is much more ethnically mixed than the Tamil north, with large numbers of Muslims and Sinhalese as well as Tamils. Both the north and east are claimed by Tamil nationalists as their 'traditional homeland', which is contested by the state in part because of the strategic importance of Trincomalee, which has the largest natural harbour in the Indian Ocean.

21 The name for Northern Ireland is contested. Legally it is 'Northern Ireland' and this is used by the UK government. Most unionists and loyalists use 'Northern Ireland' but many also use 'Ulster' (though seemingly less so now than in the past). Nationalists and republicans tend to use 'the north' or 'the six counties' for Northern Ireland and 'the south' or 'the 26 counties' for the Republic of Ireland. Republicans studiously avoid using 'Northern Ireland'. On the whole I use 'Northern Ireland' but liberally use other terms as well. No political judgement is implied by my use of various terms.

22 Source: Northern Ireland Statistics website: www.nisra.gov.uk. Crown copyright material is reproduced with the permission of the Controller of HMSO. See key statistics tables, available online at: www.nisranew.nisra.gov.uk/Census/pdf/Key%20Statistics%20ReportTables.pdf.

23 The IRA came into being from about 1917 through the re-organization of the Irish Volunteers, an Irish nationalist military organization central to the 1916 Easter Rising against British rule in Ireland. With the establishment of the rebel Irish parliament the Dáil Éireann, set up by the abstentionist Sinn Féin MPs elected in the 1918 general election, the IRA became the army of the declared Irish Republic.

24 The new Northern Ireland government was not given control of security and policing until 1923.

25 After a 1955 UK general election in which the biggest anti-partition vote was cast since 1921 (for abstentionist Sinn Féin candidates), the IRA launched a six-year guerrilla campaign against the northern statelet. By September 1958 almost all the IRA Army Council were interned in the south. However, '[t]he decisive factor in the defeat of the campaign was the leadership's realization that … the Northern nationalist community's support for violence had waned.' In February 1962 the IRA announced it was ending the campaign (Hennessey 1997: 104–7).

26 Paisley founded the Free Presbyterian Church of Ulster in 1951 and is both a political and religious leader. See Bruce (1986).

27 Survey results on this question are available online at: www.ark.ac.uk/nilt/2002/Political_Attitudes/NIRELAND.html.

28 Survey results on this question are available online at: www.ark.ac.uk/nilt/2002/Political_Attitudes/NIRELAND.html.

29 On PIRA, among many others see English (2003); Bell (1989, 2000); Coogan (1995); Patterson (1997); Maloney (2002).

30 The UDR was a part-time Northern Ireland-based security force, predominantly recruited from the local Protestant community. It was the successor to the B-Specials,

which was the only remaining unit of the almost exclusively Protestant and notoriously violent USC, which was established in 1920.

31 See http://cain.ulst.ac.uk/issues/politics/election/elect.htm for Northern Ireland election results since 1968.

32 The UK government did not proscribe the UDA until 1992.

33 7,000 refugees were reported to have crossed the border to the Republic, with the Lynch government setting up refugee camps and calling for a United Nations peacekeeping force (Kennedy-Pipe 2000: 27–8).

34 The IRA had earlier taken over policing in 'Free Derry', one of its 'no-go' areas, and had set up its own traffic courts (Clarke and Johnston 2001: 72).

35 The name of Long Kesh prison was changed to the Maze in the mid-1970s but republicans often still refer to it as Long Kesh or 'the Kesh'.

36 On the hunger strikes, see O'Malley (1990); McKeown (2001: Chs 6–7); Campbell *et al.* (1994); Beresford (1994).

37 The famous phrase coined by Danny Morrison, Sinn Féin's publicity director in the 1980s.

38 The aftermath of the Agreement showed that unionism had lost some of its influence with the British government, as its actions did not have the effect they achieved against Sunningdale the previous decade. Unionist support in Westminster was waning, as it was in the wider British community (see Arthur 2000: 224–31).

39 The Orange Order is a Protestant (and anti-Catholic) organization, founded in 1795 after a clash between Protestants and Catholics in County Armagh. Its festivities held on 12 July celebrate William of Orange's victory over King James at the Battle of the Boyne in 1690. Some of the Order's annual summer parades march through Catholic/nationalist areas and are viewed by those communities as oppressive.

40 A September 1997 opinion poll showed 93 per cent of UUP supporters and 76 per cent of DUP supporters wanted their party to stay in the talks – compared with between 99 and 100 per cent of SDLP, Sinn Féin and APNI supporters (Irwin 2002: 155 and Ch. 7).

41 *UTV Live at Six*, 25 June 2003, UTV, 6 p.m. This is according to testimony by David Rupert, an FBI agent who had undercover contact with RIRA, in the Dublin trial of Michael McKevitt (allegedly the head of RIRA) for directing terrorism.

42 See Northern Ireland Prison Service: www.niprisonservice.gov.uk/index.cfm/area/information/page/earlyrelease. For monthly release breakdowns see www.niprisonservice.gov.uk/index.cfm/area/information/page/Earlyreleasefigures

43 See the Northern Ireland Office website on decommissioning: www.nio.gov.uk/decommissioning.

44 For the text of the St Andrews Agreement see www.taoiseach.gov.ie/index.asp?locID=199&docID=2931.

45 In May 2008 Paisley stepped down as First Minister, succeeded by DUP deputy leader Peter Robinson.

3 Theorizing women-and-peace, nationalism and female combatants

1 See Richards (1990) for an interesting philosophical argument that critiques cultural feminism (or rather, radical feminism more broadly) and attempts to show just how difficult it is to sustain a reasonable, reliable and consistent argument that the pursuit of peace is necessarily entailed in the feminist movement.

2 For a searing indictment of women's varied participation in the 1994 Rwandan genocide see African Rights (1995). See also Coomaraswamy (1998) and Jones (2002: section vi).

3 They give an example of one such existing grassroots peace group, the Sudanese Women's Voice for Peace, which addresses women's as well as men's violence in the context of war in the Sudan.

4 See Caldicott (1985), a medical doctor and anti-nuclear activist, for an argument that women are *innately* pacifists and nurturers because of their biological capacity for motherhood.
5 This surprises me about Ruddick's work on maternal thinking because in other work, when discussing feminism, she herself recognizes the complex nature of identity.
6 An international development non-governmental organization.
7 See Enloe's works, in particular 2000a.
8 One could also argue that militarism and militaries are usually equally 'unfriendly' to homosexuals, both male and female, as they tend to assert a particularly narrow form of hetero-masculinity which has no room for homosexuality. However, as I have noted elsewhere (2007: 77 fn. 11), Goldstein has shown that homophobia and intolerance towards gay soldiers has not been universal cross-culturally or throughout history, giving examples of some militaries where homosexual behaviour was tolerated or encouraged (2001: 374–6).
9 For an exploration of rape and sexual harassment in the US armed forces that draws on personal accounts see Nelson (2002).
10 Feinman admits to having previously 'used the powerful symbols and stories of women as nonviolent' in her activism. However, in the context of the Gulf War and women's increased visibility and pride in the US armed forces, she 'found it increasingly difficult to use the framework of an automatic, easily recognizable linkage between feminism and antimilitarism' (1998: 132).
11 Elshtain was responding to a 1980 US poll on whether the draft should be reintroduced, which found that more women than men favoured its reinstatement. However, when asked if *women* should be subject to the draft, a solid majority of women said no while a similar majority of men said yes (1987: 243–4).
12 Hegemonic masculinity is generally conceptualized as norms and institutions that seek to maintain men's authority over women and over subordinate masculinities (Tosh 2004: 51). It is in a tense and unstable relationship with other masculinities, constantly needing shoring up (ibid.: 43). Tosh cites Connell (1983) as having been the first to outline the concept.
13 It is also worth noting here that biological research on the connection between the male hormone (testosterone) and aggression shows that the relationship is extremely complex and not well understood. Different studies have produced variable and inconclusive findings; it seems the jury is still out on whether testosterone leads to aggression or acts of aggression lead to production of testosterone (Archer and Lloyd 2002: Ch. 6).
14 Particularly notable examples are Kumari Jayawardena, Nira Yuval-Davis, Valentine Moghadam, Cynthia Enloe, V. Spike Peterson, Marysia Zalewski, Carol Cohn, Jan Pettman and J. Ann Tickner.
15 As discussed earlier in this chapter, in stark contrast to maternalist feminist arguments it is clear that motherhood is definitely not a guarantee of pacifism. Reproduction is highly politicized and motherhood frequently 'militarized', both by state and non-state nationalist movements, in a 'demographic race' to encourage the 'right' women to produce more children to be combatants in the conflict and to discourage the 'wrong' sort from reproducing. On Israel and Palestine see Sharoni (1995) and Abdo (1994). On Northern Ireland see Dowler (1997). On the former Yugoslavia see Zajovic (1993), Korac (1996), Meznaric (1994), Corrin (1999), Enloe (1993: Ch. 8); Bracewell (1996); Lilly and Irvine (2002); Rejali (1996).
16 This dynastic tradition can also be seen in ex-colonial South Asian political systems. In regard to Sri Lanka see Kirimabune (1999) and Kamalawathie (1990).
17 A moving fictionalized representation of this is a play by Jane Harrison called *Stolen*, based on the factual accounts of Koori people of the 'stolen generation'.
18 For an autobiographical account of a Lakota (Native American nation) woman who experienced this and later became politically involved with the American Indian Movement, see Crow Dog and Erdoes (1991).

19 Yuval-Davis makes a similar point about the failure of primordialists to pick up on this (1998: 23).

20 It should be noted that after a predominantly non-essentialist discussion West suddenly makes some surprising and unsubstantiated statements: 'women see the world globally in terms of antimilitarism' (1997a: xxxi) and '[a]rmed feminists in guerilla movements are not antimilitarist, but where women have children, they certainly are' (ibid.: xxxii). This is odd on many levels. First, she appears to be assuming that women in guerrilla movements are feminists, which is not necessarily true. Second, she assumes that they are not anti-militarist, whereas I would argue that just because a person chooses to take up arms in a particular context for particular reasons does not automatically mean they are militarist. It is surely possible that some are overall anti-militarist but feel that there are certain circumstances under which political violence is necessary. To be anti-militarist does not necessarily make one a principled pacifist. Finally, she assumes that mothers are necessarily anti-militarist; again this is not always the case, as I have argued already. This is a disappointing and incongruous end to an otherwise interesting article. It is all the more odd when one considers that earlier in the chapter she criticized Walby's work for concluding 'that women are somehow more pacifist than men' and for ignoring 'the cultural contexts in which women have been revolutionary, armed guerillas' (ibid.: xx).

21 On the development of a feminist nationalism in Palestine, particularly the 'flowering' of this during the *intifada* that began in 1987, see Abdo (1994); Gluck (1997); Sharoni (1995, 2001). On movements for women's rights and nationalism in Ireland in the late nineteenth and early twentieth centuries see Ward (1989); Coulter (1993). On the nationalist mobilization of (mostly Catholic) women in Northern Ireland and their political involvement and development of a feminist consciousness see Sharoni (2001). On the history of the Northern Irish feminist movement since the 1970s, the paralysis of the movement over the 'national question', and ongoing feminist-nationalist tensions, see Roulston (1997). On the splintering of the Yugoslav feminist movement in the context of the early 1990s wars see Boric (1997). On how trans-national/inter-ethnic feminism was seen as a fundamental threat to the nationalist project by nationalist leaders in the former Yugoslavia see Boric (1997); Bunch and Reilly (1994); Korac (1996). On the development of a feminist nationalism with strong socialist elements in the Philippines, and the ongoing internal debates over the primacy of gender versus nationalist interests, see Kwiatkowski and West (1997). On the difficulty of pursuing a feminist agenda in the context of Black nationalism in South Africa, and the gap between reality and the rhetoric of sexual equality in the new Constitution, see Mangaliso (1997).

22 Elsewhere, Saint-Germain argues that although periods of democratic transition can provide space for increased political participation of women, after the transition period women's participation often decreases. She argues that whether or not this happens depends on the form of women's participation in the transition period, seeing three conditions as being necessary for women to be able to consolidate their gains from the transition period and participate more fully in politics after the transition: women must be present and contribute to the transition, they must form autonomous organizations but remain engaged with the state, and they must transform their political behaviour from opposition to interaction with the new state (1997).

23 Women were active as nationalist combatants in Vietnam during anti-colonial resistance in the nineteenth and twentieth centuries, in the struggle against the Japanese during the occupation in the Second World War and in the later socialist revolution and struggle against America. It has been argued that women's history of participation in popular uprisings in Vietnam goes back to ancient times and that remembrance of many famous resistance heroines has been preserved in Vietnamese society and may have contributed to a greater acceptance of female combatants in modern times (Jayawardena 1986) – though, as noted earlier, this does not seem to have gained them much post-conflict as it has also been argued that in the current historical

moment women's participation in the socialist revolution has been 'forgotten' in state remembrance (Tétreault 1994b: 434–5).

4 Enlistment of women in paramilitary organizations in Sri Lanka and Northern Ireland

1 For years her murder was commonly attributed to the LTTE but I have also been told that in 1998 two members of the EPRLF confessed that their group had carried out the murder, under orders of the IPKF.
2 From transcripts of interviews with Sri Lankan women, undertaken for the Panos oral testimony project. Access to transcripts with kind permission from Olivia Bennett, Panos, London. (Hereafter referred to as 'Panos interviews'.)
3 A note on the RUC: female officers were not armed until April 1994, after a court case against discrimination in this respect was pursued by female officers (Coulter 1999: 132). On women in the RUC, see Brewer (1991); Brewer and Magee (1991); Brown (2000).
4 Some of this material was older women's narratives of their childhoods in Northern Ireland. Some of it relates to their views on the peace process and the devolved Assembly. Another intriguing aspect related to republican and loyalist women's perceptions of the 'other'. Although I did not usually specifically ask about this, as I was more interested in participants' thoughts about themselves and their own communities than their thoughts about the 'enemy', when the subject came up it frequently revealed more about the speaker than the subject of their comments. For example, one republican woman maintained that loyalist paramilitary women were 'less politicized' than republican women, reflecting a common republican stereotype about loyalists. More frequently recurring was the loyalist stereotype that republicans (male and female) wanted 'glory' and 'praise', 'were in it for the bravo' and wanted to 'brag' about their activities, while loyalist (*women*) were happy to contribute what they could, without seeking praise or recognition. (This was also given by Alison, a loyalist woman with a history of paramilitary involvement, as a reason for loyalist paramilitary women to not discuss their participation.)
5 As a counterpoint, for interesting work on contrasting British film and media representations of republican paramilitary women see Edge (1998) and Steel (1998).
6 On the 1798 women, see Keogh and Furlong (1998). On women and the Young Irelanders of the 1840s, see Cannavan (1997). On women in the 1916 Easter Rising, see Taillon (1999) and McCoole (1997). On some gendered aspects of the Anglo-Irish/Independence War, see Ryan (2000) (also more generally Ryan 1999 and 1997).
7 The IRA men attacked an RUC station and were shot. An inquest in 1995 (later abandoned) heard that 600 bullets were fired by the SAS during the ambush (Elliott and Flackes 1999: 317).
8 Catholic women have suffered political violence from within their own community, often signalling communal concern to maintain boundaries through the regulation of sexual conduct. A particularly well-known manifestation of this, especially in the early years of the conflict, was the punishment of young Catholic women who had relationships with British soldiers (or supposedly committed other 'offences', such as extra-marital affairs and informing on the IRA). Some were tied to lampposts, had their heads shaved, and were tarred and feathered (Coulter 1999: 135; McCann 1993: 153; Fairweather *et al.* 1984: 247–51; MacDonald 1991).

5 Women's experiences in the LTTE in Sri Lanka: gender relations and feminist nationalism

1 As de Alwis (1998a) has argued (using the phrase 'moral mother'), Maunaguru agrees that similar developments happened in southern Sri Lanka in the late 1980s in the context of Sinhala mobilization into the state military.

2 Women in the Sri Lankan state military are also not allowed to marry until three years after they enlist (Sebastian 1996).
3 Molyneux argues that women's interests, strategic or practical, are historically and culturally constituted and politically and discursively constructed rather than given, objective or *a priori*; processes of their 'formation and articulation are clearly subject to cultural, historical and political variation and cannot be known in advance' (1998: 231, 233).

6 Women's experiences in paramilitary organizations in Northern Ireland: gender relations and feminist nationalism

1 'Till' is often used instead of 'to' in local speech.
2 On the women's prison protest, see D'Arcy (1981); McCafferty (1981); Aretxaga (1995; 1997: Ch. 6).
3 For some testimonies of sexual molestation and harassment during interrogation, see Calamati (2002).
4 Ward cites *An Phoblacht*, 17 November 1979, introduction to the report on the Sinn Féin Women's Conference. On gender and Irish nationalism in the early twentieth century see also Ryan (1997, 1999).
5 The party has been divided on the issue of abortion. Many women members pushed for a liberal stance on the matter but were stymied by conservative elements and the concern about alienating conservative nationalist and religious Catholic voters.
6 The exceptions are Emma, who being INLA-aligned supports the Irish Republican Socialist Party (though she was always more interested in the military side of things than the political); Teresa, who became disillusioned with Sinn Féin and the Provisional movement as a whole in the late 1980s/early 1990s as she saw the leadership moving towards peace negotiations and feels Sinn Féin has betrayed the republican ideal by calling a ceasefire and entering into government; and Mary, who like Teresa also became disillusioned with the Provisional movement. Though she has no problem necessarily with a ceasefire and peace deal she feels the leadership should have been more 'honest' about this, admitting surrender, giving up the republican label and acknowledging that they were moving into constitutional nationalist politics.
7 See the Centre for Advancement of Women in Politics (available online at: www.qub.ac.uk/cawp/UKhtmls/MLA2007.htm).
8 This theme was echoed in 2008 media discussion about the pregnancy of Michelle Gildernew, when she commented that there was no crèche at Stormont and no maternity leave.
9 On women's involvement in formal unionist politics, see Wilford and Galligan (1999); Wilford (1999); Ward (2002, 2006).
10 Robinson's husband, Peter, became PUP Party Leader and Northern Ireland's First Minister in 2008.
11 Witness the 2008 controversy over various extremely homophobic comments she made publicly, which included explicitly describing homosexuality as comparable to child sexual abuse.
12 The fact that searching through the DUP's website fails to reveal the name of their current spokesperson for women's issues, or indeed whether they even still have one, is a clear indication of their stance. Despite the cheerful photograph of a pretty young woman on the second page of the Party's 2007 manifesto (available online at www.dup.org.uk/), there is absolutely no mention anywhere in the document of anything relating to gender or to women's issues, no matter how this is conceptualized.
13 The Malone Road is a very wealthy area of Belfast and the Falls Road is a working-class Catholic area.

7 Conclusions and reflections

1 As discussed in Chapter 3, Skjelsbæk (2001) found this to also be the case in El Salvador and Vietnam.

2 Indeed, since the 2007 death of David Ervine the PUP is now headed by a woman, Dawn Purvis.

Bibliography

Abdo, Nahla (1994) 'Nationalism and feminism: Palestinian women and the *intifada* – no going back?', in V.M. Moghadam (ed.) *Gender and National Identity: women and politics in Muslim societies*, London: Zed Books and Oxford University Press for the United Nations University World Institute for Development Economics Research.

Abeyesekera, Sunila (1995) 'Organizing for peace in the midst of war: experiences of women in Sri Lanka', in M.A. Schuler (ed.) *From Basic Needs to Basic Rights: women's claim to human rights*, Washington, DC: Women, Law & Development International.

African Rights (1995) *Rwanda: not so innocent: when women become killers*, Kigali: African Rights.

Afshar, Haleh (2003) 'Women and wars: some trajectories towards a feminist peace', *Development in Practice*, 13(2–3): 178–88.

Alcoff, Linda and Potter, Elizabeth (1993) 'Introduction: when feminisms intersect epistemology', in L. Alcoff and E. Potter (eds) *Feminist Epistemologies*, New York: Routledge.

Alegria, Claribel (1987) *They Won't Take Me Alive: Salvadorean women in struggle for national liberation [no me agarran viva]*, London: Women's Press.

Alison, Miranda (forthcoming) '"That's equality for you dear": gender, small arms and the Northern Ireland conflict', in V. Farr and A. Schnabel (eds) *Sexed Pistols: gender perspectives on small arms and light weapons*, Tokyo: United Nations University Press.

—— (2007) 'Wartime sexual violence: women's human rights and questions of masculinity', *Review of International Studies*, 33: 75–90.

—— (2004a) *Armed Violence and Poverty in Sri Lanka: a mini case study for the Armed Violence and Poverty Initiative*, Centre for International Cooperation and Security, University of Bradford and the UK Department for International Development (DFID). Online, available at: www.brad.ac.uk/acad/cics/publications/AVPI/poverty/ (accessed 3 May 2005).

—— (2004b) 'Women as agents of political violence: gendering security', *Security Dialogue*, 35(4): 447–63.

—— (2003a) 'Cogs in the wheel? Women in the Liberation Tigers of Tamil Eelam', *Civil Wars*, 6(4): 37–54.

—— (2003b) 'Uncovering the girls in "the boys": female combatants in the Liberation Tigers of Tamil Eelam', *Nivedini: a journal on gender studies*, 10: 41–70.

—— (2003c) '"We are fighting for the women's liberation also": a comparative study of female combatants in the nationalist conflicts in Sri Lanka and Northern Ireland', unpublished thesis, Queen's University Belfast.

Alles, A.C. (1977) *Insurgency – 1971 (an account of the April insurrection in Sri Lanka)*, 2nd edn, Colombo: The Colombo Apothecaries' Co. Ltd.

Amnesty International (2006) *Sri Lanka: a climate of fear in the east*, ASA 37/001/2006, London: Amnesty International. Online, available at: www.amnesty.org/en/library/asset/ASA37/001/2006/en/dom-ASA370012006en.pdf (accessed 15 April 2008).

—— (2002) *Sri Lanka: rape in custody*, ASA 37/001/2002, London: Amnesty International. Online, available at: www.amnesty.org/en/library/asset/ASA37/001/2002/en/dom-ASA370012002en.html (accessed 15 April 2008).

—— (1999) *Sri Lanka: torture in custody*, ASA 37/10/99, London: Amnesty International. Online, available at: www.amnesty.org/en/library/asset/ASA37/010/1999/en/dom-ASA370101999en.pdf (accessed 12 May 2006).

Anderson, Benedict (1991) *Imagined Communities: reflections on the origin and spread of nationalism*, 2nd edn, London: Verso.

Anderson, Kathryn and Jack, Dana C. (1991) 'Learning to listen: interview techniques and analyses', in S.B. Gluck and D. Patai (eds) *Women's Words: the feminist practice of oral history*, New York: Routledge.

Angell, Marisa (1998) 'Understanding the Aryan theory', in M. Tiruchelvam and Dattathreya C.S. (eds) *Culture and Politics of Identity in Sri Lanka*, Colombo: International Centre for Ethnic Studies.

Ann, Adele (1993) *Women Fighters of Liberation Tigers*, Jaffna: LTTE Publication Section, Thasan Printers (see also Balasingham, Adele).

—— (1990) 'Women fighters of liberation tigers: women and the struggle for Tamil Eelam', EelamWeb. Online, available at: www.eelamweb.com/women/ (accessed 10 May 2002).

Anthias, Floya and Yuval-Davis, Nira (1989) 'Introduction', in N. Yuval-Davis and F. Anthias (eds) *Woman–Nation–State*, Basingstoke: Macmillan.

Archer, John and Lloyd, Barbara (2002) *Sex and Gender*, 2nd edn, Cambridge: Cambridge University Press.

Aretxaga, Begoña (1997) *Shattering Silence: women, nationalism, and political subjectivity in Northern Ireland*, Princeton, NJ: Princeton University Press.

—— (1995) 'Dirty protest: symbolic overdetermination and gender in Northern Ireland ethnic violence', *Ethos*, 23(2): 123–48.

Arthur, Paul (2000) *Special Relationships: Britain, Ireland and the Northern Ireland problem*, Belfast: Blackstaff Press.

—— (1999) 'Anglo-Irish relations and constitutional policy', in P. Mitchell and R. Wilford (eds) *Politics in Northern Ireland*, Boulder, CO: Westview Press in cooperation with PSAI Press.

Aughey, Arthur (2000) 'The 1998 Agreement: Unionist reponses', in M. Cox, A. Guelke and F. Stephen (eds) *A Farewell to Arms? From 'long war' to long peace in Northern Ireland*, Manchester: Manchester University Press.

—— (1997) 'The character of Ulster Unionism', in P. Shirlow and M. McGovern (eds) *Who Are 'the People'? Unionism, Protestantism and Loyalism in Northern Ireland*, London: Pluto Press.

Bairner, Alan (1999) 'Masculinity, violence and the Irish peace process', *Capital and Class*, 69: 125–44.

Balasingham, Adele (2001) *The Will to Freedom: an inside view of Tamil resistance*, Mitcham: Fairmax Publishing (see also Ann, Adele).

Ballinger, A. (2000) *Dead Woman Walking*, Dartmouth: Ashgate.

—— (1996) 'The guilt of the innocent and the innocence of the guilty: the cases of Marie Fahmy and Ruth Ellis', in A. Myers and S. Wight (eds) *No Angels: women who commit violence*, London: Pandora.
Bar On, Bat-Ami (1993) 'Marginality and epistemic privilege', in L. Alcoff and E. Potter (eds) *Feminist Epistemologies*, New York: Routledge.
Basu, Amrita (1998a) 'Appropriating gender', in P. Jeffery and A. Basu (eds) *Appropriating Gender: women's activism and politicized religion in South Asia*, New York: Routledge.
—— (1998b) 'Hindu women's activism in India and the questions it raises', in P. Jeffery and A. Basu (eds) *Appropriating Gender: women's activism and politicized religion in South Asia*, New York: Routledge.
Bell, J. Bowyer (2000) *The IRA 1968–2000: analysis of a secret army*, London: Frank Cass.
—— (1989) *The Secret Army: the IRA 1916–1979*, revised and updated edn, Dublin: Poolbeg Press.
Benderly, Jill (1997) 'Rape, feminism, and nationalism in the war in Yugoslav successor states', in L.A. West (ed.) *Feminist Nationalism*, New York: Routledge.
Bennett, Olivia, Bexley, Jo and Warnock, Kitty (eds) (1995) *Arms to Fight, Arms to Protect: women speak out about conflict*, London: Panos Publications.
Beresford, David (1994) *Ten Men Dead: the story of the 1981 Irish hunger strike*, new edn, London: HarperCollins.
Berkman, Joyce (1990) 'Feminism, war, and peace politics: the case of World War I', in J.B. Elshtain and S. Tobias (eds) *Women, Militarism and War: essays in history, politics, and social theory*, Savage, MD: Rowman & Littlefield.
Berrington, Eileen and Honkatukia, Päivi (2002) 'An evil monster and a poor thing: female violence in the media', *Journal of Scandinavian Studies in Criminology and Crime Prevention*, 3(1): 50–72.
Bew, Paul (2000) 'The Belfast Agreement of 1998: from ethnic democracy to a multicultural, consociational settlement?', in M. Cox, A. Guelke and F. Stephen (eds) *A Farewell to Arms? From 'long war' to long peace in Northern Ireland*, Manchester: Manchester University Press.
—— (1994) *Ideology and the Irish Question: Ulster Unionism and Irish Nationalism*, Oxford: Clarendon Press.
Bew, Paul, Gibbon, Peter and Patterson, Henry (2002) *Northern Ireland 1921–2001: political forces and social classes*, revised and updated edn, London: Serif.
Bloomfield, David (1998) *Political Dialogue in Northern Ireland: the Brooke Initiative, 1989–92*, Basingstoke: Macmillan.
Bock, Gisela (1983) 'Racism and sexism in Nazi Germany: motherhood, compulsory sterilization, and the state', *Signs*, 8(3): 400–21.
Boric, Rada (1997) 'Against the war: women organizing across the national divide in the countries of the former Yugoslavia', in R. Lentin (ed.) *Gender and Catastrophe*, London: Zed Books.
Borland, Katherine (1991) '"That's not what I said": interpretive conflict in oral narrative research', in S.B. Gluck and D. Patai (eds) *Women's Words: the feminist practice of oral history*, New York: Routledge.
Bose, Sumantra (1994) *States, Nations, Sovereignty: Sri Lanka, India and the Tamil Eelam movement*, New Delhi: Sage.
Bouatta, Cherifa (1994) 'Feminine militancy: *moudjahidates* during and after the Algerian war', in V.M. Moghadam (ed.) *Gender and National Identity: women and politics in*

Muslim societies, trans. A. Bensouiah, London: Zed Books and Oxford University Press for the United Nations University World Institute for Development Economics Research.

Boulding, Elise (1990) *Building a Global Civic Culture: education for an interdependent world*, New York: Syracuse University Press.

Boulton, David (1973) *The UVF 1966–73: an anatomy of Loyalist rebellion*, Dublin: Gill & Macmillan.

Bracewell, Wendy (1996) 'Women, motherhood, and contemporary Serbian nationalism', *Women's Studies International Forum*, 19(1–2): 25–33.

Breuilly, John (1993) *Nationalism and the State*, 2nd edn, Manchester: Manchester University Press.

Brewer, J.D. (1991) 'Hercules, Hippolyte and the Amazons – or policewomen in the RUC', *British Journal of Sociology*, 42: 231–47.

Brewer, J.D. and Magee, K. (1991) *Inside the RUC: routine policing in a divided society*, Oxford: Clarendon Press.

Brown, Jennifer (2000) 'Discriminatory experiences of women police: a comparison of officers serving in England and Wales, Scotland, Northern Ireland and the Republic of Ireland', *International Journal of the Sociology of Law*, 28: 91–111.

Brown, Kris and Hauswedell, Corinna (2002) *Burying the Hatchet: the decommissioning of paramilitary arms in Northern Ireland*, Brief 22, Bonn: Bonn International Center for Conversion.

Bruce, Steve (1992a) 'The problems of "pro-state" terrorism: Loyalist paramilitaries in Northern Ireland', *Terrorism and Political Violence*, 4(1): 67–88.

—— (1992b) *The Red Hand: Protestant paramilitaries in Northern Ireland*, Oxford: Oxford University Press.

—— (1986) *God Save Ulster! The religion and politics of Paisleyism*, Oxford: Clarendon Press.

Bryman, Alan (1984) 'The debate about quantitative and qualitative research: a question of methods or epistemology?', *The British Journal of Sociology*, 35(1): 75–92.

Buckley, Suzann and Lonergan, Pamela (1984) 'Women and the Troubles, 1969–1980', in Y. Alexander and A. O'Day (eds) *Terrorism in Ireland*, London: Croom Helm.

Bunch, Charlotte and Reilly, Niamh (1994) *Demanding Accountability: the global campaign and Vienna Tribunal for Women's Human Rights*, New Brunswick, NJ: Center for Women's Global Leadership and the United Nations Development Fund for Women.

Bush, Kenneth (2003) *The Intra-Group Dimensions of Ethnic Conflict in Sri Lanka: learning to read between the lines*, Basingstoke: Palgrave Macmillan.

Butler, Judith (1992) 'Contingent foundations: feminism and the question of "postmodernism"', in J. Butler and J.W. Scott (eds) *Feminists Theorize the Political*, New York: Routledge.

Byrne, Anne and Lentin, Ronit (2000a) 'Introduction: feminist research methodologies in the social sciences', in A. Byrne and R. Lentin (eds) *(Re)searching Women: feminist research methodologies in the social sciences*, Dublin: Institute of Public Administration.

—— (eds) (2000b) *(Re)searching Women: feminist research methodologies in the social sciences*, Dublin: Institute of Public Administration.

Calamati, Silvia (2002) *'The Trouble We've Seen …' women's stories from the north of Ireland*, Belfast: Beyond the Pale.

Caldicott, Helen (1985) *Missile Envy*, New York: Bantam Books.

Cameron, D.S.C., the Honourable Lord (1969) *Disturbances in Northern Ireland: Report of the Commission appointed by the Governor of Northern Ireland*, Belfast: HMSO. Online, available at: http://cain.ulst.ac.uk/hmso/cameronx.htm (accessed 20 September 2001).
Campbell, Brian, McKeown, Lawrence and O'Hagan, Felim (eds) (1994) *Nor Meekly Serve My Time: the H-Block struggle 1976–1981*, Belfast: Beyond the Pale Publications.
Campbell, Patricia J. (2005) 'Gender and post conflict civil society', *International Feminist Journal of Politics*, 7(3): 377–99.
Cannavan, Jan (1997) 'Romantic revolutionary Irishwomen: women, young Ireland and 1848', in M. Kelleher and J.H. Murphy (eds) *Gender Perspectives in Nineteenth-Century Ireland: public and private spheres*, Dublin: Irish Academic Press.
Carroll, Berenice and Hall, Barbara Welling (1993) 'Feminist perspectives on women and the use of force', in R.H. Howes and M.R. Stevenson (eds) *Women and the Use of Military Force*, Boulder, CO: Lynne Rienner Publishers.
Carter, April (1998) 'Should women be soldiers or pacifists?', in L.A. Lorentzen and J. Turpin (eds) *The Women and War Reader*, New York: New York University Press.
Centre for Policy Alternatives (2002) 'Political and conflict resolution perspectives on de-proscription of the LTTE', unpublished background note, Colombo: Conflict and Peace Unit, Centre for Policy Alternatives.
Chandraprema, C.A. (1991) *Sri Lanka: the years of terror: the JVP insurrection 1987–1989*, Colombo: Lake House.
Chatterjee, Partha (1993) *The Nation and Its Fragments: colonial and postcolonial histories*, Princeton, NJ: Princeton University Press.
—— (1991) 'Whose imagined community?', *Millennium: Journal of International Studies*, 20(3): 521–5.
Chenoy, Anuradha M. (1998) 'Militarization, conflict, and women in South Asia', in L.A. Lorentzen and J. Turpin (eds) *The Women and War Reader*, New York: New York University Press.
Chinchilla, Norma Stoltz (1997) 'Nationalism, feminism, and revolution in Central America', in L.A. West (ed.) *Feminist Nationalism*, New York: Routledge.
Clarke, Liam and Johnston, Kathryn (2001) *Martin McGuinness: from guns to government*, Edinburgh: Mainstream Publishing.
Clayton, Pamela (1998) 'Religion, ethnicity and colonialism as explanations of the Northern Ireland conflict', in D. Miller (ed.) *Rethinking Northern Ireland: culture, ideology and colonialism*, London: Longman.
Cochrane, Feargal (1997) *Unionist Politics and the Politics of Unionism since the Anglo-Irish Agreement*, Cork: Cork University Press.
Cockburn, Cynthia (2001) 'The gendered dynamics of armed conflict and political violence', in C.O.N. Moser and F.C. Clark (eds) *Victims, Perpetrators or Actors? Gender, armed conflict and political violence*, London: Zed Books.
—— (1998) *The Space between Us: negotiating gender and national identities in conflict*, London: Zed Books.
Cohn, Carol (1990) '"Clean bombs" and clean language', in J.B. Elshtain and S. Tobias (eds) *Women, Militarism and War: essays in history, politics, and social theory*, Savage, MD: Rowman & Littlefield.
—— (1987) 'Sex and death in the rational world of defense intellectuals', *Signs*, 12(4): 687–718.
Connell, R.W. (1983) *Which Way Is Up?* Sydney: Allen and Unwin.
Connolly, Clara (1995) 'Ourselves alone? Clár na mBan conference report', *Feminist Review*, 50: 118–26.

Connolly, Linda (1999) 'Feminist politics and the peace process', *Capital and Class*, 69: 145–59.

Coogan, Tim Pat (1995) *The IRA*, revised and expanded edn, London: HarperCollins.

Coomaraswamy, Radhika (2002) 'Violence, armed conflict and the community', in S. Jayaweera (ed.) *Women in Post-Independence Sri Lanka*, New Delhi: Sage.

—— (1998) *Report of the Special Rapporteur on Violence against Women, its Causes and Consequences: Addendum: Report of the Mission to Rwanda on the Issues of Violence against Women in Situations of Armed Conflict*, E/CN.4/1998/54/Add.1, United Nations Economic and Social Council, 4 February. Online, available at: http://daccess-dds.un.org/doc/UNDOC/GEN/G98/103/85/PDF/G9810385.pdf?OpenElement (accessed 22 March 2008).

—— (1997a) 'LTTE women: is this liberation?', Rajani Thiranagama Memorial Lecture 1996, printed in *Sunday Times* (Colombo), 5 January. Online, available at: www.sundaytimes.lk/970105/plus2.html#LTTE (accessed 11 May 2002).

—— (1997b) 'Tiger women and the question of women's emancipation', *Pravada*, 4(9): 8–10.

Corrin, Chris (1999) 'Gender and identity in Central and Eastern Europe', *Journal of Communist Studies and Transition Politics*, 15(1): 64–82.

Coulter, Carol (1998) 'Feminism and nationalism in Ireland', in D. Miller (ed.) *Rethinking Northern Ireland: culture, ideology and colonialism*, London: Longman.

—— (1993) *The Hidden Tradition: feminism, women and nationalism in Ireland*, Cork: Cork University Press.

Coulter, Chris (2008) 'Female fighters in the Sierra Leone war', *Feminist Review*, 88: 54–73.

Coulter, Colin (1999) *Contemporary Northern Irish Society: an introduction*, London: Pluto Press.

—— (1997) 'The culture of contentment: the political beliefs and practice of the Unionist middle classes', in P. Shirlow and M. McGovern (eds) *Who Are 'the People'? Unionism, Protestantism and Loyalism in Northern Ireland*, London: Pluto Press.

Cox, Michael, Guelke, Adrian and Stephen, Fiona (eds) (2000) *A Farewell to Arms? From 'long war' to long peace in Northern Ireland*, Manchester: Manchester University Press.

Crawford, Colin (1999) *Defenders or Criminals? Loyalist prisoners and criminalisation*, Belfast: Blackstaff Press.

Crosby, Christina (1992) 'Dealing with differences', in J. Butler and J.W. Scott (eds) *Feminists Theorize the Political*, New York: Routledge.

Crothers, Jim (1998) *Reintegration: the problems and the issues*, EPIC Research Document no. 2, Belfast: EPIC.

Crow Dog, Mary and Erdoes, Richard (1991) *Lakota Woman*, New York: HarperPerennial.

Cusack, Jim and McDonald, Henry (1997) *UVF*, Dublin: Poolbeg Press.

D'Amico, Francine (2000) 'Citizen-soldier? Class, race, gender, sexuality and the US military', in S. Jacobs, R. Jacobson and J. Marchbank (eds) *States of Conflict: gender, violence and resistance*, London: Zed Books.

—— (1998) 'Feminist perspectives on women warriors', in L.A. Lorentzen and J. Turpin (eds) *The Women and War Reader*, New York: New York University Press.

D'Arcy, Margaretta (1981) *Tell Them Everything: a sojourn in the prison of Her Majesty Queen Elizabeth II at Ard Macha (Armagh)*, London: Pluto Press.

de Alwis, Malathi (1998a) 'Motherhood as a space of protest: women's political participation in contemporary Sri Lanka', in P. Jeffery and A. Basu (eds) *Appropriating Gender: women's activism and politicized religion in South Asia*, New York: Routledge.

—— (1998b) 'Moral mothers and stalwart sons: reading binaries in a time of war', in L.A. Lorentzen and J. Turpin (eds) *The Women and War Reader*, New York: New York University Press.
de Laine, Marlene (2000) *Fieldwork, Participation and Practice: ethics and dilemmas in qualitative research*, London: Sage.
de Mel, Neloufer (2001) *Women and the Nation's Narrative: gender and nationalism in twentieth century Sri Lanka*, Colombo: Social Scientists' Association.
de Pauw, Linda Grant (1998) *Battle Cries and Lullabies: women in war from prehistory to the present*, Norman, OK: University of Oklahoma Press.
de Silva, Chandra (1999) 'A historical overview of women in Sri Lankan politics', in S. Kirimabune (ed.) *Women and Politics in Sri Lanka: a comparative perspective*, Kandy: International Centre for Ethnic Studies.
de Silva, K.M. (1993) 'The making of the Indo-Sri Lanka Accord: the final phase – June–July 1987', in K.M. de Silva and S.W.R. de A. Samarasinghe (eds) *Peace Accords and Ethnic Conflict*, London: Pinter Publishers for the International Centre for Ethnic Studies, Sri Lanka.
de Silva, Mangalika (1994) 'Women in the LTTE: liberation or subjugation?', *Pravada*, 3(7): 27–31.
de Silva, P.L. (1999) 'The growth of Tamil paramilitary nationalisms: Sinhala chauvinism and Tamil responses', in S. Gamage and I.B. Watson (eds) *Conflict and Community in Contemporary Sri Lanka: 'pearl of the east' or the 'island of tears'?*, New Delhi: Sage India.
—— (1995) 'The efficacy of "combat mode": organisation, political violence, affect and cognition in the case of the Liberation Tigers of Tamil Eelam', in P. Jeganathan and Q. Ismail (eds) *Unmaking the Nation: the politics of identity and history in modern Sri Lanka*, Colombo: Social Scientists' Association.
DeVotta, Neil (2002) 'Illiberalism and ethnic conflict in Sri Lanka', *Journal of Democracy*, 13(1): 84–98.
Dillon, Martin (1989) *The Shankill Butchers: a case study of mass murder*, London: Hutchinson.
Dowler, Lorraine (1997) 'The mother of all warriors: women in West Belfast, Northern Ireland', in R. Lentin (ed.) *Gender and Catastrophe*, London: Zed Books.
Edge, Sarah (1998) 'Representing gender and national identity', in D. Miller (ed.) *Rethinking Northern Ireland: culture, ideology and colonialism*, London: Longman.
Edrisinha, Rohan (1998) 'Trying times: constitutional attempts to resolve armed conflict in Sri Lanka', in J. Armon and L. Philipson (eds) *Demanding Sacrifice: war and negotiation in Sri Lanka*, London: Conciliation Resources (London) in association with the Social Scientists' Association (Colombo).
Edwards, Rosalind and Ribbens, Jane (1998) 'Living on the edges: public knowledge, private lives, personal experience', in J. Ribbens and R. Edwards (eds) *Feminist Dilemmas in Qualitative Research: public knowledge and private lives*, London: Sage.
Eichacker, Joanne Mooney (2003) *Irish Republican Women in America: lecture tours, 1916–1925*, Dublin: Irish Academic Press.
Elliott, Sydney and Flackes, W.D. (1999) *Northern Ireland: a political directory 1968–1999*, revised and updated edn, Belfast: Blackstaff Press.
Ellison, Graham and Smyth, Jim (2000) *The Crowned Harp: policing Northern Ireland*, London: Pluto Press.
Elshtain, Jean Bethke (1991) 'Sovereignty, identity, sacrifice', *Millennium: Journal Of International Studies*, 20(3): 395–406.

—— (1990) 'The problem with peace', in J.B. Elshtain and S. Tobias (eds) *Women, Militarism and War: essays in history, politics, and social theory*, Savage, MD: Rowman & Littlefield.
—— (1987) *Women and War*, New York: Basic Books.
English, Richard (2003) *Armed Struggle: the history of the IRA*, London: Macmillan.
—— (1996) 'The same people with different relatives? Modern scholarship, Unionists and the Irish nation', in R. English and G. Walker (eds) *Unionism in Modern Ireland: new perspectives on politics and culture*, Dublin: Gill & Macmillan.
Enloe, Cynthia (2000a) *Bananas, Beaches and Bases: making feminist sense of international politics*, updated edn, Berkeley, CA: University of California Press.
—— (2000b) *Maneuvers: the international politics of militarizing women's lives*, Berkeley, CA: University of California Press.
—— (1998) 'All the men are in the militias, all the women are victims: the politics of masculinity and femininity in nationalist wars', in L.A. Lorentzen and J. Turpin (eds) *The Women and War Reader*, New York: New York University Press.
—— (1993) *The Morning After: sexual politics at the end of the Cold War*, Berkeley, CA: University of California Press.
Evans, Judith (1986a) 'Feminism and political theory', in J. Evans, J. Hills, K. Hunt, E. Meehan, T. ten Tusscher, U. Vogel and G. Waylen (eds) *Feminism and Political Theory*, London: Sage.
—— (1986b) 'Feminist Theory and Political Analysis', in J. Evans, J. Hills, K. Hunt, E. Meehan, T. ten Tusscher, U. Vogel and G. Waylen (eds) *Feminism and Political Theory*, London: Sage.
Fairweather, Eileen, McDonough, Roisín and McFadyean, Melanie (1984) *Only the Rivers Run Free: Northern Ireland: the women's war*, London: Pluto Press.
Fay, Brian (ed.) (1996) *Contemporary Philosophy of Social Science: a multicultural approach*, Oxford: Blackwell.
Fearon, Kate (2000) 'Whatever happened to the women? Gender and peace in Northern Ireland', in M. Cox, A. Guelke and F. Stephen (eds) *A Farewell to Arms? From 'long war' to long peace in Northern Ireland*, Manchester: Manchester University Press.
Feenan, Dermot (2002) 'Researching paramilitary violence in Northern Ireland', *International Journal of Social Research Methodology*, 5(2): 147–63.
Feeney, Brian (2002) *Sinn Féin: a hundred turbulent years*, Dublin: O'Brien Press.
Feinman, Ilene Rose (1998) 'Women warriors/women peacemakers: will the real feminists please stand up!', in L.A. Lorentzen and J. Turpin (eds) *The Women and War Reader*, New York: New York University Press.
Finlayson, Alan (1997) 'Discourse and contemporary Loyalist identity', in P. Shirlow and M. McGovern (eds) *Who Are 'the People'? Unionism, Protestantism and Loyalism in Northern Ireland*, London: Pluto Press.
Fitzsimons, Lily (1996) *Women in Ireland: the unsung heroes of conflict in Ireland's six north-east counties*, place of publication and publisher unknown.
Flax, Jane (1992) 'The end of innocence', in J. Butler and J.W. Scott (eds) *Feminists Theorize the Political*, New York: Routledge.
—— (1987) 'Postmodernism and gender relations in feminist theory', *Signs*, 12(4): 621–43.
Fraser, T.G. (2000) *Ireland in Conflict 1922–1998*, London: Routledge.
Gallagher, Michael (1995) 'How many nations are there in Ireland?', *Ethnic and Racial Studies*, 18(4): 715–39.

Galligan, Yvonne and Wilford, Rick (1999) 'Women's political representation in Ireland', in Y. Galligan, E. Ward and R. Wilford (eds) *Contesting Politics: women in Ireland, north and south*, Boulder, CO: Westview Press.
Galtung, Johan (1985) 'Twenty-five years of peace research: ten challenges and some responses', *Journal of Peace Research*, 22(2): 141–58.
—— (1969) 'Violence, peace, and peace research', *Journal of Peace Research*, 6(3): 167–91.
Gamage, Siri (1999) 'Post-independent political conflicts in Sri Lanka: élites, ethnicity, and class contradictions', in S. Gamage and I.B. Watson (eds) *Conflict and Community in Contemporary Sri Lanka: 'pearl of the east' or the 'island of tears'?*, New Delhi: Sage India.
Gilliam, Angela (1991) 'Women's equality and national liberation', in C.T. Mohanty, A. Russo and L. Torres (eds) *Third World Women and the Politics of Feminism*, Bloomington: Indiana University Press.
Gilligan, Carol (1982) *In a Different Voice: psychological theory and women's development*, Cambridge, MA: Harvard University Press.
Gluck, Sherna Berger (1997) 'Shifting sands: the feminist-nationalist connection in the Palestinian movement', in L.A. West (ed.) *Feminist Nationalism*, New York: Routledge.
Goldblatt, Beth and Meintjes, Sheila (1998) 'South African women demand the truth', in M. Turshen and C. Twagiramariya (eds) *What Women Do in Wartime: gender and conflict in Africa*, London: Zed Books.
Goldstein, Joshua (2001) *War and Gender: how gender shapes the war system and vice versa*, Cambridge: Cambridge University Press.
González-Pérez, Margaret (2006) 'Guerrilleras in Latin America: domestic and international roles', *Journal of Peace Research*, 43(3): 313–29.
Graham, Brian (1997) 'Ulster: a representation of place yet to be imagined', in P. Shirlow and M. McGovern (eds) *Who Are 'the People'? Unionism, Protestantism and Loyalism in Northern Ireland*, London: Pluto Press.
Grant, Rebecca (1992) 'The quagmire of gender and international security', in V.S. Peterson (ed.) *Gendered States: feminist (re)visions of international relations theory*, Boulder, CO: Lynne Rienner Publishers.
Green, Marion (1998) *The Prison Experience: a Loyalist perspective*, EPIC Research Document no. 1, Belfast: EPIC.
Guelke, Adrian (2000) '"Comparatively peaceful": South Africa, the Middle East and Northern Ireland', in M. Cox, A. Guelke and F. Stephen (eds) *A Farewell to Arms? From 'long war' to long peace in Northern Ireland*, Manchester: Manchester University Press.
—— (1999) 'Political violence and the paramilitaries', in P. Mitchell and R. Wilford (eds) *Politics in Northern Ireland*, Boulder, CO: Westview Press in cooperation with PSAI Press.
—— (1995) *The Age of Terrorism and the International Political System*, London: Tauris.
—— (1988) *Northern Ireland: the international perspective*, Dublin: Gill & Macmillan.
Gunaratna, Rohan (2001) *International Dimension of the Sri Lankan Conflict: Threat and Response*, Marga Monograph Series on Ethnic Reconciliation no. 27, Colombo: Marga Institute.
—— (1999) 'Internationalisation of the Tamil conflict (and its implications)', in S. Gamage and I.B. Watson (eds) *Conflict and Community in Contemporary Sri Lanka: 'pearl of the east' or the 'island of tears'?*, New Delhi: Sage India.

—— (1990) *Sri Lanka: a lost revolution? The inside story of the JVP*, Kandy: Institute of Fundamental Studies.

—— (1987) *War and Peace in Sri Lanka, with a post-accord report from Jaffna*, Colombo: Institute of Fundamental Studies.

Gunawardana, R.A.L.H. (1990) 'The people of the lion: the Sinhala identity and ideology in history and historiography', in J. Spencer (ed.) *Sri Lanka: history and the roots of conflict*, London: Routledge.

Hackett, Claire (1995) 'Self-determination: the Republican feminist agenda', *Feminist Review*, 50: 111–16.

Haggis, Jane (1990) 'The feminist research process – defining a topic', in L. Stanley (ed.) *Feminist Praxis: research, theory and epistemology in feminist sociology*, London: Routledge.

Hall, Michael (2000a) *Left in Limbo: the experience of prisoners' children*, Island Pamphlets no. 31, Newtownabbey: Island Publications.

—— (2000b) *Seeds of Hope*, Island Pamphlets no. 27, Newtownabbey: Island Publications.

Handrahan, Lori (2004) 'Conflict, gender, ethnicity and post-conflict reconstruction', *Security Dialogue*, 35(4): 429–45.

Harding, Sandra (1991) *Whose Science? Whose Knowledge? Thinking from women's lives*, Milton Keynes: Open University Press.

—— (1987a) 'Conclusion: epistemological questions', in S. Harding (ed.) *Feminism and Methodology: social science issues*, Milton Keynes: Open University Press.

—— (1987b) 'Introduction: is there a feminist method?', in S. Harding (ed.) *Feminism and Methodology: social science issues*, Milton Keynes: Open University Press.

Harris, Simon (2004) 'Gender, participation, and post-conflict planning in northern Sri Lanka', *Gender and Development*, 12(3): 60–9.

Harstock, Nancy (1987) 'The feminist standpoint: developing the ground for a specifically feminist historical materialism', in S. Harding (ed.) *Feminism and Methodology: social science issues*, Milton Keynes: Open University Press.

Hayes, Bernadette C. and McAllister, Ian (2001) 'Sowing dragon's teeth: public support for political violence and paramilitarism in Northern Ireland', *Political Studies*, 49(5): 901–22.

Hellmann-Rajanayagam, Dagmar (1990) 'The politics of the Tamil past', in J. Spencer (ed.) *Sri Lanka: history and the roots of conflict*, London: Routledge.

Hennessey, Thomas (2000) *The Northern Ireland Peace Process: ending the Troubles?*, Dublin: Gill & Macmillan.

—— (1997) *A History of Northern Ireland 1920–1996*, Dublin: Gill & Macmillan.

—— (1996) 'Ulster Unionism and loyalty to the Crown of the United Kingdom, 1912–74', in R. English and G. Walker (eds) *Unionism in Modern Ireland: new perspectives on politics and culture*, Dublin: Gill & Macmillan.

Henry, Marsha (2007) 'If the shoe fits: authenticity, authority and agency feminist diasporic research', *Women's Studies International Forum*, 30(1): 70–80.

Hettige, Siri (1999) 'Economic liberalisation, social class and ethnicity: emerging trends and conflicts', in S. Gamage and I.B. Watson (eds) *Conflict and Community in Contemporary Sri Lanka: 'pearl of the east' or the 'island of tears'?*, New Delhi: Sage India.

Hinds, Bronagh (1999) 'Women working for peace in Northern Ireland', in Y. Galligan, E. Ward and R. Wilford (eds) *Contesting Politics: women in Ireland, north and south*, Boulder, CO: Westview Press.

Holland, Jack and McDonald, Henry (1994) *INLA: deadly divisions*, Dublin: Torc.

Holt, Maria (2003) 'Palestinian women, violence and the peace process', *Development in Practice*, 13(2–3): 223–38.

Hoole, Rajan, Somasundaram, Daya, Sritharan, K. and Thiranagama, Rajani (1990) *The Broken Palmyra: the Tamil crisis in Sri Lanka – an inside account*, revised edn, Claremont, CA: Harvey Mudd College Press.

Hooper, Charlotte (2001) *Manly States: masculinities, international relations, and gender politics*, New York: Columbia University Press.

Horowitz, Donald L. (2000) *Ethnic Groups in Conflict*, 2nd edn, Berkeley and Los Angeles: University of California Press.

Human Rights Watch (2008) *Recurring Nightmare: state responsibility for 'disappearances' and abductions in Sri Lanka*, HRW 20(2). Online, available at: http://hrw.org/reports/2008/srilanka0308/srilanka0308web.pdf (accessed 20 April 2008).

—— (2006) *Funding the 'Final War': LTTE intimidation and extortion in the Tamil diaspora*, HRW 18(1). Online, available at: www.hrw.org/reports/2006/ltte0306/ltte0306web.pdf (accessed 16 April 2007).

—— (2004) *Living in Fear: child soldiers and the Tamil Tigers in Sri Lanka*, HRW 16(13). Online, available at: www.hrw.org/reports/2004/srilanka1104/srilanka1104.pdf (accessed 16 April 2007).

Ibáñez, Ana Cristina (2001) 'El Salvador: war and untold stories – women guerrillas', in C.O.N. Moser and F.C. Clark (eds) *Victims, Perpetrators or Actors? Gender, armed conflict and political violence*, London: Zed Books.

IICD (2006) *Report of the Independent International Commission on Decommissioning*, 19 January. Online, available at: www.nio.gov.uk/report_of_the_independent_commission_on_decommissioning_19_january_2006.pdf (accessed 22 February 2006).

—— (2003) *Report of the Independent International Commission on Decommissioning*, 21 October. Online, available at: www.nio.gov.uk/iicd_report_21oct03.pdf (accessed 22 February 2006).

Irwin, Colin (2002) *The People's Peace Process in Northern Ireland*, Basingstoke: Palgrave Macmillan.

Ismail, Qadri (1995) 'Unmooring identity: the antinomies of elite Muslim self-representation in modern Sri Lanka', in P. Jeganathan and Q. Ismail (eds) *Unmaking the Nation: the politics of identity and history in modern Sri Lanka*, Colombo: Social Scientists' Association.

—— (1992) 'Boys will be boys: gender and national agency in Fanon and the LTTE', *Pravada*, 1(7): 6–10.

Jacobs, Susie, Jacobson, Ruth and Marchbank, Jen (eds) (2000) *States of Conflict: gender, violence and resistance*, London: Zed Books.

Jacobson, Ruth (2000) 'Women and peace in Northern Ireland: a complicated relationship', in S. Jacobs, R. Jacobson and J. Marchbank (eds) *States of Conflict: gender, violence and resistance*, London: Zed Books.

Jacobson, Ruth, Jacobs, Susie and Marchbank, Jen (2000) 'Introduction: states of conflict', in S. Jacobs, R. Jacobson and J. Marchbank (eds) *States of Conflict: gender, violence and resistance*, London: Zed Books.

Jayawardena, Kumari (1986) *Feminism and Nationalism in the Third World*, London: Zed Books.

—— (1985) *Ethnic and Class Conflicts in Sri Lanka: some aspects of Sinhala Buddhist consciousness over the past 100 years*, Dehiwala: Centre for Social Analysis.

Jeffreys, Sheila (2007) 'Double jeopardy: women, the US military and the war in Iraq', *Women's Studies International Forum*, 30(1): 16–25.

Jeganathan, Pradeep (1992) 'Students, soldiers, the princess and the tiger', *Pravada*, 1(4): 18–19.

Jeganathan, Pradeep and Ismail, Qadri (1995) 'Introduction: unmaking the nation', in P. Jeganathan and Q. Ismail (eds) *Unmaking the Nation: the politics of identity and history in modern Sri Lanka*, Colombo: Social Scientists' Association.

Jipson, Arthur J. and Litton, Chad E. (2000) 'Body, career and community: the implications of researching dangerous groups', in G. Lee-Treweek and S. Linkogle (eds) *Danger in the Field: risk and ethics in social research*, London: Routledge.

Jones, A. (2002) 'Gender and genocide in Rwanda', *Journal of Genocide Research*, 4(1): 65–94.

Kamalawathie, I.M. (1990) 'Women in parliamentary politics in Sri Lanka', in S. Kiribamune and V. Samarasinghe (eds) *Women at the Crossroads: a Sri Lankan perspective*, New Delhi: International Centre for Ethnic Studies in association with Vikas Publishing House.

Kandiyoti, Deniz (1991) 'Identity and its discontents: women and the nation', *Millennium: Journal of International Studies*, 20(3): 429–43.

—— (1988) 'Bargaining with patriarchy', *Gender and Society*, 2(3): 274–90.

Keairns, Yvonne E. (2003) *The Voices of Girl Child Soldiers: Sri Lanka*, Quaker United Nations Office, January. Online, available at: www.quno.org/newyork/Resources/girlSoldiersSriLanka.pdf (accessed 5 May 2004).

—— (2002) *The Voices of Girl Child Soldiers: summary*, Quaker United Nations Office/Coalition to Stop the Use of Child Soldiers, October. Online, available at: www.quno.org/newyork/Resources/QUNOchildsoldiers.pdf (accessed 5 May 2004).

Kelly, Liz (2000) 'Wars against women: sexual violence, sexual politics and the militarised state', in S. Jacobs, R. Jacobson and J. Marchbank (eds) *States of Conflict: gender, violence and resistance*, London: Zed Books.

Kelly, Liz, Burton, Sheila and Regan, Linda (1994) 'Researching women's lives or studying women's oppression? Reflections on what constitutes feminist research', in M. Maynard and J. Purvis (eds) *Researching Women's Lives from a Feminist Perspective*, London: Taylor & Francis.

Kennedy-Pipe, Caroline (2000) 'From war to peace in Northern Ireland', in M. Cox, A. Guelke and F. Stephen (eds) *A Farewell to Arms? From 'long war' to long peace in Northern Ireland*, Manchester: Manchester University Press.

Keogh, Dáire and Furlong, Nicholas (eds) (1998) *The Women of 1798*, Dublin: Four Courts Press.

Kerber, Linda K. (1990) 'May all our citizens be soldiers and all our soldiers citizens: the ambiguities of female citizenship in the new nation', in J.B. Elshtain and S. Tobias (eds) *Women, Militarism and War: essays in history, politics, and social theory*, Savage, MD: Rowman & Littlefield.

Kirimabune, Sirima (1999) 'Climbing the greasy pole: opportunities and challenges in women's access to electoral politics in Sri Lanka', in S. Kirimabune (ed.) *Women and Politics in Sri Lanka: a comparative perspective*, Kandy: International Centre for Ethnic Studies.

Korać, Maja (1996) 'Understanding ethnic-national identity and its meaning: questions from women's experience', *Women's Studies International Forum*, 19(1–2): 133–43.

Kwiatkowski, Lynn M. and West, Lois A. (1997) 'Feminist struggles for feminist nationalism in the Philippines', in L.A. West (ed.) *Feminist Nationalism*, New York: Routledge.

Lal, Jayati (1996) 'Situating locations: the politics of self, identity, and "other" in living and writing the text', in D.L. Wolf (ed.) *Feminist Dilemmas in Fieldwork*, Boulder, CO: Westview Press.

Lee, Raymond M. (1995) *Dangerous Fieldwork*, Thousand Oaks, CA: Sage.

—— (1993) *Doing Research on Sensitive Topics*, London: Sage.

Lentin, Ronit (1997a) 'Introduction: (en)gendering genocides', in R. Lentin (ed.) *Gender and Catastrophe*, London: Zed Books.

—— (1997b) 'Women, war and peace in a culture of violence: the Middle East and Northern Ireland', in B. Kašic (ed.) *Women and the Politics of Peace: contributions to a culture of women's resistance*, Zagreb: Centre for Women's Studies.

Lijphart, Arend (1977) *Democracy in Plural Societies: a comparative exploration*, New Haven, CT: Yale University Press.

Lilly, Carol S. and Irvine, Jill A. (2002) 'Negotiating interests: women and nationalism in Serbia and Croatia, 1990–1997', *East European Politics and Societies*, 16(1): 109–44.

Liyanage, Kamala (1999) 'Women in political parties: the Sri Lankan experience', in S. Kirimabune (ed.) *Women and Politics in Sri Lanka: a comparative perspective*, Kandy: International Centre for Ethnic Studies.

Liyanage, Priyath (1998) 'Popular Buddhism, politics and the ethnic problem', in J. Armon and L. Philipson (eds) *Demanding Sacrifice: war and negotiation in Sri Lanka*, London: Conciliation Resources (London) in association with the Social Scientists' Association (Colombo).

Lorentzen, Lois Ann and Turpin, Jennifer (eds) (1998) *The Women and War Reader*, New York: New York University Press.

McAuley, Chrissie (ed.) (1989) *Women in a War Zone: twenty years of resistance*, Dublin: Sinn Féin Book Bureau.

McBride, Ian (1996) 'Ulster and the British problem', in R. English and G. Walker (eds) *Unionism in Modern Ireland: new perspectives on politics and culture*, Dublin: Gill & Macmillan.

McCafferty, Nell (1981) *The Armagh Women*, Dublin: Co-op Books.

McCann, Eamonn (1993) *War and an Irish Town*, 3rd edn, London: Pluto Press.

McClintock, Anne, Mufti, Aamir and Shohat, Ella (eds) (1997) *Dangerous Liaisons: gender, nation, and postcolonial perspectives*, Minneapolis, MN: University of Minnesota Press.

McClure, Kirstie (1992) 'The issue of foundations: scientized politics, politicized science, and feminist critical practice', in J. Butler and J.W. Scott (eds) *Feminists Theorize the Political*, New York: Routledge.

McCoole, Sinead (1997) *Guns and Chiffon: women revolutionaries and Kilmainham Gaol 1916–1923*, Dublin: Government of Ireland Stationery Office.

MacDonald, Eileen (1991) *Shoot the Women First*, London: Fourth Estate.

McGarry, John and O'Leary, Brendan (1995) *Explaining Northern Ireland: broken images*, Oxford: Blackwell Publishers.

McGilvray, Dennis B. (1999) 'Tamils and Muslims in the shadow of war: schism or continuity?', in S. Gamage and I.B. Watson (eds) *Conflict and Community in Contemporary Sri Lanka: 'pearl of the east' or the 'island of tears'?*, New Delhi: Sage India.

McKeown, Laurence (2001) *Out of Time: Irish Republican prisoners Long Kesh 1972–2000*, Belfast: Beyond the Pale.

McKittrick, David (1994) *Endgame: the search for peace in Northern Ireland*, Belfast: Blackstaff Press.

McKittrick, David and McVea, David (2001) *Making Sense of the Troubles*, London: Penguin.

Mac Stiofáin, Seán (1974) *Revolutionary in Ireland*, Farnborough: Saxon Press.

Mallie, Eamonn and McKittrick, David (1996) *The Fight for Peace: the secret story behind the Irish peace process*, London: Heinemann.

Maloney, Ed (2002) *A Secret History of the IRA*, London: Penguin.

Mangaliso, Zengie A. (1997) 'Gender and nation-building in South Africa', in L.A. West (ed.) *Feminist Nationalism*, New York: Routledge.

Manoharan, N. (2006) *Mission Impossible: Sri Lanka monitoring mission in crisis*, article 2099, New Delhi: Institute of Peace and Conflict Studies South Asia. Online, available at: www.ipcs.org/South_Asia_articles2.jsp?action=showView&kValue=2114&country=1017&status=article&mod=b (accessed 16 April 2007).

Mason, T.D. (1992) 'Women's participation in Central American revolutions – a theoretical perspective', *Comparative Political Studies*, 25(1): 63–89.

Maunaguru, Sitralega (1995) 'Gendering Tamil nationalism: the construction of "woman" in projects of protest and control', in P. Jeganathan and Q. Ismail (eds) *Unmaking the Nation: the politics of identity and history in modern Sri Lanka*, Colombo: Social Scientists' Association.

Maynard, Mary (1994) 'Methods, practice and epistemology: the debate about feminism and research', in M. Maynard and J. Purvis (eds) *Researching Women's Lives from a Feminist Perspective*, London: Taylor & Francis.

Maynard, Mary and Purvis, June (1994) 'Doing feminist research', in M. Maynard and J. Purvis (eds) *Researching Women's Lives from a Feminist Perspective*, London: Taylor & Francis.

Mazali, Rela (2003) '"And what about the girls?" What a culture of war genders out of view', *Nashim: A Journal of Jewish Women's Studies and Gender Issues*, 6: 39–50.

Mazurana, Dyan E. and McKay, Susan R. (1999) *Women and Peacebuilding*, Essays on Human Rights and Democratic Development no. 8, Montreal: International Centre for Human Rights and Democratic Development.

Meehan, Elizabeth (2000) 'Europe and the Europeanisation of the Irish question', in M. Cox, A. Guelke and F. Stephen (eds) *A Farewell to Arms? From 'long war' to long peace in Northern Ireland*, Manchester: Manchester University Press.

—— (1986) 'Women's studies and political studies', in J. Evans, J. Hills, K. Hunt, E. Meehan, T. ten Tusscher, U. Vogel and G. Waylen (eds) *Feminism and Political Theory*, London: Sage.

Meznaric, Silva (1994) 'Gender as an ethno-marker: rape, war, and identity politics in the former Yugoslavia', in V.M. Moghadam (ed.) *Identity Politics and Women: cultural reassertions and feminisms in international perspective*, Boulder, CO: Westview Press.

Mies, Maria, and Shiva, Vandana (1993) *Ecofeminism*, London: Zed.

Miller, David (1998) 'Colonialism and academic representations of the Troubles', in D. Miller (ed.) *Rethinking Northern Ireland: culture, ideology and colonialism*, London: Longman.

Miller, David W. (1978) *Queen's Rebels: Ulster loyalism in historical perspective*, Dublin: Gill & Macmillan.

Miller, Robert L. (1998) 'Conclusion', in R. Wilford and R.L. Miller (eds) *Women, Ethnicity and Nationalism: the politics of transition*, London: Routledge.

Miller, Robert L., Wilford, Rick and Donoghue, Freda (1996) *Women and Political Participation in Northern Ireland*, Aldershot: Avebury.

Mitchell, Claire (2006) *Religion, Identity and Politics in Northern Ireland*, Aldershot: Ashgate.

Mitchell, Paul, O'Leary, Brendan and Evans, Geoffrey (2001) 'Northern Ireland: flanking extremists bite the moderates and emerge in their clothes', *Parliamentary Affairs*, 54: 725–42.

Moghadam, Valentine M. (1994a) 'Introduction and overview', in V.M. Moghadam (ed.) *Gender and National Identity: women and politics in Muslim societies*, London: Zed Books and Oxford University Press for the United Nations University World Institute for Development Economics Research.

—— (ed.) (1994b) *Gender and National Identity: women and politics in Muslim societies*, London: Zed Books and Oxford University Press for the United Nations University World Institute for Development Economics Research.

—— (1993) *Modernising Women: gender and social change in the Middle East*, Boulder, CO: Lynne Rienner.

Molyneux, Maxine (1998) 'Analysing women's movements', *Development and Change*, 29: 219–45.

—— (1985) 'Mobilisation without emancipation? Women's interests, the state and revolution in Nicaragua', *Feminist Studies*, 11: 227–54.

Montgomery, Tommie Sue (1982) *Revolution in El Salvador: origins and evolution*, Boulder, CO: Westview Press.

Mookherjee, Nayanika (2008) 'Gendered embodiments: mapping the body politic of the raped woman and the nation in Bangladesh', *Feminist Review*, 88: 36–53.

Morrissey, Belinda (2003) *When Women Kill: questions of agency and subjectivity*, London: Routledge.

Moser, Caroline O.N. (2001) 'The gendered continuum of violence and conflict: an operational framework', in C.O.N. Moser and F.C. Clark (eds) *Victims, Perpetrators or Actors? Gender, armed conflict and political violence*, London: Zed Books.

Moser, Caroline O.N. and Clark, Fiona C. (eds) (2001) *Victims, Perpetrators or Actors? Gender, armed conflict and political violence*, London: Zed Books.

Mukta, Parita (2000) 'Gender, community, nation: the myth of innocence', in S. Jacobs, R. Jacobson and J. Marchbank (eds) *States of Conflict: gender, violence and resistance*, London: Zed Books.

Mulholland, Marc (2000) *Northern Ireland at the Crossroads: Ulster Unionism in the O'Neill years 1960–9*, Basingstoke: Macmillan.

Narayan Swamy, M.R. (1994) *Tigers of Lanka, from Boys to Guerrillas*, Delhi: Konark Publishers.

Naylor, B. (1995) 'Women's crime and media coverage', in R.E. Dobash, R.P. Dobash and L. Noakes (eds) *Gender and Crime*, Cardiff: University of Wales Press.

Nelson, Sarah (1984) *Ulster's Uncertain Defenders: Protestant political, paramilitary and community groups and the Northern Ireland conflict*, Belfast: Appletree Press.

Nelson, T.S. (2002) *For Love of Country: confronting rape and sexual harassment in the US military*, Binghamton, NY: The Haworth Maltreatment and Trauma Press.

Nesiah, Devanesan (2001) *Tamil Nationalism*, Marga Monograph Series on Ethnic Reconciliation no. 6, Colombo: Marga Institute.

Nissan, Elizabeth and Stirrat, R.L. (1990) 'The generation of communal identities', in J. Spencer (ed.) *Sri Lanka: history and the roots of conflict*, London: Routledge.

Nordstrom, Carolyn (1998) 'Girls behind the (front) lines', in L.A. Lorentzen and J. Turpin (eds) *The Women and War Reader*, New York: New York University Press.

O'Doherty, Malachi (1998) *The Trouble With Guns: republican strategy and the Provisional IRA*, Belfast: Blackstaff Press.

Ognibene, Elaine R. (1998) 'Imagining peace', in L.A. Lorentzen and J. Turpin (eds) *The Women and War Reader*, New York: New York University Press.

O'Hearn, Denis, Porter, Sam and Harpur, Alan (1999) 'Turning agreement to process: republicanism and change in Ireland', *Capital and Class*, 69: 7–25.

O'Leary, Brendan (2001) 'The character of the 1998 Agreement: results and prospects', in R. Wilford (ed.) *Aspects of the Belfast Agreement*, Oxford: Oxford University Press.

O'Leary, Brendan and McGarry, John (1996) *The Politics of Antagonism: understanding Northern Ireland*, 2nd edn, London: Athlone Press.

O'Malley, Padraig (1990) *Biting at the Grave: the Irish hunger strikes and the politics of despair*, Belfast: Blackstaff Press.

Orde, Hugh (2003) *Report of the Chief Constable 2002–2003*, Police Service of Northern Ireland. Online, available at: www.psni.police.uk/report_of_the_chief_const.doc (accessed 23 May 2007).

Pankhurst, Donna (2003) 'The "sex war" and other wars: towards a feminist approach to peacebuilding', *Development in Practice*, 13(2–3): 154–76.

Papandreou, Margarita (1997) 'Are women more peace-loving than men?', in B. Kašic (ed.) *Women and the Politics of Peace: contributions to a culture of women's resistance*, Zagreb: Centre for Women's Studies.

Patai, Daphne (1991) 'US academics and Third World women: is ethical research possible?', in S.B. Gluck and D. Patai (eds) *Women's Words: the feminist practice of oral history*, New York: Routledge.

Pateman, Carole (1988) *The Sexual Contract*, Cambridge: Polity Press.

Patterson, Henry (1997) *The Politics of Illusion: a political history of the IRA*, new edn, London: Serif.

Peel, Michael and Salinsky, Mary (2000) *Caught in the Middle: a study of Tamil torture survivors coming to the UK from Sri Lanka*, London: Medical Foundation for the Care of Victims of Torture.

Perera, Sasanka (1998) *Political Violence in Sri Lanka: dynamics, consequences and issues of democratization*, Colombo: Centre for Women's Research.

Peries, Sharmini 'Metamorphosis of the Tamil woman in the nationalist war for Eelam', paper presented at York University, Toronto, 11 December 1998.

Peterson, V. Spike (1998) 'Gendered nationalism: reproducing "us" versus "them"', in L.A. Lorentzen and J. Turpin (eds) *The Women and War Reader*, New York: New York University Press.

Pettman, Jan Jindy (1996) *Worlding Women: a feminist international politics*, London: Routledge.

Phoenix, Ann (1994) 'Practising feminist research: the intersection of gender and "race" in the research process', in M. Maynard and J. Purvis (eds) *Researching Women's Lives from a Feminist Perspective*, London: Taylor & Francis.

Pickering, Sharon (2002) *Women, Policing and Resistance in Northern Ireland*, Belfast: Beyond the Pale.

Pierson, Ruth Roach (1987) '"Did your mother wear army boots?" Feminist theory and women's relation to war, peace and revolution', in S. Macdonald, P. Holden and S. Ardener (eds) *Images of Women in Peace and War: cross-cultural and historical perspective*, Basingstoke: Macmillan Education.

Piyadasa, L. (1988) *Sri Lanka: the unfinished quest for peace*, London: Marram Books.

Porter, Elisabeth (1998) 'Identity, locality, plurality: women, nationalism and Northern Ireland', in R. Wilford and R.L. Miller (eds) *Women, Ethnicity and Nationalism: the politics of transition*, London: Routledge.

Powers, Janet (2003) 'Women and peace dialogue in the Middle East', *Peace Review*, 15(1): 25–31.

Pringle, Peter and Jacobson, Philip (2000) *Those Are Real Bullets, Aren't They? Bloody Sunday, Derry, 30 January 1972*, London: Fourth Estate.

Racioppi, Linda and O'Sullivan See, Katherine (2000) 'Ulstermen and Loyalist ladies on parade: gendering Unionism in Northern Ireland', *International Feminist Journal of Politics*, 2(1): 1–29.

Rajasingham-Senanayake, Darini (2001a) 'Ambivalent empowerment: the tragedy of Tamil women in conflict', in R. Manchanda (ed.) *Women, War and Peace in South Asia: beyond victimhood to agency*, New Delhi: Sage.

—— (2001b) *Identity on the Borderline: multicultural history in a moment of danger*, Marga Monograph Series on Ethnic Reconciliation no. 12, Colombo: Marga Institute.

Randall, Margaret (1992) *Gathering Rage: the failure of twentieth-century revolutions to develop a feminist agenda*, New York: Monthly Review Press.

Randall, Vicky (1991) 'Feminism and political analysis', *Political Studies*, 39(3): 513–32.

Reardon, Betty A. (1998) 'Women or weapons?', in L.A. Lorentzen and J. Turpin (eds) *The Women and War Reader*, New York: New York University Press.

—— (1993) *Women and Peace: feminist visions of global security*, Albany, NY: State University of New York Press.

—— (1985) *Sexism and the War System*, reprinted 1996, Syracuse, NY: Syracuse University Press.

Rejali, Darius M. (1996) 'After feminist analyses of Bosnian violence', *Peace Review*, 8(3): 365–71.

Richards, Janet Radcliffe (1990) 'Why the pursuit of peace is no part of feminism', in J.B. Elshtain and S. Tobias (eds) *Women, Militarism and War: essays in history, politics, and social theory*, Savage, MD: Rowman & Littlefield.

Roberts, Michael (2001a) *Sinhala-ness and Sinhala Nationalism*, Marga Monograph Series on Ethnic Reconciliation no. 4, Colombo: Marga Institute.

—— (2001b) *Primordialist Strands in Contemporary Sinhala Nationalism in Sri Lanka: Urumaya as Ur*, Marga Monograph Series on Ethnic Reconciliation no. 20, Colombo: Marga Institute.

Rooney, Eilish (1995a) 'Political division, practical alliance: problems for women in conflict', *Journal of Women's History*, 6(4): 42–8.

—— (1995b) 'Women in political conflict', *Race and Class*, 37(1): 51–6.

Rose, Richard (1971) *Governing without Consensus: an Irish perspective*, London: Faber and Faber.

Roulston, Carmel (1997) 'Women on the margin: the women's movements in Northern Ireland, 1973–1995', in L.A. West (ed.) *Feminist Nationalism*, New York: Routledge.

Ruane, Joseph (1999) 'The end of (Irish) history? Three readings of the current conjuncture', in J. Ruane and J. Todd (eds), *After the Good Friday Agreement: analysing political change in Northern Ireland*, Dublin: University College Dublin Press.

Ruane, Joseph and Todd, Jennifer (eds) (1999) *After the Good Friday Agreement: analysing political change in Northern Ireland*, Dublin: University College Dublin Press.

—— (1996) *The Dynamics of Conflict in Northern Ireland: power, conflict and emancipation*, Cambridge: Cambridge University Press.

Ruddick, Sara (1998) '"Woman of peace": a feminist construction', in L.A. Lorentzen and J. Turpin (eds) *The Women and War Reader*, New York: New York University Press.

—— (1990) 'The rationality of care', in J.B. Elshtain and S. Tobias (eds) *Women, Militarism and War: essays in history, politics, and social theory*, Savage, MD: Rowman & Littlefield.

—— (1989) *Maternal Thinking: toward a politics of peace*, New York: Ballantine Books.

—— (1983) 'Pacifying the forces: drafting women in the interests of peace', *Signs*, 8(3): 471–89.

Ryan, Louise (2000) '"Drunken Tans": representations of sex and violence in the Anglo-Irish War (1919–21)', *Feminist Review*, 66: 73–94.

—— (1999) '"Furies" and "die-hards": women and Irish Republicanism in the early twentieth century', *Gender and History*, 11(2): 256–75.

—— (1997) 'A question of loyalty: war, nation, and feminism in early twentieth-century Ireland', *Women's Studies International Forum*, 20(1): 21–32.

Saint-Germain, Michelle A. (1997) '*Mujeres '94*: democratic transition and the women's movement in El Salvador', *Women and Politics*, 18(2): 75–99.

—— (1994) 'Women, democratization, and public policy' [book review essay], *Policy Sciences*, 27(2–3): 269–76.

Sales, Rosemary (1997a) 'Gender and Protestantism in Northern Ireland', in P. Shirlow and M. McGovern (eds) *Who Are 'the People'? Unionism, Protestantism and Loyalism in Northern Ireland*, London: Pluto Press.

—— (1997b) *Women Divided: gender, religion and politics in Northern Ireland*, London: Routledge.

Salla, Michael (2001) 'Women and war, men and pacifism', in I. Skjelsbæk and D. Smith (eds) *Gender, Peace and Conflict*, London: Sage.

Samarasinghe, Vidyamali (1996) 'Soldiers, housewives and peace makers: ethnic conflict and gender in Sri Lanka', *Ethnic Studies Report*, 14(2): 203–27.

Samuel, Kumudini (2001) 'Gender difference in conflict resolution: the case of Sri Lanka', in I. Skjelsbæk and D. Smith (eds) *Gender, Peace and Conflict*, London: Sage.

Sathananthan, Sachithanandam (1998) 'Self-determination: a Ceylon Tamil perspective', in J. Armon and L. Philipson (eds) *Demanding Sacrifice: war and negotiation in Sri Lanka*, London: Conciliation Resources (London) in association with the Social Scientists' Association (Colombo).

Schalk, Peter (1994) 'Women fighters of the Liberation Tigers in Tamil Īlam. The martial feminism of Aṭēl Pālacinkam', *South Asia Research*, 14(2): 163–83.

—— (1992) 'Birds of independence: on the participation of Tamil women in armed struggle', *Lanka*, 7: 44–142.

Scheper-Hughes, Nancy (1998) 'Maternal thinking and the politics of war', in L.A. Lorentzen and J. Turpin (eds) *The Women and War Reader*, New York: New York University Press.

—— (1992) *Death Without Weeping: the violence of everyday life in Brazil*, Berkeley, CA: University of California Press.

Schreiner, Olive (1978 [orig. 1911]) *Woman and Labour*, 1st edn reprinted, London: Virago.

Schrijvers, Joke (1999) 'Fighters, victims and survivors: constructions of ethnicity, gender and refugeeness among Tamils in Sri Lanka', *Journal of Refugee Studies*, 12(3): 307–33.

Schwarz, Walter (1983) *The Tamils of Sri Lanka*, 2nd revised edn, London: Minority Rights Group.

Scott, David (1995) 'Dehistoricising history', in P. Jeganathan and Q. Ismail (eds) *Unmaking the Nation: the politics of identity and history in modern Sri Lanka*, Colombo: Social Scientists' Association.

Segal, Lynne (2008) 'Gender, war and militarism', *Feminist Review*, 88: 21–35.
—— (1990) *Slow Motion: changing masculinities, changing men*, London: Virago.
Sharoni, Simona (2001) 'Rethinking women's struggles in Israel-Palestine and in the north of Ireland', in C.O.N. Moser and F.C. Clark (eds) *Victims, Perpetrators or Actors? Gender, armed conflict and political violence*, London: Zed Books.
—— (1995) *Gender and the Israeli-Palestinian Conflict: the politics of women's resistance*, Syracuse, NY: Syracuse University Press.
Shirlow, Peter and McGovern, Mark (1997) 'Introduction: who are "the people"? Unionism, Protestantism and Loyalism in Northern Ireland', in P. Shirlow and M. McGovern (eds) *Who Are 'the People'? Unionism, Protestantism and Loyalism in Northern Ireland*, London: Pluto Press.
Shirlow, Peter and Shuttleworth, Ian (1999) '"Who is going to toss the burgers"? Social class and the reconstruction of the Northern Irish economy', *Capital and Class*, 69: 27–46.
Singer, Linda (1992) 'Feminism and postmodernism', in J. Butler and J.W. Scott (eds) *Feminists Theorize the Political*, New York: Routledge.
Sjoberg, Laura and Gentry, Caron E. (2007) *Mothers, Monsters, Whores: women's violence in global politics*, London: Zed Books.
Skjelsbæk, Inger (2001) 'Is femininity inherently peaceful? The construction of femininity in war', in I. Skjelsbæk and D. Smith (eds) *Gender, Peace and Conflict*, London: Sage.
Smith, Anthony D. (1996) 'Culture, community and territory: the politics of ethnicity and nationalism', *International Affairs*, 72(3): 445–58.
—— (1993) 'The ethnic sources of nationalism', in M. Brown (ed.) *Ethnic Conflict and International Security*, Princeton, NJ: Princeton University Press.
—— (1991a) *National Identity*, London: Penguin.
—— (1991b) 'The nation: invented, imagined, reconstructed?', *Millennium: Journal Of International Studies*, 20(3): 353–68.
—— (1986) *The Ethnic Origins of Nations*, Oxford: Basil Blackwell.
—— (1971) *Theories of Nationalism*, London: Duckworth.
Smith, Chris (2003) *In the Shadow of a Cease-fire: the impacts of small arms availability and misuse in Sri Lanka*, Occasional Paper no. 11, Geneva: Small Arms Survey, Graduate Institute of International Studies.
Smith, Dan (2001) 'The problem of essentialism', in I. Skjelsbæk and D. Smith (eds) *Gender, Peace and Conflict*, London: Sage.
Smith, Dorothy E. (1987) 'Women's perspective as a radical critique of sociology', in S. Harding (ed.) *Feminism and Methodology: social science issues*, Milton Keynes: Open University Press.
Spence, Louise (2002) *Unheard Voices: the experiences and needs of the children of Loyalist political ex-prisoners*, Belfast: EPIC.
Spencer, Jonathan (1990) 'Introduction: the power of the past', in J. Spencer (ed.) *Sri Lanka: history and the roots of conflict*, London: Routledge.
Stack-O'Connor, Alisa (2007) 'Lions, tigers and freedom birds: how and why the Liberation Tigers of Tamil Eelam employs women', *Terrorism and Political Violence*, 19(1): 43–63.
Stanley, Liz (1990a) 'Feminist praxis and the academic mode of production: an editorial introduction', in L. Stanley (ed.) *Feminist Praxis: research, theory and epistemology in feminist sociology*, London: Routledge.
—— (ed.) (1990b) *Feminist Praxis: research, theory and epistemology in feminist sociology*, London: Routledge.

Stanley, Liz and Wise, Sue (1990) 'Method, methodology and epistemology in feminist research processes', in L. Stanley (ed.) *Feminist Praxis: research, theory and epistemology in feminist sociology*, London: Routledge.

Stavenhagen, Rodolfo (1990) *The Ethnic Question: conflicts, development, and human rights*, Tokyo: United Nations University Press.

Stedman, Stephen John (1997) 'Spoiler problems in peace processes', *International Security*, 22(2): 5–53.

Steel, Jayne (1998) 'Vampira: representations of the Irish female terrorist', *Irish Studies Review*, 6(3): 273–84.

Stevenson, Jonathan (1996) *'We Wrecked the Place': contemplating an end to the Northern Irish Troubles*, New York: The Free Press.

Swerdlow, Amy (1982) 'Ladies' day at the Capitol: Women Strike for Peace versus HUAC', *Feminist Studies*, 8(3): 493–520.

Taillon, Ruth (1999) *When History Was Made: the women of 1916*, Belfast: Beyond the Pale.

Tennekoon, Serena (1990) 'Newspaper nationalism: Sinhala identity as historical discourse', in J. Spencer (ed.) *Sri Lanka: history and the roots of conflict*, London: Routledge.

Tétreault, Mary Ann (1994a) 'Women and revolution: a framework for analysis', in M.A. Tétreault (ed.) *Women and Revolution in Africa, Asia, and the New World*, Columbia, SC: University of South Carolina Press.

—— (1994b) 'Women and revolution: what have we learned?', in M.A. Tétreault (ed.) *Women and Revolution in Africa, Asia, and the New World*, Columbia, SC: University of South Carolina Press.

Thangarajah, Yuvi (1995) 'Narratives of victimhood as ethnic identity among the Veddas of the east coast', in P. Jeganathan and Q. Ismail (eds) *Unmaking the Nation: the politics of identity and history in modern Sri Lanka*, Colombo: Social Scientists' Association.

Thiruchandran, Selvy (1997) *The Politics of Gender and Women's Agency in Post-Colonial Sri Lanka*, Colombo: Women's Education and Research Centre.

Tilly, Charles (ed.) (1975) *The Formation of National States in Western Europe*, Princeton, NJ: Princeton University Press.

Tiruchelvam, M. and Dattathreya, C.S. (eds) (1998) *Culture and Politics of Identity in Sri Lanka*, Colombo: International Centre for Ethnic Studies.

Todd, Jennifer (1987) 'Two traditions in Unionist political culture', *Irish Political Studies*, 2: 1–26.

Tosh, John (2004) 'Hegemonic masculinity and the history of gender', in S. Dudink, K. Hagemann and J. Tosh (eds) *Masculinities in Politics and War: gendering modern history*, Manchester: Manchester University Press.

Trawick, Margaret (1999) 'Reasons for violence: a preliminary ethnographic account of the LTTE', in S. Gamage and I.B. Watson (eds) *Conflict and Community in Contemporary Sri Lanka: 'pearl of the east' or the 'island of tears'?*, New Delhi: Sage India.

Turpin, Jennifer (1998) 'Many faces: women confronting war', in L.A. Lorentzen and J. Turpin (eds) *The Women and War Reader*, New York: New York University Press.

Turshen, Meredeth (1998) 'Women's war stories', in M. Turshen and C. Twagiramariya (eds) *What Women Do in Wartime: gender and conflict in Africa*, London: Zed Books.

Turshen, Meredeth and Twagiramariya, Clotilde (eds) (1998) *What Women Do in Wartime: gender and conflict in Africa*, London: Zed Books.

UNDP (United Nations Development Programme) (2002) 'Small arms and light weapons', *Essentials*, 9: 1–12.
Urbina, Yance (1994) 'Building a feminist organization inside the social movement', in G. Kuppers (ed.), *Companeras: voices from the Latin American women's movement*, London: Latin American Bureau (Research and Action).
Uyangoda, Jayadeva (2001) *Beyond the Talks: towards transformative peace in Sri Lanka*, Marga Monograph Series on Ethnic Reconciliation no. 13, Colombo: Marga Institute.
Uyangoda, Jayadeva and Perera, Morina (eds) (2003) *Sri Lanka's Peace Process 2002: critical perspectives*, Colombo: Social Scientists' Association.
Vickers, Jeanne (1993) *Women and War*, London: Zed Books.
Walby, Sylvia (1996) 'Woman and nation', in G. Balakrishnan (ed.) *Mapping the Nation*, London: Verso.
Walker, Clive (2001) 'The Patten Report and post-sovereignty policing in Northern Ireland', in R. Wilford (ed.), *Aspects of the Belfast Agreement*, Oxford: Oxford University Press.
Ward, Margaret (2000) *The Northern Ireland Assembly and Women: assessing the gender deficit*, Belfast: Democratic Dialogue.
—— (1999) '"Ulster was different?" Women, feminism, and nationalism in the north of Ireland', in Y. Galligan, E. Ward and R. Wilford (eds) *Contesting Politics: women in Ireland, north and south*, Boulder, CO: Westview Press.
—— (1995) 'Finding a place: women and the Irish peace process', *Race and Class*, 37(1): 41–50.
—— (1989) *Unmanageable Revolutionaries: women and Irish nationalism*. London: Pluto Press.
Ward, Rachel (2006) *Women, Unionism and Loyalism in Northern Ireland: from 'tea-makers' to political actors*, Dublin: Irish Academic Press.
—— (2002) 'Invisible women: the political roles of Unionist and Loyalist women in contemporary Northern Ireland', *Parliamentary Affairs*, 55: 167–78.
West, Lois A. (1997a) 'Introduction: feminism constructs nationalism', in L.A. West (ed.) *Feminist Nationalism*, New York: Routledge.
—— (ed.) (1997b) *Feminist Nationalism*, New York: Routledge.
Whyte, John (1990) *Interpreting Northern Ireland*, Oxford: Oxford University Press.
—— (1983) 'How much discrimination was there under the Unionist regime, 1921–68?', in T. Gallagher and J. O'Connell (eds) *Contemporary Irish Studies*, Manchester: Manchester University Press. Online, available at: http://cain.ulst.ac.uk/issues/discrimination/whyte.htm (accessed 21 June 2003).
Wickramagamage, Carmen (1999) 'Sri Lankan organisations for women: a critical appraisal', in S. Kirimabune (ed.) *Women and Politics in Sri Lanka: a comparative perspective*, Kandy: International Centre for Ethnic Studies.
Wickramasinghe, Nira (2006) *Sri Lanka in the Modern Age: a history of contested identities*, London: Hurst and Company.
Wilford, Rick (1999) 'Women and politics', in P. Mitchell and R. Wilford (eds) *Politics in Northern Ireland*, Boulder, CO: Westview Press in cooperation with PSAI Press.
—— (1998) 'Women, ethnicity and nationalism: surveying the ground', in R. Wilford and R.L. Miller (eds) *Women, Ethnicity and Nationalism: the politics of transition*, London: Routledge.
Wilford, Rick and Galligan, Yvonne (1999) 'Gender and party politics in Northern Ireland', in Y. Galligan, E. Ward and R. Wilford (eds) *Contesting Politics: women in Ireland, north and south*, Boulder, CO: Westview Press.

Wilson, Alfred J. (1988) *The Break-up of Sri Lanka: the Sinhalese–Tamil conflict*, London: C. Hurst & Co.
Wilson, Alfred J. and Chandrakanthan, A. Joseph (1998) 'Tamil identity and aspirations', in J. Armon and L. Philipson (eds) *Demanding Sacrifice: war and negotiation in Sri Lanka*, London: Conciliation Resources (London) in association with the Social Scientists' Association (Colombo).
Winslow, Deborah and Woost, Michael D. (eds) (2004) *Economy, Culture, and Civil War in Sri Lanka*, Bloomington, IN: Indiana University Press.
Wolf, Diane L. (1996) 'Situating feminist dilemmas in fieldwork', in D.L. Wolf (ed.) *Feminist Dilemmas in Fieldwork*, Boulder, CO: Westview Press.
Wollstonecraft, Mary (1975 [orig. 1792]) *A Vindication of the Rights of Woman*, 2nd edn reprinted, edited with an introduction by M.B. Kramnick, Harmondsworth: Penguin.
Woolf, Virginia (1943 [orig. 1938]) *Three Guineas*, new edn, London: Hogarth Press.
York, Jodi (1998) 'The truth about women and peace', in L.A. Lorentzen and J. Turpin (eds) *The Women and War Reader*, New York: New York University Press.
Yuval-Davis, Nira (1998) 'Gender and nation', in R. Wilford and R.L. Miller (eds) *Women, Ethnicity and Nationalism: the politics of transition*, London: Routledge.
—— (1997) *Gender and Nation*, London: Sage.
—— (1996) 'Women and the biological reproduction of "the nation"', *Women's Studies International Forum*, 19(1–2): 17–24.
—— (1994) 'Identity politics and women's ethnicity', in V.M. Moghadam (ed.) *Identity Politics and Women: cultural reassertions and feminisms in international perspective*, Boulder, CO: Westview Press.
Yuval-Davis, Nira and Anthias, Floya (eds) (1989) *Woman–Nation–State*, Basingstoke: Macmillan.
Zajovic, Staša (ed.) (1993) *Women for Peace*, Belgrade: Women in Black.
Zalewski, Marysia (2000) *Feminism after Postmodernism: theorising through practice*, London: Routledge.
Zedalis, Debra D. (2004) 'Female suicide bombers', *Carlisle Papers in Security Strategy*, Carlisle, PA: Strategic Studies Institute. Online, available at: www.strategicstudiesinstitute.army.mil/pdffiles/PUB408.pdf (accessed 25 February 2008).

News articles, documentaries and audio-visual material

(2002) 'Agreement on a ceasefire between the Government of the Democratic Socialist Republic of Sri Lanka and the Liberation Tigers of Tamil Eelam'. Online, available at: www.peaceinsrilanka.org/insidepages/Agreement/PV.htm (accessed 12 April 2007).
(2002) 'LTTE to impose dress code for Jaffna women', *Sunday Times* (Colombo), 28 April. Online, available at: www.sundaytimes.lk/020428/front/ltte.html (accessed 11 May 2002).
(2002) 'Towards a totalitarian peace: the human rights dilemma', excerpt from Special Report No. 13 of the University Teachers for Human Rights (Jaffna), 10 May 2002, *The Island* (Colombo), 11 May. Online, available at: www.island.lk/2002/05/11/featur01.html (accessed 21 May 2002).
Athas, Iqbal (2002) 'Inside story of female tigers', *Sunday Times* (Colombo), 16 June. Online, available at: www.sundaytimes.lk/020616/columns/sitrep1.html (accessed 1 July 2002).
BBC1 Northern Ireland (2003) *Spotlight: Loyalists at War*, television documentary aired BBC1 Northern Ireland, 28 January 2003, 10.35 p.m.

Benedict, Helen (2007) 'The private war of women soldiers', *Salon*, 6 March. Online, available at: www.salon.com/news/feature/2007/03/07/women_in_military (accessed 5 February 2008).

Buerk, Roland (2007) 'A date with a renegade rebel Tiger', *BBC News*, 4 April. Online, available at: http://news.bbc.co.uk/1/hi/world/south_asia/6524869.stm (accessed 5 February 2008).

Bulathsinghala, Frances (2002a) 'Life under the LTTE', *Sunday Observer* (Colombo), 5 May. Online, available at: www.sundayobserver.lk/2002/05/05/fea01.html (accessed 11 May 2002).

—— (2002b) 'Armed virgins getting ready to celebrate life', *Sunday Observer* (Colombo), 21 April. Online, available at: www.sundayobserver.lk/2002/04/21/fea13.html (accessed 9 May 2002).

Coiste na n-Iarchimí (2001) *Inside Stories* (documentary on republican ex-prisoners, copy held by the author).

—— (date unknown) *What is the Journey?* (documentary on republican ex-prisoners, copy held by the author).

Farrell, Stephen (2001) 'Women at war', *The Times*, 25 June: 2, 2–3.

Farrell, Tom (2002) 'Can Tigers enter the mainstream?', *Fortnight*, March: 16–17.

Fernando, Manjula (2002) 'NE Interim Council should include women', *Daily News* (Colombo), 24 April. Online, available at: www.dailynews.lk/2002/04/24/new36.html (accessed 9 May 2002).

Gopalakrishnan, Ramesh (2004) 'Profile: Colonel Karuna', *BBC News*, 5 March. Online, available at: http://news.bbc.co.uk/1/hi/world/south_asia/3537025.stm (accessed 15 May 2008).

Harrison, Jane *Stolen*, Ilbijerri Aboriginal and Torres Strait Islander Theatre Co-operative and Playbox Theatre, play performed in Belfast 29–30 October 2001 at the Waterfront Hall.

Hettiarachchi, Kumudini (2001) 'Women are joining the army to fight insurgency', Inter Press Service, 12 July. Online, available at: www.ips.org/index.htm (accessed 28 April 2002).

LTTE (2001) 'LTTE leader makes special plea to the Sinhalese: reject racist forces: offer justice to the Tamils', Tamil Eelam Home Page, 27 November. Online, available at: www.eelam.com/freedom_struggle/ltte_press_releases/2000/november/27.html (accessed 21 May 2002).

—— (2000) 'Urgent press release', Tamil Eelam Home Page, 27 November. Online, available at: www.eelam.com/freedom_struggle/ltte_press_releases/2000/november/27.html (accessed 21 May 2002).

Pirapaharan, V. (1996) 'Tamil national leader Hon. V. Pirapaharan's Women's International Day message', EelamWeb, 8 March. Online, available at: www.eelamweb.com/leader/messages/women/1996/ (accessed 21 May 2002).

—— (1993) 'Tamil national leader Hon. V. Pirapaharan's Women's International Day message', EelamWeb, 8 March. Online, available at: www.eelamweb.com/leader/messages/women/1993/ (accessed 21 May 2002).

—— (1992) 'Tamil national leader Hon. V. Pirapaharan's Women's International Day message', EelamWeb, 8 March. Online, available at: www.eelamweb.com/leader/messages/women/1992/ (accessed 21 May 2002).

Pirapaharan, Velupillai and Mazumdar, Sudip [interviewer] (1986) 'The eye of the tiger: Tamil national leader Velupillai Pirapaharan's interview', excerpt from *Newsweek*,

11 August 1986, Tamil Eelam Home Page. Online, available at: www.eelam.com/interviews/leader_august_86.html (accessed 21 May 2002).

Samaranayake, Ajith (2002) 'A short history of Velupillai Prabhakaran', *Sunday Observer* (Colombo), 21 April. Online, available at: www.sundayobserver.lk/2002/04/21/fea04.html (accessed 9 May 2002).

Samath, Feizal (2001) 'Cynicism, violence mark poll campaign', Inter Press Service, 27 November. Online, available at: www.ips.org/index.htm (accessed 28 April 2002).

—— (1998) 'Radical left group returns to haunt', Inter Press Service, 23 January. Online, available at: www.ips.org/index.htm (accessed 28 April 2002).

—— (1997) 'Child warriors in a lingering war', Inter Press Service, 7 October. Online, available at: www.ips.org/index.htm (accessed 28 April 2002).

Sebastian, Rita (1996) 'Do women soldiers go against feminist ideology of working for peace?', Inter Press Service, 2 March. Online, available at: www.ips.org/index.htm (accessed 28 April 2002).

Seevaratnam, Chandran (2002) 'Tamil women back in shackles?', *Sunday Times Plus* (Colombo), 19 May. Online, available at: www.sundaytimes.lk/020519/plus/let.html (accessed 16 June 2002).

Sivan, Santosh (dir.) (2000) *The Terrorist* (fictional film).

Subramaniam, Sarita (1997) 'Women lead rebel attacks, but Tiger leaders are men', Inter Press Service, 11 August. Online, available at: www.oneworld.org/ips2/aug/srilanka.html or from www.ips.org/index.htm (accessed 16 February 2002).

Thompson, Melissa (dir.) (2000) *The Road of Women: voices of Irish women political prisoners* (documentary).

UNHCR (2004) 'UNHCR calls for renewed attention to plight of displaced Sri Lankans', *UNHCR News Stories*, 29 April.

—— (2003a) 'Sri Lanka: discussions on IDP and refugee returns', *UNHCR Briefing Notes*, 17 January.

—— (2003b) 'UNHCR in talks on Sri Lankans uprooted by civil war', *UNHCR News Stories*, 16 January.

Index

CPSIA information can be obtained at www.ICGtesting.com
Printed in the USA
LVOW030419100112

263146LV00002B/17/P